Programmable Logic
Designer's Guide

RELATED TITLES

For the retailer nearest you, or to order directly from the publisher,
call 800-428-SAMS. In Indiana, Alaska, and Hawaii call 317-298-5699.

Programmable Logic Designer's Guide

Roger C. Alford

HOWARD W. SAMS & COMPANY

A Division of Macmillan, Inc.
4300 West 62nd Street
Indianapolis, Indiana 46268 USA

FIRST EDITION
FIRST PRINTING—1989

International Standard Book Number: 0-672-22575-1
Library of Congress Catalog Card Number: 89-60596

Acquisitions Editor: *Greg Michael*
Development Editor: *C. Herbert Feltner*
Technical Reviewer: *Forrest M. Mims*
Manuscript Editor: *A. Tony Melendez*
Illustrators: *Wm. D. Basham & Sally Copenhaver*
Cover Design: *Meridian Design Studio*
Indexer: *Sherry Massey*
Composition: *Cromer Graphics*

Printed in the United States of America

To Nathan, Matthew, and Amy

Contents

5. PLD Development Systems and Support

6. Designing with PLDs

7. Production with PLDs   *219*

8. PLD Application Examples   *243*

Foreword

Roger Alford has seen the future of electronics and he knows that programmable logic devices (PLDs) will be a big part of it.

There's a revolution going on which has turned the traditional approach to electronics design upside down. Previously, one started with a device and tried to design a circuit around it. There were limitations due to the capabilities of the device (whether vacuum tube, transistor, or integrated circuit) and some compromises in circuit design were inevitable. But no more. Today, one can start with a circuit and design a device to provide the logic functions the circuit requires. In effect, the device itself is "compromised" to meet the needs of the circuit design. Design engineers are no longer at the mercy of merchant and "jellybean" logic IC manufacturers.

Programmable logic techniques offer advantages for manufacturers of electronic devices, as well as design engineers. Stocking a large inventory of standard logic devices can be an expensive proposition and an administrative nightmare. PLD technology requires only a modest number of "foundation" devices to be kept on hand. These can be rapidly programmed to meet changing production and design requirements, giving manufacturers great flexibility and cost savings.

If you intend to be active in electronics in the 1990s, you'd better become familiar with PLDs. This is the book to help you do just that.

If you're a design engineer, you'll find this book covers the crucial design philosophy for using PLDs as well as the purely "hardware" aspects. Also included is coverage of the software involved with successfully using PLDs, programming languages and design tools, production runs of PLDs, and patents and copyrights.

I like the way Roger Alford eases the way into the world of PLDs. He reviews such topics as Boolean algebra and Karnaugh maps which you studied in school long ago and have now forgotten—but which are essential to understanding PLDs. And Roger relates all the material back to the real world instead of the blackboard, giving you information you can put to work *today* instead of someday.

Every revolution in electronics technology has left behind those who didn't keep up. The list is long and depressing—transistors in the Fifties, ICs in the Sixties, microprocessors in the Seventies—all of which resulted in some people and their skills becoming "obsolete." Roger Alford has done his part to prevent this from happening to you.

Harry L. Helms

Preface

"Wake up. Rub the silicon from your baby blues. A new programmable logic day is dawning. And to cut the mustard, engineers must have PLDs in their repertoires." This insightful statement came from Stan Baker in his "Silicon Bits" column in the February 2, 1987, issue of *Electronic Engineering Times*. Indeed, digital design engineers who are not well versed in programmable logic design will quickly find themselves handicapped as they step into new designs while limiting themselves to yesterday's IC technologies. The rapid growth of the programmable logic industry—approaching $1 billion per year—has clearly driven home its point: Programmable logic is crucial to modern circuit design, and it's here to stay!

A technology which has been available for a few years is currently undergoing a level of development and growth which is firmly establishing it as the most significant advance in the electronics industry since the advent of the microprocessor. Programmable logic is the next generation technology for millions of engineers around the world presently designing with discrete TTL, and it is available today. Dedicated R&D has resulted in denser, higher speed, low power devices and programming tools of increasing sophistication to support them. With decreasing costs also becoming apparent, it is now clear that programmable logic is here to stay. (Colin, Pizey, Technitron Ltd., *New Electronics*, April 29, 1986.)

Since their introduction in the late-1970s, programmable logic devices, or *PLDs*, have come a long way, offering a wide variety of complexities, architectures, and configurations. While initial acceptance of the first PLDs was slow, the ubiquitous *PAL* introduced by Monolithic Memories (MMI) created a spark which quickly exploded into the expanding industry it is today. Although the PAL concept initially met with lackluster enthusiasm within MMI, PAL inventor John Birkner championed his brainchild to the marketplace; the result exceeded all expectations.

The growth of the PLD industry has been further kindled by myriad new devices. Compared to the choices available in the 1970s and early 1980s, today's programmable logic designer can select from a vast number of device options to meet design needs. PLD selection tradeoff issues now include architecture, packaging, semiconductor technology, power consumption, speed, and development support. Price, availability, and sourcing options are also always concerns for the designer.

To support the onslaught of new PLD devices and architectures, many software packages have been developed to help designers. The importance of "good" support software has become increasingly important as device complexities have increased. In addition, the huge amount of documentation required to support this rapidly growing industry has been primarily in the form of manufacturer data sheets and application notes, with a little help from the electronics industry trade journals.

Although programmable logic has been around since the 1970s, it has been slow in becoming a part of the repertoire of many digital designers for two primary reasons. First, designing with programmable logic involves a new approach that requires a learning curve many designers are reluctant to undertake. The *Electronic Engineering Times'* 1987 PLD Survey revealed that PLD designers considered "learning" to be the biggest obstacle in using programmable logic. Second, universities have been slow in developing programs that teach programmable logic design to their engineering students. This has been partly because universities have had little more than (biased) manufacturer data books to use as text resources.

The *Programmable Logic Designer's Guide* is designed to overcome both of these obstacles. It allows students and practicing engineers to quickly learn about the whole programmable logic industry, and how to apply programmable logic to digital circuit design. This guide is also designed to support engineers already familiar with programmable logic. It is a complete resource of programmable logic information, including a detailed look at all existing PLD architectures, families, and development tools.

Because existing PLD information is primarily scattered among manufacturer data books and industry journal articles, it is difficult for designers to keep abreast of all available PLD device alternatives and design support options. Additionally, without a great deal of studying and using a wide variety of devices, it is difficult to get a clear understanding of how different device features and architectures compare, as well as how well the various software packages succeed in supporting PLD designs. In order to create the best possible designs, the designer requires a knowledge and understanding of *all* available device architectures and software packages, and the comparative tradeoffs between the various alternatives. This guide covers these issues.

Here is the chapter breakdown:

Chapter 1 presents an introduction to programmable logic, a look at its history, and a comparison with other device alternatives.

Chapter 2 provides an intermediate-level review of digital logic design, including a look at some of the logic minimization algorithms that are used in some PLD software packages.

Chapters 3 and 4 discuss all of the currently available PLD families and architectures, and compare the features and tradeoffs of each. Chapter 3 concentrates on the primary PLD architectures, while Chapter 4 looks more closely at application-specific device architectures.

Chapter 5 describes the available software development aids for supporting PLD designs. It also discusses design entry alternatives and the JEDEC PLD file format standard.

Chapter 6 covers how to design with PLDs, including defining design goals, comparing the PLD alternative to other device options, choosing the right PLDs and the right development tools, and other related issues. An example is provided to help the designer better visualize and understand the PLD design process.

Chapter 7 discusses issues related to using PLDs in a production environment. This includes device selection, testing, security, and PLD-production economics.

Chapter 8 provides several proven, real-life PLD application examples, which designers can use to implement in their own designs or use as examples to get a better understanding of how PLD designs are realized.

Chapter 9 concludes the text portion with a look at industry trends and the future of the PLD industry.

Four appendices have also been included to provide helpful quick-reference information for the designer. Appendices A and B provide the names and addresses of PLD device manufacturers and development aid manufacturers, respectively. Appendix C provides the names and addresses of PLD device-programmer manufacturers. Appendix D provides a bibliography broken down by chapter that can be used for further research.

Although the PLD industry has experienced tremendous growth during the past decade, in many ways it still seems to be in its infancy. As the PLD industry continues to mature, it will have an increasing impact on the SSI/MSI device market and the gate array market. Programmable logic's ability to simplify and speed up circuit design will make it essential for most products, further increasing its demand. If this book fulfills its intent, both new and veteran logic designers will experience the fun, excitement, and rewards of using programmable logic.

Roger C. Alford

Acknowledgments

The development of an extensive work such as this requires a great deal of research and the cooperation and assistance of many individuals and corporations. While it is impossible to list everyone who contributed to this work, I would like to mention with gratitude many of the individuals, and their respective corporations, who made a substantial contribution to the completion of this work. I would especially like to acknowledge the patience and encouragement provided by my wife, Valerie, and by our children, Nathan, Matthew, and Amy, to whom this book is dedicated.

The following individuals and corporations contributed to this work:

Mike Hansen	Altera
Clive McCarthy	Altera
Napoleone Cavlan	AMD/MMI
Cheryl Hall	AMD/MMI
Keith H. Gudger	Atmel
Don Campbell	CMP Publications
Bill Kittle	COM2
Richard Lundy	Control-O-Mation
Robert Wallace	Control-O-Mation
Dane Elliot	Cypress Semiconductor
Mark Kuenster	Data I/O
Victor Nowakowski	DuKane
Eric Goetting	Exel Microelectronics
Bob Hartwig	Fairchild/NSC
Thomas Wnorowski	IM-Press Publishing
Lawrence S. Palley	Intel
Robin J. Jigour	International CMOS Technology
Paul Hoy	Kontron Electronics
Paul Kollar	Lattice Semiconductor
George Kriegl	Marquette Electronics
Jay Kamdar	National Semiconductor
Bob Nelson	National Semiconductor
Joseph Vithayathil	National Semiconductor
Robert LaJeunesse	Nematron
Tracy Kahl	Personal CAD Systems
Nancy Mazza	Pioneer Electronics

Mike Salameh	PLX Technology
Ed McCarron	Programmable Devices
Sue Mauretti	Sensors
John Birkner	Structured Design
Bruce Graham	Symplex
Philip B. Doherty	Texas Instruments
John Haller	VLSI Technology
Dave Lautzenheiser	Xilinx

Trademark Acknowledgments

All terms mentioned in this book that are known to be trademarks or service marks are listed below. In addition, terms suspected of being trademarks or service marks have been appropriately capitalized. Howard W. Sams & Company cannot attest to the accuracy of this information. Use of a term in this book should not be regarded as affecting the validity of any trademark or service mark.

ACT, PLICE, and Action Logic are trademarks of Actel Corporation
A + PLUS and LogiCaps are trademarks of Altera Corporation
UNIX is a trademark of AT&T
PLD Master is a trademark of Daisy Systems Corp.
ABEL and Logic Fingerprint are trademarks of Data I/O Corp.
VAX and VMS are trademarks of Digital Equipment Corp.
LOG/IC is a trademark of Elan Digital Systems
ERASIC, Multi-Map, Multi-Sim, and SecurityPlus are trademarks of Exel Microelectronics, Inc.
FutureNet DASH and FutureNet FutureDesigner are trademarks of FutureNet Corp.
HPL, PCSD, and Silicon Breadboard are trademarks of Harris Corporation
CADAT is a trademark of HHB Softron
IBM, XT, and AT are trademarks and IBM Personal Computer is a registered trademark of International Business Machines Corp.
PEEL and APEEL are trademarks of International CMOS Technology Inc. (ICT)
GAL is a registered trademark and Generic Array Logic is a trademark of ComPALibility Lattice Semiconductor Corp.
SmartModel is a registered trademark of Logic Automation, Inc.
C.A.S.T is a trademark of Logical Devices, Inc.
MS-DOS is a registered trademark of Microsoft Corp.
PAL, HAL, PALASM, and SKINNYDIP are registered trademarks and Diagnostics-On-Chip, DOC, and PROSE are trademarks of Monolithic Memories, Inc.
Tri-state is a registered trademark of National Semiconductor Corp.
P-CAD, CUPL, and PC-CAPS are trademarks of Personal CAD Systems, Inc.
VAMP, IFL, and FPLS are trademarks of Signetics Corp.
Silos is a trademark of Simucad Corp.
Viewlogic, Viewdraw, and Viewsim are registered trademarks of Viewlogic Systems, Inc.
Xilinx, Logic Cell, XACT, XACTOR and Logic Processor are trademarks of Xilinx, Inc.

Chapter 1

Introduction

What is a *programmable logic device* (PLD)? This is a worthwhile question to answer before proceeding further. A PLD is a digital integrated circuit capable of being programmed to provide a variety of different logical functions. The programming may be in the form of on-chip fuses, EPROM (UV-Erasable/ Programmable Read-Only Memory) circuits, EEPROM (Electrically Erasable/ Programmable Read-Only Memory) circuits, or RAM (Random-Accessed Memory, or read/write memory) circuits. Possessing this quality of programmability, a PLD can be used in a large number of unique applications where common silicon is employed and only the chip's internal programming is distinct.

Under this definition, high-speed Programmable Read-Only Memory (PROM) devices qualify and are useful as PLDs. The slower, higher-density MOS/ CMOS cousins, EPROMs and EEPROMs, also fall under this definition, although these devices are not traditionally considered PLDs. Some high-speed MOS EPROMs are available, but standard devices generally have relatively slow access times—typically 200 ns (nanoseconds) or greater—making them impractical as logic devices in most applications. EPROMs and EEPROMs will not be discussed as PLDs in this book. We will discuss PROMs, however, with the understanding that EPROMs or EEPROMs may substitute if speed requirements are met.

Our PLD definition precludes special-purpose LSI devices, such as UARTs and interrupt controllers, since they are designed to be used only for a single, particular function, and their logical design cannot be altered to permit different functionality in different systems. Ironically, PLDs exist that can be programmed to operate as UARTs, interrupt controllers, and other special functions, potentially resulting in a notable impact on the microprocessor peripheral market.

Figure 1-1 is a photo of many popular PLDs and shows the wide variety of packages. The range of PLD architectures currently available and in development is equally diverse and capable of meeting the logical requirements of innumerable systems and subsystems. The application of these devices is, indeed, limited only by the designer's imagination. This variety of packages and architectures is complemented with a wide selection of speed (propagation delay), power consumption, temperature rating, and sourcing options. With such a selection, PLDs can be found to fit into virtually every possible application.

Figure 1-1. Photo of many popular PLDs.

Why Use Programmable Logic Devices?

Today's digital logic designer has the opportunity to design from any of six primary categories:

- Standard SSI/MSI devices.
- Standard LSI/VLSI devices.
- Gate array devices.
- Standard-cell devices.
- Full-custom devices.
- Programmable logic devices.

To see where PLDs fit into the designer's picture, and to see how they have filled an important niche, let's take a look at each of these device categories individually, particularly noting the (inevitable) tradeoffs that exist between the various alternatives.

Standard SSI/MSI Devices

The standard SSI/MSI (Small Scale Integration, Medium Scale Integration) device category includes such devices as the 4000-series CMOS devices and the 74XX00-series TTL/CMOS devices—common, relatively inexpensive, logic building blocks. Prior to the availability of programmable logic and the widespread acceptance of gate arrays and standard-cells, these devices were the primary lifeblood of most digital systems. Even today, they are widely used in digital systems, providing buffers, shift-registers, counters, flip-flops, gates, and other logic functions.

Standard SSI/MSI devices are inexpensive when viewed from a *cost-per-chip* standpoint (typically being in the under 20-cent range for simple gates), but are expensive and inefficient when viewed from a *cost-per-gate* standpoint. The low unit cost is a result of their being produced in very high volume, assisted by their small die size and mature semiconductor technologies.

Standard LSI/VLSI Devices

The second category listed above, standard LSI/VLSI (Large Scale Integration, Very Large Scale Integration) devices, includes such devices as microprocessors and related peripheral devices (UARTs, interrupt controllers, DMA controllers, etc.). With reasonable volume production yields, these devices quickly provide high-level functionality at comparatively low cost (again, measured on a cost-per-gate basis). Devices in this category, microprocessors in particular, have revolutionized the digital design industry. Digital systems are rarely designed today without some form of microprocessor control.

With the 8-bit Z80 microprocessor available for about $1.00, the 8031 8-bit microcontroller (with on-chip memory, I/O, timers, interrupt support, UART, and crystal oscillator) in the $2.00 range, and the highly integrated 16-bit 80186 microprocessor (with on-chip interrupt controller, DMA controller, timers, wait-state generator, crystal oscillator, bus buffer control logic, and programmable peripheral and memory chip select logic) under $20.00, it is little wonder these devices have had such an awe-inspiring impact on the digital design world.

Devices in this category provide the best cost-per-gate value of any category. Because they are full-custom devices, they use their silicon area very efficiently—only *necessary* gates are included on the chip, no unused gates are included (unlike gate arrays and PLDs). Large scale integration also reduces packaging and silicon overhead wastes (silicon space for bonding pads, etc.) that are especially dominant with the devices in the SSI/MSI category. This helps to further establish the low cost-per-gate device cost the standard LSI/VLSI devices enjoy.

These devices also reflect lower cost because they are manufactured in high volume. High-volume production reduces per-unit overhead costs, resulting in a lower per-unit manufacturing cost. Further production cost reductions will be realized with improved manufacturing know-how and more mature technology.

Gate-Array Devices

Gate arrays—devices that contain a "sea of gates"—have become increasingly popular as the number of suppliers has increased, prices have come down, and software has become available that permits faster, lower-cost development. These devices are generally prefabricated, with the silicon dies complete except for the final two or three metallization layers. Final layers on a gate array then provide the interconnect wiring for the gates, thereby defining the logic functions to be implemented by the array. Gate arrays are available from under 1,000 gates to as many 50,000 or more, with the most popular devices currently being the under-10,000 gate sizes.

While the number of gates in a gate array may initially seem large, a design requiring 2,000 "real" gates would most likely require a gate array with approximately 5,000 gates, since the architecture of these devices does not permit very efficient use of the chips' gates. Typical gate-usage efficiency has been around 40%, although newer gate array designs claim over 75% gate usage. Translated into dollars and cents, the inefficient use of gates typically results in a significant amount of "wasted" silicon real-estate on a gate array—a cost that must be reflected and absorbed in the selling price of the devices.

Nonetheless, gate arrays are an attractive alternative to using myriad SSI/MSI devices, and the functions of many such devices can be conveniently amalgamated onto a single gate array.

Because the gate interconnections must be defined, gate array designs also involve *nonrecurring engineering (NRE)* charges—mask tooling charges and charges for the use of a computer-aided design (CAD) system. Although the cost can vary greatly, depending on a variety of factors, typical gate array NRE charges are in the $10,000–$50,000 range, though they can be as high as $250,000. Note that NRE charges *do* recur if the design process is repeated due to a change in the gate array logic requirements (to implement a bug fix, or to institute an important or essential functional change, for example).

Because of the sizable NRE charges, gate arrays are generally used only in applications involving medium- to high-volume production (typically more than 5,000 units), allowing the NRE charges to be amortized over a large number of devices. Some low-volume, space-critical applications also use gate arrays. This is because of the space savings the devices afford, despite the significant NRE charges involved.

Once a gate array design is complete, a wait of up to several weeks is typical before functional gate arrays are available. Depending on complexity, technology, packaging, testing requirements and purchase volume, gate array devices can cost from a few dollars to hundreds of dollars each.

Standard-Cell Devices

Standard-cell devices, like gate arrays, are *semicustom* devices involving NRE charges for design generation. Unlike gate arrays, however, these devices are not prefabricated and do not contain "seas of gates." Instead, the CAD system used for the design of these devices contains a *cell library*, where many standard SSI, MSI, and LSI functional blocks are defined. By using the system to define the interconnection of different *standard cells*—like interconnecting the pieces of a puzzle—a "board on a chip" can be designed. Once designed, a computer is used to generate the appropriate masks for producing the desired standard-cell devices.

It would not be unreasonable, for example, to define a standard-cell device containing a Z80 microprocessor, three timers, an interrupt controller, a DMA controller, and some address decoding and bus buffering logic. Each of the individual functional blocks (the Z80, the DMA controller, the bus buffers, etc.) would be a separate *cell* in the cell library, and the cells would be interconnected to operate together as a system. The resulting chip can then replace what might otherwise be an entire P.C. (printed circuit) board full of components. The chip not only saves a remarkable amount of board space, it costs less than the individual components it replaces, providing the production volume is sufficiently large.

As might be expected, NRE charges for standard-cell designs are somewhat higher than those for gate array designs. This is because more-advanced software is required to properly handle the interconnection of library cells, and to perform logical simulations of standard-cell designs. Also, a *complete* set of masks must be developed to manufacture the dies. In general, standard-cell designs are limited to large volume applications.

In addition to the building-block advantage offered by standard-cell devices, a second feature is also notable, namely efficient die usage. Each cell in the cell library is a separate, distinct circuit, efficiently designed using only the components required to implement the particular cell function. Each cell, then, acts as a separate, *standard* SSI, MSI, or LSI device (without separate bonding pads), possessing the high circuit density common to these types of devices. Because of this, standard-cell devices—like standard LSI/VLSI devices—do not contain unused gates, thereby maintaining very efficient usage of the silicon area.

Since die size is proportional to device cost (for sufficiently large volumes), standard-cell devices generally cost less than gate arrays for large volumes. Thus, for large volume applications, standard-cell devices are commonly chosen where gate arrays would suffice, simply because of lower production costs. Notice that as production volume increases, a standard-cell device becomes more and more like a standard SSI/VLSI device in all respects.

Standard-cell designs may incur repeated NRE charges for changes made to the device design specifications. Lead times for obtaining working standard-cell devices are generally much longer than those for gate arrays, and may take several months.

Full-Custom Devices

Full-custom, as the name implies, involves device design from "scratch." This approach involves the largest NRE costs and the longest lead times of any of the device alternatives, and is suitable only for very-high volume applications.

Typical applications might include certain automotive uses and some very-high volume consumer items, such as calculators and digital watches.

Again, for sufficiently high production volumes, these devices can be very economical to manufacture, due to extremely efficient use of die space.

Programmable Logic Devices

Programmable logic devices combine features found in standard devices with those found in gate arrays, resulting in a great deal of versatility and utility.

Like standard devices, PLDs are manufactured in large volumes with standard architectures. As a result, they can achieve the traditional cost reductions familiar to these types of devices. Similar to gate arrays (and standard-cell devices), PLDs are *Application-Specific Integrated Circuits* (ASICs) since they function differently, depending on how they're programmed. Thus PLDs provide the flexibility of specialized, semicustom devices, allowing designers to specify their logical operation according to their needs. Also, like a gate array, a PLD can replace many standard SSI/MSI logic devices, depending on the complexity of the PLD and the circuitry implemented in the device.

Device Type Comparisons

While there are several similarities between gate arrays and PLDs, it should be noted that most PLDs do not have a gate array "sea of gates" type of architecture (there are some that do). PLD architectures vary considerably among different families, and will be described in detail in Chapters 3 and 4.

PLDs offer certain advantages over gate arrays. First, PLD NRE charges are either nonexistent or very small (aside from the engineer's time, which is a constant involved with all ASIC designs), compared with relatively high charges for gate-array designs. This important feature becomes even more paramount as design changes occur. PLD design changes are simple, fast, and cost-free, compared to repeated NRE charges for gate-array designs.

Second, PLD "turn-around" time (the time from design completion to having usable devices available) is very fast, ranging from a few minutes to a few hours. This compares to a few weeks for gate arrays. Again, design changes multiply the turn-around time savings, allowing many PLD design alterations to be made and tested during the time required to receive the first pass on a gate-array design. Ultimately, this can result in a significant reduction in the time-to-market of a product.

Finally, PLDs, unlike gate arrays, are practical for use in small designs (where a single PLD might replace only 4 or 5 SSI devices), or designs involving low-volume production.

Despite their advantages over gate arrays in some areas, PLDs are far from replacing or making gate arrays obsolete. They are, however, sure to take a chunk out of the gate array market. One problem with PLDs is that they have not yet been able to attain densities above low-end gate arrays. Current high-density PLDs contain under 10,000 gates—far short of the 50,000 or more gates available on new high-density gate arrays. Also, there comes a point in production volume where gate-array NRE charges have been sufficiently amortized to allow gate arrays to be more cost-effective than high-density PLDs. While the *changeover volume* (the volume at which gate arrays become more cost-effective to use) varies depending on several factors (particularly, device costs and NRE charges), some estimates show this to be typically between 5,000 and 10,000 units (assuming a single-design iteration on the gate-array design).

Although high-end, 9,000-gate PLDs do not reach the complexity of high-end gate arrays, it should be noted that 9,000 gates is still sufficient for many complex circuits that might typically be considered gate-array candidates. Also, the number of gates is not *everything*, since the architecture of a device plays an important role in determining the number of gates actually required to implement a desired function. PLDs also offer multiple sourcing, providing alternate device suppliers and competitive pricing. Multiple-sourcing is typically a costly feature for other types of ASIC devices.

Other Factors

In addition to the many PLD features already described, there are other advantages worth mentioning. Let's first look at the cost savings permitted by PLDs when used in place of standard SSI/MSI devices. Since a single PLD replaces several SSI/MSI devices, and since several PLDs may be included on a single P.C. board, it is clear that PLDs can significantly reduce parts count, thereby reducing inventory requirements and inventory-related costs. Since PLDs are (almost always) inventoried as blank, unprogrammed devices, they are not affected by design changes that occur anytime before production. Such changes would not require any PLD devices to be destroyed because they are no longer usable, as would be the case with other "hard logic" ASICs (gate arrays, standard-cell devices or full-custom devices).

Because of reduced chip count, PLDs can decrease testing requirements and related costs, both for incoming devices and for manufactured boards.

In addition to allowing higher board logic densities than standard SSI/MSI devices, PLDs also increase system reliability as a result of fewer components being used, thereby reducing maintenance and repair costs. Additionally, PLDs lower printed circuit board costs in many cases, by either reducing the required board size, or permitting the use of fewer board layers to implement a circuit.

Reduction in development time and effort is another area in which PLDs shine. PLDs permit any number of design change/test iterations without the penalty of cumulative NRE charges, and without long delays. In addition, the development process can be executed using erasable devices to eliminate parts waste and reduce development costs, switching to lower-cost, one-time programmable devices for production. When working with existing P.C. boards, during development or otherwise, board functional changes often require only alterations in PLD programming because of the PLD's programmable nature, eliminating the need to alter P.C. board traces.

Prototyping, similarly, is improved using PLDs. Not only is the amount of time and effort required (and, consequently, the number of errors made) to build a prototype significantly reduced over using equivalent SSI/MSI logic, but many (often most) prototype changes require only PLD reprogramming, reducing the time-consuming, error-prone task of circuit-rewiring.

Finally, some PLDs have a special "personality" feature that permits in-circuit reprogramming. Thus, the function of a PLD could be dynamically altered while operating in-circuit. This can be done with RAM-based PLDs, as well as with certain EEPROM-based devices.

This discussion should provide at least a basic understanding of the advantages of PLDs, and afford a first view of why PLDs should be used. The reasons will become clearer as we look at device architectures in detail in Chapters 3 and 4, and other aspects of PLD design and usage throughout the book.

History of PLDs

In the pre-programmable logic era, traditional digital logic designs consisted of many SSI and MSI TTL chips being combined to form the desired logic functions. Designers relied on *The TTL Databook* from Texas Instruments, and other similar databooks, for finding device specifications and determining what devices were available for "design in." Debugging was often complex and tedious, consisting of numerous "cuts and jumpers," and sometimes even "piggybacked" add-on chips.

In 1975, Signetics Corp. introduced the first nonmemory programmable logic device—the 82S100 (now PLS100) *Field-Programmable Logic Array* (*FPLA*). Napoleone Cavlan (Fig. 1-2), "the father of programmable logic"—then Signetics' PLA (Programmable Logic Array) applications manager—had the insight to realize that there must be a better way to design and modify digital systems. While PROMs—introduced earlier at Harris—showed promise and were already being used in some logic applications, there was still no PROM-like programmable substitute for standard logic gates. Such a device could potentially reduce the number of devices on a printed circuit (P.C.) board and minimize the amount of effort necessary to make logic changes to digital designs. Instead of myriad cuts and jumpers, designers could opt instead to change the programming of on-board logic devices.

National Semiconductor had been producing mask-programmable *PLAs* (*Programmable Logic Arrays*)—logic devices consisting of a programmable AND-array followed by a programmable OR-array, allowing standard Sum-of-Products (SOP) logic implementation. By combining fused-based PROM technology with the PLA concept, Cavlan conceived the first field-programmable logic device, the *field-programmable PLA* (*FPLA*). Since PLAs were already available (albeit, in mask-programmable form) and PROM technology was available and promising, a field-programmable PLA seemed the next logical step. The management at Signetics was convinced that the idea was viable, and agreed to proceed with the project.

The pioneering 82S100 FPLA—the initial member of Signetics' *Integrated Fuse Logic* (*IFL*) family—resided in a 28-pin fat (0.6-inch wide) DIP. Its architecture—in keeping with its PLA ancestry—consisted of a programmable AND-

Figure 1-2. Napoleone Cavlan, the "father of programmable logic." *Photo courtesy Advanced Micro Devices, Inc.*

array followed by a programmable OR-array, permitting straightforward SOP logic implementation.

Though flexible, the new FPLA received only mild acceptance from digital designers. The P.C. board space-hogging 28-pin fat DIP was not especially popular for a device intended to save space. More importantly, it was very difficult and tedious to specify the logic for the device since software support was not available. The designer was required to fill in a chart with 1s, 0s, Hs, Ls, and dashes (see Fig. 1-3) to specify the internal logic—a long, tedious, and error-prone process. Modifications to the logic table were similarly tedious and prone to errors. Device prices were also relatively high, starting at about $30 for relatively low quantities (100 pieces). This was mostly due to the fact that fuses require substantial silicon area, resulting in large dies. Finally, the dual programmable-array architecture also resulted in relatively slow propagation times (50 ns max.). While the benefits of the FPLA were many, its drawbacks provided a resistance in the marketplace that was not overcome until 1978.

In the early 1970s, John Martin Birkner (see Fig. 1-4) worked for Computer

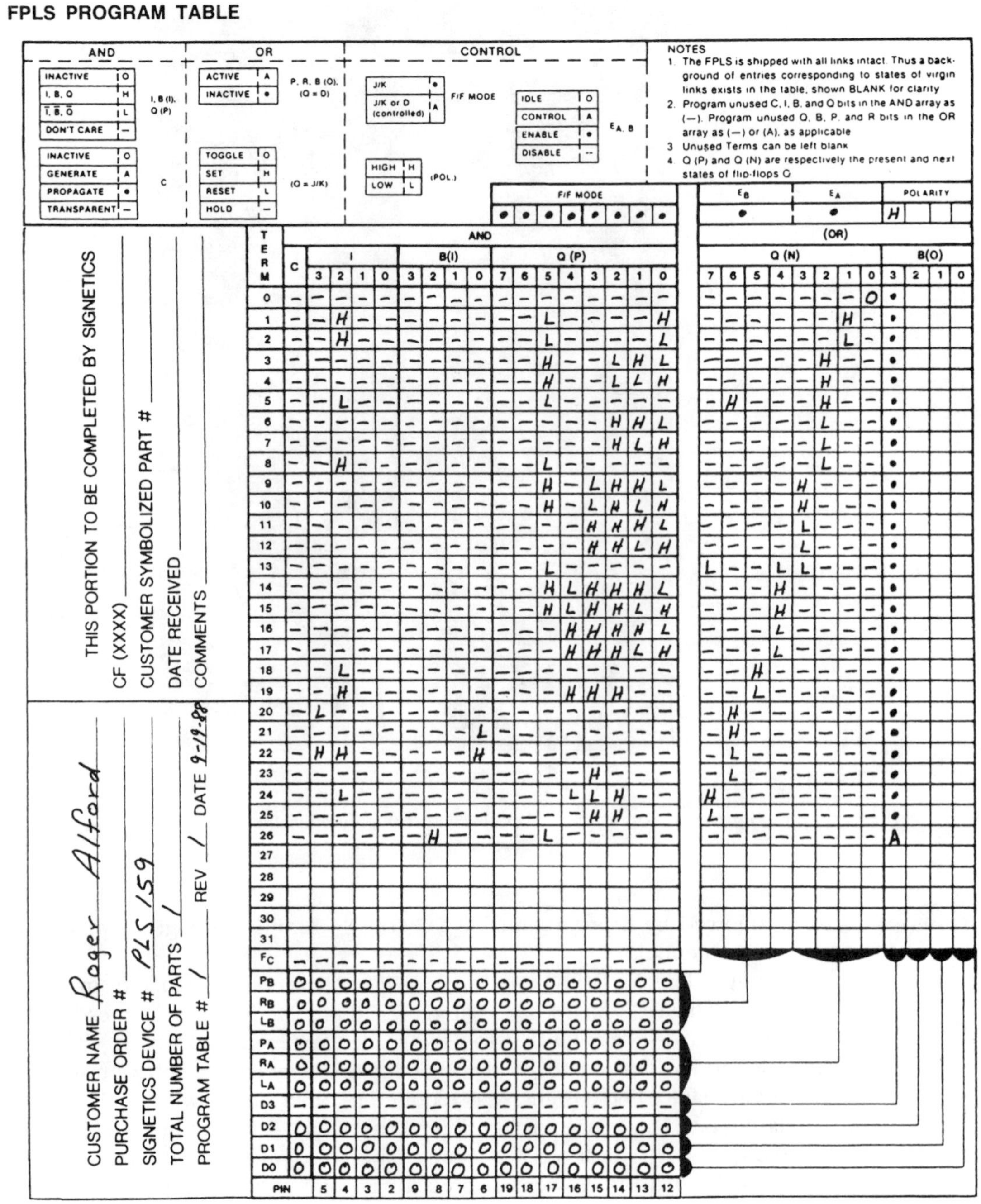

FPLS PROGRAM TABLE

Legend boxes:

AND

INACTIVE	O
I, B, Q	H
Ī, B̄, Q̄	L
DON'T CARE	—
INACTIVE	O
GENERATE	A
PROPAGATE	•
TRANSPARENT	—

I, B (I), Q (P) / C

OR

ACTIVE	A
INACTIVE	•
TOGGLE	O
SET	H
RESET	L
HOLD	—

P, R, B (O), (Q = O) / (Q = J/K)

CONTROL

J/K, J/K or D (controlled) — F/F MODE

IDLE	O
CONTROL	A
ENABLE	•
DISABLE	--

E A, B

HIGH H / LOW L (POL.)

NOTES

1. The FPLS is shipped with all links intact. Thus a background of entries corresponding to states of virgin links exists in the table, shown BLANK for clarity
2. Program unused C, I, B, and Q bits in the AND array as (—). Program unused Q, B, P, and R bits in the OR array as (—) or (A), as applicable
3. Unused Terms can be left blank
4. Q (P) and Q (N) are respectively the present and next states of flip-flops Q

THIS PORTION TO BE COMPLETED BY SIGNETICS

CF (XXXX) ___
CUSTOMER SYMBOLIZED PART # ___
DATE RECEIVED ___
COMMENTS ___

CUSTOMER NAME *Roger Alford*
PURCHASE ORDER # ___
SIGNETICS DEVICE # *PLS 159*
TOTAL NUMBER OF PARTS ___
PROGRAM TABLE # *1*   REV *1*   DATE *9-19-88*

Figure 1-3. Example of a completed Signetics FPLS logic specification chart.

Figure 1-4. John Martin Birkner, the "father of the PAL."

Automation as a designer of minicomputer circuits. Through many designs he came to realize that much of the logic design methodology taught in college was not of much practical use. Instead, designs consisted of mixing and matching standard TTL chips until the desired design was achieved. Texas Instruments' *The TTL Databook* was one of the favorite references for logic designers of that time.

Circuit boards were riddled with the inescapable "cuts and jumpers" necessary to achieve proper operation. The engineering change notice (ECN) became the standard procedure for documenting circuit changes, and was a constant source of conflict between engineering and manufacturing. Even after product release, additional changes were not uncommon—often due to circuit problems uncovered by customers.

Convinced that there must be a better way to design digital circuits, Birkner left for Silicon Valley in 1975. Arriving on the doorstep of Monolithic Memories, Inc. (MMI), a manufacturer of PROMs and standard logic devices, Birkner began considering the idea of programmable logic. After studying Signetics' FPLA he realized the benefits of the concept, but also perceived its drawbacks. He then set out to conceive a new approach to programmable logic devices that would overcome the primary hurtles of the FPLA.

Birkner eventually conceived the concept of *Programmable Array Logic (PAL)* devices—devices that were similar to, yet architecturally simpler than, the

FPLA. The simplicity of the PAL concept was, in many ways, its primary feature. Instead of having two programmable arrays, PAL would have a programmable AND-array followed by a fixed (nonprogrammable) OR-array. Thus, each OR gate would have a fixed number of product (AND) terms connected to its inputs. This would reduce die size (i.e., cost) substantially and permit faster signal propagation, while still allowing SOP logic implementation. PAL would also fit into a space-saving, 20-pin SkinnyDIP package (having a 0.3-inch width). Other PAL features would include a data sheet that paralleled those found in the familiar *The TTL Databook*—to help designers feel more at home with the parts—as well as software support to facilitate PAL logic designs. The PALs would also be designed to "look" like PROMs, to allow them to be programmed on existing PROM programmers with the addition of an adapter module.

Birkner also had to determine what a reasonable number of product terms would be for each output (sum term). He did this by empirically working through many of the circuit problems he had faced during his minicomputer design days at Computer Automation. He determined that a majority of the logic functions would fit nicely using eight or fewer product terms. This number was, then, chosen as the goal for the initial PAL devices.

Birkner's initial attempt to convince management to go with his PAL concept was met with skepticism and apprehension. In view of the fact that Signetics' FPLAs hadn't generated a lot of market interest, and the fact that the expense of tooling a new package type (a 20-pin, 0.3-inch-wide DIP) would be substantial, the management at MMI found it difficult to be optimistic. Birkner presented his idea at industry conferences, but realized that the way to a boss' heart is through his customers. He therefore took his ideas to some large computer companies, including Data General[1] and Digital Equipment Corp., and convinced them of the merits of his PAL concept. Their support helped Birkner get the internal balls rolling—however slowly—to turn his concept into working silicon. With Birkner heading the project and H. T. Chua handling the circuit design, the PAL project was under way.

Ironically, Cavlan and Birkner started out as adversaries but, according to Cavlan, "we came to realize that we shared a common vision and developed a cordial professional relationship."[2] Birkner urged Cavlan to join MMI, which he eventually did in February, 1986, as its manager of PAL product planning.

Even though the PAL project had begun, it was still an uphill effort. Because of initial low yields due to fuse difficulties, it was difficult to convince the wafer fabrication manager to "run" the PAL wafers. With a little coercing (and a few lunch expenditures), Birkner got his working parts into the hands of his customers. The first PAL devices were the now-popular PAL16L8, PAL16R4, PAL16R6, and PAL16R8, having 35 ns input-to-output propagation delays. Each of these devices had eight outputs, and up to 16 inputs. The 'L' device had eight "active low" combinatorial outputs, while the 'R' devices had four, six, or eight registered outputs, respectively (with the remaining outputs being combinatorial).

---

[1] In *The Soul of a New Machine*, Tracy Kidder describes the development of a Data General minicomputer and the decision of the designers to use PALs.
[2] "Semiconductors," *Electronics*, October 16, 1986, p. 83.

HOWARD W. SAMS & COMPANY

fff

Bookmark

DEAR VALUED CUSTOMER:

Howard W. Sams & Company is dedicated to bringing you timely and authoritative books for your personal and professional library. Our goal is to provide you with excellent technical books written by the most qualified authors. You can assist us in this endeavor by checking the box next to your particular areas of interest.

We appreciate your comments and will use the information to provide you with a more comprehensive selection of titles.

Thank you,

Vice President, Book Publishing
Howard W. Sams & Company

COMPUTER TITLES:

Hardware
☐ Apple 140   ☐ Macintosh 101
☐ Commodore 110
☐ IBM & Compatibles 114

Business Applications
☐ Word Processing J01
☐ Data Base J04
☐ Spreadsheets J02

Operating Systems
☐ MS-DOS K05   ☐ OS/2 K10
☐ CP/M K01   ☐ UNIX K03

Programming Languages
☐ C L03   ☐ Pascal L05
☐ Prolog L12   ☐ Assembly L01
☐ BASIC L02   ☐ HyperTalk L14

Troubleshooting & Repair
☐ Computers S05
☐ Peripherals S10

Other
☐ Communications/Networking M03
☐ AI/Expert Systems T18

ELECTRONICS TITLES:
☐ Amateur Radio T01
☐ Audio T03
☐ Basic Electronics T20
☐ Basic Electricity T21
☐ Electronics Design T12
☐ Electronics Projects T04
☐ Satellites T09

☐ Instrumentation T05
☐ Digital Electronics T11

Troubleshooting & Repair
☐ Audio S11   ☐ Television S04
☐ VCR S01   ☐ Compact Disc S02
☐ Automotive S06
☐ Microwave Oven S03

Other interests or comments: _____

_____

_____

Name_____
Title _____
Company _____
Address _____
City _____
State/Zip _____
Daytime Telephone No. _____

A Division of Macmillan, Inc.

4300 West 62nd Street   Indianapolis, Indiana 46268

22575

Bookmark

HOWARD W. SAMS
& COMPANY

After a slow start, the PALs were finally designed into real systems. The minicomputer companies were finding that the PALs allowed them to reduce the number of boards needed to implement their designs, and also permitted logic changes without "cuts and jumpers." Once the parts were designed in, however, MMI found itself in a pinch. Production yields on the PAL devices were still unacceptable, and were insufficient to meet customer demand. Production problems also made the $5.00 target price unattainable.

With Data General and Digital Equipment breathing heavily down their necks, MMI was forced to come up with another alternative. Realizing that the fuse links presented the primary manufacturing problem, MMI chose to go with mask-programmable PALs to satisfy the production requirements of its customers. This led to the introduction of the *Hard Array Logic* (*HAL*) family of devices. To produce HAL parts for Data General and Digital Equipment, MMI removed the fuse mask layers and replaced them with metal link layers corresponding to the logic patterns required for its customers. The resulting parts had several benefits, including high yields and easier testability. The customers also benefited by not having to be concerned with programming or testing the parts.

MMI eventually improved its PAL manufacturing processes, achieving acceptable yields for producing PALs in high volume. In 1978, MMI published its first *PAL Handbook*, launching PALs to the open world of logic designers. Among other things, the *PAL Handbook* had the task of explaining its concept to designers in a way that would help them realize the benefits without being intimidating. Significantly, the book also included the Fortran source listing for PALASM (PAL ASseMbler)—a software package designed for entering PAL logic equations. PALASM could compile a logic definition into a format that could then be downloaded (transferred) to a PAL programmer—making PAL development relatively simple and straightforward. PALASM was also capable of simulating the operation of the PAL based on the logic equations. In conjunction with designer-specified "test vectors," PALASM could verify proper (essential) logic operation before programming real parts.

Reflecting on his dedicated efforts in pushing PAL from conception to production, Birkner's business cards read, "Champion of PALs."

All of the features of the PAL—including the absence of many of the FPLA drawbacks—combined to accelerate PAL acceptance to a level much higher than expected. PALs quickly overtook Signetics' IFL devices in popularity, and the term *PAL* became synonymous with *PLD* in many circles.

In the meantime, Signetics continued its IFL family development. In 1977, Signetics introduced its 82S103 *Field-Programmable Gate Array* (*FPGA*), and in 1979 its 82S105 *Field-Programmable Logic Sequencer* (*FPLS*). The FPGA consisted of a single-level array of AND gates with programmable input and output polarity selection, allowing any basic logic function (AND, OR, NAND, NOR, INVERT) to be implemented. The FPLS contained flip-flops to implement state machine and sequencer functions.

Realizing the importance of software for assisting PLD designers—particularly in light of MMI's PAL success—Signetics introduced its *AMAZE* (Automated Map And Zap Equations) PLD compiler in 1984 to support its devices. Similarly, other PLD manufacturers began offering software support to encourage use of their own devices.

Both Signetics and MMI continued to introduce new PLDs to meet a greater variety of design requirements, and PALs showed steadily increasing sales. As programmable logic entered into the early 1980's, a wide variety of IFLs and PALs were available to designers, and many parts were alternate-sourced by other manufacturers (such as National Semiconductor and Advanced Micro Devices (AMD)). Despite the initial success of the first PLDs, however, only a relatively small number of digital designers were familiar with programmable logic—at least from the standpoint of feeling comfortable designing with PLDs—and few universities were covering programmable logic in their digital design courses.

Nonetheless, programmable logic technology continued to improve and second-generation devices were soon being introduced, led by the 1983 intro-duction of AMD's PAL22V10. The PAL22V10 introduced a number of features previously not available on programmable logic devices. The most notable feature was the inclusion of flexible *output macrocells* on each of its 10 output pins. Each macrocell was capable of being a combinatorial or registered output (with programmable output polarity), or a pin input. The tri-state output buffer was controlled by a separate product term, allowing bidirectional operation. All registers were automatically reset during power-up, and the registers also fea-tured "preload" capability to facilitate more-advanced post-programming test-ing. It took little time for the PAL22V10 to become popular, and for other PLDs to begin implementing many of its features.

With new devices appearing regularly, it became increasingly clear that software support was a key issue in making PLDs usable for design engineers. One man, Bob Osann, saw the need for a universal PLD compiler that could support all of the PLDs from all manufacturers. In 1981, Osann started Assisted Technology to develop PLD support tools. In September, 1983 Assisted Tech-nology released version 1.01a of its *CUPL* (Universal Compiler for Programm-able Logic) PLD compiler, supporting 29 devices.

Having vision for its universal compiler, Assisted Technology approached Data I/O Corp.—the world's largest manufacturer of device (EPROM, PROM, and PLD) programming equipment—about marketing the product. Impressed with the product, Data I/O wanted to acquire Assisted Technology, but the privately held Assisted Technology refused to sell. Assisted Technology chose, instead, to market CUPL themselves. (Ironically, Assisted Technology later allowed itself to be acquired by Personal CAD Systems.)

In the meantime, Data I/O—realizing the potential for a universal PLD compiler—decided to develop its own software. In 1984, Data I/O introduced its *ABEL* (Advanced Boolean Expression Language) PLD compiler. Having simi-lar features to its CUPL competitor, but with a much stronger financial backing for marketing, ABEL soon overtook CUPL in the marketplace. Both are still popular universal compilers, although ABEL is clearly the industry leader in terms of units sold.

The availability of universal PLD compilers spurred the digital design indus-try to more-readily accept and use PLDs in new designs. The universal com-pilers were much more advanced than MMI's popular PALASM compiler and Signetics' AMAZE compiler, and they allowed designers to support devices from multiple vendors while becoming familiar with only a single compiler. CUPL and ABEL also allowed designers to specify the logic equations for a device, then find the least expensive PLD that could implement the logic. Logic minimization and device simulation were standard features of both universal compilers.

In 1983, the PLD industry showed that it had learned an important lesson from the EPROM industry. Over the previous several years, myriad computer systems had taken advantage of EPROMs for storing programs and data. To program the EPROMs, an object file containing the desired binary bit patterns had to be created (typically using an assembler or compiler) and (somehow) transferred to an EPROM programmer. Numerous object file formats bloomed for this purpose because no formal standard existed. Intel's hex/ASCII format was probably the most dominant of the various formats, although Motorola's S-record format also proved popular, as did Tektronix's Tek-Hex format. Many software manufacturers chose to support multiple object file formats to meet customer requirements, requiring extra development effort. Similarly, EPROM programmer manufacturers were forced to either limit their market share by supporting a single object file format, or to support multiple formats, resulting in greater development effort and ultimately higher product cost.

As the PLD industry began to mature, it became clear that a similar situation would again develop unless a standard was created. Thus, while the PLD industry was still in its infancy, the Joint Electron Device Engineering Council (JEDEC) set out to produce a PLD compiler output file standard that could be used by all current and future PLD manufacturers. This would prevent duplicate effort, and would require PLD programmer manufacturers to support only a single format. In October, 1983 the JEDEC Solid State Products Engineering Council released JEDEC Standard No. 3, "Standard Transfer Format Between Data Preparation System and Programmable Logic Device Programmer." The standard was later revised to JEDEC Standard No. 3-A in May, 1986. To the benefit of all, the standard has become universally accepted by the entire PLD industry.

The next significant advance in programmable logic took place in July, 1984, with the introduction of the first product from start-up Altera Corp., the EP300. The primary significance of the EP300 was its implementation using CMOS EPROM technology, which offered not only low-power operation, but also erasability (using ultraviolet light). The EP300's erasability allowed it to be fully programmed and tested at the factory—unlike the bipolar PLDs of the day—and permitted designers to reuse parts during the development cycle, saving the expense of discarding devices containing old-version logic. The EP300 also implemented output macrocells, with extended features over the PAL22V10. Altera's later devices further improved the flexibility of output macrocells.

Altera called its devices *Erasable, Programmable Logic Devices*, or *EPLDs*. As UV-erasable PLDs became available from other manufacturers, such as Cypress and Atmel, the term 'EPLD' became generic, and is now commonly used to refer to all PLDs that are implemented using EPROM technology. Intel served both as the foundry and as an alternate-source for Altera's EPLDs.

A similar, yet distinct, PLD family was also introduced in 1985 by Lattice Semiconductor Corp. With the introduction of its *Generic Array Logic (GAL)* family, Lattice offered programmable logic designers yet another technology from which to choose, namely CMOS EEPROM. Like the EPLDs introduced by Altera, Lattice's GALs (initially the GAL16V8) offered the low-power operation common to CMOS technology, as well as erasability. Unlike the EPLDs, however, the GALs were *electrically* erasable, allowing them to be erased in a matter of seconds using an applied voltage, compared to the 20 minutes or so of UV-light exposure typically required for EPLD erasure. Also, GALs were capable of being erased even when residing in inexpensive molded plastic packages, whereas EPLDs required expensive windowed ceramic packages to facilitate erasure.

GALs, like all other *Electrically Erasable PLDs*, became generically known as *EEPLDs*. As its name implies, Generic Array Logic was designed with a flexible "generic" architecture (i.e., using macrocells), similar to that of Altera's EPLDs. The primary intent of its generic architecture was to get a piece of the PAL pie by providing devices that could functionally replace existing PALs. The GAL16V8, for example, was capable of functionally replacing nearly every existing 20-pin PAL. Lattice coined the term *ComPALibility* to emphasize this point.

Gradually more and more companies entered the PLD marketplace, often with special features or different technologies. Numerous companies began offering erasable CMOS PLDs (EPLDs and EEPLDs), and even fast ECL parts became available. For the most part all of the new devices being introduced were architecturally similar to existing devices, building on either an FPLA or PAL foundation.

As PLD manufacturers looked for ways to use device silicon area more efficiently, the discovery of new PLD architectures was inevitable. The first radical change in PLD architecture came in 1985 from the start-up company, Xilinx. Founded in February, 1984, the company's goal was to "develop a family of CMOS user-programmable gate arrays and associated development systems."[3] Unlike existing PLDs, the Xilinx *Logic Cell Array (LCA)* did not contain product terms and sum terms. Its third-generation PLD architecture consisted of a matrix of Configurable Logic Blocks (CLBs) surrounded by Input/Output Blocks (IOBs), with an interconnect network for connecting blocks. Called a programmable gate array, the Xilinx LCA was indeed architecturally similar to traditional, mask-programmed gate arrays, especially in comparison to previous PLDs.

Its unique architecture was not the only distinguishing feature of the Logic Cell Array. The LCA was also the first PLD to use static RAM (SRAM) cells for configuring its logic functionality. Prior to this, PLDs were configured using bipolar fuses, CMOS fuses, EPROM cells, or EEPROM cells. The use of SRAM cells for device configuration had both its advantages and disadvantages. On the positive side, the device was completely factory (and customer) testable, and was dynamically, in-system reconfigurable. On the negative side, the LCA's volatile nature required external memory to store its configuration, which needed to be loaded each time the device was powered up. This precluded the

---

[3] *The Programmable Gate Array Design Handbook, First Edition*, Xilinx, Inc., p. iii.

LCA from being used in situations where its functionality was required immediately at power-up time.

Because of the relatively complex—and unique—nature of the LCA, it was clear to Xilinx that existing third-party PLD software packages would be inadequate to support their devices. The software support was, therefore, developed internally, and introduced with the LCA. It included the XACT design editor and a simulator package (P-SILOS). Xilinx also offered another development feature, which was unavailable from any other PLD manufacturer: an in-circuit emulator. The LCA in-circuit emulator presented the logic designer with an advanced hardware tool (with software support) to aid in developing and debugging LCA-based designs.

Another new, third-generation PLD architecture was announced in 1985, although initial parts did not begin to appear until 1986. At WESCON 1985, Signetics introduced its *Programmable Macro Logic (PML)* concept. PML is a *foldback* architecture, consisting of a single array of NAND gates, with the outputs of the NAND gates "folded back" into the NAND-array. This allows multiple logic levels to be implemented, and also permits efficient use of device silicon. Once logic functions are internally defined, they can be routed to any output pin via on-chip interconnects. The first PML device from Signetics, the PLHS501 Random Logic Unit, was implemented using bipolar technology, and resided in a 52-pin package.

Another foldback family was introduced in 1986 by Exel Microelectronic, although production did not begin until 1987. Exel's *ERASIC* (Erasable Application-Specific IC) family is based on CMOS EEPROM technology, and uses a NOR-foldback array for best performance. The first ERASIC device, the XL78C800, was released in the popular, space-saving 0.3-inch, 24-pin package, and is able to functionally replace virtually every existing 24-pin PAL and FPLA (except for speed). The XL78C800 includes transparent input latches and flexible output macrocells to form a truly flexible device. Exel also developed ERASIC software to work with ABEL for supporting their devices.

A new trend in PLDs appeared around 1986, although the first devices existed before that time. The trend was toward function-specific or application-specific PLDs *(ASPLDs)*. Instead of having general-purpose architectures, devices were being streamlined for specific functions, allowing more-efficient usage of on-chip resources and more-advanced functionality in special applications. The two primary areas experiencing the proliferation of ASPLDs were bus interface applications and state machine and sequencer applications. Devices soon appeared from Intel, Altera, AMD, MMI, Texas Instruments, and others.

Realizing that its IFL family name had become virtually lost in the popularity of PAL and other similar family names (HAL, GAL, etc.), Signetics decided in 1986 to change the name (and image) of its PLD family to something that designers might readily associate with programmable logic. It decided on *PLS (Programmable Logic from Signetics)* as its new name, and correspondingly changed its part numbering system; part numbers changed, for example, from 82S100 to PLS100, and from 82S157 to PLS157.

Several other significant announcements were made in 1988 from two new entrants into the PLD marketplace. The first announcement came from Actel Corp., which introduced a new series of programmable gate-array devices.

Unlike the RAM-based Xilinx LCAs, the Actel parts are one-time-programmable (OTP), eliminating the need for configuring the devices each time they are powered up.

The second important announcement came from Gazelle Microcircuits, which announced the first PLD based on GaAs (gallium arsenide) technology. This technology features an improved speed-power product over silicon-based technologies, allowing very fast devices with only moderate power consumption. The first part released by Gazelle was a GaAs version of the popular PAL22V10, which was first introduced in silicon by AMD. Gazelle had two primary hurtles to overcome in developing its GaAs-based programmable logic technology. First, the company had to develop circuitry that would permit its GaAs devices to have TTL-compatible inputs and outputs, without a substantial performance degradation. The second hurtle was to develop an acceptable method of programming the parts. To do this, the company developed a laser-based programmer that blows selected fuses using a directed laser beam. Unfortunately, since the programming unit is elaborate and costly, customers wishing to use the Gazelle parts must have them programmed at the factory, eliminating some of the flexibility generally offered by the use of programmable logic.

Throughout the early-to-mid 1980s, the market for PLDs grew steadily as more-advanced devices and software became available, and as more designers became aware of PLDs. Universities began offering PLD courses, even though little more than manufacturer data books were available as texts, and manufacturers became increasingly aggressive in offering short design courses to engineers around the United States, and in other countries. It was clear by the mid-1980s that the PLD market had begun its explosive growth, which is still continuing unabated. PLDs had become essential tools for digital designers, leaving behind the "optional" status dominant in previous years.

The growth in the PLD industry—as with the semiconductor industry in general—was not without its conflicts, mergers, and acquisitions, although such things did not (formally) begin until 1986. In that year, MMI sued both Altera and Lattice for infringement of its PAL patent. In a precedent-setting move, Altera conceded its infringement and settled out of court with a patent exchange agreement. Lattice, similarly, settled out of court with a patent cross-licensing agreement.

Nineteen eighty six and 1987 were active years in terms of mergers and acquisitions. In 1986, MMI purchased stock in Xilinx and became an alternate-source for the company's LCAs; later, in 1987, MMI merged with AMD. AMD and MMI are maintaining their separate names for the time being—particularly because of the name-association MMI enjoys in the PLD industry—although they will likely fall entirely under the AMD name later. AMD and MMI are addressed individually here to clarify the pre-merger contributions of each company.

National Semiconductor also acquired Fairchild in 1987, giving Fairchild's FASTPLA PAL family a new home with a potentially stronger marketing backing.

Nineteen eighty seven also saw the first victim of the increasing competition in the PLD industry. Sprague Electric Co. withdrew its CMOS PAL family from the market due to lower than expected demand. Sometime later VLSI

Technology also decided to retreat from the PLD marketplace, withdrawing its GAL devices, which were being sold as an alternate-source for Lattice.

The history of PLDs has certainly been interesting and dynamic, and its future will predictably be even more so. In Chapter 9 we speculate about the future of the industry.

Chapter 2

Logic Design Review

To fully understand and appreciate how programmable logic devices can revolutionize digital logic design, it is important to have at least a modest understanding of what is involved with traditional logic design. This includes the techniques and terminology that have become its trademark. Although it is assumed that the reader already understands the basics of digital logic design, this chapter provides an intermediate-level logic design review to act as a foundation for PLD design discussions in later chapters. A complete understanding of the digital design information presented here is not absolutely essential to use PLDs, but would permit using the devices more effectively.

Chapter Overview

We will begin by taking a look at combinatorial logic, including basic logic gates, truth tables, Boolean equations, and DeMorgan's theorem. From there we will go on to the SOP and POS forms of describing Boolean equations, and logic minimization using Karnaugh maps and other techniques. This will be followed by an examination of sequential logic, including state machine descriptions; a look at synchronization and metastability; and a discussion of "nasty realities," race conditions, and hang-up states. We will then briefly look at open-collector and three-state outputs, and the concept of busses. Finally, we will conclude with a comparison of some common IC technologies.

Terminology

Terminology is sometimes confusing when talking about Boolean logic, particularly when referring to actual circuit designs. The terms "high," "one," "true," "active," and "asserted" sometimes have the same meaning and sometimes have different meanings. For example, the terms "true," "active," and "asserted" have different meanings depending on how they are used. Likewise the terms "low," "zero," "false," "active," and "asserted" have inconsistent meanings, with "false" being a term that maintains a particularly inconsistent interpretation. For consistency and to avoid confusion, the terms "high" and "low" or "one" and "zero" will be used initially. The terms "active" and "asserted" will be defined later, and will then be used where appropriate. The term "true" will only be used to refer to an uncomplemented signal.

Logic Gates and Truth Tables

The basic *logic gates* used in digital design are shown symbolically in Fig. 2-1, along with their respective *truth tables*. The output of an *AND gate* (Fig. 2-1A) is high only when both inputs are high, otherwise it is low. The truth table next to the AND gate symbol shows the gate's logical *transfer function* by indicating its output state for every possible combination of input states.

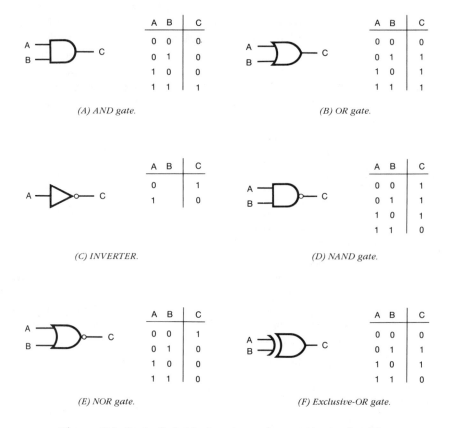

(A) AND gate.

(B) OR gate.

(C) INVERTER.

(D) NAND gate.

(E) NOR gate.

(F) Exclusive-OR gate.

Figure 2-1. Basic digital logic gates and respective truth tables.

The output of an *OR gate* (Fig. 2-1B) is high when either input (or both) is high, and is low otherwise. The output of an *inverter* (Fig. 2-1C) is always the opposite (complement) of its input; when its input is high, its output is low, and vice-versa.

A *NAND gate* (Fig. 2-1D) acts like an AND gate with an inverter connected to its output. This is reflected in its truth table, which has outputs exactly inverted from those shown in the truth table for the AND gate. Similarly, a *NOR gate* (Fig. 2-1E) acts like an OR gate with an inverter connected to its output.

Another gate, the *exclusive-OR* (*XOR gate*, Fig. 2-1F), is similar to the OR gate, but relates more closely to "real life" than the OR gate. The output of an *OR* gate is high when input A is high or input B is high, or *both* are high. The output of an *XOR* gate, on the other hand, is high when input A is high or input B is high, but *not* when both are high. If, for example, someone says, "I will cook fish *or* chicken tomorrow," he means he will cook one or the other, but not both—the exclusive-OR function is being applied in this "real life" situation. Because the output of an XOR gate is low when the inputs match and high when the inputs differ, XOR gates are commonly used for digital "equal to" comparisons.

Although the AND, OR, NAND, and NOR gates in Fig. 2-1 are shown with only two inputs, these gates can have any number of inputs.

Truth tables can be created for any combinatorial logic circuit, to describe the circuit's outputs in terms of its inputs. The truth tables for the basic gates in Fig. 2-1 are simple and very easy to understand, having only one or two inputs and a single output. For complex circuits, however, very large truth tables can be generated, having many inputs and outputs. It is frequently the case that for some input signal combinations, the state of one or more outputs is unimportant. These are called *don't-care* states, and are generally denoted with an 'X'. Having *don't-care* states generally makes logic reduction easier.

While truth tables are very useful for smaller logic circuits and some special applications (e.g., a BCD to 7-segment decoder), circuits with many inputs (or outputs) would be prohibitively difficult to define using a truth table. Each time a new input term is added to a circuit, the size of the truth table *doubles*! A truth table with four inputs requires 16 lines to describe all input combinations; one with five inputs requires 32 lines; and a truth table with 10 inputs requires 1,024 lines to completely describe!

Boolean Equations

In order to describe, manipulate, and minimize circuits effectively, a two-valued (binary) mathematical approach must be used. Use of *Boolean equations*[1] provides such a mathematical method to describe the logical operation of a digital circuit. *Boolean algebra*—the mathematics of two-valued variables—can be used to manipulate Boolean equations for minimization and other purposes.

---

[1]George Boole (1815–1864) was the son of a shoemaker. His formal education ended in third grade. Despite this, he was a brilliant scholar, teaching Greek and Latin in his own school, and an accepted mathematician who made lasting contributions in the areas of differential and difference equations as well as algebra.

Figure 2-2 shows the common theorems applicable to Boolean algebra. An additional theorem that has special significance in Boolean algebra, *DeMorgan's theorem*,[2] is shown in Fig. 2-3.

$$
\begin{array}{ll}
a + 0 = a & a \cdot 1 = a \\
a + a' = 1 & a \cdot a' = 0 \\
a + a = a & a \cdot a = a \\
a + 1 = 1 & a \cdot 0 = 0 \\
(a')' = a & \\
a + b = b + a & a\,b = b\,a \\
a + (b + c) = (a + b) + c & a(b\,c) = (a\,b)\,c \\
a(b + c) = a\,b + a\,c & a + b\,c = (a + b)(a + c) \\
a + a\,b = a & a(a + b) = a
\end{array}
$$

Figure 2-2. Common Boolean algebra theorems and postulates.

$$(a + b)' = a'\,b' \qquad (a\,b)' = a' + b'$$

Figure 2-3. DeMorgan's theorem.

In Boolean algebra, the multiplication symbol (the dot or asterisk) is used to represent variables being ANDed together. ANDed variables, therefore, are algebraically multiplied and, for the most part, normal algebra multiplication rules apply (as seen by the theorems and laws in Fig. 2-2). A group of signals ANDed together is called a *product term*. The addition symbol ($+$) is used to represent variables being ORed together. While the addition symbol can, for the most part, be used in the traditional algebraic manner for equation manipulation, when determining the logical output of a Boolean equation it must be remembered that the "added" variables are not actually added together (though the term "sum" is used). They are ORed to provide a binary (one or zero) result.

DeMorgan Equivalents

Figure 2-4 shows four more gates along with their respective truth tables, which are similar in appearance to the gates shown in Fig. 2-1. Looking at the truth tables, we see that the gates are indeed logically equivalent to gates in Fig. 2-1. For example, the NOR gate with a *bubble* at each input in Fig. 2-4A is logically equivalent to the AND gate in Fig. 2-1A. The *inverting bubbles* at the gate inputs have the logical effect of inverting the input signals. The AND gate in Fig. 2-1A and the gate shown in Fig. 2-4A are logically identical because they are *DeMorgan equivalents*; that is, applying DeMorgan's theorem to the Boolean equation of an AND gate (C = A * B) gives us the DeMorgan equivalent version (C' = A' + B' or C = (A' + B')') shown in Fig. 2-4A. (Note, the suffix prime symbol (') is used here to specify a complemented variable. Also, the multiplication asterisk (*) will be largely dropped from the remainder of this discussion, realizing that x * y = xy and x' * y' = x'y'.)

---

[2]Augustus DeMorgan (1806–1871), like George Boole, was an English mathematician and logician, and made a significant contribution to Boolean algebra with his famous theorem.

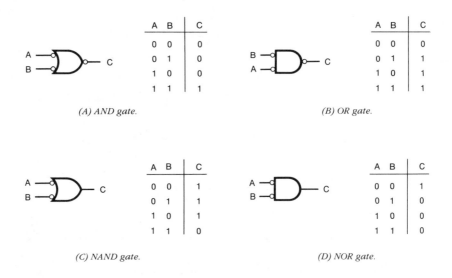

(A) AND gate.

(B) OR gate.

(C) NAND gate.

(D) NOR gate.

Figure 2-4. DeMorgan gate equivalents.

Minterms and Maxterms

It seems appropriate at this point to introduce the concept of *minterms* and *maxterms*. A binary variable may appear in either of two forms, true (x) or complemented (x'). Any two binary variables can appear in any of four possible combinations, with neither, one, or both variables complemented (xy, xy', x'y, x'y'). This expands similarly to any number of binary variables, where 2^n combinations (product terms) are possible with n variables. Each of these product terms is called a *minterm* or *standard product*, containing exactly one occurrence of each variable (true or complemented).

In a similar way, any n binary variables can be summed (ORed) together in 2^n different combinations, with the resulting terms called *maxterms* or *standard sums*. Figure 2-5 shows all of the three-variable minterms and maxterms. By definition, a minterm or maxterm cannot contain both the true and complemented version of the same signal. For example, the term xyx' is *not* considered a minterm since it contains both the true and complemented version of the variable 'x'; indeed, such a product term will always have a zero value.

Any Boolean function can be expressed as a sum of minterms or a product of maxterms. An equation in either of these forms is said to be in *canonical form*, and conversion from one canonical form to the other is straightforward.

Sum-of-Products and Product-of-Sums

While logical expressions in canonical form often possess only minimal usefulness, there are two general forms of Boolean equations having greater usefulness in digital logic design, the Sum-of-Products (SOP) form and the Product-of-Sums (POS) form; these are called *standard forms*. The SOP and POS forms

			Minterms	
a	b	c	Term	Designation
0	0	0	$a'b'c'$	m_0
0	0	1	$a'b'c$	m_1
0	1	0	$a'bc'$	m_2
0	1	1	$a'bc$	m_3
1	0	0	$ab'c'$	m_4
1	0	1	$ab'c$	m_5
1	1	0	abc'	m_6
1	1	1	abc	m_7

			Maxterms	
a	b	c	Term	Designation
0	0	0	$a+b+c$	M_0
0	0	1	$a+b+c'$	M_1
0	1	0	$a+b'+c$	M_2
0	1	1	$a+b'+c'$	M_3
1	0	0	$a'+b+c$	M_4
1	0	1	$a'+b+c'$	M_5
1	1	0	$a'+b'+c$	M_6
1	1	1	$a'+b'+c'$	M_7

Figure 2-5. All three-variable minterms and maxterms.

have one primary (and very important) advantage over the corresponding sum of minterms and product of maxterms forms. The individual terms need not contain a true or complemented version of *all* variables. Thus, for example, the equation

$$a = xy + yz$$

is in standard SOP form, but is not in canonical (sum of minterms) form. The canonical equivalent would be:

$$a = xyz + xyz' + x'yz \ .$$

The following two equations are logically equivalent, but are presented in different standard forms:

$$(x' + y') * (x + y) \qquad \text{POS form}$$

$$(xy') + (x'y) \qquad \text{SOP form}$$

As in algebra, the multiplication (AND) operator has precedence over the addition (OR) operator, so the parentheses in the second equation are redundant. Most PLD architectures are optimized for Boolean equations in the SOP form.

Karnaugh Maps

The map method for minimizing logic equations was first introduced in 1952 by E. W. Veitch[3] and was improved in 1953 by M. Karnaugh.[4] The *Karnaugh map* (*K-map*) or *Veitch diagram* has proven to be a popular tool for logic reduction in logic circuits involving up to five or six variables.

---

[3]Veitch, E. W., "A Chart Method for Simplifying Truth Functions." *Proceedings of the ACM* (May 1952), pp. 127–33.

[4]Karnaugh, M., "A Map Method for Synthesis of Combinational Logic Circuits." *Trans. AIEE, Communications and Electronics*, Vol. 72, Part I (November 1953), pp. 593–99.

An n-variable Karnaugh map requires 2^n squares, each of which holds the output value of the logic circuit for a specific combination of input signals. Circuits having multiple outputs require a separate map for each output. Because the size of the map doubles for each additional input variable, K-maps become somewhat impractical above about six variables. The best way to describe the operation of the Karnaugh map is by example, so let's look at a circuit problem to be minimized using the K-map.

Figure 2-6 shows the circuit function to be created, namely a BCD to 7-segment decoder. Thus, with a 4-bit BCD input, we need to determine the logic equation for each of the seven outputs—one output corresponding to each of the seven display segments (a–g). To do this, we must first prepare a truth table to show the state of each output for every combination of inputs. The truth table should be consistent with the desired 7-segment patterns shown in Fig. 2-6, with the additional requirement that all segments be off when the binary value 1111_2 is input to the circuit. Notice that there are five input combinations where all of the outputs are don't cares. The desired truth table is shown in Fig. 2-7.

We begin by creating a blank four-variable map, as shown in Fig. 2-8. Notice the numbering next to the squares on the top and left sides of the map, corresponding to the possible variable combinations (two-variable minterms). The order of the binary coding—from left to right or top to bottom—is important. It does not ascend in the normal binary counting order (00, 01, 10, 11). Instead, the order is chosen so that exactly one bit changes when going from one square to the next. Thus, for a K-map having three variables on a single side, an acceptable order would be 000, 001, 011, 010, 110, 111, 101, 100.

The reason for the odd K-map numbering approach becomes apparent after studying the annotated map in Fig. 2-9. Because only a single bit changes when going from one row to the next, or one column to the next, horizontal and vertical variable fields are created. This fact provides the key to using K-maps for logic minimization. The overlap of the various fields determines the product term of a square or group of squares on the map. For example, the square in the lower left corner of the map in Fig. 2-9 forms the product term A'B'C'D, since it is the overlap of the A', B', C' and D fields. Similarly, the block of four squares in the upper right corner of the map forms the product term BD', since it overlaps the B and D' fields.

This product term determination can be accomplished for any *rectangular* group of 2^n squares, where n is between zero and the number of map variables (four in our example), inclusive. Rectangles meeting this requirement will be referred to as *valid map rectangles*. The "rectangular group" requirement mentioned above is somewhat more flexible than is first obvious. This is because the map acts in a *modulo* fashion, where the left and right sides effectively wrap around to meet each other, and the top and bottom sides effectively wrap around to meet each other. Thus, for example, the middle two squares in the right-most column and the middle two squares in the left-most column together form a valid map rectangle, resulting in the A'C product term. Similarly, even the four corners together form a valid map rectangle (forming the A'C' product term).

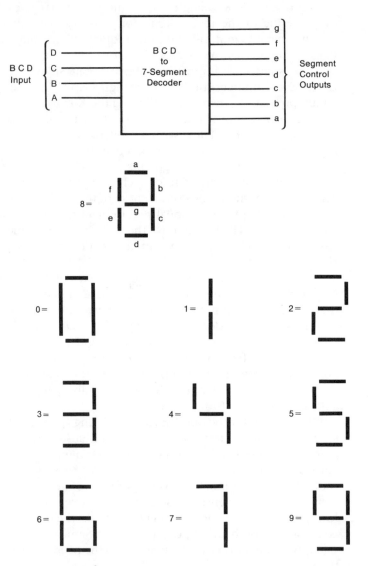

Figure 2-6. Example circuit function, a 7-segment decoder.

Let's move on with our design example to see how all this applies to solving the problem at hand. Figure 2-10A shows the K-map for output 'a' filled-in according to the truth table presented in Fig. 2-7. Since each square on the map represents a unique combination of the inputs (A–D), one has merely to place the desired output value for each input combination in the appropriate, corresponding square. Notice that Xs are included for the don't-care terms, so that all of the K-map boxes are filled in.

The next step is where we actually determine a minimized Boolean expression for the function specified in the map. The goal is to create the Boolean expression using as few product terms as possible, and also using as few inputs per product term as possible. To do this, we study the map looking for the

D	C	B	A	a	b	c	d	e	f	g
0	0	0	0	1	1	1	1	1	1	0
0	0	0	1	0	1	1	0	0	0	0
0	0	1	0	1	1	0	1	1	0	1
0	0	1	1	1	1	1	1	0	0	1
0	1	0	0	1	1	0	0	1	0	1
0	1	0	1	1	0	1	1	0	1	1
0	1	1	0	1	0	1	1	1	1	1
0	1	1	1	1	1	1	0	0	0	0
1	0	0	0	1	1	1	1	1	1	1
1	0	0	1	1	1	1	1	0	1	1
1	0	1	0	X	X	X	X	X	X	X
1	0	1	1	X	X	X	X	X	X	X
1	1	0	0	X	X	X	X	X	X	X
1	1	0	1	X	X	X	X	X	X	X
1	1	1	0	X	X	X	X	X	X	X
1	1	1	1	0	0	0	0	0	0	0

Figure 2-7. Truth table for 7-segment decoder.

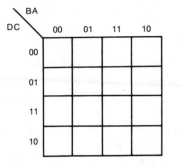

Figure 2-8. Blank, four-variable Karnaugh map.

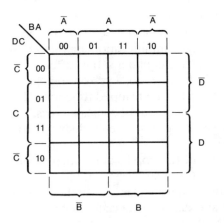

Figure 2-9. Annotated four-variable Karnaugh map.

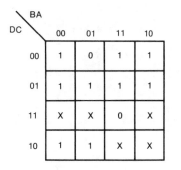

(A) K-map for output 'a' of 7-segment decoder.

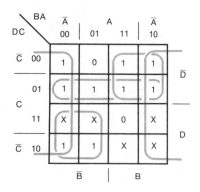

(B) K-map minimization of 7-segment decoder output 'a'.

$\overline{A}$, $\overline{B}D$, $B\overline{D}$, $C\overline{D}$

(C) Product terms determined by output 'a' K-map minimization.

$a = \overline{A} + \overline{B}D + B\overline{D} + C\overline{D}$

(D) Final equation for output 'a' of the 7-segment decoder.

Figure 2-10. Karnaugh map for output 'A.'

largest possible valid map rectangles that do not have 0s. Enough rectangles must be defined to include all '1' bits in the map. Once every '1' bit has been included in at least one valid map rectangle—defining the least number of valid map rectangles possible (it is OK for the valid map rectangles to overlap)—the logic minimization operation is complete (see Fig. 2-10B). The final step (referring back to Fig. 2-9) is to convert the defined valid map rectangles into product terms, as shown in Fig. 2-10C. The final equation for output 'a', based on our K-map minimization, is shown in Fig. 2-10D. Completed maps for the remaining six outputs are presented in Fig. 2-11.

While K-map minimization to the SOP standard form has been shown (and is the most common), it is simple to create a POS standard equation as well. To do this, minimize the 0s (and don't-cares, if any), instead of the 1s, then invert the resulting SOP expression. The result will be the minimized function in POS form.

The K-map minimization method described above is very effective for minimizing logic equations, but suffers from one significant drawback, namely, it requires a fairly good "eye" on the part of the designer to find the best logic minimization for the mapped function. This is not too much of a problem for a four-variable map, but becomes increasingly more of a problem as the number of variables increases. Five- and six-variable maps become tedious, and larger maps are rare.

Due to the drawbacks of the map method, and because it is desirable to find algorithms that can be easily implemented on computers, other algorithms for logic reduction have been researched and developed. Take a brief look at some of these alternatives, especially since logic minimization is an important issue in the use of PLDs.

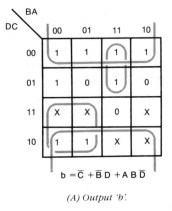

$$b = \overline{C} + \overline{B}\,D + A\,B\,\overline{D}$$

(A) Output 'b'.

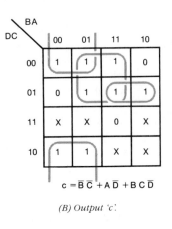

$$c = \overline{B}\,\overline{C} + A\,\overline{D} + B\,C\,\overline{D}$$

(B) Output 'c'.

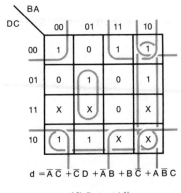

$$d = \overline{A}\,\overline{C} + \overline{C}\,D + \overline{A}\,B + B\,\overline{C} + A\,\overline{B}\,C$$

(C) Output 'd'.

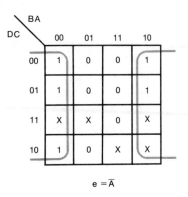

$$e = \overline{A}$$

(D) Output 'e'.

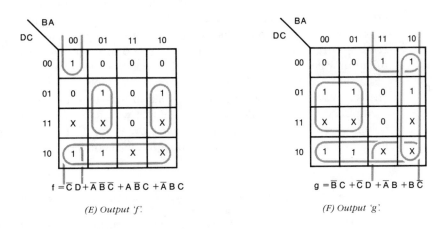

$$f = \overline{C}\,D + \overline{A}\,\overline{B}\,\overline{C} + A\,\overline{B}\,C + \overline{A}\,B\,C$$

(E) Output 'f'.

$$g = \overline{B}\,C + \overline{C}\,D + \overline{A}\,B + B\,\overline{C}$$

(F) Output 'g'.

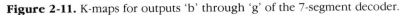

Figure 2-11. K-maps for outputs 'b' through 'g' of the 7-segment decoder.

Other Logic Minimization Algorithms

Due to advancements in computing, the past few decades have seen a lot of research in logic reduction algorithms that reduce even large Boolean equations efficiently, and are easily adaptable to numerical implementation. The Quine-McCluskey method is perhaps the most established algorithm, but newer algorithms, including ESPRESSO II-MV (from the University of California at Berkeley) and PRESTO (developed by Antonin Svoboda of Tektronix), are being used more and more. Let's explore two popular algorithms—Quine-McCluskey and PRESTO.

Quine-McCluskey Method

The *Quine-McCluskey method* for logic reduction, also known as the *tabulation method*, was originally developed by W. V. Quine[5] in 1952, and was later improved by E. J. McCluskey, Jr.[6] It provides a step-by-step procedure that is guaranteed to generate a simplified standard-form expression for the function being minimized.

The procedure begins with a list of the minterms for the function to be minimized (the function must, therefore, be defined in the sum of minterms canonical form). From the list of minterms, an iterative procedure takes place where each minterm is compared with every other minterm. Minterms that differ by only a single variable are removed from the list, while a new term with one less literal (variable) is created in their place. After the first pass, the same procedure is repeated for the new terms created. This iterative process continues until a single pass through the most recent list results in no further reductions. Upon collecting all terms remaining after the completion of the iterative process, a final list of *prime-implicants* is achieved.

The minimized function in some cases will be the Boolean sum of the prime-implicants (creating a result in SOP form). However, this is not always the case. The Quine-McCluskey method, therefore, goes a step further to determine the minimum list of prime implicants acceptable to specify the function. This is done by creating a *prime-implicant table*, where the original minterm values are listed across the top as columns, and the prime-implicants are listed along the left side. For each prime-implicant row, an 'X' is placed in each column that represents a minterm value that participated in the reduction to that prime-implicant (this discussion can be confusing—clarification will come shortly). Once this is done, a check is placed at the bottom of each column that has only a single 'X'. A check is then placed next to each prime-implicant that was reduced from a minterm whose column is checked; these are the *essential prime-implicants*. The essential prime-implicants are required terms in the final Boolean equation.

---

[5]Quine, W. V., "The Problem of Simplifying Truth Functions." *American Mathematics Monthly*, Vol. 59, No. 8 (October, 1952), pp. 521–31.

[6]McCluskey, E. J., Jr., "Minimization of Boolean Functions." *Bell System Technical Journal*, Vol. 35, No. 6 (November, 1956), p. 14.

The next step is to place a check at the bottom of each column that is covered by one of the essential prime-implicants (i.e., an 'X' from an essential prime-implicant exists in that column). The final step is to verify by observation (or computation) which one or more of the nonessential prime-implicants can be chosen to minimally cover all of the remaining unchecked columns. Once this is determined, the minimized expression is merely the Boolean sum of the essential prime-implicants and the chosen nonessential prime-implicants (in SOP standard form).

The minimization can also be performed so as to result in a POS form equation. To do this, the complements of the original minterms are chosen for the minimization, and the resulting SOP equation can be complemented to get the POS form of the function.

It is also possible to include don't-care states when using the Quine-McCluskey minimization method. To do this, the don't-care minterms should be included in the original list of minterms, for the determination of the prime-implicants. However, they should be excluded from the prime-implicant table, since they do not need to be covered by the final prime-implicants.

As was the case with the Karnaugh map described above, little can substitute for a good example to fully explain and clarify the operation of the Quine-McCluskey minimization method just described. Figure 2-12 shows the Quine-McCluskey reduction procedure, with explanations of the various steps. Because this discussion is intended to be primarily a review or brief introduction to the Quine-McCluskey reduction method, it is recommended that the sources specified in Appendix D be referenced for more in-depth coverage of the topic. The Quine-McCluskey method, sometimes with slight deviations, is one of the most popular algorithms in use today for computerized logic reduction.

PRESTO Algorithm

The PRESTO algorithm for logic minimization was developed by Antonin Svoboda and was presented in 1981 by Douglas W. Brown.[7] It is used in Data I/O's ABEL PLD language and Logical Devices' CUPL language, making it worthy of a brief look.

PRESTO's primary "claim to fame" is its fast operation with minimal memory requirements, making it particularly valuable for use with compilers that run on microprocessor-based systems. PRESTO accepts as input incompletely specified multiple-output equations in sum-of-products form—that is, output equations with don't-care terms permitted; PRESTO outputs a reduced set of equations. Brown presented an extended version of PRESTO that improved on Svoboda's original algorithm by using a tree method of checking product term coverage, resulting in greatly reduced execution time with a negligible increase in memory usage.

The PRESTO algorithm is order-dependent; that is, the reduction results depend on the order in which the product terms are entered and processed.

[7]Brown, Douglas W., "A State Machine Synthesizer—SMS" *Proceedings of the 18th Design Automation Conference, IEEE* (June, 1981), pp. 301–305.

PROBLEM: Minimize the Boolean function $F = \Sigma (0, 1, 2, 3, 5, 11, 12, 13, 14)$.

(1) Put minterms into a table, separating the terms by the number of ones, then combine terms that differ by only one bit into a second table, placing a dash (-) in place of the differing bit. Place an asterisk by each term that was involved in a combination. Continue the process until no further combinations can be made; this results in the <u>prime-implicants</u>:

(A)

term	d	c	b	a	
0	0	0	0	0	*
1	0	0	0	1	*
2	0	0	1	0	*
3	0	0	1	1	*
5	0	1	0	1	*
12	1	1	0	0	*
11	1	0	1	1	*
13	1	1	0	1	*
14	1	1	1	0	*

(B)

terms	d	c	b	a	
0,1	0	0	0	–	*
0,2	0	0	–	0	*
1,3	0	0	–	1	*
1,5	0	–	0	1	
2,3	0	0	1	–	*
3,11	–	0	1	1	
5,13	–	1	0	1	
12,13	1	1	0	–	
12,14	1	1	–	0	

(C)

terms	d	c	b	a
0,1,2,3	0	0	–	–
0,2,1,3	0	0	–	–

The terms without asterisks are the prime-implicants, namely:
    $ab'd'$, abc', $ab'c$, $b'cd$, $a'cd$, $c'd'$

(2) Create a prime-implicants table, and determine the <u>minimum</u> terms that can be used to represent the Boolean function. Place an asterisk by the <u>essential prime-implicants</u>, which are required in order to cover minterms that appear in only a single prime-implicant (as indicated by an asterisk in the column). Then indicate with a plus sign (+) all of the minterms that are covered by the essential prime-implicants. Finally, determine the last remaining prime-implicant(s) (mark with an equals sign [=]) needed to cover any remaining minterms:

P I	Terms	0	1	2	3	5	11	12	13	14
$ab'd'$	1,5		X			X				
* abc'	3,11				X		X			
= $ab'c$	5,13					X			X	
$b'cd$	12,13							X	X	
* $a'cd$	12,14							X		X
* $c'd'$	0,1,2,3	X	X	X	X					
		*	+	*	+		*	+		*

This provides the terms for the final, minimized Boolean equation:

$$F = abc' + ab'c + a'cd + c'd'$$

Figure 2-12. Example of the Quine-McCluskey reduction procedure.

Altering the product term order could result in greater reduction in some cases, although adding this step to the algorithm would substantially increase the execution time of the algorithm, and the small improvement in minimization would not likely justify the tradeoff.

Sequential Logic and State Machines

It seems that the best way to begin our discussion on *sequential logic* is to first take a look at Boolean storage or memory devices, namely, two-state *flip-flops*. There are five basic types of flip-flops we will discuss here, each having its own peculiarities and usefulness. It should be noted that for the clocked flip-flops, some versions of a particular flip-flop will *trigger* using the rising edge of the input clock, while others will trigger using the falling edge of the input clock. For purposes of discussion, a rising-edge trigger will be assumed for all clocked flip-flops.

The first, and probably most popular, flip-flop is the *D flip-flop*, shown in Fig. 2-13. Its primary characteristic is that the logic level at the 'D' input appears at the 'Q' output after the next rising edge of the input clock, thereby *latching* the value at the 'D' input. If the signal at the 'D' input changes after the rising clock edge, the output will not change until the following rising edge of the clock. The operation of the D flip-flop is also shown in the table in Fig. 2-13.

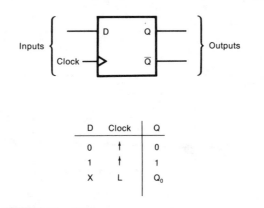

D	Clock	Q
0	↑	0
1	↑	1
X	L	Q_0

Figure 2-13. The D flip-flop.

The D flip-flop comes in a variety of flavors, typically having both true and inverted outputs. It also commonly has *reset* and/or *preset* inputs, which are generally *asynchronous* with respect to the input clock, i.e., the reset or preset operation occurs as soon as the respective input goes active, without waiting for a clock edge to occur. However, one or both of these inputs may be synchronous with the input clock.

Another popular flip-flop is the *J-K flip-flop*, shown in Fig. 2-14. This clocked flip-flop has two inputs, with the output changing at the rising edge of the input clock, as a function of the J-input, the K-input, *and* the current output, as shown in the table in Fig. 2-14. If the J-input is low and the K-input is low, the output will remain unchanged after the input clock. If the J-input is low and the K-input is high, the output will always go low after the input clock. If the J-input is high and the K-input is low, the output will always go high after the rising edge of the input clock. Finally, if both the J- and K-inputs are high, the output will *toggle* at the rising edge of the input clock; that is, the output will change to the opposite state.

As with the D flip-flop described above, the J-K flip-flop typically (not always) has both true and inverted outputs available and may have asynchronous or synchronous reset and/or preset inputs.

Another clocked flip-flop is the *T flip-flop* (or *Toggle flip-flop*), shown with its state table in Fig. 2-15. This simple device toggles its output if the 'T' input is high at the rising edge of the clock, and leaves the output unchanged if the 'T' input is low. Again, reset and preset are options that may be present.

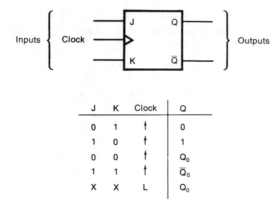

J	K	Clock	Q
0	1	↑	0
1	0	↑	1
0	0	↑	Q_0
1	1	↑	$\overline{Q}_0$
X	X	L	Q_0

Figure 2-14. The J-K flip-flop.

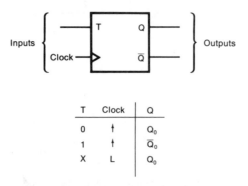

T	Clock	Q
0	↑	Q_0
1	↑	$\overline{Q}_0$
X	L	Q_0

Figure 2-15. The T flip-flop.

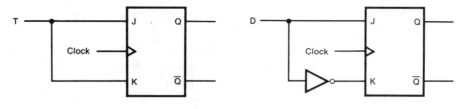

(A) T flip-flop emulation using a J-K flip-flop.   (B) D flip-flop emulation using a J-K flip flop.

Figure 2-16. Flip-flop emulations

Reviewing the operation of the three flip-flops presented above, it should be clear that the J-K flip-flop is the most versatile. This observation comes from the fact that it can perform the same functions as the D and T flip-flops, and other functions as well. The J-K flip-flop can emulate a T flip-flop (see Fig. 2-16A) merely by tying the J and K inputs together, and using the combination as a single flip-flop input. Similarly, the J-K flip-flop can emulate a D flip-flop by connecting an inverter from the J-input to the K-input, using the J-input as the 'D' input (see Fig. 2-16B).

The *R-S flip-flop*—better known as the *R-S latch*—is quite different from those described above. As shown in Fig. 2-17, this flip-flop merely consists of a pair of NAND gates (though a pair of NOR gates can similarly be used). Typically, both inputs are normally high. When the R (Reset) input goes low (while the S input remains high), the Q output goes low (reset state). Q will remain low even after the R input returns high; thus, the state is latched. When the S (Set) input goes low (while the R input remains high), the Q output goes high (set state). Once again, Q will remain high even after the S input returns high. Since its operation does not involve synchronization with an input clock, the R-S latch is not a clocked flip-flop—it is an asynchronous flip-flop.

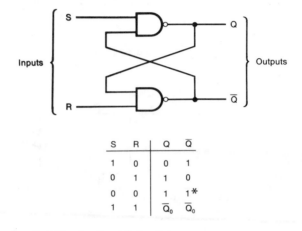

S	R	Q	$\overline{Q}$
1	0	0	1
0	1	1	0
0	0	1	1*
1	1	$\overline{Q}_0$	$\overline{Q}_0$

✱ = Unstable when R and S changed

Figure 2-17. The R-S latch.

During normal operation of the R-S flip-flop, where the R and S inputs are not both simultaneously low, the Q and Q′ outputs shown in Fig. 2-17 will always be opposite each other—i.e., true complements. A complication arises, however, when both inputs go low simultaneously. When this happens, both the Q and Q′ outputs go high, no longer being complements of each other. This is generally considered an undesirable state, since the final latch output state will be determined by which input signal remains active the longest. In designs where this situation may cause a problem, it is best to use *only* the Q output, adding an external inverter to provide a "real" Q′ if necessary.

Note that a J-K flip-flop can also emulate an R-S latch if it has asynchronous reset and preset inputs.

The final flip-flop to be discussed here is the *clocked R-S flip-flop*, as shown in Fig. 2-18. As indicated by its name, this is merely a clocked version of the R-S latch described above. Thus, the R and S inputs do not affect the flip-flop output until the next rising edge of the input clock. The clocked R-S flip-flop can be emulated by a J-K flip-flop by adding the input gates shown in Fig. 2-19, as derived from the accompanying truth table.

To provide maximum flexibility, some PLDs incorporate support for several different types of flip-flops (generally by including a J-K flip-flop with the extra logic required to emulate the other flip-flops, as described above). This allows the

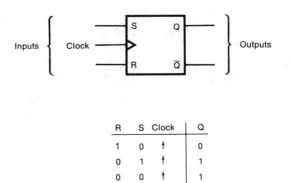

R	S	Clock	Q
1	0	↑	0
0	1	↑	1
0	0	↑	1
1	1	↑	Q_0

Figure 2-18. The clocked R-S flip-flop.

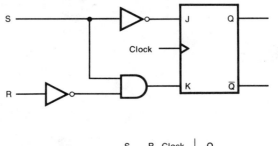

S	R	Clock	Q
1	0	↑	0
0	1	↑	1
0	0	↑	1
1	1	↑	Q_0

Figure 2-19. Clocked R-S flip-flop emulation using a J-K flip-flop.

designer, or design software, to select the flip-flop type that best accommo-
dates the logic being defined. In effect, this flip-flop selection flexibility is
another form of logic minimization for sequential logic designs.

While flip-flops are often used to simply latch signals (to demultiplex a
combined address/data bus, for example), the primary use of flip-flops is
probably in the development of *sequencers* and *state machines*. A sequencer is
a circuit that generates synchronized signals that allow various logic operations
to occur in a defined sequence. A sequencer might, for example, be used as part
of a disk-controller circuit to generate several clocks with varying duty cycles
and phase relationships. State machines direct system operations so that they
occur in appropriate sequences synchronized by one or more digital clock
signals, and are present in one form or another in almost all digital systems.
Microprocessors, for example, make extensive use of internal state machines,
with each program instruction causing a number of internal *microinstructions*
to be executed in a sequence determined by the processor's *microcode*.

Sequencers and state machines can be implemented using standard SSI/MSI logic, but PLDs—and the advanced software packages that are now available for them—give the designer an alternate approach that offers shorter design time and easier changes.

To aid our discussion of state machines, it is worthwhile to look at the two primary models for state machines, the *Mealy model* and the *Moore model*. Since PLDs are used extensively for state machine implementation, and because they greatly simplify and expedite state machine development, it is important to present some of the basics of state machine design here. This chapter provides only a brief look at state machine models and design concepts. Other sources, such as those listed in Appendix D should be consulted for more-detailed information.

The Mealy Model

Figure 2-20A illustrates a typical Mealy state machine model, with the corresponding *state table* shown in Fig. 2-20B. This model is known as a *transition-assigned circuit* because the output of the circuit is related to the state transitions. In Fig. 2-20, the letters in the circles represent the different state machine states, while the "x/y" indicators along the path lines provide transitional change information. The 'x' portion specifies the state machine inputs, while the 'y' portion specifies the state machine outputs. Thus, for the path line from state A *to* state B (note arrow indicating path direction) with the 0/1 identifier, if the state machine is in state A and the input is 0 at the next state machine transition, the state machine will proceed to state B and the output will go to 1, regardless of its previous value.

Note that the value of the state machine output does *not* correspond to its current state. The state machine output value can, for example, be either 0 or 1 in state B, depending on whether the previous state was state C or state A.

The Moore Model

A typical Moore state machine model, with its corresponding state table, is illustrated in Fig. 2-21. Unlike the Mealy model, the outputs of a Moore circuit correspond directly to the *current state* of the state machine. Thus, whenever the state machine is in state X, the output of the state machine will always be the same, without regard to the previous state. For example, referring to Fig. 2-21, whenever the state machine is in state C, the output is *always* 1, and whenever it is in state B, the output is *always* 0, regardless of the previous state. Notice how the state table (Fig. 2-21B) is shown differently because of the difference in operation of the Moore state machine.

Combinatorial logic is used together with flip-flops to generate state machines. After a state machine has been defined, the combinatorial logic (inputs to the flip-flops) can be minimized using the same minimization techniques described earlier.

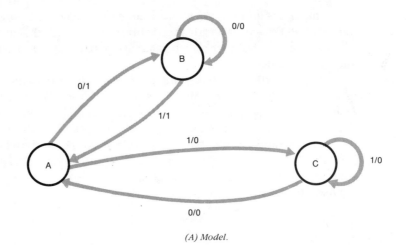

(A) Model.

	Input X	
Present State	0	1
A	B/1	C/0
B	B/0	A/1
C	A/0	C/0

Next State /Output Y

(B) State table.

Figure 2-20. Mealy state machine.

A State Machine Example

In order to describe the sequential logic design process, let's look at an example circuit problem and how it can be solved with a sequential circuit.

Let's assume we are developing a system that supports dual-ported (shared) memory; i.e., memory that can be directly accessed by two independent, asynchronous devices (typically two different processors). Since either of the two processors may attempt to access the shared memory at any time, even simultaneously, a circuit must be designed that will arbitrate access to the shared memory, and force one of the processors to wait if both attempt to access the memory simultaneously. To develop such a system, we choose to break the arbitration circuitry into two functional blocks, as shown in Fig. 2-22.

The first block in Fig. 2-22 (block A) looks at the shared memory access request signals coming from the two processors and generates acknowledge ("access O.K.") signals to indicate when each processor may access the shared memory. The second block (block B) takes care of controlling the address and data bus buffers and access strobes (chip select, read and write) for proper access to the shared memory. For this example we will only concern ourselves

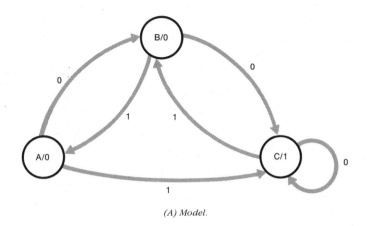

(A) Model.

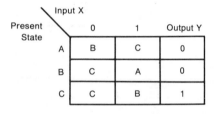

(B) State table.

Figure 2-21. Moore state machine.

with the operation of block A. For simplicity, we will also assume that once a processor has completed its access to the shared memory, it will remove its access request signal for at least two clock cycles (of the state machine clock).

A Moore state diagram for circuit block A is shown in Fig. 2-23, along with its accompanying state table. Only three states are required to implement the desired state machine (A, B, and C), but a fourth state (D) has been added for completeness, to define all four states in a two-bit state machine. This fourth state should never occur, but if it somehow does (due, perhaps, to a system electrical noise problem), the state machine will always return to a known state, state A.

The state machine will remain in state A until an access request is received from one or both of the processors. Processor 1 has priority if both processors request access simultaneously. When processor 1 requests access to the shared memory, the state machine proceeds to state B, generating the "access 1 O.K." signal. It remains in state B until processor 1 completes its access cycle and removes its access request. Similarly, when processor 2 requests access to the shared memory (and processor 1 is not simultaneously requesting access), the state machine advances to state C, generating the "access 2 O.K." signal. It then remains in state C until processor 2 completes its access cycle and removes its access request. Notice that once an access cycle has begun (the state machine has entered state B or state C), an incoming request from the nonaccessing

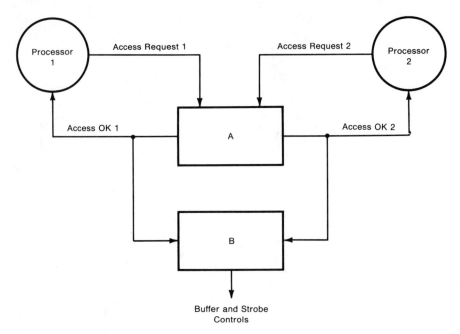

Figure 2-22. Functional breakdown of example memory arbitration circuit.

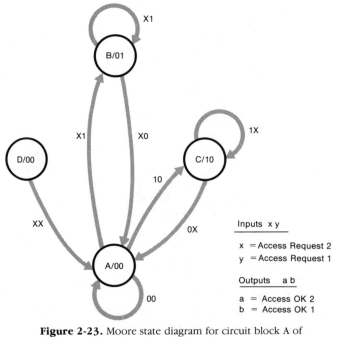

Figure 2-23. Moore state diagram for circuit block A of
example memory arbitration circuit.

processor will not be recognized until after the completion of the current access cycle, when the state machine returns to state A.

Since we need a two-bit state machine, let's first arbitrarily assign a unique two-bit binary *state number* to each defined state: state A = 00, state B = 01, state C = 10 and state D = 11. These can be referred to as state 0, state 1, state 2 and state 3, respectively.

Using two D flip-flops to implement the state machine, let's determine the combinatorial logic required for the state machine. Figure 2-24 shows the K-maps for the state machine logic. The first (Fig. 2-24A) is for the low-order state machine bit (bit 0), and the second (Fig. 2-24B) is for the high-order state machine bit (bit 1). The resulting state machine circuit is shown in Fig. 2-25; Q_0 and Q_1 are the low-order and high-order bits of the state machine, respectively.

Now that we have the state machine circuit determined, we must determine the appropriate logic to generate the desired output signals, OK1 and OK2. Since we used the Moore model to specify the state machine, the OK1 and OK2 outputs are simply a function of the state machine outputs. The simple K-maps used to determine the logic for OK1 and OK2 from the two state machine outputs are shown in Fig. 2-26. Figure 2-27 shows the entire circuit, including the OK signals, as developed thus far.

Depending on certain system specifics, the design may be finished, but it probably is not quite yet. Two potential problem areas exist in the design that are common when interfacing with asynchronous subsystems. The first problem area involves the flip-flop inputs. Since it is possible for the R1 input to go active (or inactive) during a state transition time (rising edge of the "clock" signal), varying gate delays and inherent differences in D flip-flop input characteristics could cause one flip-flop to see R1 as 1 at transition time, while the other flip-flop sees R1 as 0. This could cause the state machine to enter an incorrect state.

To prevent such a tragedy, it is important to *synchronize* the R1 input signal with the state machine circuitry. This can be done by merely adding an input flip-flop for R1, the output of which goes to the state machine circuitry. The modified circuit is shown in Fig. 2-28. While this resolves the synchronization problem, it also means that R1 will not be seen by the state machine logic until at least one clock cycle after it actually goes high. Note that the state flip-flop synchronization problem does not exist with the R2 input, because only one state machine flip-flop uses R2 in its logic. R2 is, however, still synchronized to the system clock in the same way as R1 to prevent the likelihood of entering a metastable state.

The second potential problem exists with the outputs of the sequential circuit, OK1 and OK2. While our design up to this point seems to indicate that OK1 and OK2 will provide the desired output values for each of the various states, we have not considered what actually happens during state transition time. Because of varying delays through the state flip-flops and the output AND gates, *any* flip-flop output combination may occur for a short period of time (usually a few nanoseconds) before the outputs stabilize to their appropriate values. This could cause undesirable *glitching* at OK1 and OK2, where an output could go high for a brief time before attaining its correct, low state. If it were known that the processors would not sample ("look at") the OK signal until

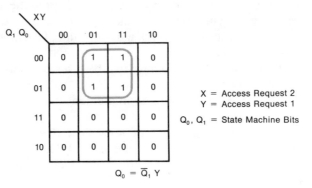

$$Q_0 = \overline{Q}_1\, Y$$

(A) K-map for state machine bit 0.

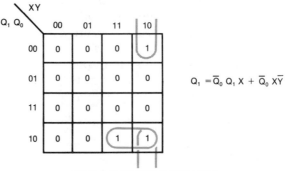

$$Q_1 = \overline{Q}_0\, Q_1\, X + \overline{Q}_0\, X\overline{Y}$$

(B) K-map for state machine bit 1.

Figure 2-24. K-maps for Moore state machine logic of example arbitration circuit.

after the transition time, the glitching would not be a problem. If this is not the case, however, the glitch could cause the processor to complete its shared memory access cycle, when it really has not yet been given authorization.

This problem can be resolved in a manner similar to that used to synchronize the R1 input. By requiring OK1 and OK2 to go through a flip-flop before getting to their respective processors, the outputs will be guaranteed correct at all times. The sequential circuit with this addition is shown in Fig. 2-29. The penalty, once again, is that the outputs to the processors will lag behind the state machine by (exactly) one clock cycle, increasing each shared memory access by this much.

Since our reason for adding the extra input and output signals is to synchronize these signals with the state machine clock, these flip-flops do not have to be clocked at the same time. The only requirement is that they must be clocked with a clock that is synchronized with the state machine clock (as long as appropriate logic setup and hold times are recognized for interacting with the state machine logic). Thus, we could reduce the input and output delays by half a clock cycle by choosing to synchronize the input and output flip-flops with the inverted state machine clock. Implementing this, the final sequential circuit to accomplish our task is shown in Fig. 2-30.

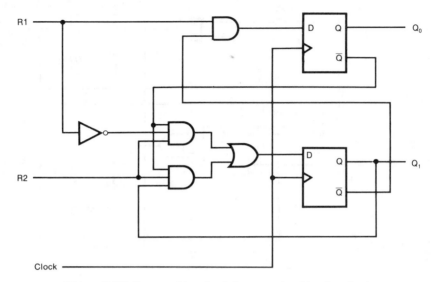

Figure 2-25. State machine circuit for example arbitration circuit.

OK1 = $Q_0 \overline{Q}_1$

(A) OK1.

OK2 = $\overline{Q}_0 Q_1$

(B) OK2.

Figure 2-26. K-maps for arbitration circuit outputs.

Synchronization and Metastability

The design of sequential circuits brings with it new concerns regarding the synchronization of asynchronous input signals. Research and practical experience have shown that if an asynchronous signal is input to a flip-flop, and the specified set-up and hold times are not met with respect to the synchronizing clock, the output of the flip-flop may do strange things. The output will often enter a *metastable* state—having an output voltage somewhere between the normal logic low and logic high output voltages—for a variable and unpredictable period of time, often much longer than the propagation delay of the flip-flop. The output then relaxes to either a logic 0 or logic 1 level, again unpredictably. Other possible output characteristics of such a circuit situation include oscillating outputs (with the true and "complement" outputs of the flip-flop not necessarily oscillating as complements of each other), and outputs that enter a

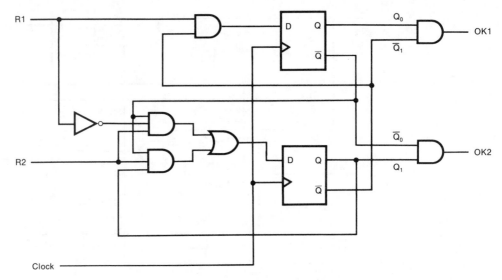

Figure 2-27. First revision of complete arbitration circuit.

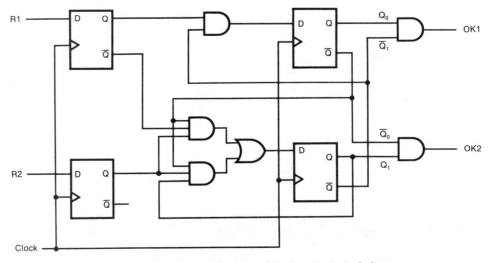

Figure 2-28. Revision 2 of the arbitration circuit, including
synchronizing input flip-flops.

stable state for a period of time, only to switch to a different, final state
sometime after the worst-case transition time of the flip-flop.

Unfortunately, the concerns of synchronization and metastable outputs
have been largely overlooked by many digital circuit designers. Although the
problems of synchronization do not frequently show themselves in slower
systems, the trend toward faster systems has made synchronization concerns
more dominant. Unfortunately, it is impossible to entirely prevent metastable
output situations from occurring in systems that synchronize incoming

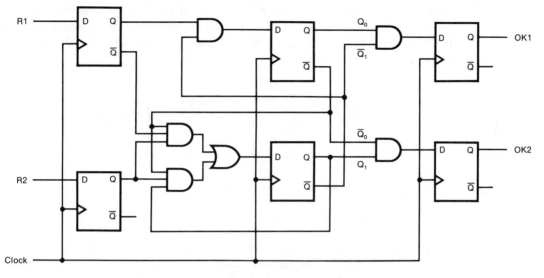

Figure 2-29. Revision 3 of the arbitration circuit, including
registered OK1 and OK2 outputs.

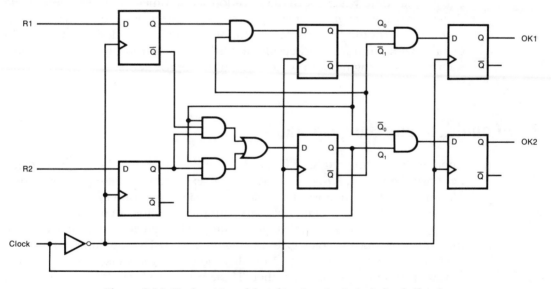

Figure 2-30. Final revision of the arbitration circuit, including half-cycle
registered R1, R2, OK1, and OK2 signals.

asynchronous signals. The designer can, however, reduce the likelihood of such
an occurrence to an acceptably low level.

Many devices are now "metastable hardened." A metastable hardened
device is one that the manufacturer has studied under asynchronous input
conditions, and can offer data that allows the designer to calculate the probability that the part will enter a metastable state in a particular circuit. A common
method of reducing the likelihood of a metastable output is by using a two-level

clocked circuit, as shown in Fig. 2-31. Based on the data provided by the manufacturer, the clock time between the two registers can be adjusted so that the probability of output Q2 entering a metastable state can be reduced to any desired level.

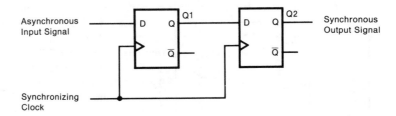

Figure 2-31. Two-level clocked circuit to minimize metastable output probability.

The introduction of PLDs has not eliminated metastability concerns in circuit designs. While flip-flops are commonly found on devices along with other, combinatorial logic, the designer must still make sure that specified set-up and hold times are met—keeping in mind the propagation time of the combinatorial circuitry. Most PLD manufacturers include the combinatorial circuit delay time when specifying flip-flop set-up times. PLDs, like other logic devices, are continually increasing in speed to meet designer demands. Synchronization should be considered carefully in any digital design—using PLDs or otherwise—and is an especially important concern in high-speed designs, such as those using modern 16- and 32-bit microprocessors.

Race Conditions and Hang-Up States

Another area of logic design involves some "nasty realities" of logic circuits: *race conditions* and *hang-up states*. Classic examples of these problems were illustrated in the example state machine design in a previous section. It is important to design *all* digital systems with these realities in mind.

Figure 2-32 shows a simple logic circuit (exclusive-OR) with its corresponding truth table. Ideally, logic gates operate with no delay; the output of the gate is always correct for its inputs. In reality, however, gates take time to make a transition from one state to another. These gate delays can (and generally do) vary slightly from gate to gate (typically by a few nanoseconds, depending on the technology used). Also, the *input threshold* of one gate (the point at which the gate recognizes an input logic change from high to low or vice-versa) can be different than that of another. This causes the different gates to switch at different times, even with the same input signal.

The result of these gate delay and threshold differences is illustrated in the timing diagram shown in Fig. 2-33. At point 'a' in the diagram, both X and Y inputs are low, with the corresponding Z output also low. At point 'b', the Y input goes high, causing the output to also go high. At 'c', the X input also goes high, causing the output to return low. Finally, at point 'd', both inputs return

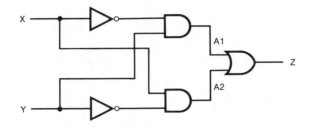

X	Y	Z
0	0	0
0	1	1
1	0	1
1	1	0

Figure 2-32. Example logic circuit—exclusive-OR function.

low *simultaneously*, but because of gate delay differences, signal A1 (at the OR gate input) goes low a short time before A2. This, in turn, causes the output to go active for that very brief period before attaining its correct, low output state. This condition, where two or more signals are "racing" each other, is known as a *race condition*.

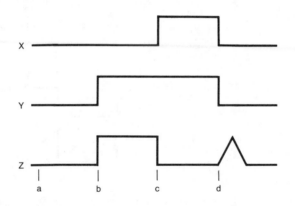

Figure 2-33. Output timing of the example circuit during a race condition.

The output glitch caused as the result of the race condition may or may not affect the system, depending on where the signal is used. If the signal is used as a flip-flop clock input, it could cause the flip-flop to be falsely triggered. If the signal is synchronized in such a way that other parts of the circuit do not use the signal until it is guaranteed stable, the glitch will not have a detrimental effect.

The concept of *hang-up states* was illustrated in the state machine circuit example. If the R1 input signals were not synchronized with the additional flip-flop, the state machine could enter an invalid state (such as state 3 in that example). If we had not have supported the unused state in our design, the circuit would operate unpredictably if that state were entered; possibly "hanging-up" the system, never being able to exit state 3. It is important to ensure that

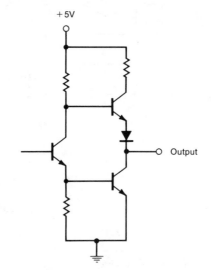

Figure 2-34. The totem-pole output stage of the 7400 NAND gate.

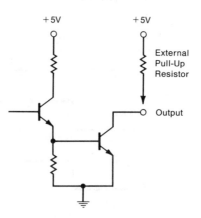

Figure 2-35. The open-collector output stage of the 7401 NAND gate.

invalid states cannot normally be entered, but it is equally important to ensure that no state (even invalid states) can possibly *hang up* the system. That is, a state machine should never get in an "infinite loop" it cannot exit. Invalid states should cause a known and prespecified action to occur, such as returning to a valid state or generating a fault signal.

Programmable logic devices can go far to simplify the logic design process, but they do not defeat the inherent realities of digital logic; thus normal digital design cautions must be observed when using them. Such problems may, in fact, be somewhat more elusive with PLDs because so much of the logic design is software-aided. Furthermore, all of the gates that implement the logic functions are typically inside a single IC package and are, therefore, unavailable for troubleshooting.

Open-Collector and Three-State Signals and Busses

The digital signals discussed so far have been two-state signals having either a low or high voltage level. The outputs of most SSI and MSI logic devices fit into this category, swinging between low and high levels depending on input conditions. There are, however, other types of digital outputs that are important in the design of real systems, particularly *open-collector* outputs and *three-state* outputs.

The output stage of a 7400 NAND gate is shown in Fig. 2-34. Notice how two transistors comprise the output stage; essentially, one functions as a pull-up transistor while the other functions as a pull-down transistor. This is called a *totem-pole* output, and is responsible for allowing the 7400 NAND gate to generate both logic high and logic low voltages.

It is desirable in many situations to be able to connect several output signals together so that the combined signal goes "active" when any one or more of the outputs goes "active." This is conveniently accomplished with the use of *open-collector* outputs. Figure 2-35 shows the output stage of the open-collector 7401 NAND gate. Notice that only a pull-down transistor is included, and the collector (output) of the transistor is floating. Since the open-collector output has no pull-up component, it can never go high. With the addition of a pull-up resistor to the supply voltage, however, the output will go high when not being pulled low by the output transistor. This approach allows several open-collector outputs to be connected together and to a common pull-up resistor. The result is a signal that goes low when any one or more of the connected outputs goes low. This is often called a *wired-OR* arrangement.

Figure 2-36A shows several signals connected together in a wired-OR arrangement. A logically equivalent circuit using totem-pole output gates is shown in Fig. 2-36B. The wired-OR approach is more beneficial in many situations, and is commonly used, for example, to connect interrupt signals together in microprocessor-based systems. Since MOS and CMOS devices use field-effect transistors (FETs) instead of bipolar transistors, they offer *open-drain* outputs instead of open-collector outputs, having essentially the same characteristics.

Another type of output used widely in microprocessor-based systems is the *three-state* or *tri-state* output. As its name implies, the three-state output includes a new state, beyond the normal high and low logic states offered by traditional logic devices. The third state is a *high-impedance* state, where the output is effectively removed from the circuit. Thus, numerous three-state outputs could be connected together, as long as no more than one is *enabled* (to be a two-state output) at any given time.

In microprocessor-based systems, some sets of signals are commonly grouped together. These signal groups are called *busses*. Most such systems have three primary busses: an address bus, a data bus, and a control bus. The data bus is used to transfer information between the processor and the system's memory and peripheral devices. Since all of these devices typically share the same data bus, three-state outputs are commonly used.

Because busses are fundamental to the operation of microprocessor-based systems, a number of PLDs have become available that are specifically designed

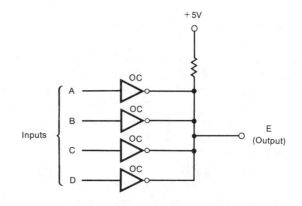

(A) Open-collector signals connected in wired-OR fashion.

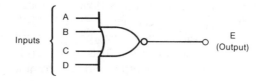

(B) Logically equivalent circuit using totem-pole output gates.

Figure 2-36. Connecting several signals.

to assist in bus-oriented applications. Busses commonly take advantage of open-collector or three-state outputs, so these output types—usually one or the other—are supported on virtually all PLDs.

IC Technologies

Digital integrated circuits are made using different IC technologies. A common tradeoff between technologies is speed and power. Faster parts tend to consume more power. The most common SSI and MSI devices first became available in *bipolar* (Transistor-Transistor Logic-TTL) technologies, offering reasonable speeds at considerable power consumption. To minimize power consumption, devices taking advantage of *CMOS* technologies have become very popular, and several logic families are now available in CMOS. *Emitter-coupled logic (ECL)* is another bipolar technology, offering greater speed than standard TTL technology, although at a higher power consumption. Finally, *gallium-arsenide (GaAs)* is the newest technology on the block, offering speed comparable to, or faster than, ECL with lower power consumption.

PLDs have followed the IC technology trends reasonably well, and devices are available in all of the standard IC technologies. This flexibility provides the designer with programmable logic choices regardless of the IC families being used in a design.

Chapter Summary

In this chapter we reviewed digital logic design, beginning with basic gates, truth tables, Boolean equations, and a description of the canonical and standard equation forms. We then looked at logic minimization using Karnaugh maps and the Quine-McCluskey and PRESTO algorithms, followed by a review of flip-flop types and sequential logic design, using a circuit example to clarify the state machine design process. We then covered metastability concerns, and some of the nasty realities of logic design: Race conditions and hang-up states. We subsequently discussed open-collector and three-state outputs and the concept of signal busses, then concluded with a brief look at some common IC technologies and their relative merits.

Chapter 3

PLD Families and Primary Architectures

One important fact that has made PLDs such effective devices for solving myriad design problems is that there are many different PLD families, architectures and technologies available that combine to give the designer a great deal of flexibility. This allows the designer to choose devices that are optimum for his or her designs. The designer can also choose devices that fit into the speed, power consumption and reprogrammability requirements demanded by particular applications.

Chapter Overview

In this chapter we will take a look at the primary PLD families currently available, study their varying architectures and the tradeoffs between them, and look at the different types of fuses or programmable links used in PLDs. We will also discuss IC technologies, and device interchangeability.

In the process of studying device families and architectures, we will look at the logic diagrams of several representative devices and will become familiar with much of the terminology and abbreviations common to the PLD industry.

The purpose of this chapter is to acquaint the reader—the PLD designer—with the device families and architectures currently available. This is the palette from which the designer must choose the devices for a design, and is therefore a focal point of this book. Many of the logic implementation intricacies of the devices presented here can be overlooked since they are generally handled by the design software (such as how the programmable links are responsible for configuring the different device operating modes). The reader should, therefore, become familiar with the essential family and device architectures presented here, in order to gain a firm foundation for the entire programmable logic design process.

The discussions on PLD families and architectures have been broken down into five sections; the first presented in this chapter, with the remaining four presented in Chapter 4. The first and most important section describes the primary device architectures present today. The next three sections describe function-specific or application-specific PLDs (ASPLDs) and state machine, bus interface, and miscellaneous architectures. The fifth and final section briefly describes some manufacturer-specific PLD families.

Families vs. Architectures

In looking at the various PLD families currently on the market, the designer should be aware that there is overlap between *families* and *architectures* in the realm of PLDs, and this is a potential point of confusion. The term "families" is used rather loosely here, and one family may encompass other families or multiple architectures. Where appropriate, distinctions will be made in the text to clarify the terminology.

As an example, *PAL*—programmable array logic—represents both an *architecture* (having a programmable AND-array and a fixed OR-array) and a *family*, with many devices varying in configuration. Similarly, the *FPLA* and *FPLS* families represent specific architectures, and are themselves families within the *PLS* (Programmable Logic from Signetics) family.

Some families simply convert existing devices from other families into a different technology, such as bipolar to CMOS. Other families duplicate (second-source) existing devices, but have a different family name simply because they are produced by a different manufacturer.

Still other family names are the same as device type identifiers that have become standard in the PLD industry. For example, the term *EPLD*—Erasable, Programmable Logic Device—has come to be a standard term for all PLDs that are U.V.- (ultraviolet light) erasable and reprogrammable. However, the same term also represents the *family* of devices available from Altera and Intel (where the term originated).

Since much of the terminology and family tree structure has evolved from manufacturers attempting to distinguish themselves or categorize their product lines, it is not important at this point to go into too much detail. Rather, it is best to study the primary architectures and to become familiar with the different IC technologies used in manufacturing the devices.

In the discussions that follow, both *family* architectures and *device* architectures will be described; these should not be confused. When the PAL family is first introduced, for example, architectural features that are generally common to all of the devices in the family are described. This is followed by other discussions centering on the architectural features of specific devices in the PAL family. In the process of studying a particular device, it may be appropriate to take a closer look at a sub-architecture of the device—such as an output *macrocell*—and describe its features. Thus, the term *architecture* should be viewed from the context in which it is being used.

Notation

Programmable logic devices tend to have many logic gates with large numbers of inputs. Since it is difficult, inefficient, and confusing to draw logic gates with many inputs, the PLD industry has adopted a notation that is more fitting for the types of architectures common to the PLD world.

Figure 3-1 shows a 16-input AND gate as it might be drawn using conventional notation. The same 16-input AND gate is shown using PLD notation in Fig. 3-2. Notice how a single line is shown going into the AND gate, with the 16 input lines intersecting the AND gate input line. The single line *does not* indicate that the 16 inputs are connected together. It is used to indicate that intersecting lines are inputs to the gate. Since the intersection points are generally fuse links in PLDs, an 'X' at an intersection point is used to indicate that a connection is to be made (i.e., the fuse is to be left intact). A new, unprogrammed device generally has all fuses intact, and is sometimes (though not usually) shown with 'X's at all intersection points.

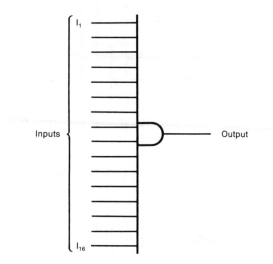

Figure 3-1. Diagram of a 16-input AND gate drawn using conventional notation.

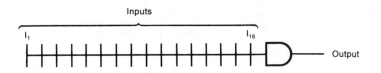

Figure 3-2. Diagram of a 16-input AND gate using PLD notation.

Perhaps the best way to understand this is by example. Let's suppose we want to implement the logic shown in Fig. 3-3 into a PLD that has the architecture shown in Fig. 3-4. The appropriate PLD connection diagram for the desired logic function is shown in Fig. 3-5; note the 'X's at the places that input connections to the AND gates are to be made.

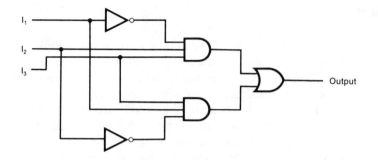

Figure 3-3. Example logic circuit to be implemented using a PLD.

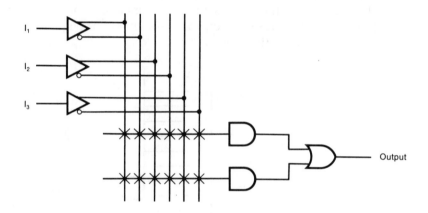

Figure 3-4. PLD architecture for example logic circuit implementation.

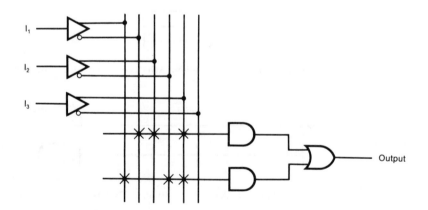

Figure 3-5. PLD connection diagram for example logic circuit implementation.

Notice how the input signals enter the product term matrix in both the true and inverted forms. This approach is typical of virtually all PLDs, since it is necessary for supporting the generation of product terms.

PLD Families—Background

As discussed in Chapter 1, PLDs got their start at Signetics in 1975, with the introduction of the field-programmable logic array (FPLA). Though flexible, the FPLA—consisting of a programmable AND-array followed by a programmable OR-array—caught on slowly among digital designers for several reasons. Because of the large number of gates and the fact that product terms (AND gate outputs) may connect to multiple OR gates, the die size was relatively large and worst case propagation delays were relatively long. The device cost was also high, being a function of die size. These drawbacks were compounded by the fact that special device programmers were required to program the devices (standard PROM programmers would not work), and no logic description languages were available for describing the logic in the FPLA. The FPLA logic description was defined by specifying the fuse configuration on a special chart or *fuse map*—a long, tedious and error-prone process. Making changes to the logic within a device was, of course, similarly time-consuming and error-prone.

In 1978 Monolithic Memories, Inc. (MMI) introduced a new family of programmable logic devices, incorporating some innovative concepts that succeeded in popularizing PLDs. MMI's Programmable Array Logic (PAL) family architecture had a programmable AND-array like the FPLA, but it had a fixed OR-array. This architecture supported logic implementation in the Sum-Of-Products (SOP) form, which all combinatorial logic equations can be expressed in. It also offered several features that made the family desirable over FPLAs in many applications.

While the logic in the first PALs was also defined using fuse maps, MMI had the insight to develop a computer-based aid to help in the logic design process. Its PALASM logic language, though simple by today's standards, quickly became almost universally accepted throughout the PLD design industry. PALs quickly took over FPLAs as the programmable logic of choice, and remains the number one PLD family, in terms of sales.

As the use of programmable logic accelerated in the early-to-mid 1980s—helped by plummeting device prices—the demand for faster devices and newer, more-flexible and more-complex devices increased. The number of manufacturers jumping into the PLD market increased as the sales volume for existing devices accelerated. With each manufacturer wanting to get a piece of the pie, PLD families using new IC technologies and often having radically different architectures began to appear. These new PLD implementations were the foundations upon which the new manufacturers hoped to find untapped niches in the marketplace, or to convert over designers using the more-established PLD architectures and families. To keep pace, the manufacturers of the mainstream families retaliated with new families and architectures of their own.

The number and variety of PLD families is increasing, and there are currently no signs of abatement. New families typically represent new architectures for the designer to consider. As PLDs become more complex, manufacturers are showing an increasing trend toward application-specific architectures. The increasing variety of devices becoming available is not without its price, however, since the large variety makes it difficult for designers to keep up with what is available. It is also difficult for a designer to feel comfortable "standardizing" on a single PLD family. The alternative of becoming proficient with multiple PLD families and architectures, though arduous, seems to be the inevitable fate of the modern PLD designer.

While PLDs designed for specific applications are, by definition, more market-limited than the general-purpose devices, they are also capable of providing a much higher level of functionality when used in the applications for which they were designed. By designing a PLD for a specific type of application, a much higher portion of the silicon comprising the device is effectively utilized. Thus, a PLD designed specifically for bus interface applications may have a complexity of only 500 gates, but may provide more functionality in that application than a more-costly, general-purpose 2,000-gate device.

Even for general-purpose devices, device architecture plays a critical role in its effective utilization. This fact has been a primary basis for the introduction of numerous new device architectures, such as foldback arrays and logic cell arrays. While some generalizations can (and will) be made about the relative merits of the different PLD architectures, it should be clear that the choice of a particular PLD is an application-specific decision, and no single device or family is the absolute best for all applications.

Of course, with such rapid and profound changes in the PLD industry, device manufacturers and third-party software producers have been challenged to keep up with adequate design software. This is particularly true where radically new architectures are involved. The software support issues are covered in Chapter 5.

Gate Equivalence

A common, though not particularly conclusive, method of specifying the complexity of a PLD is to indicate its *equivalent gate count*. This number approximates the number of two-input gates (typically NAND gates) the PLD replaces, and is frequently used in PLD articles and manufacturers' data.

Primary PLD Architectures

The remainder of this chapter describes the primary programmable logic device architectures, and discusses a few representative devices. Even the application-specific architectures described in the next chapter are founded on the primary PLD architectures described here.

Programmable Read-Only Memory (PROM, PLE)

Programmable Read-Only Memories (PROMs) were the first devices to be used as programmable logic devices. It was from these devices that the concept of the more-conventional logic device families originated.

The architecture of a PROM is very simple. It consists of an array of memory cells with address lines for inputs and data lines for outputs. The number of address lines and data lines together indicate the matrix of the PROM. A simple PROM is shown in Fig. 3-6. The five address lines allow 32 distinct locations to be selected (addressed), while the eight data lines indicate that eight memory cells (bits) reside at each location. Thus, the PROM has a *32 × 8* matrix, with a total of 256 (32 * 8) memory storage cells (bits).

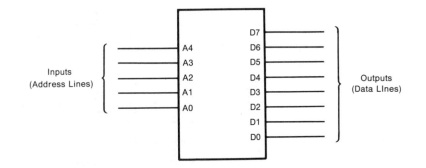

Figure 3-6. Simple PROM with 5 inputs and 8 outputs.

In terms of logic conception, PROMs consist of a fixed AND-array followed by a programmable OR-array, as illustrated in Fig. 3-7 for a 16 × 4 PROM. The 'X's in the figure indicate programmable (fused) points, while the dots indicate fixed connections. Since the AND-array is fixed, one of 16 product terms is selected (output high) based on the logic pattern present at the four PROM address inputs.

As shown in Fig. 3-7, all 16 product term outputs connect—via fuse links—to each of the four output sum (OR) terms. Wherever a fuse link is removed, the corresponding product term output is removed from the respective sum term. The sum term output will be logically high when product terms with intact fuses (for that sum term) are addressed, and will be logically low when product terms with removed fuses are addressed. Figure 3-8 illustrates this concept, showing a programmed PROM and the logic equations corresponding to the outputs.

Use of PROMs has been primarily limited to address decoding and state machine control store applications. Other, more-imaginative uses have also been found, although they are relatively few in comparison.

When designing with PROMs, the designer must beware of the output state uncertainty that exists for a short period of time when changing the (address) inputs. Since a change at the inputs causes a new memory location to be selected, the output logic level cannot be guaranteed until after the access time of the PROM. Thus, output glitches are common when changing input states, and are another design consideration.

Registered PROMs—standard PROMs with registered (latched) outputs— also exist. With these devices, the outputs of the sum terms are not transferred to the respective PROM output pins until a synchronizing clock signal is

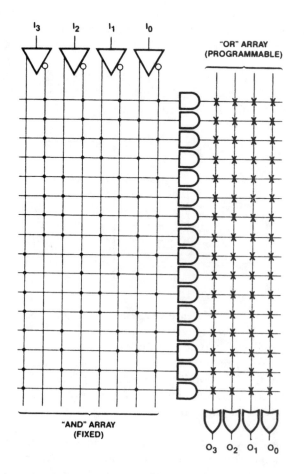

Figure 3-7. PROM conceptual logic diagram: a fixed AND-array followed by a programmable OR-array. *Copyright © 1986 Advanced Micro Devices, Inc. Reprinted with permission of copyright owner. All rights reserved.*

received. This feature can be used to overcome the address-selection glitch problem common to standard PROMs.

Because of the access speed necessary to make PROMs viable as logic devices—typically requiring sub-60 ns access times—PROMs using high-speed bipolar technology have been traditionally used for such applications. Recently, however, high-speed CMOS technologies have permitted the development of fast-access EPROMs (ultraviolet-Erasable PROMs), such as the 32Kx8 WS57C256F EPROM from WaferScale Integration, with an access time of 55 ns. The Cypress Semiconductor 2048x8 CY7C245 reprogrammable registered PROM (EPROM), with its 25 ns access time and 12 ns clock-to-output time, is another example of a high-speed CMOS PROM acceptable for logic applications.

MMI manufactures a variety of PROMs. It calls these devices *Programmable Logic Elements (PLEs)*. The MMI PLE family, while perhaps optimized in some respects for logic applications, should be considered simply a family of PROMs from a designer's standpoint.

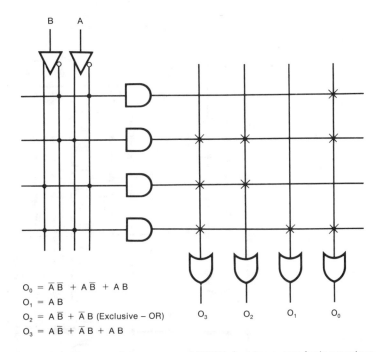

$O_0 = \overline{A}\,\overline{B} + A\,\overline{B} + A\,B$

$O_1 = A\,B$

$O_2 = A\,\overline{B} + \overline{A}\,B$ (Exclusive – OR)

$O_3 = A\,\overline{B} + \overline{A}\,B + A\,B$

Figure 3-8. Diagram of a programmed PROM showing output logic equations.

Field-Programmable Logic Array (FPLA)

Field-Programmable Logic Arrays (FPLAs) were the first non-PROM programmable logic devices. They were the first field-programmable (that is, programmable at the customer site) devices primarily intended to be used for logic design applications. Signetics introduced the FPLA in 1975, with its 28-pin 82S100 (now PLS100) device—kicking off the PLD industry. While programmable logic arrays (PLAs) were already available in mask-programmable versions, the FPLA was the first such device to be field-programmable.

The basic FPLA architecture consists of a programmable AND-array followed by a programmable OR-array, as shown in Fig. 3-9. Again, as is typical of PLDs, the inputs enter the AND-array in true and complemented forms. Unlike the PROM described above, the AND-array is programmable, so that product terms with any combination of the input signals (true or complemented) can be easily created. The product term outputs feed into the programmable OR-array, which allows any of the product terms to connect to any of the sum terms. A single product term can even connect to multiple sum terms.

To illustrate the concept of the FPLA, Fig. 3-10 shows the logic diagram of a programmed device, along with the equations corresponding to its outputs.

Whenever a device has a programmable AND-array, like the FPLA (and the PAL described later), half the fuses in the AND array will need to be blown (removed), except for fuses connected to unused product terms. This is true because half of the fuses come from true input signals, while the other half come from complemented input signals. Since the logical product of a signal and its complement is

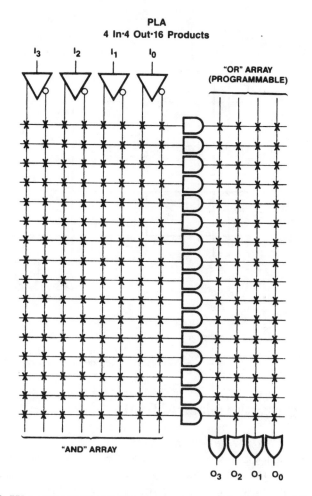

PLA
4 In·4 Out·16 Products

Figure 3-9. FPLA conceptual logic diagram: a programmable AND-array followed by a programmable OR-array. *Copyright © 1986 Advanced Micro Devices, Inc. Reprinted with permission of copyright owner. All rights reserved.*

always false, no signal can be connected to a product term with its complement. Thus, at least half—and generally many more—of the fuses must be removed to have valid product terms. Since the fuses take up considerable silicon space, particularly with bipolar PLDs, it is clear to see how silicon space-inefficient typical PLDs tend to be, and why new architectures are being researched and developed.

While the FPLA model just discussed is helpful in understanding the basic structure of FPLA devices, looking at the logic diagram of a real FPLA will show some of the intricacies of the architecture that make it especially flexible. Fig. 3-11 shows the logic diagram for the popular Signetics Corp. 20-pin PLS153 FPLA. The configuration of this device is similar to Signetics' original 28-pin PLS100, with the notable exception of programmable output buffers.

The shaded areas in Fig. 3-11 show where programmable connections exist on the device. The top-left and bottom-left shaded areas indicate the programmable AND-array and programmable OR-array, respectively. Another significant

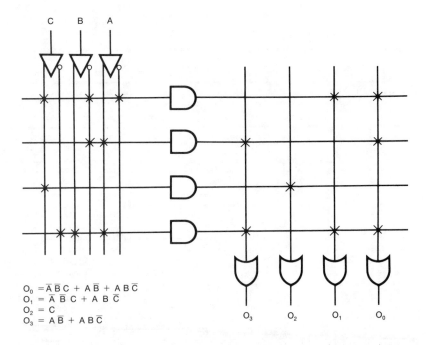

$$O_0 = \overline{A}\,\overline{B}\,C + A\,\overline{B} + A\,B\,\overline{C}$$
$$O_1 = \overline{A}\,\overline{B}\,C + A\,B\,\overline{C}$$
$$O_2 = C$$
$$O_3 = A\,\overline{B} + A\,B\,\overline{C}$$

Figure 3-10. Diagram of a programmed FPLA showing output logic equations.

feature of the PLS153 design common to most FPLAs is its *programmable output polarity*. The output of each sum term connects to one input of a two-input Exclusive-OR (XOR) gate; the second input of which is connected to ground via a fuse. If the fuse is kept intact, the output of the sum term is passed unchanged to the output of the XOR gate. If the fuse is removed (causing the XOR gate input to go high), the sum term output is inverted as it passes through the XOR gate. Programmable output polarity is a very desirable feature, since it permits more-efficient use of the logic on the chip. PLDs that do not support the programmable output polarity feature—like many of the popular PAL devices—often require a DeMorgan transformation to convert an equation to the proper polarity for an output. This frequently results in a new equation that exceeds the product-term capacity of the PLD.

Referring again to the PLS153 logic diagram in Fig. 3-11, the XOR outputs pass through tri-state output buffers before reaching the output pins. Each buffer has an associated product term used to enable the output. When the product term output is true (high), the buffer output is enabled, otherwise the buffer remains in its high-impedance state.

The output pins feed back into the AND-array. This is common, and serves a dual purpose. First, it gives flexibility to the output pins, allowing them to be used as inputs, outputs, or bidirectional input/output pins, as appropriate for the application. Second, it allows logic feedback, so that the output of a sum term can be routed back to the AND-array and used as an input to other product terms. When these pins are used as inputs, the tri-state buffers must remain in the high-impedance state, and the associated sum terms cannot be used. When used as outputs or input/output pins, the tri-state buffers must be controlled as

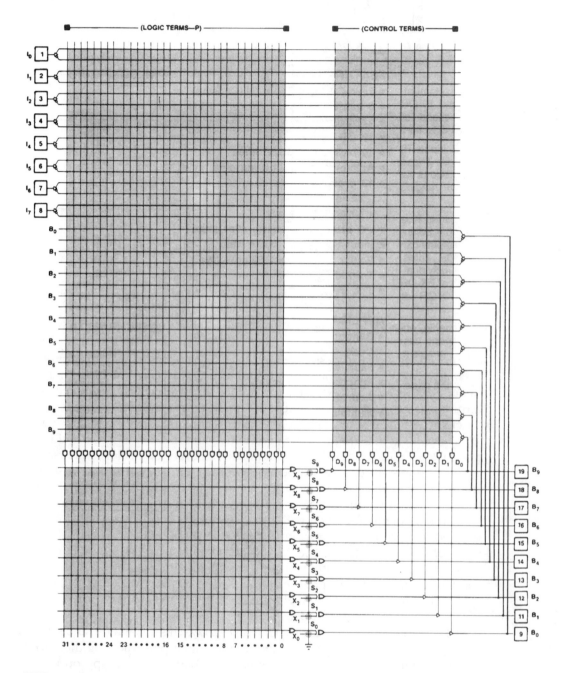

Figure 3-11. PLS153 FPLA logic diagram. *Courtesy Signetics Corp.*

necessary using the on-chip buffer-control product terms. One caution must be observed when using the feedback signal for logic feedback; whenever a tri-state buffer enters the high-impedance state, the corresponding sum term output is no longer fed back into the programmable AND-array, and thus is not available to be used as an input to a product term.

The fact that the OR-array is programmable adds considerable flexibility to the FPLA. In typical applications, the number of product terms required per output (logic equation) varies. Some may require only one or two, while others may require 10 or more. The ability to use the exact number of needed product terms for each output provides for efficient use of the on-chip resources. In contrast, most PALs (with few exceptions) have a fixed number of product terms connected to each sum term. In most cases, many of the product terms remain unused, and are thus wasted. When more product terms are needed for an output, the unused product terms are unavailable, disallowing the implementation of complex equations. The ubiquitous PAL16L8 is a typical example. Even though it provides seven product terms for each of its eight outputs—56 product terms total—the PLS153, with its 32 product terms, is better suited for many applications because of its flexibility in sharing product terms. The PAL16L8 also lacks programmable output polarities, giving the PLS153 added flexibility in that area, as well.

Acceptance of the FPLA was impeded by a number of factors, including lack of design software, relatively slow propagation delays, and relatively high cost resulting from its large die size. Since both the AND- and OR-arrays were placed on the same chip, the number of fuses, and thus the size of the chip, was large. Also, because each product term could connect to multiple sum terms, the additional capacitance of multiple sum terms slowed the worst-case propagation delay through the device. The extra delay associated with supporting programmable output polarities compounded the problem. Due to IC technology improvements, device speeds are picking up, and die sizes are becoming smaller, making these concerns less of a problem for FPLAs. Nonetheless, these drawbacks prompted the later conception and development of the PAL architecture, which continues to benefit from its simplicity.

FPLAs are often described in terms of their matrix configuration. The PLS153 is described as an 18 × 42 × 10 FPLA, since it has 18 inputs into the AND-array (each, of course, in true and complemented form), 42 product terms (only 32 of which enter the OR-array), and 10 outputs.

While Signetics, like other manufacturers, has a *family* of FPLA devices, the FPLA also represents an *architecture* that is present in other PLD families.

Field-Programmable Logic Sequencer (FPLS)

The *Field-Programmable Logic Sequencer (FPLS)* was first introduced by Signetics in 1979, and is a take-off from the basic FPLA architecture, with registers added to allow state machine implementation. Some FPLSs merely have registered outputs with feedback into the programmable AND-array; others have *buried registers* with feedback (that is, registers that can be used on the chip without any connection to input or output pins) in addition to registered outputs with or without feedback. Some FPLS devices have a mixture of registered and combinatorial outputs, allowing combinational logic to be included on the same chip with other, latched signals or state machines.

The logic diagram of the 20-pin Signetics PLS157 FPLS is shown in Fig. 3-12. The PLS157 is a representative FPLS device, with a 16 × 45 × 12 configuration. As with the PLS153 logic diagram described earlier, the shaded areas indicate programmable connections.

The PLS157 has six registered outputs and six standard, combinatorial outputs. The combinatorial outputs are functionally identical to those described above for the PLS153 FPLA. The registers can be dynamically or permanently configured as D, J-K, or T flip-flops, because of the flexibility offered by the inclusion of the "M" inverters (M_0–M_5). The outputs of the registers are fed back into the AND-array *before* reaching the tri-state output buffers, allowing for Mealy and Moore state machine development.

The design of the PLS157 has several other features worth noting. First, the registers have provisions that allow them to latch input signals from their corresponding pins, and present the latched signals as inputs to the AND-array. Second, the device also has a *complement* array. This is a sum term that is complemented and presented as an input to the AND-array, allowing the development of more-complex, multilevel logic. Of course, the use of such a feature adds additional propagation delays to the associated signals, which must be considered in the design.

Field-Programmable Gate Array (FPGA)

In 1977 Signetics introduced the first *Field-Programmable Gate Array (FPGA)*, used simply as a replacement for standard, multiple-input gates. The basic concept is illustrated in Fig. 3-13. As shown, the FPGA contains a programmable AND-array with programmable-polarity outputs. Since an AND gate can easily become a NAND gate (by inverting the output), a NOR gate (by inverting all inputs), or an OR gate (by inverting all inputs and the output), each of the FPGA AND gates can become any of these gates. They can also function as simple inverters. The AND gate inputs are easily inverted, since the true and complemented form of each input signal is present in the AND-array. The AND gate outputs are also easily inverted, since the exclusive-OR gate on the output provides for programmable polarity selection.

The FPGA is also more flexible than multiple-input standard gates, since it can function like standard gates with only certain inputs inverted; the circuit shown in Fig. 3-14, for example, can be incorporated using a single FPGA output.

The Signetics 20-pin PLS151, the logic diagram of which is shown in Fig. 3-15, is a good example of an existing FPGA. The device has six dedicated inputs, 12 logic product terms, and 12 outputs which are fed back into the AND-array and can also be used as inputs. There are three additional product terms, each of which controls the tri-state output buffers for four outputs. Separate fuses allow the tri-state output buffers to be individually hard-enabled.

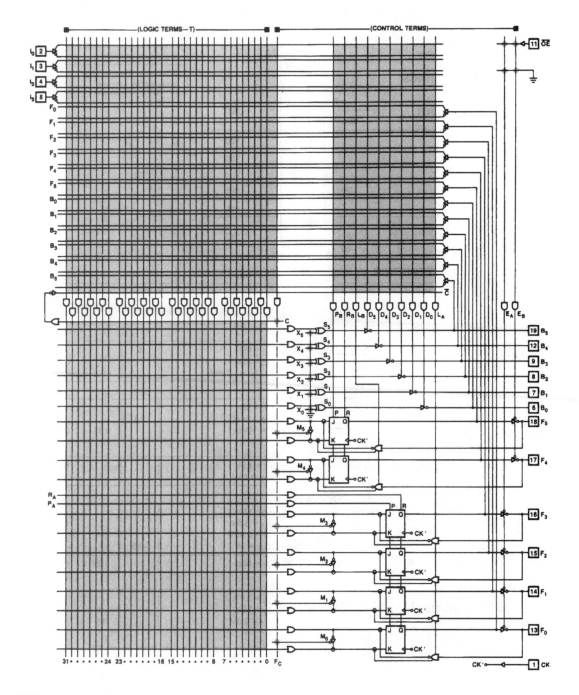

NOTES:
1. All OR gate inputs with a blown link float to logic "0".
2. All other gates and control inputs with a blown link float to logic "1".
3. ⊕ denotes WIRE-OR.
4.  Programmable connection.

Figure 3-12. PLS157 FPLS logic diagram. *Courtesy Signetics Corp.*

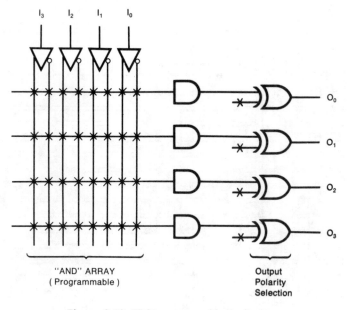

Figure 3-13. FPGA conceptual logic diagram.

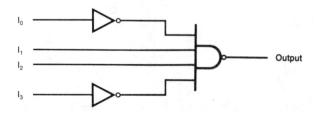

Figure 3-14. Example logic circuit that can be easily incorporated into an FPGA.

By using the feedback feature of the PLS151 outputs, it is simple to create multilevel gate functions, such as XOR gates or AND-OR-INVERT gates. The extra propagation delays resulting from feedback through the AND-array must be figured into the design. The simple architecture of the FPGA is well-suited for address decoder applications, in addition to other logic functions.

Field-Programmable Address Decoder (FPAD)

Field-Programmable Address Decoders (FPADs) are architecturally and functionally identical to FPGAs.

Programmable Array Logic (PAL, ZPAL, HAL, ZHAL, NML)

The *Programmable Array Logic (PAL)* family has become the most popular PLD family available. Introduced by Monolithic Memories, Inc. (MMI) in 1978,

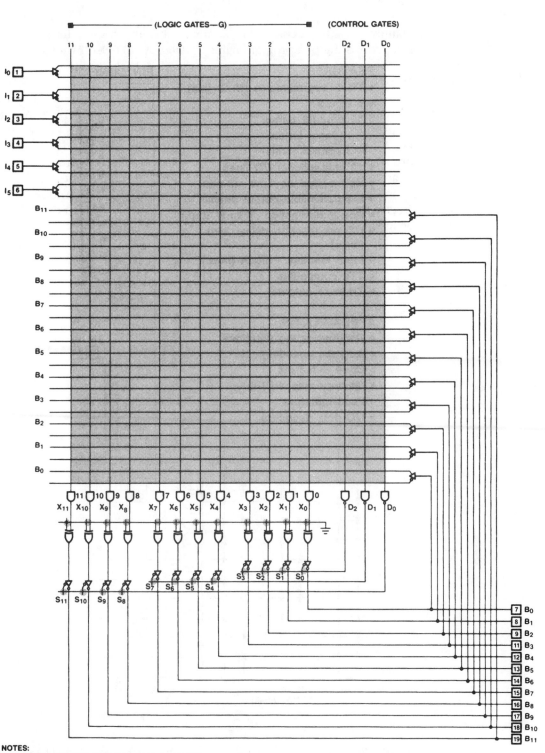

Figure 3-15. PLS151 FPGA logic diagram. *Courtesy Signetics Corp.*

NOTES:
1. All gate inputs with a blown link float to a logic "1".
2. 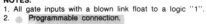 Programmable connection.

the PAL family was the second PLD family to be introduced. Its patented architecture, consisting of a programmable AND-array followed by a fixed OR-array, was conceived to overcome some of the drawbacks presented by the FPLA—the only other existing PLD at that time.

Figure 3-16 illustrates the basic PAL architecture. As shown, the AND-array is programmable—like that of the FPLA—but the OR-array is fixed. A set number of product terms are connected to each OR gate and product terms are not shared. As mentioned earlier, fuses are responsible for occupying a considerable portion of the silicon real estate. Since the PAL architecture precludes the use of OR-array fuses, the amount of silicon required to implement devices of similar complexity is considerably less with PALs than with FPLAs. And since IC cost is directly related to the amount of silicon real estate used by a chip, PALs tend to be less costly to manufacture.

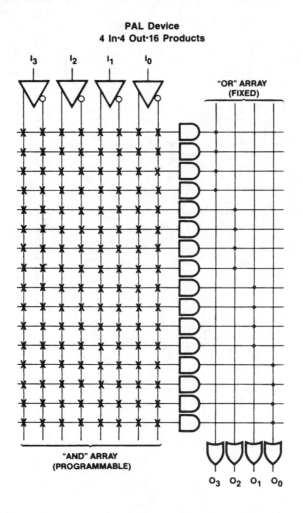

**PAL Device
4 In·4 Out·16 Products**

Figure 3-16. PAL conceptual logic diagram: a programmable AND-array followed by a fixed OR-array. *Copyright © 1986 Advanced Micro Devices, Inc. Reprinted with permission of copyright owner. All rights reserved.*

The PAL's simpler architecture also results in shorter propagation delays than those specified for FPLAs, since the FPLA's second programmable array and its product-term sharing among different sum terms increase the propagation time.

Another PAL feature, applicable particularly to the early devices, is that they were designed to "look" like standard PROMs from a fuse standpoint, and could therefore be programmed on standard PROM programmers. This alleviated the special programming requirements common to FPLAs.

Because of the impact PALs have had in the PLD industry, it is worth taking a look at a few specific devices, as well as the numbering system that has been adopted by the PAL manufacturers.

Figure 3-17 shows the logic diagram of the 20-pin PAL16L8 from MMI. This device has eight combinatorial outputs. Each output is an inverted sum term with seven product term inputs. An eighth product term at each output controls the state of the tri-state buffer for that output. Six of the eight output pins are fed back into the AND-array, allowing these pins to also be used as inputs or bidirectional input/output pins.

Notice that the logic function implemented by the PAL16L8 is the AND-OR-INVERT, since the outputs are inverted. The outputs are considered "active low" and thus best support logic functions that are low when asserted (true). The PAL16L8 is commonly used for address decoding, for example, since most microprocessor memory and peripheral devices have active-low chip select inputs. Logic functions requiring active-high outputs can also be supported by the PAL16L8, as long as the new logic equations resulting from a DeMorgan transformation do not exceed the seven product term limitation of the device. Unfortunately, this is often a problem.

The PAL16L8 has become very popular because it has a medium level of complexity, and the seven product terms available for each output are adequate for many general-purpose decoding and logic applications. It also provides this functionality at low cost and relatively high speed. Parts with propagation times as fast as 7.5 ns have been developed, and faster parts are promised in the future.

One feature that was first established in the PAL family, and has since spread to other PLD families, is the inclusion of a *last fuse* or *security fuse*. If this fuse is blown, device verification is inhibited, preventing the device from being easily copied. While the security fuse does not make it impossible to determine the logic in a PLD, it certainly makes it much more difficult, and is nearly impossible for complex PLDs. Security fuses and their implications are discussed further in Chapter 7.

The PAL16R6 is also a medium-complexity 20-pin PAL, and is similar in many respects to the PAL16L8 described above. Figure 3-18 shows the logic diagram for the PAL16R6. Like the PAL16L8, it has eight outputs. Six of the outputs, however, are *registered* using D-type flip-flops, while the remaining two outputs are combinatorial. Because the flip-flop outputs are returned to the AND-array, this device can be used not only for latching output signals, but also for the development of Moore and Mealy state machines. A separate input pin is used to control the output enable for the six registered outputs, while each of the combinatorial outputs has a separate product term to control the tri-state output buffer.

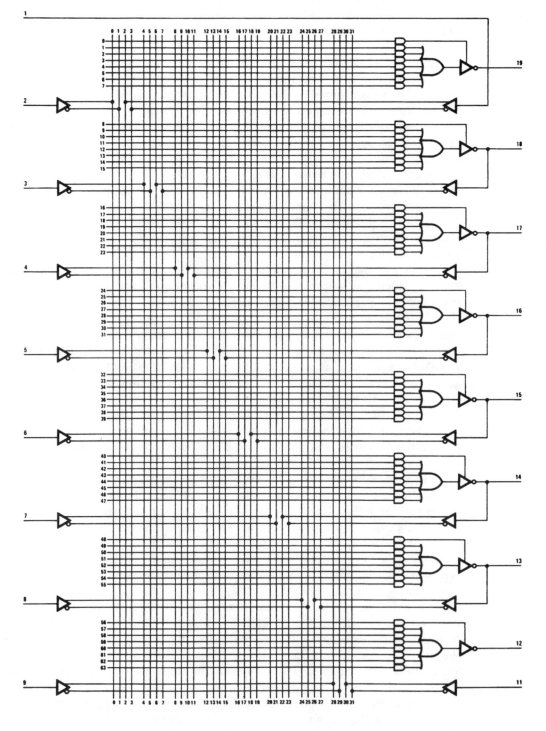

Figure 3-17. PAL16L8 logic diagram. *Copyright © 1986 Advanced Micro Devices, Inc.*
Reprinted with permission of copyright owner. All rights reserved.

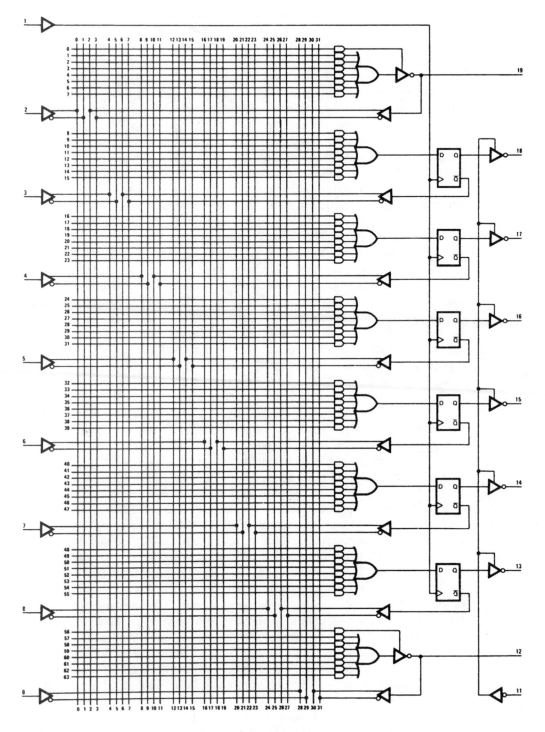

Figure 3-18. PAL16R6 logic diagram. *Copyright © 1986 Advanced Micro Devices, Inc.*
Reprinted with permission of copyright owner. All rights reserved.

The "Medium 20" PAL series includes two additional PALs, the PAL16R4, with four registered outputs and four combinatorial outputs, and the PAL16R8, having eight registered outputs. The four Medium 20 series PALs, PAL16L8, PAL16R4, PAL16R6 and PAL16R8, together make up the most-used group of PLDs in the PLD industry. These devices are available in numerous speed and power consumption versions, and have been converted from bipolar to other technologies as well. When a faster technology is developed, these are generally the first parts to be implemented using the new technology, and are very economical as a result of their popularity. Although they are architecturally simple by today's PLD standards, they are adequate for many simple logic design applications. Because of their importance, PLD designers should become familiar with the architectures of the devices in this small group of PALs.

Another PAL worth looking at that is a generation ahead of the Medium 20 series devices described above and has achieved similar popularity, is the 24-pin PAL22V10 from Advanced Micro Devices (AMD). The logic diagram for the PAL22V10 is shown in Fig. 3-19. The PAL22V10 incorporates *programmable macrocells*, which have become popular among PLD users. They add considerable flexibility to PLDs, and have accounted for the wide acceptance of the PAL22V10 and other devices. Several other manufacturers are now also producing the PAL22V10 in bipolar and CMOS technologies because of its popularity. Atmel has introduced an improved version of the PAL22V10, the V750, as will be described later in the section on EPLDs.

Referring to the logic diagram, we see that the PAL22V10 has 12 dedicated inputs into the programmable AND-array, and 10 output macrocells, any of which can also be used as inputs. Each output has an inverting tri-state output buffer that is controlled by its own product term.

In addition to the macrocells, the PAL22V10 also has several other features worth noting. First, pin 1 serves a dual purpose. If any of the output macrocells are configured as registered outputs, pin 1 is used as the clock input to the registers; otherwise it acts as a standard input into the AND-array. Second, the sum terms have differing numbers of product term inputs, ranging from eight to 16. This is commonly referred to as *variable product term distribution*. The higher number of product terms over first-generation PALs gives the device much more capability in implementing complex logic functions. The PAL22V10 also supports programmable output polarities, further enhancing its ability support complex logic functions.

Figure 3-20 shows a close-up logic diagram of the macrocell structure found in the PAL22V10. The output of the sum term enters the macrocell on the left. The output of the macrocell exits on the right, entering the inverting, tri-state output buffer. The macrocell also has a feedback term, exiting at the lower-left, which returns to the AND-array. Determined by the programmed configuration of the two fuses in the macrocell, one of four output configurations can be achieved. The four configurations, shown in Fig. 3-21, include registered/active-low, registered/active-high, combinatorial/active-low, and combinatorial/active-high. If a registered output is selected, the feedback term comes from the register, allowing Mealy and Moore state machines to be developed. If a combinatorial output is selected, the feedback term comes from the pin, allowing the pin to be used as an output with feedback, an input, or a bidirectional input/output signal.

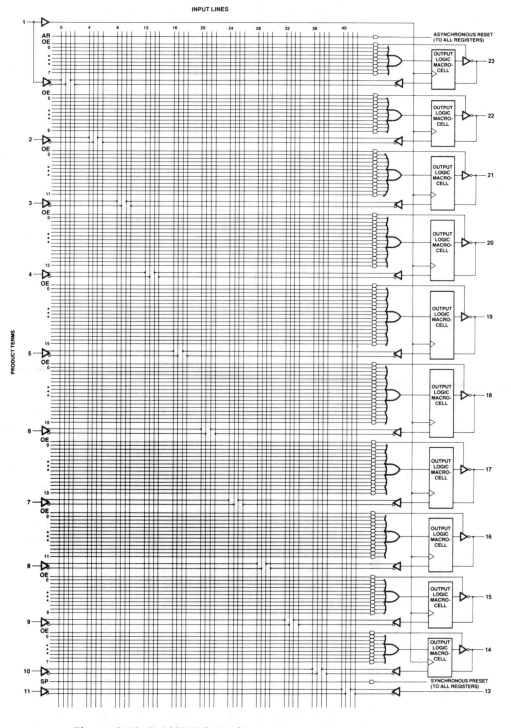

Figure 3-19. PAL22V10 logic diagram. *Copyright © 1987 Advanced Micro Devices, Inc. Reprinted with permission of copyright owner. All rights reserved.*

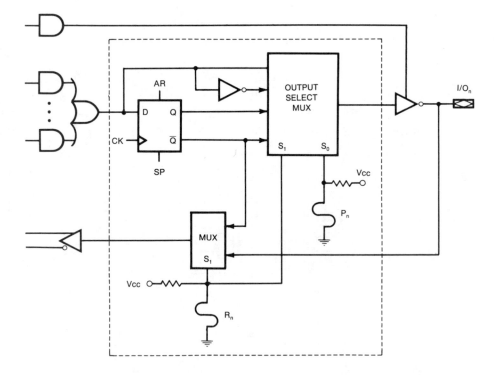

Figure 3-20. PAL22V10 macrocell logic diagram. *Copyright © 1987 Advanced Micro Devices, Inc. Reprinted with permission of copyright owner. All rights reserved.*

Each of the 10 macrocells in the PAL22V10 are individually configurable. This allows the device to be configured to the input, output, and register requirements of different applications. The flexibility also provides for easier device changes during the development and prototype stages of new designs. This is because signals connected to macrocell pins can easily be changed from inputs to outputs, or from combinatorial outputs to registered outputs, with only a change in the device programming.

The features of the PAL22V10 do not stop there. The registers on the chip are automatically reset during power-up. There is also a programmable product term that provides an asynchronous reset signal to all of the registers, and another product term that supplies a synchronous preset (synchronized to the register clock from pin 1) to all of the registers. The logic level that appears *at the pin* when a register is reset (or preset) is determined by whether the true or inverted register output is selected to be output to the pin. In a design, it may be appropriate for some signals to go to the logic high level when reset, while other signals may need to go low when reset. The PAL22V10 supports this flexibility.

The PAL22V10 also supports *register preloading*, allowing the registers to be preset to a given state for testing. This allows more-complete testing, as described in detail in Chapter 7.

Many other PAL devices exist, and additional ones are being introduced regularly. Clearly, the attempt is to provide a PAL to meet nearly every need of the programmable logic designer. PAL variations include:

- Number of inputs
- Number of outputs
- Number of registers
- Number of product terms
- Output polarity (high, low, or programmable)
- Product term sharing capability
- Inclusion of special gates (e.g., XOR)
- Arithmetic function support
- Macrocells
- Others

Unlike some of the other PLD manufacturers, PAL manufacturers have adopted a device numbering system that provides at least some information about the devices. PAL device numbers generally consist of two numbers separated by one or two letters (e.g., PAL*16L8*). The first indicates the number of entries into the programmable AND-array. Although this is *often* the same as the maximum number of inputs (from pins) the device can support, the two are not always the same and should not be confused. The second indicates the number of outputs the device provides, or at least the number of outputs with a particular attribute. The intervening letter or two indicates a significant attribute about some or all of the device outputs. Some of the letter codes and corresponding meanings are:

- H = Active High
- L = Active Low
- C = Complementary
- P = Programmable polarity
- R = Registered
- RA = Registered asynchronous
- S = Shared product terms or Sequencer
- X = Exclusive-OR registered
- A = Arithmetic registered
- V = Versatile (i.e., macrocell)

The single-letter codes are combined to form two-letter codes. For example, a PAL16RP8 has eight registered outputs with programmable output polarity. Of course, only limited information can be put into a part number, so the PAL numbering system should be used only as a basic guide for remembering certain devices, or for determining special device characteristics. Because of the information limitation in the part number, it is easy to become confused or misled when only looking at a device part number. For example, from its part number it is simple to determine that the PAL16R4 has 16 AND-array inputs (and probably supports up to 16 pin inputs), and has four registered outputs. What is not clear is that the device also has four combinatorial outputs. Thus the PAL part numbers should be used as guides. Manufacturer device logic diagrams and data sheets should always be consulted before considering devices for real designs.

PAL part numbers also often include a suffix providing information about device speed and power consumption. Many of the suffixes currently apply only to the popular Medium 20 series PALs described earlier. The device speed increases as the suffix letter increases. Numbers that also have a '−n' numeric extension to the suffix indicate reduced power: −2 indicates "half power" and −4 indicates "quarter power." Reducing the power consumption, however, also causes the device to revert back to the speed of the previous suffix letter For example, a device with a 'B-2' suffix has the same speed as a device with an 'A' suffix. A table showing the propagation delays and power consumptions for the various part number suffixes will clarify the suffix numbering system. The suffixes and associated propagation delays and current consumptions for the Medium 20 series PALs are:

- (no suffix) = 35 ns, 180 mA
- A   = 25 ns, 180 mA
- A-2   = 35 ns, 90 mA
- A-4   = 55 ns, 50 mA
- B   = 15 ns, 180 mA
- B-2   = 25 ns, 90 mA
- B-4   = 35 ns, 55 mA
- D   = 10 ns, 180 mA
- E   = 7.5 ns, 180 mA

Notice that the letter 'C' is absent from the speed suffix list. The letter was intentionally left out of the sequence to avoid confusion with CMOS devices, which frequently include the letter 'C' in the part number.

ZPALs are "zero power" CMOS versions of standard PALs. These devices, being CMOS, have low operating current requirements. They offer a very-low-current standby mode, requiring not more than 100 μA (microamps) of supply current, and typically less than 10 μA. The part numbers for the ZPAL devices generally have a 'Z' suffix and a 'PALC' prefix (indicating 'CMOS') instead of the standard 'PAL' prefix. Thus, for example, the PALC20R8Z is a ZPAL version of the standard PAL20R8.

Other CMOS PALs exist. An example is the PALC22V10 from Cypress Semiconductor. These others often do not offer a "zero power" standby mode, and therefore lack the 'Z' suffix. Device data sheets should be consulted to determine CMOS PAL standby current requirements. Some CMOS PALs, like the Cypress PALC22V10, are erasable and reprogrammable, while others are not; even devices that are erasable are also often offered in *one-time programmable (OTP)* versions to reduce production costs. Remember, device data sheets should be consulted to determine the erasability and reprogrammability of specific programmable logic devices.

If a design developed using PAL devices is later slated for medium-to-high volume production, it is sometimes wise to use *mask-programmed PALs*, effectively offloading the programming and testing responsibilities to the

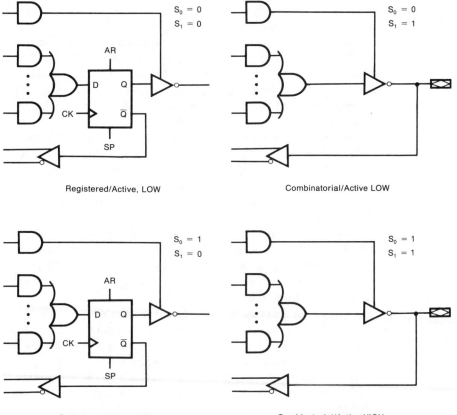

$S_0 = 0$
$S_1 = 0$

Registered/Active, LOW

$S_0 = 0$
$S_1 = 1$

Combinatorial/Active LOW

$S_0 = 1$
$S_1 = 0$

Registered/Active HIGH

$S_0 = 1$
$S_1 = 1$

Combinatorial/Active HIGH

Figure 3-21. The four possible PAL22V10 output macrocell configurations.
Copyright © 1987 Advanced Micro Devices, Inc. Reprinted with permission of copyright owner.
All rights reserved.

manufacturer, as well as reducing other production costs. Several manufacturers, such as MMI, allow such a mask-programmed option for PAL devices. MMI calls their mask-programmed parts *HAL* and *ZHAL* devices. The HAL (*Hard Array Logic*) devices are merely mask-programmed versions of the standard PALs, while the ZHAL (*Zero-power Hard Array Logic*) devices are mask-programmed "zero power" CMOS versions of the standard PAL devices. National Semiconductor also offers mask-programmed PALs, which it calls its *NML (National Masked Logic)* devices.

Generic Array Logic (GAL)

The *Generic Array Logic (GAL)* family is a group of *EEPLDs*—Electrically Erasable PLDs, also called *E²PLDs*. These were originally developed and introduced by Lattice Semiconductor Corp., but are now also alternate-sourced by a number of other manufacturers. These devices attempt to present the PLD designer with a "generic" architecture by incorporating programmable macro-cells, such as those found in the PAL22V10 described earlier. Lattice calls them *output logic macrocells (OLMCs)*.

As a result of the flexibility offered by the programmable macrocell architecture, a single GAL device can emulate numerous different PAL devices. This, of course, is a primary marketing point for the GAL family. This, combined with the fact that the GAL devices are electrically erasable and reprogrammable, should not be overlooked. Many of the benefits offered by the GAL family, as well as other, similar devices, are described in Chapter 7.

Figure 3-22 shows the logic diagram for the GAL16V8, a popular 20-pin GAL device. Each OLMC has eight product terms entering it, as well as a feedback signal from the corresponding pin and a feedback signal from an *adjacent* pin. There is also an output enable signal distributed to all of the OLMCs from pin 11, as well as a clock signal distributed from pin 1. Each OLMC also returns a feedback term to the AND-array.

Figure 3-23 shows the logic of the OLMC for the GAL16V8. Two "fuse" (EEPROM cell) connections or *architecture control bits* (AC0 and AC1) are associated with each OLMC to configure it as desired. In addition, a bit in each OLMC connects to one input of the XOR gate to allow programmable output polarity selection. There is also a 'SYN' bit associated with the chip that affects the architectural configuration of the OLMCs.

The OLMCs can achieve five different configurations, determined by the values of the AC0, AC1 and 'SYN' fuses. The five configurations are shown in Fig. 3-24. In each configuration, the XOR fuse determines the output polarity, although its setting is meaningless for the 'Dedicated Input Mode' configuration (Fig. 3-24A).

All existing GAL devices support register preloading, like the PAL22V10. This feature is very useful for improving device testability, and is described in Chapter 7.

Another development that originated with the GAL family is the *in-system programmable (ISP)* EEPLD. The first such device, the ispGAL16Z8, is architecturally identical to the GAL16V8 described above, with four pins added to control in-system programming. The ispGAL16Z8 permits a minimum of 10,000 erase/write cycles, and specifies data retention in excess of 20 years—double that specified for conventional EPROM-based devices.

The GAL family is clearly a takeoff from the popular PAL family with its architectural attempt to woo would-be PAL designers. Other GAL features also parallel those associated with PAL devices. This is particularly reflected in the GAL part numbering system and the inclusion of a security cell in GAL devices.

The similarity between GALs and PALs, particularly in terms of basic architecture—programmable AND-array followed by a fixed OR-array—has not been without its cost. It was the basis of a law suit brought against Lattice by MMI for infringement against its PAL patent.

Programmable, Electrically Erasable Logic (PEEL)

Programmable, Electrically Erasable Logic (PEEL), introduced by International CMOS Technology, Inc., and alternate-sourced by Gould and Hyundai,

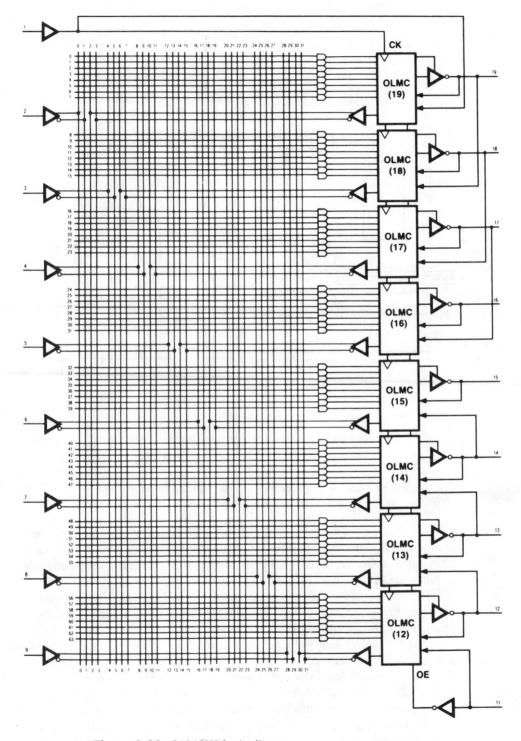

Figure 3-22. GAL16V8 logic diagram. *Courtesy Lattice Semiconductor.*

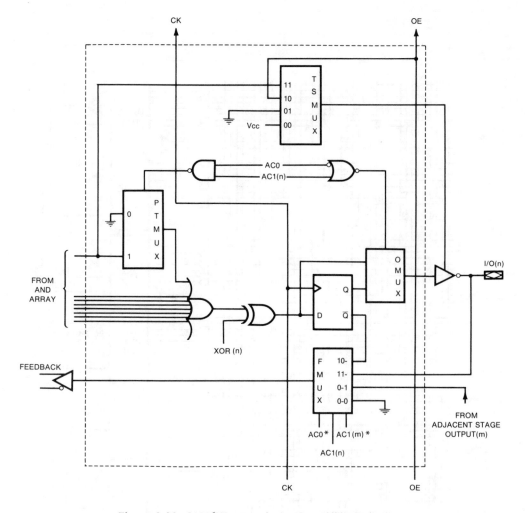

Figure 3-23. GAL16V8 output logic macrocell logic diagram.
Courtesy Lattice Semiconductor.

incorporates EEPROM technology to offer electrically erasable, reprogramm-able PLDs, like the GAL family described above. In fact the first device in the EEPLD PEEL family, the PEEL18CV8, is also architecturally very similar to the PAL-like GAL16V8.

The PEEL18CV8 logic diagram is shown in Fig. 3-25. The 20-pin device offers eight output macrocells, like the GAL16V8, and is similarly designed to emulate a number of different PAL devices. Similar to the GAL device, each PEEL18CV8 output has eight product terms entering the sum term, and has a separate product term to control the tri-state output buffer.

The macrocell logic diagram for the PEEL18CV8 is shown in Fig. 3-26. The macrocell allows either combinatorial or registered output, with programmable output polarity. The feedback term can be generated by the pin, the sum term output or the register output. Like the PAL22V10, the PEEL18CV8 has product terms for asynchronous reset and synchronous preset of its macrocell registers.

With its flexible architecture, the PEEL macrocell allows its register to be buried for internal signal-latching or state machine use, while the output is driven by the sum term. This is not supported on the GAL16V8 or the PAL22V10.

Erasable Programmable Logic Device (EPLD)

The term *Erasable Programmable Logic Device (EPLD)* was first introduced by Altera (and alternate-source Intel), for its family of CMOS UV-erasable PLDs. It has since become a generic term in the PLD industry, referring to all UV-erasable devices, i.e., devices incorporating EPROM cell technology. The similar term *EEPLD* was later coined to refer to EEPROM cell-based devices, which are *electrically* erasable. These should not be confused.

Since *EPLD* has become a generic term, numerous companies have adopted it to describe their devices, including Cypress, Atmel, PLX Technology, Gould, Panatech, and others. Since most EPLDs seem to fit better in other family categories, this discussion will center primarily around devices from Altera, Cypress and Atmel.

From its beginning, Altera has been an innovator in high-density, reprogrammable PLDs. Of all current PLD IC technologies, EPROM technology is the most space-efficient (in terms of die size). Thus, for a given IC die size, more circuitry can be placed onto a chip using EPROM technology than with EEPROM or bipolar technologies. Altera's product line reflects this, with its general-purpose devices having complexities ranging from about 300, to as much as 5,000 gates. They also offer application-specific devices for state machine and bus interface applications. For comparison, the PAL16L8 has a complexity of around 100–150 gates, while the PAL22V10 has a 500–600 gate complexity. As with the GAL devices, all of Altera's initial general-purpose chips include macrocell architectures to increase effective device usage over earlier FPLA and PAL devices.

Figure 3-27 shows the block diagram of the 20-pin EP310 EPLD, a low-end offering in the Altera product line. This device includes eight programmable macrocells, along with asynchronous clear and synchronous preset product terms. Figure 3-28 shows a close-up of the macrocell structure, including the *I/O Architecture Control Block (ACB)*.

Note the slight terminology difference between earlier macrocell discussions and this discussion of Altera's macrocells. In Fig. 3-28, Altera refers to the product term/sum term section and the configurable I/O logic block together as the *logic array macrocell*. The configurable I/O block that was referred to as a macrocell in the PAL22V10 and GAL discussions is referred to by Altera as the *I/O Architecture Control Block*, and is a sub-section of the macrocell. Altera's terminology will be used for the discussion of its devices, but the previously established terminology will be used when discussing all other device families, since it has become standard in the industry.

As shown in Fig. 3-28, each macrocell has eight product terms entering the sum term, with a ninth term used to control the tri-state output buffer. By configuring the ACB, the device can output an active-high or active-low combinatorial signal, or an active-high or active-low registered signal. The ACB

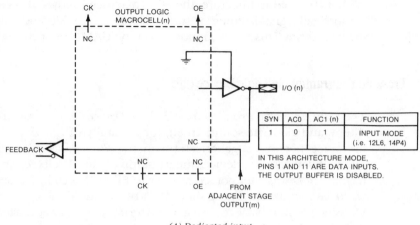

(A) Dedicated input.

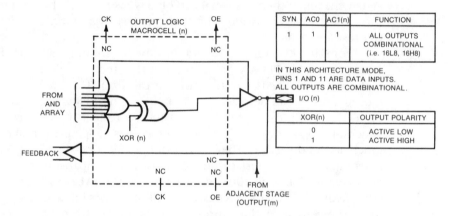

(C) Combinational output.

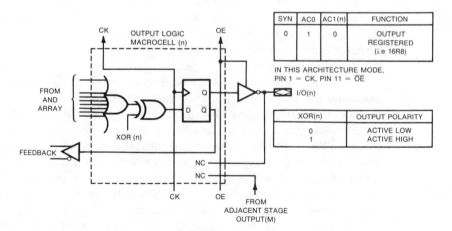

(E) Registered active high or low output.

Figure 3-24. GAL16V8 OLMC configurations.

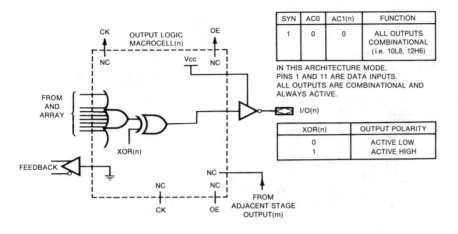

SYN	AC0	AC1(n)	FUNCTION
1	0	0	ALL OUTPUTS COMBINATIONAL (i.e. 10L8, 12H6)

IN THIS ARCHITECTURE MODE,
PINS 1 AND 11 ARE DATA INPUTS.
ALL OUTPUTS ARE COMBINATIONAL AND
ALWAYS ACTIVE.

XOR(n)	OUTPUT POLARITY
0	ACTIVE LOW
1	ACTIVE HIGH

(B) Dedicated combinational output.

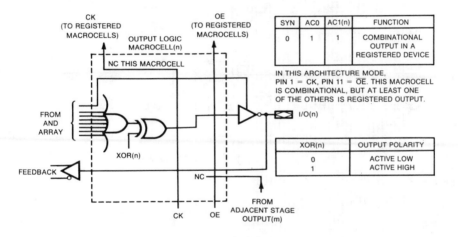

SYN	AC0	AC1(n)	FUNCTION
0	1	1	COMBINATIONAL OUTPUT IN A REGISTERED DEVICE

IN THIS ARCHITECTURE MODE,
PIN 1 = CK, PIN 11 = $\overline{OE}$. THIS MACROCELL
IS COMBINATIONAL, BUT AT LEAST ONE
OF THE OTHERS IS REGISTERED OUTPUT.

XOR(n)	OUTPUT POLARITY
0	ACTIVE LOW
1	ACTIVE HIGH

(D) Combinational output in a registered device.

Courtesy Lattice Semiconductors.

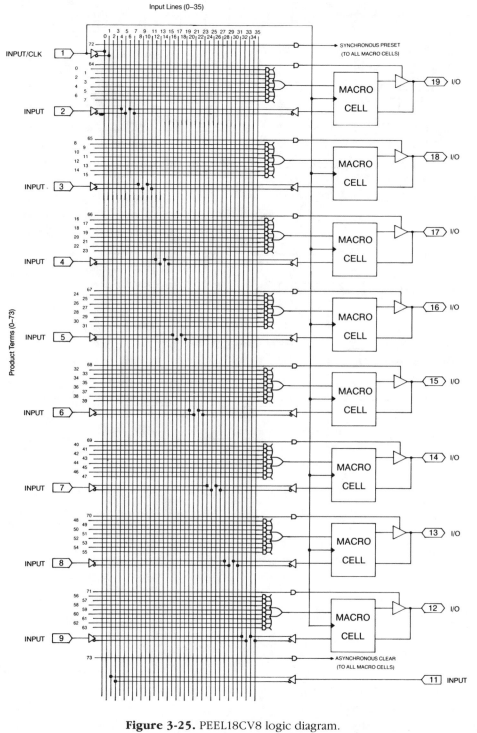

Figure 3-25. PEEL18CV8 logic diagram.
Courtesy International CMOS Technology, Inc.

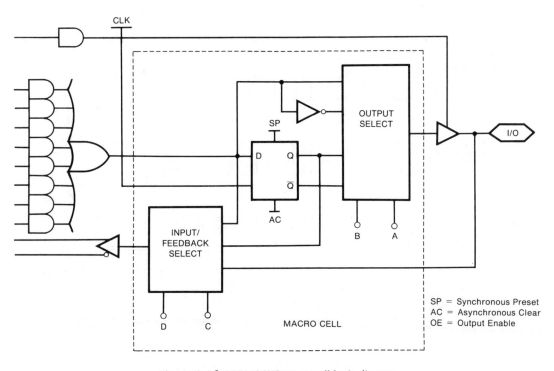

Figure 3-26. PEEL18CV8 macrocell logic diagram.
Courtesy International CMOS Technology, Inc.

feedback term to the AND-array can come from the pin, the register output, or the sum term output. The tri-state output buffer, being controlled by its own product term, allows each macrocell pin to be used as an output, an input, or a bidirectional input/output pin.

A brief glance at the EP310 macrocell diagram in Fig. 3-28 clearly shows the device's PAL architecture (programmable AND-array followed by a fixed OR-array); as with Lattice, this prompted a law suit from MMI for PAL patent infringement.

The EP310, like Altera's other EPLDs, also includes a security fuse, which has become standard for nearly all new PLDs.

A mid-range device in Altera's line-up is the 40-pin EP900; its block diagram is shown in Fig. 3-29. Its 24 exceptionally flexible ACBs are responsible for its high level of functionality. As shown in Fig. 3-30, each ACB has a programmable control that allows a special product term to either control the tri-state output buffer or to provide the clock input to the macrocell register, thus allowing asynchronous register clocking. If the product term is connected to the output buffer, the register clock input is connected to one of two synchronous clock signals (CLK1 or CLK2, depending on the ACB). If the product term is connected to the register, the output buffer is always enabled.

As shown in Fig. 3-31, the EP900's I/O Architecture Configuration Block supports five basic configurations, with the feedback options to the AND-array based on the selected configuration. In addition to the combinatorial output

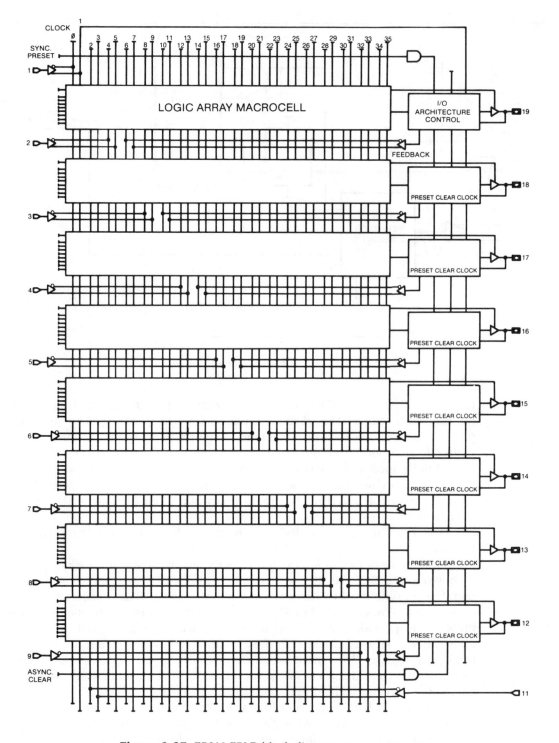

Figure 3-27. EP310 EPLD block diagram. *Courtesy Altera Corp.*

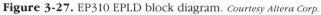

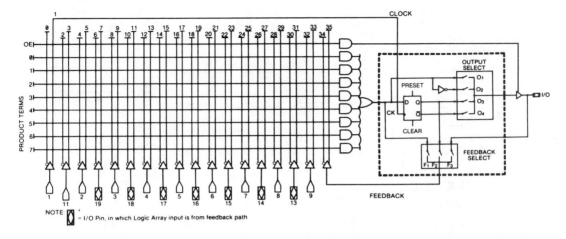

NOTE ▯ = I/O Pin, in which Logic Array input is from feedback path

Figure 3-28. EP310 EPLD macrocell logic diagram. *Courtesy Altera Corp.*

(with pin feedback) option, the ACB supports four output flip-flop types: D, T, J-K, and clocked S-R. Because the J-K and S-R flip-flops have two control inputs (J and K, or S and R), the eight product terms are split between two sum terms, one sum term for each flip-flop control input. The eight product terms can be distributed as desired between the two sum terms.

The D and T flip-flop configurations permit feedback from either the pin or the flip-flop output, while the J-K and S-R flip-flop configurations only support feedback from the register output. Register feedback enables Mealy and Moore state machines to be supported. All EP900 output configurations also support programmable polarity selection for enhanced flexibility.

The EP900 also has 12 dedicated inputs, in addition to its 24 macrocells and I/O pins, and two dedicated clock inputs for synchronous register clocking.

Altera's EP1800 EPLD, packaged in a 68-pin J-leaded chip carrier (JLCC), provides roughly double the number of gates as the EP900. Because of its large size, and because AND-array size increases geometrically as the number of array inputs increases, the EP1800 is necessarily broken down into four functionally identical quadrants. Each quadrant can be considered a separate PLD, with only a certain, limited number of global signal lines included to support inter-quadrant signal and information transfers. While the EP1800 will not be described in detail here, suffice it say that it supports a great deal of logic and is a high-end device in the PLD industry.

Programmable logic devices that reach into the 1,000-plus gate density, like the EP1800, are beginning to affect the low-end gate-array market. This trend should continue, with PLD manufacturers promising more-advanced devices and higher gate densities. Altera will likely stay at the forefront of the high-end PLD market, promising to deliver 10,000-gate PLDs in the future.

Cypress Semiconductor Corp. is known for its high-speed CMOS products, and was a natural entrant into the PLD industry. Its initial offerings were simply CMOS EPROM-based PAL devices—particularly the four Medium 20 series PALs and the PAL22V10. This offered the PLD industry the opportunity to use low-power, CMOS PALs where needed. It also gave logic designers the opportunity

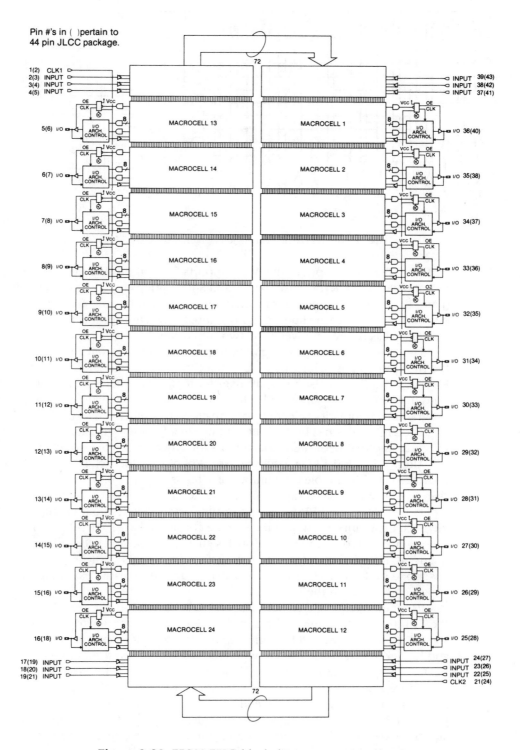

Figure 3-29. EP900 EPLD block diagram. *Courtesy Altera Corp.*

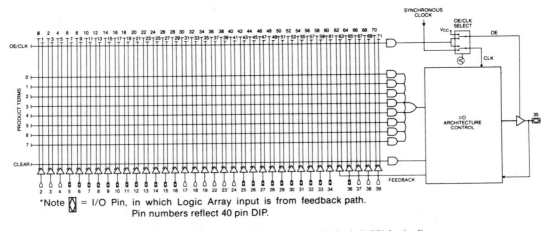

*Note ▧ = I/O Pin, in which Logic Array input is from feedback path.
Pin numbers reflect 40 pin DIP.

Figure 3-30. EP900 EPLD Architecture Control Block (ACB) logic diagram.
Courtesy Altera Corp.

to use erasable, reprogrammable devices for development work, while reverting back to the standard bipolar, OTP devices for production.

Cypress' devices still offer these benefits, although similar devices are now also available from other sources. In an attempt to overcome the "me too" image as just another PAL supplier, Cypress has taken the plunge into deeper waters, designing new devices with their own, unique architectures. These include the CY7C330 Synchronous State Machine, the CY7C331 Asynchronous Registered EPLD, and the CY7C332 Combinatorial Registered EPLD. (Clearly, the numbering system was not adopted from the PAL family!)

Atmel Corp. is another supplier of CMOS EPLDs, and like Cypress manufactures a CMOS EPLD version of the PAL22V10. Also like Cypress, Atmel wants to break the "me too" barrier, and has introduced or announced several devices to help achieve that goal. The first device to hit the market, the V750, purports a 750 gate level of complexity, and is essentially a souped-up PAL22V10.

The notable difference between the PAL22V10 and the V750 is the structure of the output macrocell, as shown in Fig. 3-32. Each macrocell has two registers, instead of the PAL22V10's one, and three feedback terms are returned to the AND-array; the pin as well as both register outputs. The PAL22V10 returns only a single feedback term to the AND-array. Each V750 register has its own sum term with multiple product term inputs, and the input to one of the registers can optionally be the sum (OR) of the register sum terms. Separate product terms are used to generate the clock signal for each register, allowing asynchronous clocking. Separate product terms are also included to provide individual asynchronous register resets. The output, of course, has programmable polarity selection, and a separate product term controls the tri-state output buffer. Atmel claims its V750 has roughly double the on-chip resources of the PAL22V10.

The architecture of the V750 permits such features as latched inputs, buried registers, and medium-complexity state machine development.

Atmel has also announced the development of its V2500 and V4000 devices, indicating an aggressive entry into the high-end PLD market. As with Cypress' EPLDs, Atmel's devices should be carefully considered for new designs.

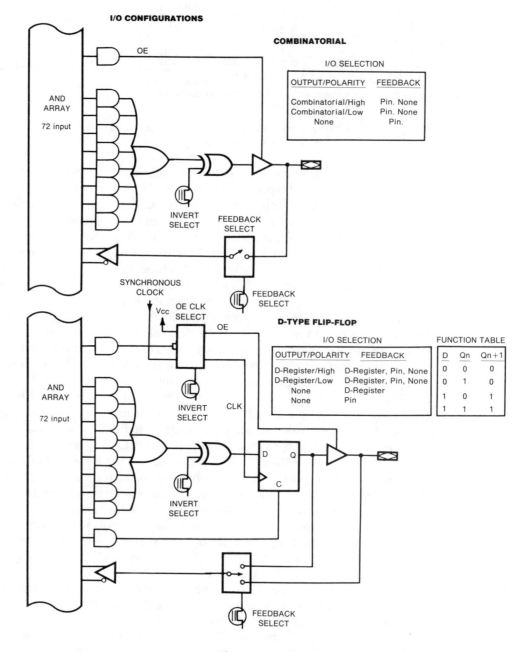

Figure 3-31. EP900 EPLD Architecture Control Block

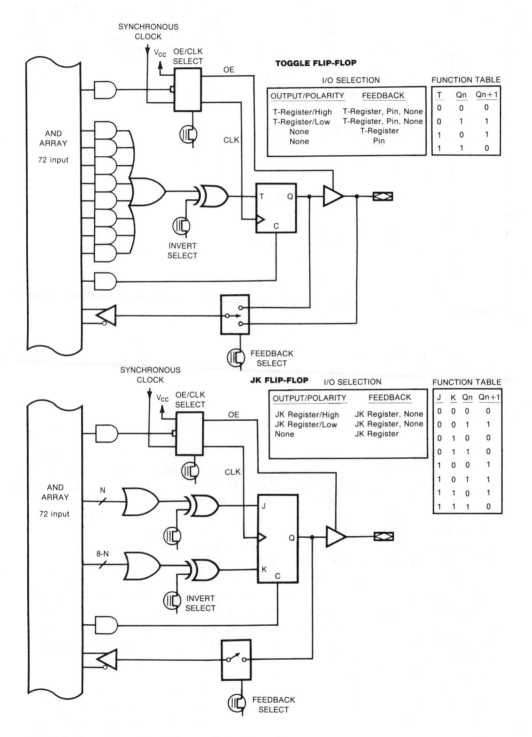

TOGGLE FLIP-FLOP

I/O SELECTION

OUTPUT/POLARITY	FEEDBACK
T-Register/High	T-Register, Pin, None
T-Register/Low	T-Register, Pin, None
None	T-Register
None	Pin

FUNCTION TABLE

T	Qn	Qn+1
0	0	0
0	1	1
1	0	1
1	1	0

JK FLIP-FLOP

I/O SELECTION

OUTPUT/POLARITY	FEEDBACK
JK Register/High	JK Register, None
JK Register/Low	JK Register, None
None	JK Register

FUNCTION TABLE

J	K	Qn	Qn+1
0	0	0	0
0	0	1	1
0	1	0	0
0	1	1	0
1	0	0	1
1	0	1	1
1	1	0	1
1	1	1	0

(ACB) logic configurations. *Courtesy Altera Corp.*

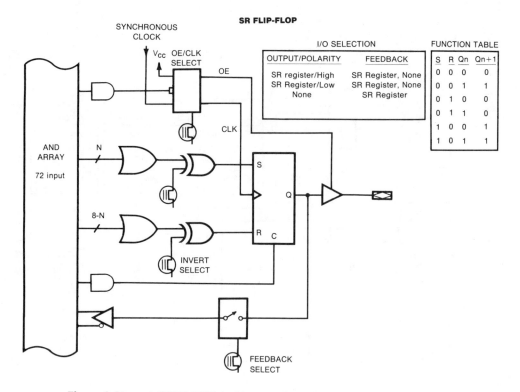

Figure 3-31. *cont.* EP900 EPLD Architecture Control Block (ACB) logic configurations.
Courtesy Altera Corp.

Programmable Macro Logic (PML)

Programmable Macro Logic (PML) is a family of devices from Signetics that features a relatively new architectural trend in programmable logic: *foldback logic*. Also called *multilevel, single-plane (MLSP)* logic, foldback logic involves the use of a single NAND- or NOR-array in conjunction with a central programmable interconnect structure, allowing multiple-level logic implementation, in addition to connections to input and output *macros*. In the case of the PML devices, a NAND-array is used. This is because NAND gates are the fastest gates buildable in the bipolar technology used to produce the initial PML devices.

The keyword *macro* refers to a functional block, and may specify an input signal, an output buffer (with perhaps an intermediate logic function, such as an inverter or XOR gate), or any logic function, such as a flip-flop, counter, or combinatorial circuit. Signetics breaks macros down into categories; inputs are *input macros*, outputs are *output macros*, and other functional blocks such as registers or combinatorial circuits are simply *functional macros*. The PML macro concept is illustrated in Fig. 3-33.

After becoming conditioned to the two-level AND/OR array logic format of the earlier-generation PLDs (such as the FPLA and PAL devices described earlier), the single-level NAND-array architecture can be somewhat confusing and difficult to grasp conceptually. The idea behind the foldback logic architecture,

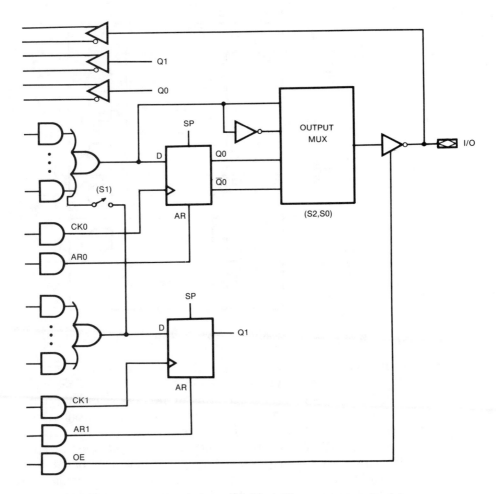

Figure 3-32. V750 output macrocell logic diagram. *Courtesy Atmel Corp.*

however, is to actually simplify complex logic functions, and to make maximum use of the on-chip logic resources. Some usage examples may help clarify the PML concept and illustrate how the logic is used.

Figure 3-34A shows a simple logic circuit using the conventional PAL AND/OR structure. A functionally identical circuit using a NAND/NAND structure is shown in Fig. 3-34B. Notice that a two-level NAND/NAND circuit is logically identical to a two-level AND/OR circuit. As a result, the PAL and FPLA logic functions can be easily implemented using the NAND-foldback architecture. Because the foldback architecture is not limited to two-level logic functions, however, it is simple to generate other logic functions, like those shown in Fig. 3-35. While such functions can be logically reduced to the Sum-of-Products form for two-level AND/OR implementation, their complexity may exceed the product term capacity of a single PAL output, and may thus require multiple outputs with external feedback to be implemented.

The PML architecture does not waste gates and other chip resources the way FPLA and PAL devices do. As mentioned earlier, PAL devices are particularly

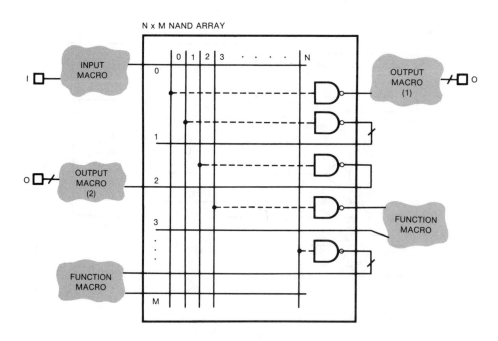

Figure 3-33. Programmable macro logic conceptual diagram. *Courtesy Signetics Corp.*

inefficient in the use of on-chip logic. Unused product terms connected to an output sum term are wasted, and cannot be used elsewhere on the chip. This is true even if additional product terms are needed by another sum term. If more product terms are needed, a sum term output has to be routed back to the AND-array and used as an input to another product term, wasting one output. Additional logic delays are also induced, since the logic not only propagates through two additional levels of logic, but must also pass through input and output buffers before re-entering the AND-array. In a similar manner, if a pin connected to a register is needed as an input, the register associated with the pin is wasted and unusable.

These problems are alleviated with the PML architecture. Within the number of NAND gates included on the chip, any number of gates can input to another gate *as required*, without gates being wasted. Some logic functions may be implemented more efficiently (i.e., using fewer gates) by using a three-level structure instead of a two-level structure, and this is permitted by the foldback architecture. As more logic levels are used, only on-chip gate delays are added to the total propagation time, since output buffers are connected only after the desired logic function has been defined using the NAND-array gates. Simple operations, such as address decoding, may only require a single level logic implementation—a NAND gate—which PML can accommodate, but still requires two levels with FPLA and PAL devices.

PML devices that have built-in macros, such as the Signetics PLHS502 with 16 on-chip register macros, do not have the macros associated with particular output pins. They are simply internal macros that can be connected to the NAND-array logic gates to form desired logic or state machine functions. Once the desired logic functions have been designed, the logic circuit output is

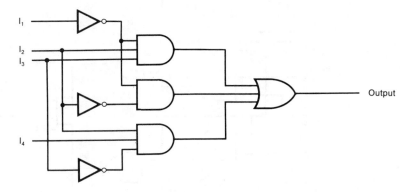

(A) Using two-level AND/OR (PAL) logic.

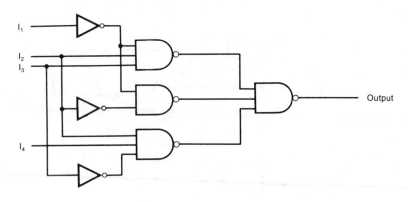

(B) Using two-level NAND/NAND logic.

Figure 3-34. Example logic circuit implementation.

assigned to an output macro. Thus, all logic functions are defined internal to the device, and are connected to output macrocells to communicate with the outside world. Signals that do not need to interact with the outside world are never connected to an output macro, and therefore never appear at a pin. This type of functionality—connecting internally defined logic functions to pins as needed—is a function common to gate-array devices, and is also a feature of the Logic Cell Array to be described shortly. By using the on-chip I/O and logic resources only as they are needed, pins, gates, and other functions are conserved, making the most efficient use of the silicon, a goal in the foldback logic concept.

When designing a circuit, it may be convenient to divide the design into smaller functional sections, then interconnect the sections to perform the desired operations. For example, if a design requires an S-R latch and a transparent D latch, such functions could be defined as macros, then interconnected with other logic functions to generate the desired output function. This concept, of course, is a basic part of the PML design, and can be handled easily *without wasting chip I/O resources!* Figure 3-36 shows how the S-R latch and transparent D latch can be implemented in PML. These can be implemented

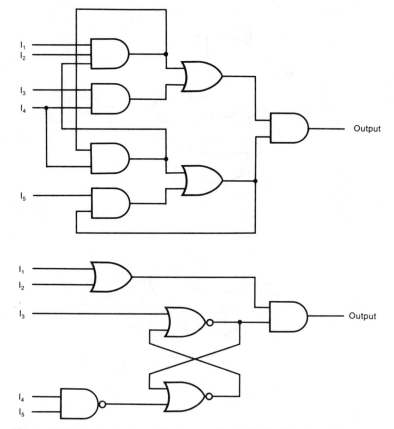

Figure 3-35. Logic circuits easily supported using foldback logic architecture.

strictly in the NAND-array, not requiring any input or output macros for implementation. In contrast, Fig. 3-37 shows how a PAL16L8 might implement an S-R latch. The PAL requires two inputs and two outputs to implement the function—wasting I/O resources—and also wastes several gates in the process.

The first member in the Signetics PML family, the PLHS501 Random Logic Unit, consists of 72 NAND gates in the primary NAND-array, and has an additional 44 NAND gates to support the output macros. The device has 24 dedicated inputs, eight XOR output buffers, four active-low output buffers, four active-high output buffers, and eight bidirectional input/output buffers. The chip is packaged in a 52-pin plastic leaded chip carrier (PLCC), and purports a complexity level of 1,200–1,500 gates. The logic diagram of the PLHS501 is shown in Fig. 3-38, and the output section (detail A) in more detail in Fig. 3-39.

The architecture of the PLHS501 is perhaps better illustrated in the functional diagram shown in Fig. 3-40. The 24 dedicated inputs simply enter the NAND-array, consisting of the entire 116 NAND gates (the *complete NAND-array*), in both true and complemented forms. The first 72 NAND gates form the *NAND-foldback array*, and the outputs of these gates simply return to the complete NAND-array. The remaining 44 NAND gates are all related to output functions, and either provide logic functions (32 NAND gates) or output buffer control functions (12 NAND gates).

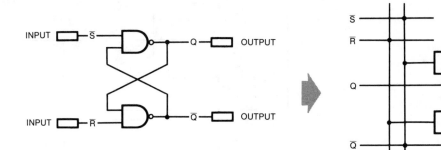

(A) S-R Latch

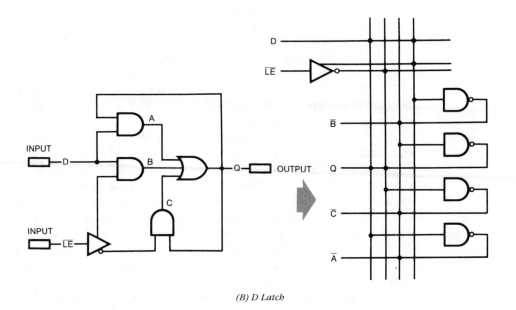

(B) D Latch

Figure 3-36. S-R latch and transparent D latch implemented using PML.
Courtesy Signetics Corp.

Eight outputs (O_0–O_7) are basic tri-state outputs—four active-high, four active-low—with separate NAND gates for controlling the tri-state output buffers for each pair of outputs. Eight more outputs (X_0–X_7) provide a true XOR function (with inverted inputs), where each XOR gate input is controlled by its own NAND gate. This provides for complex logic implementation. Again, separate NAND gates control the tri-state output buffers for each pair of outputs. The final set of eight output buffers is actually bidirectional input/output buffers, with pin feedback into the complete NAND array. Half of the outputs are active high with individual NAND gates controlling the tri-state output buffers, while the other half of the outputs is active low with individual fuses controlling the tri-state output buffers. Pins with fuse-controlled buffers,

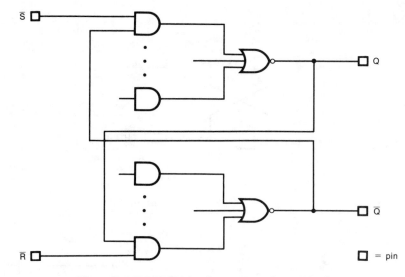

Figure 3-37. PAL16L8 implementation of an S-R latch.

of course, can only function as input or output pins, while those with NAND-controlled buffers can also provide true bidirectional operation, dynamically changing the input/output functions of the pins.

Notice how diverse the outputs are. The intention, of course, is to provide the maximum flexibility to encompass the largest number of applications. The wide variety of different output types may actually be a drawback in some designs, but such a determination is application-dependent. The outputs are even a little more versatile than they initially appear. If a design requires more active-low outputs than are available, for example, an additional pass through a NAND gate in the NAND-array will invert the output, creating the desired active-low output function using an active-high output pin. Similarly, if the XOR output functions are not needed, one of the XOR inputs can be held at a steady-state level, while the other input is passed through the gate as a standard output (either true or inverted, depending on the logic level chosen for the steady-state input).

In terms of timing, the speed of the PLHS501 is faster than generally realized. A complete, single-level pass through the device, including input and output buffers, involves an 18 ns (maximum) propagation delay. Additional levels—i.e., additional passes through the NAND-array—add 8 ns per pass (maximum) to the total propagation time. This is because the foldback architecture avoids input and output buffer delays for additional passes, incurring only NAND gate delays.

As a final comment, the fuse structure of the Signetics bipolar PML devices is rather unique. The company's Vertical Avalanche Migration Programmed (VAMP) fuses are initially all *open*. As the device is programmed, selected fuses are closed to create circuit connections where needed. Most bipolar processes, in contrast, have all fuses intact (closed) when a device is blank, and selected fuses are blown (opened) to create the desired logic functions. PML devices, of course, also include a security fuse.

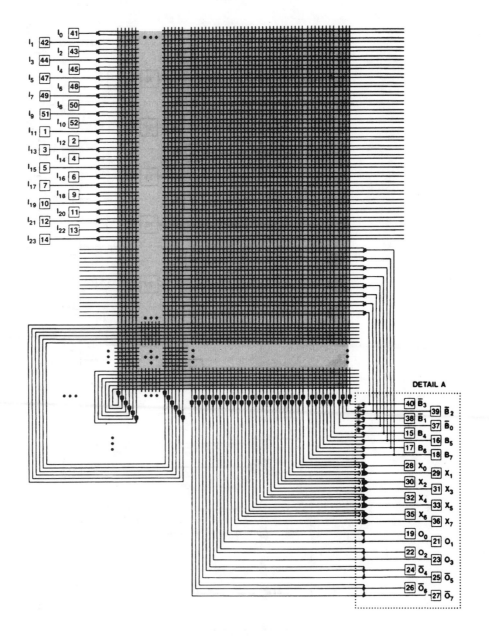

Figure 3-38. PLHS501 logic diagram. *Courtesy Signetics Corp.*

Erasable, Programmable Application-Specific IC (ERASIC)

The *Erasable, Programmable Application-Specific IC (ERASIC)* family from Exel Microelectronics is a family of EEPLDs with a foldback architecture similar to that of the PML family described above. In comparison to the bipolar technology used in the first PML family offerings, however, the ERASIC family

DETAIL A

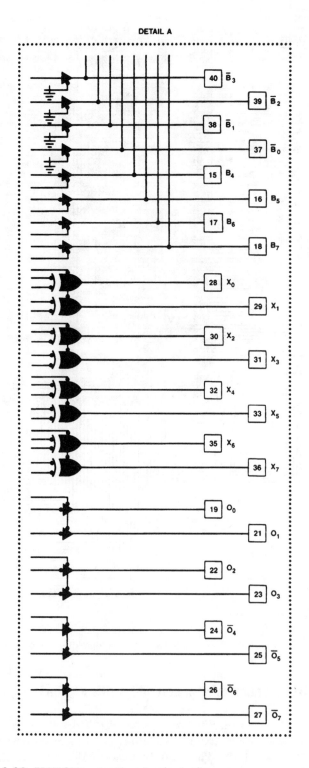

Figure 3-39. PLHS501 output section logic diagram. *Courtesy Signetics Corp.*

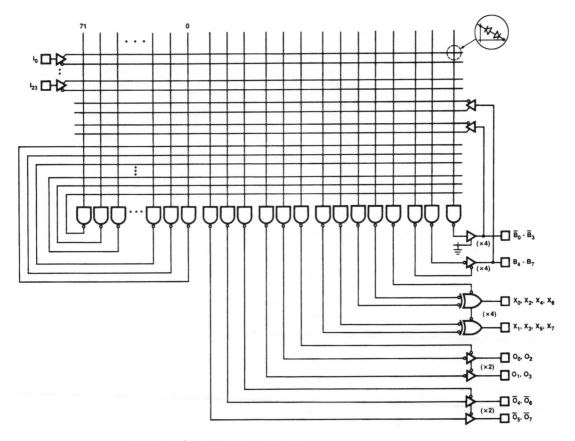

Figure 3-40. PLHS501 functional diagram. *Courtesy Signetics Corp.*

employs CMOS EEPROM technology to produce low-power, erasable devices. Whereas NAND gates provide the fastest propagation times in bipolar technologies, CMOS technologies see the fastest times from NOR gates. For this reason, the ERASIC family incorporates a NOR-foldback architecture, as opposed to the NAND-foldback architecture of the PML family.

Because both the input and output macros include inverters, the ERASIC's NOR/NOR structure can easily function like the AND/OR structure of the conventional PAL and FPLA devices. This is illustrated in Fig. 3-41.

The initial ERASIC device offered by Exel, the XL78C800, comes in a 24-pin package and purports a complexity level of approximately 800 gates. The logic diagram of the XL78C800 is shown in Fig. 3-42. This rather impressive device continues in the tradition of the gate array-like structure of the PLHS501 PML foldback device, but provides a number of on-chip macro functions to enhance the flexibility of the device. The added functionality comes in the form of the device's two 4-bit transparent input latches and ten I/O macrocells.

A point concerning notation: Exel uses diamonds on its logic diagrams to indicate *Polarity Control Elements (PCEs)*—programmable polarity selection points. Signals passing through PCEs can either pass through unchanged, or can be inverted as they pass through, determined by "fuse" (EEPROM cell) programming.

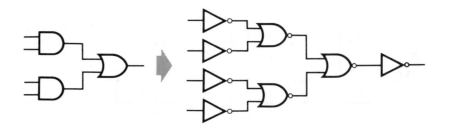

Figure 3-41. AND/OR (PAL) logic circuit implementation using
NOR/NOR logic structure.

The XL78C800 has 12 dedicated inputs and ten I/O pins connected to
macrocells. All the dedicated inputs may be used as general-purpose inputs into
the NOR array, although two can optionally be used for special, dedicated
purposes. Pin 1 can be used as the clock signal for the J-K flip-flops in the ten
I/O macrocells. Pin 13 can be used to control the tri-state output buffers of any
or all of the ten I/O macrocells. Eight of the dedicated input pins enter the NOR
array through transparent latches. Two NOR gates control the latch enable
signal for the transparent latches, with each gate controlling four latches. The
NOR gate outputs also have PCEs to increase their logic flexibility. This NOR
term-controlled input-latch feature permits the respective inputs to enter the
NOR array directly (transparent mode operation) or to be latched (latch mode
operation), controlled by device logic.

The XL78C800 has 32 NOR terms in its foldback array, with two additional
NOR terms for input latch control, two for flip-flop clear generation, and 30 to
support the I/O macrocells. Thus, a total of 66 NOR terms are present on the
chip. Since one NOR term from each output macrocell can be fed back into the
NOR array—effectively becoming another term in the NOR-foldback array—the
device can support up to 42 levels of logic implementation (not including
registers).

Figure 3-43 shows the XL78C800 macrocell logic diagram, another key to
the flexibility and capability of the ERASIC device. As shown, a number of
signals enter and exit the macrocell. Three NOR gate outputs from the NOR
array enter the macrocell. They are J, K, and O. The J and K terms control the J
and K inputs of the macrocell J-K flip-flop, respectively. The O term is a
combinatorial output term, which can be optionally fed back into the NOR
array (via the IN MUX) to act as another NOR foldback term.

The macrocell also has two signals entering the NOR array: an input (i)
signal and the flip-flop output (Q). The device pin associated with the macrocell
connects to both the tri-state output buffer and the input multiplexer, IN MUX.
Separate signals provide asynchronous clear and clocking to the J-K flip-flop,
and an OE* signal can optionally be programmed to control the tri-state output
buffer.

The beauty of the XL78C800's macrocell design may not be immediately
apparent, but a closer look reveals the cleverness of the design. First, since the
J-K flip-flop control inputs (J and K) are controlled by separate NOR terms (each
having a PCE on its output), the flip-flop can easily be programmed to operate

as a D or T flip-flop as well. Also, notice that the output of the flip-flop is always fed back into the NOR array, independent of the input signal (selected by IN MUX). The macrocell flip-flop can, thus, be buried (for state machine use or signal latching) and connected to *any level* of logic implementation; this permits some extravagant logic circuits, while still permitting use of the O NOR term and the I/O pin!

The output multiplexer, OUT MUX, permits either combinatorial (O NOR term) or registered output. The input multiplexer, IN MUX, permits input into the NOR array from either the pin or the O NOR term (feedback). The output enable multiplexer, OE MUX, allows the tri-state output buffer to be always enabled (two-state operation), always disabled (high-impedance state), or controlled by the OE* signal (tri-state operation).

The macrocell diagram in Fig. 3-43 also shows three "code" boxes. These represent the three programmable links used to configure the macrocell multiplexers. Since only eight multiplexer combinations can exist with three programmable links, obviously not all possible combinations of multiplexer configurations are possible. The most useful combinations, however, are possible. Table 3-1 indicates the various multiplexer configurations corresponding to the eight macrocell code patterns.

Table 3-1. XL78C800 Macrocell Configuration Codes and Corresponding Multiplexer Configurations.

Code	IN MUX	OUT MUX	OE MUX
000	PIN	O TERM	DISABLED
001	O TERM	O TERM	DISABLED
010	O TERM	FF	ENABLED
011	O TERM	O TERM	ENABLED
100	PIN	FF	OE*
101	PIN	O TERM	OE*
110	O TERM	FF	OE*
111	O TERM	O TERM	OE*

Being CMOS, the XL78C800 is slower than the PML PLHS501 described earlier. Single-pass propagation time through the initial ERASIC device offering requires up to 35 ns, and additional passes (through the NOR-foldback array) require 20 ns (maximum) each. The tradeoff, of course, comes in terms of power consumption, with the XL78C800 consuming only 35 mA, compared to the PLHS501's 250 mA. Faster ERASIC parts are also available, and Exel is planning higher-density and faster parts for the future. The company expects to have devices with 10 ns NOR gate propagation times for applications requiring higher speed.

The XL78C800 incorporates an interesting twist to the traditional security fuse approach. Its SecurityPlus security system has a security fuse (EEPROM cell) that prevents the logic configuration from being read from the device. The function does not go into effect, however, until the device is powered down then powered up again. Thus when programming the ERASIC, the entire fuse

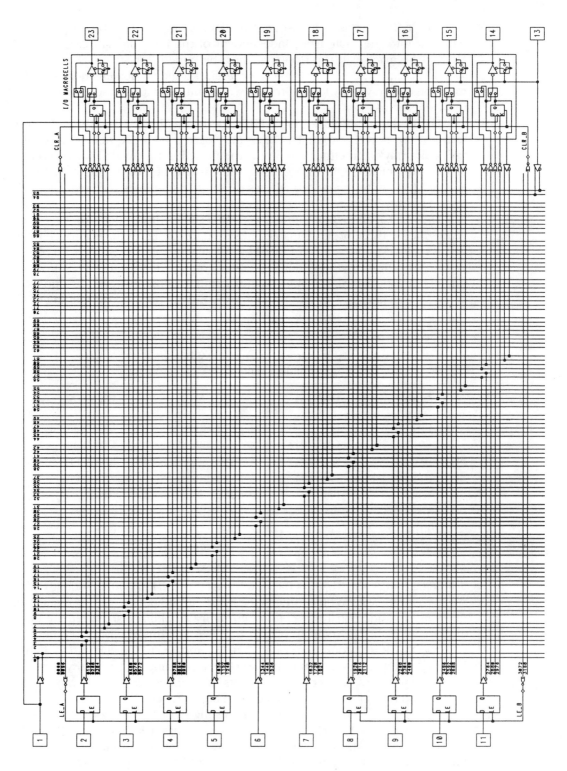

Figure 3-42. XL78C800 ERASIC

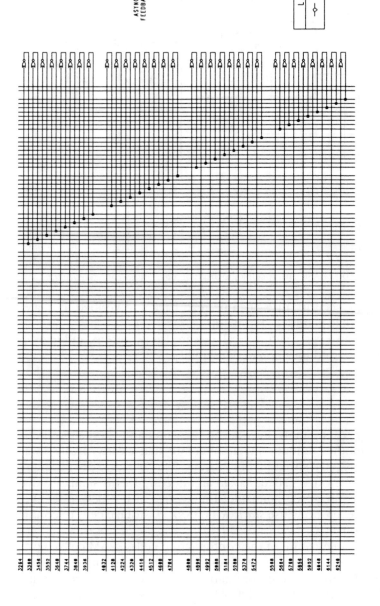

logic diagram. *Courtesy Exel Microelectronics.*

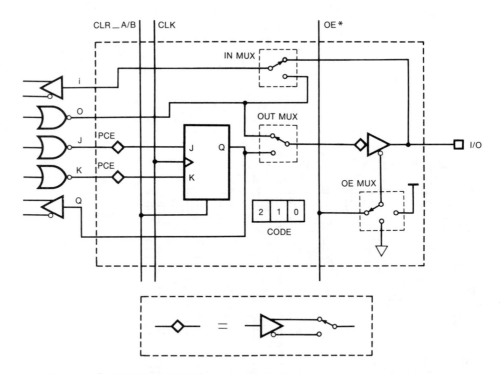

Figure 3-43. XL78C800 ERASIC macrocell logic diagram. *Courtesy Exel Microelectronics.*

pattern—including the security fuse—can be read back and verified, but later attempts to read the logic pattern are fruitless.

The XL78C800 registers are automatically cleared at power-up, and register preloading is also supported for improved testability.

Logic Cell Array (LCA)

The *Logic Cell Array (LCA)* family, introduced by Xilinx and alternate-sourced by MMI, presents another unique PLD architecture that clearly breaks away from the traditional AND/OR structure of FPLA and PAL devices. The "programmable gate array," as it is often called, has an architecture that is similar to that of a gate array, but is user-programmable. Unlike any of the device families described so far, however, LCAs use *static RAM (SRAM)* storage cells to configure their logic functionality.

Because of the volatile nature of the configuration cells (SRAM cells), LCAs must be initialized when they are powered-up. The devices support several modes to accomplish this, and the configuration code can be stored in any convenient medium, such as ROM, EPROM or EEPROM. The configuration information can even be stored on a system disk drive. The SRAM configuration cells do, however, provide the benefit of allowing LCAs to be dynamically reconfigured in a system.

The structure of the LCA, illustrated in Fig. 3-44, consists of a number of *user-configurable I/O blocks (IOBs)* around the chip periphery, with a matrix of

Configurable Logic Blocks (CLBs) in the center of the device. Programmable interconnects are then routed throughout the chip to facilitate CLB and IOB interconnection.

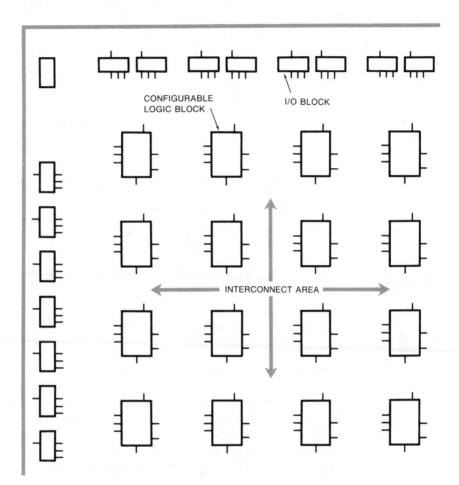

Figure 3-44. Logic Cell Array structure. *Courtesy Xilinx, Inc.*

The two initial devices in this family, the XC2064 and the XC2018, are very similar. The XC2064—the first LCA device—purports a complexity of approximately 1,200 gates, and includes 58 IOBs and an eight-by-eight matrix of 64 CLBs. The XC2018, claiming a complexity of around 1,800 gates, has 74 IOBs and a ten-by-ten matrix of 100 CLBs. The devices also have special reset and clock signal inputs, and include crystal oscillator circuitry for generating an on-chip clock signal, when used in conjunction with an externally connected crystal.

Figure 3-45 shows a diagram of the user-configurable I/O block. As shown, the IOB includes an input buffer which buffers the input signal from the pin and connects the buffered signal to the input of a multiplexer (the *input multiplexer*) and to the input of an edge-triggered D flip-flop. The logic voltage threshold of the input buffer is programmable for TTL (1.4-V threshold level) or CMOS (2.2-V threshold level) compatibility. The output of the flip-flop also connects to the input multiplexer, and the output of the multiplexer (signal 'IN' in Fig. 3-45) can be connected as needed to one or more CLBs. The clock for the IOB flip-flop comes from a dedicated I/O clock line, which connects to all of the IOB registers on a given edge of the chip. Thus four such I/O clock lines exist on the LCA, one along each of the four edges of the die.

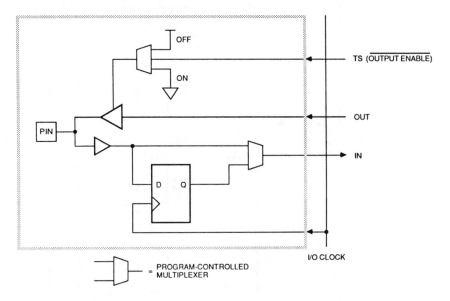

Figure 3-45. LCA user-configurable I/O Block (IOB). *Courtesy Xilinx, Inc.*

The output portion of the IOB consists of a tri-state output buffer connected to the pin. The output buffer input (signal 'OUT' in Fig. 3-45) can be connected to the output of a CLB via the programmable interconnect. The control signal for the output buffer enable comes from a multiplexer, which allows the buffer to be always enabled, always disabled, or controlled by the IOB 'TS' input, which can be connected to a CLB output. This, of course, allows dynamic, bidirectional input/output operation.

The buffer enable portion of the IOB diagram in Fig. 3-45 can be somewhat misleading. The presence or absence of an "inverting bubble" at the point the output buffer control line meets the buffer symbol is traditionally used to indicate the control signal polarity required to *enable* the buffer (that is, to *exit* the high-impedance state). The Xilinx diagram, however, indicates the polarity required to *disable* the buffer (to enter the high-impedance state). Thus, the output buffer is actually enabled when the control signal is low (logical '0').

The two IOB multiplexers shown in Fig. 3-45, as well as the multiplexers found in the CLB described below, are program-configured, being defined when the SRAM cells are configured at device initialization time.

The structure of the Configurable Logic Block is shown in Fig. 3-46. The CLB has four general-purpose logic inputs (A, B, C, and D), a clock input (K) and two outputs (X and Y). It includes a combinatorial logic section and a D flip-flop (or *storage element*, as Xilinx calls it). The D flip-flop can be configured for edge-triggered or level-triggered (transparent latch) operation.

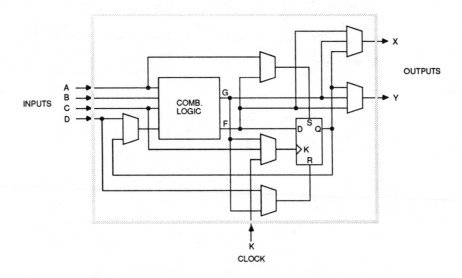

Figure 3-46. LCA configurable logic block (CLB). *Courtesy Xilinx, Inc.*

The combinatorial logic section has four inputs (A, B, C, and either D or the flip-flop output, Q) and two outputs (F and G). It consists of 16 storage cells that can be programmed like a PROM to support any logical function of four variables (acting like a four-input, single-output PROM—see Fig. 3-47), or any two logical functions of three variables (acting like two three-input, single-output PROMs—see Fig. 3-48).

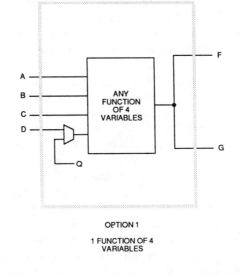

OPTION 1

1 FUNCTION OF 4
VARIABLES

Figure 3-47. CLB combinatorial logic section supporting a four-variable logic function.
Courtesy Xilinx, Inc.

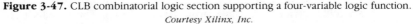

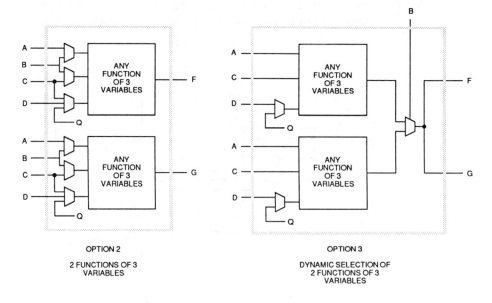

OPTION 2

2 FUNCTIONS OF 3
VARIABLES

OPTION 3

DYNAMIC SELECTION OF
2 FUNCTIONS OF 3
VARIABLES

Figure 3-48. CLB combinatorial logic section supporting two three-variable
logic functions. *Courtesy Xilinx, Inc.*

The CLB flip-flop has several control options, as shown in Fig. 3-46. The D
input of the flip-flop is the F output of the combinatorial logic section. The
clock for the flip-flop can be generated by the G output of the combinatorial
section (for asynchronous clocking), the C CLB input (for synchronous or
asynchronous clocking), or the K clock input (for synchronous clocking). The
flip-flop also includes asynchronous preset (S) and reset (R) inputs. The preset
input can be controlled either by the F output of the combinatorial logic
section, or by the A input to the CLB. Similarly, the reset input can be controlled
by the combinatorial logic section's G output, or by the D input to the CLB.

The outputs of the CLB, which can be routed to other CLBs or to IOBs via
the programmable interconnect, can come from several sources within the
CLB. Either output can be generated by the F combinatorial section output, the
G combinatorial section output, or the flip-flop output.

The programmable interconnection resources on the LCA are critical to the
flexibility of the device, and certainly required considerable thought on the
part of the chip designers. Three types of interconnect resources are included
on the LCA, to provide for different types of logical networks: *general-purpose
interconnect, long lines,* and *direct interconnect.*

General-purpose interconnect consists of multiple metal segments running
horizontally and vertically between CLB and IOB rows and columns. A *switch
matrix* is then included at each intersection to provide programmable signal
routing. The general-purpose interconnect operation is illustrated in Fig. 3-49.

Long lines run parallel to the general-purpose interconnect lines, both
horizontally and vertically, the full width or height of the interconnect area.
Unlike the general-purpose interconnect lines, however, long lines bypass the
switch matrices, and are primarily intended for signals that must travel long

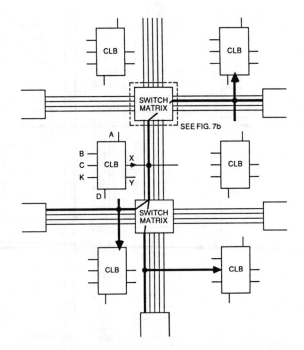

Figure 3-49. LCA general-purpose interconnect. *Courtesy Xilinx, Inc.*

distances with minimum skew among multiple destinations. The LCA incorporates a global buffer that can drive a single signal to all B and K CLB inputs. Using the global buffer for a system clock provides a low skew, high fan-out synchronized clock for use at any or all of the CLBs. Figure 3-50 illustrates the routing of the long lines.

Direct interconnect allows adjacent CLBs or IOBs to be connected using minimum interconnect resources, and results in minimum signal propagation delays. For each CLB, the X output can be directly connected to the C or D inputs of the CLB above it, and to the A or B inputs of the CLB below it. The Y output can directly connect to the B input of the CLB immediately to its right. A limited amount of direct interconnect capability is also supported for CLBs adjacent to IOBs.

Xilinx has also developed a more-advanced XC3000-series of LCA devices. While architecturally similar to the earlier XC2000-series parts, the XC3000-series devices offer improvements in several areas, substantially increasing overall device functionality. The newer devices feature improved IOBs with two registers and greater flexibility; improved CLBs with two registers, a 5-bit combinatorial section, and more-flexible signal routing; and with improved interconnects. The XC3000-series of LCAs offers devices with complexities of up to 9,000 equivalent gates.

The complexity and uniqueness of the Logic Cell Array architecture precludes its support in the standard third-party PLD software packages. Being aware of this, Xilinx has developed extensive software support for its devices, and even offers a real-time emulator for development. This is something no

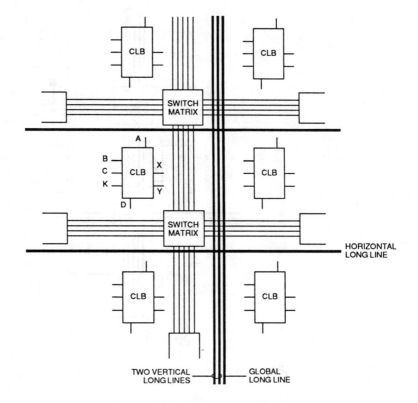

Figure 3-50. LCA long lines. *Courtesy Xilinx, Inc.*

other PLD family can offer. Of course, all of this elegant support software and hardware comes at a price, costing more than most third-party PLD compilers.

The LCA architecture is catching on and will likely continue to gain popularity, particularly with MMI's support behind it. If the cost of the development software comes down and nonvolatile EPROM or EEPROM versions of the LCA become available, as anticipated, the market for LCAs may very well explode.

Desktop-Configurable Channeled Gate Array

In 1988, Actel Corp. introduced its *desktop-configurable channeled gate arrays*. Similar to the Xilinx LCAs, the Actel devices consist of an array of *configurable logic modules* that can be interconnected to create desired logic functions. Unlike the LCAs, however, the Actel devices are configured using fuse links (based on the company's proprietary *PLICE*—Programmable Low Impedance Circuit Element—antifuse technology). Using fuse links allows the devices to be permanently programmed so that they are immediately ready for operation at power-up. In contrast, the LCA devices from Xilinx are based on volatile SRAM memory cells that must be configured each time the devices are powered. The first two devices from Actel, *ACT 1010* and *ACT 1020*, are part of the company's *ACT 1* family and offer 1,200 and 2,000 equivalent gate complexity, respectively.

Chapter Summary

In this chapter we covered the primary families and architectures that make up the PLD world. Several specific device architectures were studied to see how the family architectures are applied to real devices, and to get a feel for the architectural variations common among different family members.

We also became familiar with many of the acronyms and abbreviations associated with the PLD industry.

Chapter 4 continues the discussions on device families and architectures, concentrating particularly on application-specific PLD architectures.

PLD Families and Application-Specific Architectures

The PLD industry has shown an increasing trend in developing *application-specific PLDs (ASPLDs)*. Such devices permit more efficient use of silicon real-estate compared to general-purpose PLDs, and also provide a higher level of functionality—in their area of optimization—compared to that of their general-purpose counterparts.

Chapter Overview

In the last chapter we looked at the primary PLD families and architectures. This chapter will continue with a discussion of application-specific PLD architectures, and a brief look at some manufacturer-specific PLD families. It will then conclude with a short discussion on some of the tradeoffs presented by the various device architectures currently available.

Since most of the ASPLDs are founded on the primary PLD architectures presented in the last chapter, the discussions presented in this chapter assume that the reader has at least a fundamental understanding of the primary architectures. Similarly, the discussions on *Families vs. Architectures* and *Notation* are applicable to the material presented here as well.

Application-Specific PLD Architectures

This discussion on application-specific PLD architectures concentrates on the two primary areas served by current PLDs: state machine applications and bus interface applications. While other application-specific areas exist and will be covered briefly, they are not as dominant as these two.

State Machine PLD Architectures

To date, state machine applications have been the primary beneficiary of the industry trend toward ASPLDs. The large market for state machine applications is enticing. Some research has indicated that more than 30% of PLD usage involves state machine or sequencer functions. Because of the complexity of advanced state machines and the need for support beyond that offered by the general-purpose PLD architectures, new PLD architectures optimized for state machine applications have been developed by numerous manufacturers. Whereas conventional PLDs can support state machines with perhaps dozens of states, some of the newer, optimized devices can handle hundreds of states.

The state machine-oriented PLDs vary considerably in their architectures, and support the whole gamut of state machine complexities. Some handle Moore and Mealy state machine models, while others are particularly designed to support only Moore machines—the simpler and more common of the two. Prices, of course, are a function of device complexity and capability. Simpler devices should be chosen where appropriate to minimize cost, while the more-complex devices should be used in particularly advanced applications.

Since there are currently only a handful of state machine PLDs available—each the first in its family—it seems beneficial to take at least a cursory look at each of the available devices and observe some of their varying features.

PAL23S8 PAL Sequencer

The 20-pin bipolar *PAL23S8 PAL sequencer* introduced by AMD is clearly designed for sequencer and state machine support, although it is probably the simplest of the available devices optimized for such purposes. A functional diagram of the PAL23S8 is shown in Fig. 4-1. Being a PAL, the device has the basic programmable AND-array, fixed OR-array structure common to PALs, and also has variable product term distribution (with 6, 8, 10, or 12 product terms per sum term). The PAL23S8 has nine dedicated inputs, a clock input (for synchronous clocking of all on-chip registers), and eight outputs. It also includes six buried registers, intended for use as internal state machine registers, and can operate at up to 33 MHz.

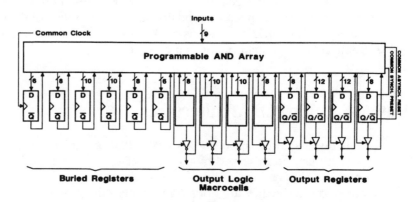

Figure 4-1. PAL23S8 functional diagram.
Copyright © 1987 Advanced Micro Devices, Inc. Reprinted with permission of copyright owner.
All rights reserved.

Of the eight PAL23S8 outputs, four are registered outputs with programmable output polarity, while the remaining four each have a programmable macrocell structure. The macrocell structure is shown in Fig. 4-2. The macrocell output can be combinatorial or registered, with programmable output polarity selectable for either. The macrocell also presents a feedback term back to the AND-array, which can come from either the pin or the register output. The tri-state output buffer is controlled by a separate product term, which also has programmable polarity selection. A unique feature of the macrocell structure, consistent with the intended application of the PAL23S8, is that the feedback multiplexer selection is independent of the output multiplexer, allowing the register to be buried for internal use, while the output is still used for combinatorial functions.

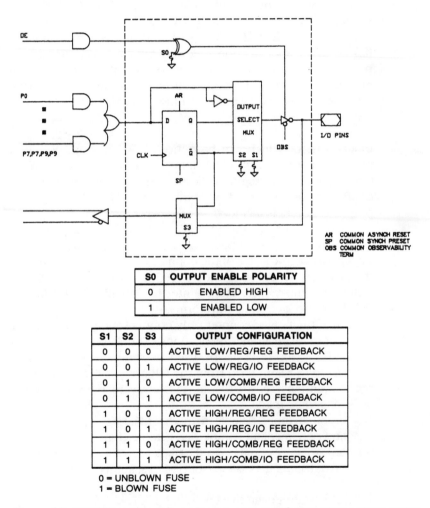

S0	OUTPUT ENABLE POLARITY
0	ENABLED HIGH
1	ENABLED LOW

S1	S2	S3	OUTPUT CONFIGURATION
0	0	0	ACTIVE LOW/REG/REG FEEDBACK
0	0	1	ACTIVE LOW/REG/IO FEEDBACK
0	1	0	ACTIVE LOW/COMB/REG FEEDBACK
0	1	1	ACTIVE LOW/COMB/IO FEEDBACK
1	0	0	ACTIVE HIGH/REG/REG FEEDBACK
1	0	1	ACTIVE HIGH/REG/IO FEEDBACK
1	1	0	ACTIVE HIGH/COMB/REG FEEDBACK
1	1	1	ACTIVE HIGH/COMB/IO FEEDBACK

0 = UNBLOWN FUSE
1 = BLOWN FUSE

Figure 4-2. PAL23S8 macrocell logic diagram. *Copyright © 1987 Advanced Micro Devices, Inc. Reprinted with permission of copyright owner. All rights reserved.*

With the eight output registers (including four in the output macrocells) and the six buried registers, the PAL23S8 provides 14 registers that can be used as needed in the state machine design. It also has an "observability" feature that allows the designer to view the states of the internal registers during debugging. The design of the PAL23S8 easily supports both Moore and Mealy state machines, although it cannot practically handle a state machine with 100-plus states like other state machine-oriented PLDs. Nonetheless, for simple-to-inter-mediate-level state machine and sequencer requirements, the PAL23S8 may very well be the best choice. The fact that some sum terms input as many as 12 product terms may also be valuable in some applications.

PSG507 Programmable Sequence Generator (PSG)

The 24-pin Texas Instruments *PSG507 Programmable Sequence Generator (PSG)* is another bipolar PLD designed especially to handle state machine and sequencer applications, offering the next higher level of capability beyond the PAL23S8. The block diagram of the PSG507 is shown in Fig. 4-3. The PSG507 has an FPLA logic section followed by state and output registers and a 6-bit binary counter. The FPLA section consists of 80 product terms, shared among 38 OR gates. The FPLA architecture, being much more flexible than the PAL architecture, supports more-complex logic functions than the PAL23S8. The PSG507 can operate at over 30 MHz.

In addition to the specified internals, the PSG507 also has 13 dedicated inputs (one of which can be optionally used as an output enable control), a programmable-polarity clock input for clocking all on-chip registers and the 6-bit counter, and eight dedicated outputs. The outputs can be individually configured as registered or combinatorial, but no feedback from the output pins or registers is included.

A key feature of the PSG507 is the 6-bit binary counter. The counter is controlled by FPLA outputs, and can be commanded to clear, hold, or count, depending on the states of the counter inputs. The six counter outputs return to the AND-array, allowing the FPLA logic to perform different operations at different count values. The counter is particularly valuable for generating time delays or special output waveforms.

Since the binary counter only counts sequentially, it cannot be used on its own for state machine applications. The PSG507 incorporates eight buried clocked S-R flip-flops to be used as state registers. Each S and R input is connected to a sum term from the OR-array for maximum flexibility. The state register outputs return to the AND-array to permit state and output control decisions to be made.

Although more flexible than the PAL23S8, the PSG507 is still capable of handling only medium-complexity state machine applications. It lacks the PROM-oriented structure common to the higher-level state machine PLDs, but is probably capable of handling a majority of typical state machine requirements.

29PL141 Fuse Programmable Controller (FPC)

The 28-pin Advanced Micro Devices (AMD) *29PL141 Fuse-Programmable Control-ler (FPC)* is a bipolar single-chip, microcode-based microcontroller, and probably the first PLD optimized for state machine applications. The block diagram of the 29PL141 is shown in Fig. 4-4. The device consists of four primary functional blocks: the microprogram memory (a 64×32 PROM), the microaddress control logic, the

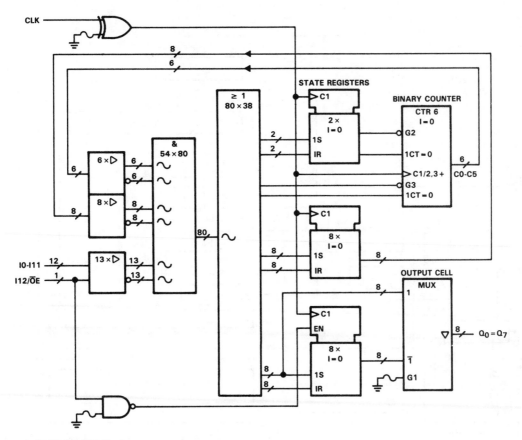

~ denotes fused inputs

Figure 4-3. PSG507 block diagram. *Reprinted by Permission of Texas Instruments.*
Copyright © 1985.

condition code selection logic, and the microinstruction decode. It also sports 7 condition test inputs, a reset input, a "zero count" indicator output, 16 registered outputs, a synchronizing clock input, and some special control signals for use with the Serial Shadow Register used for debugging and diagnostic functions. The device operates at up to 20 MHz.

The pipeline register simply latches the 32 outputs of the microprogram memory (PROM) at the rising edge of each clock. The lower 16 bits of the pipeline register are presented as chip outputs, indicating a Moore machine functionality. The upper 16 bits of the pipeline register are returned to the microprogram address sequencer. The 16 bits are separated into *fields*, each having its own purpose. The fields include output enable (1 bit), microinstruction opcode (5 bits), test polarity select (1 bit), test condition select (3 bits), and data (6 bits).

The output enable field controls the tri-state output buffers for the high-order eight pipeline bits of the 16 that are output from the chip (P8–P15). The low-order eight outputs are always enabled. The opcode bits are the instruction code to the microinstruction decode, and determine the next microinstruction

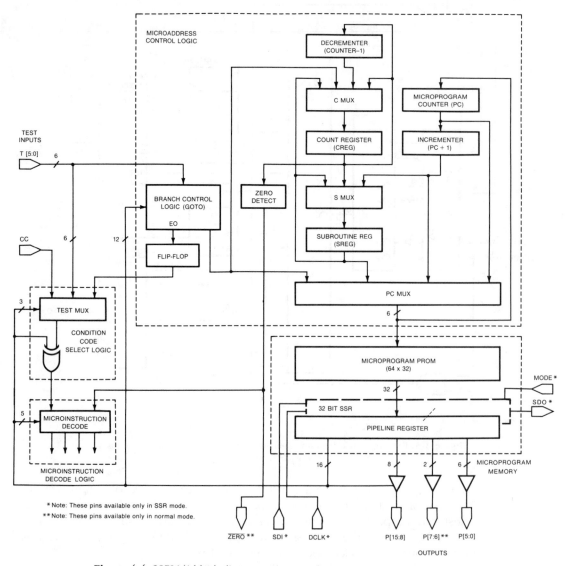

Figure 4-4. 29PL141 block diagram. *Copyright © 1987 Advanced Micro Devices, Inc.*
Reprinted with permission of copyright owner. All rights reserved.

to be executed of the 29 supported by the 29PL141. The test polarity select bit
determines whether the test bit should be tested for high or low polarity. The
test condition select bits determine what test input will be tested. The 6-bit data
field is used for branch addresses, test input masks, and counter values.

Upon reset, the 29PL141 begins executing microinstructions from microprogram address 63 (the highest address in the PROM). Execution then
proceeds based on conditional input values and the microprogram instructions
and data presented to the microprogram address sequencer. The device supports 29 opcodes, including single-level subroutine calls, loops, and multiway

conditional branches. The 64 words of control store limit the 29PL141 to 64 states in a state machine design.

AMD also offers its 29PL142 FPC, which has twice the PROM storage of the '141—128 words—but is otherwise only slightly different than the '141.

PMS14R21 Programmable Sequencer (PROSE)

The 24-pin, bipolar *PMS14R21 Programmable Sequencer (PROSE)* is the first entry in MMI's *Programmable Memory-based Sequencer (PMS)* family. The architecture of the PMS14R21 combines a PAL front-end, followed by a 21-output registered PROM with feedback. The device operates at up to 30 MHz when used in stand-alone mode, or up to 25 MHz when used with external feedback or in conjunction with a similar sequencer.

The block diagram of the PMS14R21 is shown in Fig. 4-5. The chip includes a Diagnostics-On-Chip (DOC) feature that allows the complete 21-bit output of the PROM to be viewed for diagnostic purposes. The DOC block will be ignored for purposes of this discussion. The PMS14R21 includes a PAL14H2 (with 14 AND-array inputs and two active-high outputs), a 128 × 21 registered PROM, and two XOR gate inputs to the PROM. Of the 21 registered PROM output bits, six are fed into the PAL AND-array, two are fed into the XOR gates—one for each gate—and five are fed back as address inputs to the PROM. The remaining two XOR gate inputs are the PAL outputs, and the XOR gate outputs generate the remaining two (high-order) PROM address inputs.

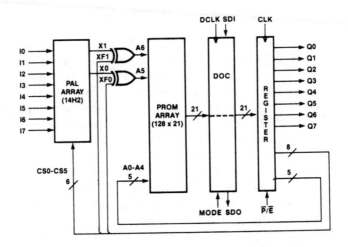

Figure 4-5. PMS14R21 block diagram. *Copyright © 1987 Advanced Micro Devices, Inc.*

For pins, the PMS14R21 has eight registered outputs from the 21-bit PROM register (the low-order eight PROM bits) and eight general-purpose inputs which enter the PAL AND-array. It also has a CLK input for synchronously clocking the 21-bit PROM register, a preset/enable pin for controlling output enables or presetting the register outputs (fuse programmable), and some miscellaneous signals for controlling the DOC.

At power-up, the PMS14R21 PROM output register is preset to all 1's, allowing the state machine to start from a known state. If the preset/enable pin is programmed for preset, the register can also be preset externally. Every rising edge of the synchronizing clock causes the PROM location addressed by the seven PROM address inputs to be latched in the 21-bit register. The low-order eight latched bits are presented as chip outputs for controlling external processes. The remaining bits are fed back internally to help determine—either directly or indirectly—the next PROM location (i.e., the next state machine state) to be addressed.

As indicated earlier, the low-order five bits of the next PROM address are generated by five latched bits from the current location. The two high-order address bits are generated by two PROM latch outputs in conjunction with the two outputs from the PAL. The PAL can therefore look at six "condition select" feedback signals from the current PROM register output, as well as the eight general-purpose inputs (from the device input pins) and make a logical decision regarding the values of the two high-order address bits. This allows for a multiway (four-way) conditional branch.

Since the PROM can store up to 128 different words, the PMS14R21 is capable of supporting up to 128 different states in a state machine application. Since the outputs are latched values determined by the current state, this device is designed to primarily support Moore state machines. In the PMS14R21 data sheet, MMI indicates that the chip supports both Moore and Mealy state machine models, but its Mealy machine support requires the outputs to lag by one clock cycle, and does not implement a true Mealy machine. The PMS14R21 does, however, have an advanced architecture that supports complex state machines with over 100 states.

EPS448 Stand-Alone Microsequencer (SAM)

The 28-pin *EPS448 Stand-Alone Microsequencer (SAM)* developed jointly by Altera and WaferScale Integration is easily the most advanced state machine device currently available. It is the first device in a family of SAMs, with a 24-pin version of the same chip, the EPS444, also available. The EPS448 is a CMOS EPLD incorporating high-speed CMOS instead of bipolar technology. The only other state machine-oriented PLD available using CMOS EPROM technology is the Cypress CY7C330 described briefly below. Despite its use of CMOS technology, the EPS448 purports 30 MHz operation.

The block diagram of the EPS448 is shown in Fig. 4-6. The device is essentially a combination of the 29PL141 and the PMS14R21. It consists of a PLD front-end (the branch control logic), a 448×36 registered PROM (EPROM), a 15×8 stack area, and a count register (CREG). There are eight general-purpose inputs which enter into the branch control logic, and the device outputs 16 registered PROM bits (compared to the PMS14R21's eight). One bit in each 36-bit microcode word is also used to specify the output enable state of the eight output buffers, allowing the enabling of the output buffers to be determined on a cycle-by-cycle basis. The remaining 19 register outputs are fed back into the branch control logic for making decisions and determining the next PROM location (state) to be addressed.

Like the 29PL141, the EPS448's branch control logic section (with the equivalent of 768 product terms) has its own instruction set, with different

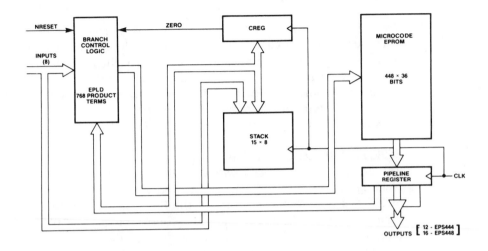

Figure 4-6. EPS448 block diagram. *Courtesy Altera Corp.*

opcodes indicating different microsequencer operations. With its 15-level stack, the EPS448 can perform subroutine calls of up to 15 levels (compared to only one for the 29PL141) and nested loops, and temporarily save data or counter information. The count register (CREG) also permits time delays and looping. Also, similar to the 29PL141 and the PMS14R21, the EPS448 supports four-way decision branching based on device input and pipeline register (i.e., PROM output register) information.

The design of the EPS448 allows it to be operated in conjunction with another EPS448 to effect more states (vertical cascading) or more outputs (horizontal cascading). The EPS448, architecturally similar to the 29PL141 and the PMS14R21, is best suited for Moore state machine implementation. This is primarily because the outputs are registered and determined by the current state. The complexity and versatility of this device, allowing up to 448 states, has raised the ceiling of single-chip state machine capability. The promise of even more-advanced SAM designs further indicates Altera's determination to maintain a leadership role in high-performance PLDs.

CY7C330 Synchronous State Machine

Cypress Semiconductor offers its *CY7C330 Synchronous State Machine* EPLD to compete with the other state machine-oriented devices already described. This 28-pin erasable, reprogrammable CMOS device offers 50 MHz operation, and is architecturally similar to the PAL23S8, though more advanced. The CY7C330 supports three synchronizing clock inputs, and all inputs to the device are registered. Its 12 I/O macrocells permit registers to be buried with feedback when the associated pin is used as an input. In addition, the device has four completely buried registers, for a total of 16 available. A variable number of product terms—up to 19—is assigned to the various sum terms. Though state machine-oriented, the CY7C330 is still based on PAL architecture and is limited to medium-complexity state machines as a result.

Bus Interface PLD Architectures

The need for bus interface-oriented PLDs was rather late in being realized, but PLD user surveys reveal that a large amount of logic is used by digital designers for implementing bus interface functions. Once the market was realized, a few firms became involved in PLD designs geared toward bus interface requirements. Since only three such devices currently exist, each in a different family and with its own unique features, it seems worthwhile to study and compare all three. Coincidentally, all three parts are CMOS EPLDs.

5CBIC Bus Interface Controller (BIC)

The *5CBIC Bus Interface Controller (BIC)* from Intel Corp. is a CMOS EPLD residing in a 44-pin PLCC package. Its block diagram is shown in Fig. 4-7. The 5CBIC has three functional blocks: the Bus Management Unit (BMU), the Programmable Logic Unit (PLU), and the control block. The BMU has three 8-bit bidirectional ports that connect to the device pins. The PLU has an 8-bit input port and an 8-bit bidirectional output port with programmable macrocells. The control block can be viewed as a switching network to switch signals generated by the PLU to control BMU functions, and to provide PLU feedback

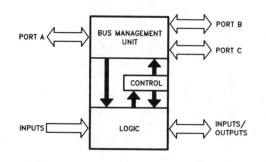

Figure 4-7. 5CBIC block diagram. *Courtesy Intel Corp. Reprinted with permission of copyright owner.*

The block diagram for the BMU is shown in Fig. 4-8. There are a number of multiplexers (*mux*es) in the BMU; some are "fuse-programmable" (i.e., EPROM cell-programmable), while others are dynamically controllable from the PLU. The MPCB multiplexer is an example of a dynamically controllable mux, as indicated by the 'SELB' control line. The MUXB multiplexer, on the other hand, is fuse-programmable, as indicated by the absence of a control signal input. Each 8-bit bidirectional bus port enters a transparent latch, allowing the signals to be optionally latched, controlled by the respective LEx signals. Ports A and B also permit direct input via MUXA and MUXB. Each port has tri-state output buffers to control the output of information onto the bus lines. The output buffers are controlled by the respective OEx signals, generated by the PLU.

The structure of the BMU permits information from any 8-bit bus to be transferred to any other 8-bit bus. Each port also has a fuse-programmable INVx mux to permit port outputs to be inverted, if desired. The BMU's FEEDBACK

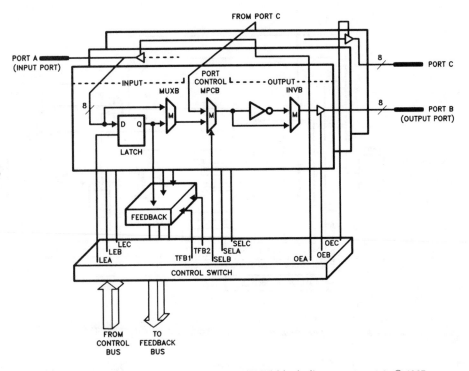

Figure 4-8. 5CBIC bus management unit (BMU) block diagram. *Copyright © 1987 Intel Corp. Reprinted with permission of copyright owner.*

mux permits the eight bits of information from any bus to be input to the PLU. The mux control bits TFB1 and TFB2, generated by the PLU, determine which port is selected to pass its information through the FEEDBACK mux.

Figure 4-9 shows the logic diagram of the PLU. The PLU is essentially a standard PLD having a complexity of about 600 gates. The eight bits entering the input port enter through transparent latches, and can thus be latched or passed straight through. Each output macrocell includes eight product terms from the AND-array, an output register, a transparent input latch, and various multiplexers. The macrocell design allows the register to be configured for D, T, S-R, or J-K operation, with the eight product terms divided in any proportion when using a two-input register option (S-R or J-K). The output of the sum term includes programmable polarity selection, and either a combinatorial or registered output can be sent to the pin. Significantly, if the pin is used as an input, the macrocell sum term and output register can still be used, since the input pin and macrocell output have separate feedback paths. This, of course, allows buried logic (a buried register or combinatorial circuit). Of the feedback paths, the MARB5 mux permits a macrocell output to be sent to the control logic to be used to control BMU functions.

The output macrocells also offer other features. The output registers have individual product terms for set and reset functions. The register clock can be generated either by a synchronous clock or a product term, for asynchronous clocking. Similarly, the tri-state output buffer can be controlled by its own product term, or by a signal common to all output macrocells.

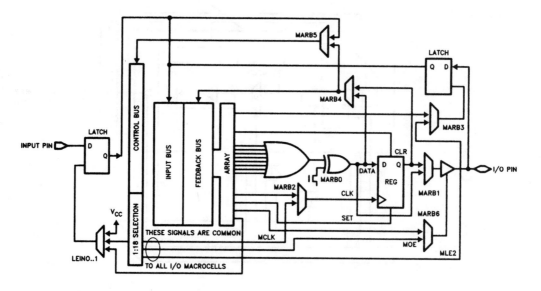

Figure 4-9. 5CBIC programmable logic unit (PLU) logic diagram. *Copyright © 1987 Intel Corp. Reprinted with permission of copyright owner.*

The 5CBIC is clearly organized to handle bus-intensive applications. Ports B and C offer higher current drive (16 mA) than Port A, and are thus intended as the system connect busses. The 5CBIC can save a considerable amount of logic in such common applications as dual-ported memory (two processors having access to a common memory or peripheral bus) and multiplexed bus interfaces.

PLX448 Bus Interface PLD

The *PLX448 bus interface PLD* from PLX Technology is rather unique among CMOS EPLDs in its offering of high-current outputs. The device has four 24 mA and four 48 mA outputs. Such high output drive currents are typically found only in bipolar devices. The device also allows its 48 mA outputs to be programmed for tri-state or open-collector operation. The logic diagram of the PLX448 is shown in Fig. 4-10. The eight outputs offer a programmable macrocell structure, with bidirectional operation. The macrocell structure is shown in Fig. 4-11.

The PLX448 has a PAL architecture with 8, 10, 12, or 14 product terms per sum term. The device has two separate synchronous clock inputs, each controlling four macrocell registers (one clock input also enters the AND-array, and can be used as a general-purpose input). Nine dedicated AND-array inputs support general-purpose signal entry into the EPLD. The nine general-purpose inputs and the clock inputs all have input hysteresis, allowing direct bus connections while minimizing potential noise and rise-time problems. Due to the high-current outputs, the 24-pin package also includes two ground pins and two +5-V pins to minimize signal noise.

As shown in the macrocell diagram (Fig. 4-11), separate feedback paths are provided for the pin and the macrocell output, allowing the macrocell function

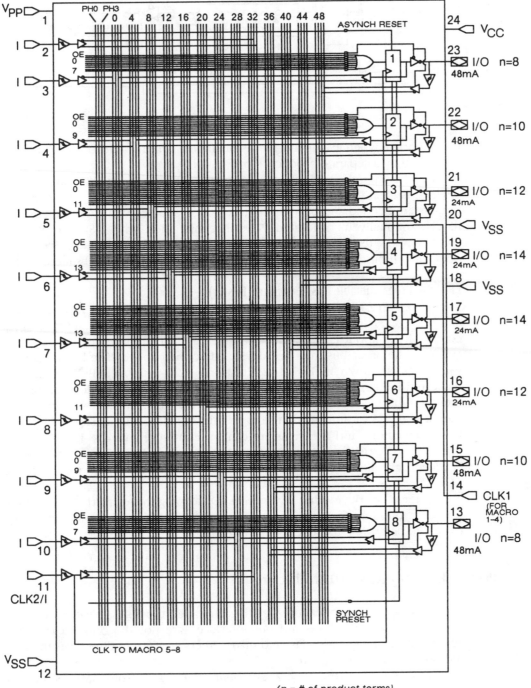

Figure 4-10. PLX448 logic diagram. *Courtesy PLX Technology.*

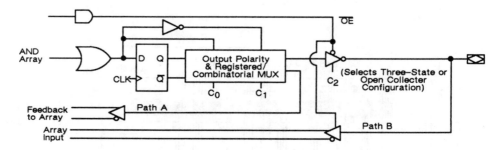

Figure 4-11. PLX448 macrocell logic diagram. *Courtesy PLX Technology.*

to be buried when using the pin as an input. The tri-state output buffer is controlled by a separate product term.

The design of the PLX448, although different from the 5CBIC and EPB1400 devices, is ideal for high-current bus designs, especially where open-collector outputs are needed and/or input hysteresis is desirable. Many applications that have traditionally incorporated PLDs in conjunction with MSI bus interface chips can now use the single-chip PLX448 solution. Directly interfacing to the popular VMEbus is one application for which the PLX448 is well-suited.

EPB1400 Programmable Bus Peripheral (Buster)

The 40-pin *EPB1400 Programmable Bus Peripheral (Buster)* from Altera is another CMOS EPLD designed for bus interface applications, purporting a complexity of about 1,400 gates. Its architecture and application is quite different from the other bus interface devices described above. The block diagram for Buster is shown in Fig. 4-12. It sports a 20-macrocell PLD with eight dedicated inputs, and an 8-bit bidirectional bus port. The device also has an internal 8-bit bus between the bus port and the PLD section, with input and output registers for information storage. The 20 macrocells all support bidirectional operation, and the registers can be configured for D, T, S-R, or J-K operation. The pin feedback into the AND-array is independent of the macrocell feedback, allowing buried registered or combinatorial logic—much like the 5CBIC.

Buster is clearly another advanced PLD, keeping in step with Altera's tradition. For bus interface applications, the EPB1400 should be studied more closely to determine its benefits.

Other Application-Specific PLD Architectures

The two primary application-specific categories the PLD market has been addressing—state machine and bus interface—are not the only areas seeing activity in the area of ASPLDs, and many others are sure to emerge as the PLD industry continues to mature.

The *2971 Programmable Event Generator (PEG)* from AMD is another application-specific PLD, featuring unique capabilities in generating output waveforms down to a 10 ns resolution. Although the PSG507 from Texas

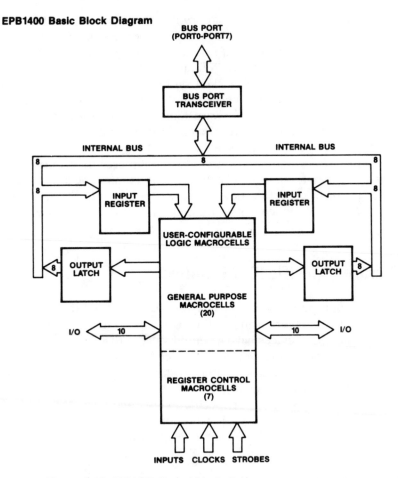

EPB1400 Basic Block Diagram

Figure 4-12. EPB1400 (Buster) block diagram. *Courtesy Altera Corp.*

Instruments, described in the section on state machines, is capable of generating special output waveforms, it cannot match the functionality offered by the 2971.

In another application-specific area, Harris has introduced two PLDs designed for chip-select (address decoder) functions. The *HPL-82C338 and HPL-82C339 Programmable Chip Select Decoders (PCSDs)* include address line, device-select, and bank-select inputs to the chip, and include an ALE (Address Latch Enable) input to support multiplexed busses. The devices output eight active-low chip-select signals for connecting to various memory and peripheral devices within a system.

Texas Instruments has also developed a device oriented toward address decoding, the *PAD16N8 Programmable Address Decoder (PAD)*. Because of its optimized architecture, the PAD16N8 can perform fast (7 ns) address decodes, while maintaining an input/output pinout compatible with the popular PAL16L8, which is also often used for address decoding.

There has not been much activity from other manufacturers to develop chip-select-oriented PLDs, since this function is generally handled adequately by many low-cost, general-purpose PLDs. In fact, both MMI and Signetics have introduced devices that are *simpler* than their standard low-end PLDs, intended for chip-select applications. These devices are simply product term arrays, without the inclusion of sum terms. (See FPGA in Chapter 3.)

Another unique ASPLD architecture was introduced by AMD to better handle situations in clocked systems where metastability is a concern. AMD's *interface protocol asynchronous cell (IPAC)* concept was especially designed to facilitate the straightforward interface of two asynchronous systems. When a separate clock is used to latch various handshake signals, metastability problems may occur if the setup and hold times relative to the latching clock are not met. To overcome this, the IPAC design uses the handshake signals themselves to generate their own latching clock, eliminating any chance of a metastability problem. The first device to incorporate the IPAC concept is AMD's 24-pin PAL22IP6, which has six outputs with IPAC-based macrocells.

Manufacturer-Specific PLD Families

Manufacturers tend to strive for autonomy and their own identity in the markets they enter, including the PLD market. Several manufacturers of programmable logic devices have invented a name that represents their PLD offerings. In some cases, the devices produced by a manufacturer are little more than alternate sources for parts produced by a different manufacturer—under a different family name.

The manufacturer-specific PLD family names are presented here to allow the reader to become familiar with them, since they are a visible part of the PLD industry and are used extensively by the respective manufacturers.

Programmable Logic from Signetics (PLS)

Signetics was responsible for introducing the first PLDs, in the form of its FPLA. Other devices followed, including varying FPLA architectures, as well as FPLSs and FPGAs. These devices were all a part of Signetics' *Integrated Fuse Logic (IFL)* family. It was not until PALs were introduced by MMI, however, that the PLD market began to take off. Soon many designers were familiar with the term "PAL" and other, similar terms (GAL, HAL), but often did not consider "IFL" in the same device category. As a result, Signetics eventually changed the family name encompassing its entire programmable logic device line to *PLS—Programmable Logic from Signetics*. It includes the company's FPLA, FPLS, PML, and other families.

Harris Programmable Logic (HPL)

Harris produces (alternate-sources) both PAL and FPLA devices, as well as some unique devices of its own. All of the programmable logic devices produced by Harris are included in the family name, *Harris Programmable Logic (HPL)*.

Sprague Programmable Logic (SPL)

Sprague has produced a group of CMOS EPLDs that functionally replace the Medium 20 series PAL devices. These devices were members of the *Sprague Programmable Logic (SPL)* family. Unfortunately, Sprague decided to pull out of the programmable logic market because of poor sales and increased competition.

Erasable Programmable Logic (EPL)

Panatech Semiconductor—the North American marketing arm of Ricoh, Electronic Device Division—produces a group of CMOS EPLD PALs that make up its *Erasable, Programmable Logic (EPL)* family.

FAST Programmable Logic Array (FASTPLA)

Fairchild Semiconductor, now part of National Semiconductor, manufactures a number of high-speed PALs, intended to complement its Fairchild Advanced-Schottky TTL (FAST) family of SSI/MSI devices. The Fairchild PALs reside under the family name of *FAST Programmable Logic Array (FASTPLA)*.

Electrically Erasable Programmable Array Logic (EEPAL)

In 1987 Seeq Technology entered into the programmable logic market with its *electrically erasable programmable array logic (EEPAL)* family. As the family name implies, Seeq's devices are PALs implemented using EEPROM technology, and are thus EEPLDs. The first device in this family was the 24-pin EEPAL20RA10Z.

CMOS Programmable Logic (CPL)

Korea-based Samsung Semiconductor produces CMOS EPLDs based on the popular PAL architecture. These devices are offered under the company's *CMOS Programmable Logic (CPL)* family name.

Family and Device Comparisons

With so many families and architectures presented all at once, both in this chapter and Chapter 3, it can be difficult to determine the relative merits of the different families, and how to select a device for a specific application. Although Chapter 6 covers device selection in depth, it seems worthwhile to briefly compare the different types of devices and present some of their inherent tradeoffs. We will look at the devices from several angles, including architecture, speed, power consumption, IC technology, cost, factory testing, and fuse security.

Architectural Comparisons

Architecture, more than anything else, determines a device's suitability for an application. Device architectures vary in many ways and also dictate how changes are handled during the design process and future product upgrades.

The simple FPLA, FPLS, and PAL devices offer only bare-bones logic functionality. The designer must select the device that has the number of registered and combinatorial outputs adequate for the design task, and also that has output polarities and adequate product terms to meet the design requirements. These simple devices offer little in terms of flexibility, and changing an output from combinatorial to registered, or vice-versa, requires a device change. Simplicity has its advantages, of course, and these are generally reflected in terms of speed and cost.

Macrocells are here to stay. It is clear from the wide acceptance of macro-cell-based devices that the flexibility of macrocells will cause them to continue to be found in new PLDs. Macrocells provide the designer with important flexibility, allowing on-chip resources to be used much more effectively, and permitting many logic functions to occupy less space. They also support changes in the design process, allowing a signal to change from a combinatorial output to a registered output to a latched input. This is done by reprogramming—eliminating the need for device or artwork changes, and saving considerable time and expense in many designs.

The newer foldback architecture devices are also designed to make the most efficient use of on-chip resources. In some respects, the foldback architecture reflects a combination of the LCA architecture (with programmable input/output connections) and the more-traditional PLD-with-macrocell architecture. The foldback architecture supports the development of internal functions—macros—that can be connected to output pins as needed. While the foldback architecture is still relatively new, its acceptance is increasing rapidly, and is likely to become a dominant PLD architecture in the future. The concept of using silicon resources efficiently is certainly one that is being almost universally sought by PLD manufacturers. The foldback approach may prove to be one of the most effective implementations to achieve such an end.

The "programmable gate array" architecture of the LCA is also an approach that supports efficient gate and I/O-resource utilization. Although the nonvolatile nature of current LCAs can be a disadvantage in many designs, the devices are easily modifiable and can support complex designs.

For special applications, designers should look carefully at the increasing number of ASPLDs. Two areas in particular have been heavily supported by the PLD industry: complex state machines, and bus interface applications. Such application-specific devices feature the most efficient use of silicon, providing high-level functionality even from devices with only medium-level complexity. These devices can, for example, replace several conventional PLDs, making them worth considering for applications that exceed the capability of a single general-purpose PLD.

Other Comparisons and Considerations

Few designs escape cost considerations, so this must be a factor during the device comparison and selection process. Of course, cost-sensitivity varies from application to application, but it may be appropriate to give up a certain amount of device flexibility (e.g., macrocells) for simpler devices that are still acceptable for the design task.

Speed and power consumption are also important considerations, and are related to device complexity and IC technology. By the nature of the technology, CMOS devices inherently offer lower power consumption than similar bipolar devices. For high-speed applications, however, the power consumption advantage of CMOS diminishes, since the power consumption of CMOS devices is proportional to operating frequency. CMOS also offers higher noise immunity, wider power supply operating range, and greater resistance to alpha-particle attack than bipolar technologies. The lower operating power of CMOS also minimizes system power supply and cooling requirements.

High-speed CMOS technology tends to be about two years behind bipolar technology speeds. The entire semiconductor industry nonetheless has seen a shift toward CMOS technology, and the PLD sector is no exception. CMOS PLDs have infiltrated areas of the PLD marketplace previously restricted to bipolar devices, and the increasing trend of designers choosing CMOS devices for their designs will likely continue.

For applications requiring especially fast PLDs, several manufacturers have introduced devices using *Emitter-Coupled Logic (ECL)* technology, offering 6 ns propagation times. Future devices are being promised with propagation delays as low as 3 ns! Gallium arsenide-based PLDs are now also available, which allow fast operation and TTL compatibility, with lower power consumption than similar ECL devices.

From development and testability standpoints, SRAM-, EPROM-, and EEPROM-based devices have distinct advantages over bipolar devices. Since these devices are erasable and reprogrammable, they can be completely tested at the factory. SRAM and EEPROM devices are the most ideal, since they can be quickly erased and reprogrammed, providing the fastest turn-around for design changes, as well as manufacturing testing. Bipolar devices, on the other hand, are not reprogrammable, and disallow complete factory testing. The programming yield and post-programming functional yield (PPFY) are higher with the reprogrammable devices, and are an important design consideration. Testability, however, tends to be a manufacturing concern more than a design concern, and is covered in detail in Chapter 7.

Device Interchangeability

Device alternate-sourcing is an important concern in many designs. In some cases, if exact alternate-sources do not exist, devices from other families can sometimes substitute on a pin-compatible basis. Alternate-sourcing in this way, of course, is application-specific, so care must be taken in selecting devices.

Pin-level functional alternate-sourcing is also valuable for development purposes. For example, a reprogrammable device such as a GAL EEPLD or an Altera EPLD may be used during the development cycle of a new design, then later replaced with a functionally identical standard PAL part to reduce cost.

Chapter Summary

In this chapter we studied application-specific PLD architectures, and how ASPLDs offer the programmable logic designer previously unavailable capability. The primary ASPLD categories are state machine devices and bus interface devices, although the manufacturers have made it clear that the types and variety of ASPLDs will be expanding. We also considered some of the implications of the various PLD architectures.

In addition to studying ASPLDs, we also took a glance at some manufacturer-specific PLD families, with the particular intention of becoming familiar with the family names.

Chapter 5

PLD Development Systems and Support

Development software is the key that has made programmable logic devices—especially complex ones—efficient for electronic designers. Since the 1978 introduction of the first programmable logic compiler, MMI's PALASM, numerous other vendors have introduced software and hardware development aids aimed at helping the designer take advantage of the application potential of today's increasingly complex PLDs. Instead of defining PLD logic in terms of a fuse map, PLD functionality can now be specified using Boolean equations, truth tables, state machine diagrams, schematics, netlists, and waveforms. This, of course, allows the designer to be more efficient in achieving a design.

Chapter Overview

In this chapter we will take a look at the available PLD development software offerings. We will also look at PLD development services, the JEDEC PLD fuse map format standard, and the EDIF file format standard.

PLD Languages

As mentioned above, PLD languages now offer a variety of competing features. Since the PLD language choice plays an important role in the PLD development process, it's worth looking at the software packages and their relative merits. It should be kept in mind that virtually every vendor is constantly improving its product. Not only are new devices supported when they become available, but the capability, efficiency, and user-interface aspects of the software packages are also improved. The product information provided here should be used as a guideline for becoming familiar with the capabilities and features of the different languages, with the realization that the specifications of these languages may change at any time.

Appendix B provides a comprehensive list of manufacturers that offer programmable logic development aids.

Chapter 9 describes some of the improvements that are likely to be incorporated into future PLD software packages.

PLD software can be broken down into two categories: PLD-manufacturer-dependent languages and PLD-manufacturer-independent (or "third-party") languages. We will look at these two categories separately.

PLD-Manufacturer-Dependent Languages

The concept of using software to support PLD designs first came from PLD manufacturers. MMI generated the first PLD language implementation—its Fortran-based PAL Assembler (PALASM). MMI's offering made it clear that software design support was a critical element for design engineers considering the use of PLDs. Since new PLDs are virtually worthless without adequate software support, every PLD manufacturer has taken the initiative to make sure adequate software coverage is available for its devices. While some manufacturers have found it preferable to coordinate support for their PLDs with independent, third-party PLD software suppliers, many have opted to create their own. In this section we will look at the PLD support languages available from PLD manufacturers.

It should be obvious that a manufacturer-dependent PLD language essentially supports only the PLDs offered by the manufacturer providing the language. Of course, if equivalent devices are offered by other manufacturers, these devices are also supported.

PALASM 2—PAL Assembler (MMI)

After establishing its PALASM language as the defacto standard for PLD software support, MMI developed a second-generation *PALASM 2* compiler to implement several improvements. PALASM 2 supports *asynchronous* devices (devices that use a separate clock for each output register, such as the PAL20RA10) and complex parts (MegaPALs) that were not supported before. It also offers less-restrictive syntax and an improved test vector simulation capability over the original PALASM.

PALASM 2 supports virtually all of the PAL devices offered by MMI, including the PMS14R21 Programmable Sequencer, although MMI's Logic Cell Array (LCA) devices are not supported. Even though MMI merged with AMD in 1987, PALASM 2 has not been updated to support parts unique to the AMD PLD line. This is primarily because AMD already has a PLD language—PLPL—to support its devices.

With the exception of its simulation capability, PALASM 2 is, for the most part, a plain vanilla PLD language offering. It lacks many of the advanced features that distinguish the third-party (manufacturer-independent) languages. While state machine input capability was incorporated beginning with version 2.20, only selected devices are supported, and the flexibility is only moderate. PALASM 2 is primarily designed for Boolean equation input, and is adequate for most low- to medium-complexity PAL applications.

The logic operators used by PALASM 2 are the conventional operators used in most Boolean logic texts. The OR operator is the '+' symbol, the AND operator is the '*' symbol, and the Exclusive-OR operator is the ': + :' symbol. A preceding slash (/) indicates negation (NOT) or an active-low signal. Active-low signals in the pinlist (the list of signals names assigned to the pins of the PAL) typically have a preceding slash to indicate their active-low nature. Like most PLD languages, there are two different assignment operators, ' = ' and ': = '. The first is used for assignment to a combinatorial output, while the second is used for assignment to a registered output.

The PALASM 2 source file created by the designer is called the PAL Design Specification file, or PDS file. This file is processed by the *PALASM2* program to verify syntax. If the syntax is ok, an output file called 'PALASM2.TRE' is generated. This file can then be used by *XPLOT* to determine if the defined logic will fit into the specified PAL device. If so, a fuse map is generated, and two output files are created: one with a '.XPT' extension, and the other with a '.JED' extension. The '.XPT' file contains the generated fuse map, and the '.JED' file contains the JEDEC output file (described later), which can be downloaded (transferred) to a PLD programmer.

The 'PALASM2.TRE' file can also be used as an input to the PALASM 2 simulator, *SIM*. The simulator then outputs information pertaining to the simulation results, and can optionally modify the JEDEC output file to add test vectors, if desired.

An example PALASM 2 design (PDS file) listing is shown in Listing 5-1. The design uses a PAL16L8 to generate four memory chip selects and four system read/write strobes. The inputs to the PAL are six address lines (A19-A14), an active-low CPU read strobe (/rd), an active-low CPU write strobe (/wr), and an I/O/memory select signal (mem_io) which is low for I/O accesses.

Listing 5-1. Example PALASM 2 Design

```
TITLE           Memory Selects/Strobes
PATTERN  PAL2BK.PDS
REVISION        A
AUTHOR          Roger C. Alford
COMPANY  none
DATE            1/16/88

CHIP MEM PAL16L8

; Pin List (pins 1-20):
        a19 a18 a17 a16 a15 a14 mem_io /rd /wr gnd
        nc /sel1 /sel2 /sel3 /sel4 /mrd /mwr /iord /iowr vcc

; Description:
;
;       This PALASM 2 file defines the memory select outputs
```

```
;        generated by a PAL16L8 device. Memory and I/O read and
;        write strobes are also generated.
;
;        Input Signals:
;           a14-a19 are address lines
;           mem_io is active low for I/O accesses
;           /wr and /rd are the write and read strobes, respectively
;
;        Output Signals:
;           /mrd is the memory read strobe
;           /mwr is the memory write strobe
;           /iord is the I/O read strobe
;           /iowr is the I/O write strobe
;           The following memory select ranges are defined:
;               /sel1 = C0000-FFFFF (256K)
;               /sel2 = B0000-B3FFF (16K)
;               /sel3 = 40000-5FFFF or 80000-9FFFF (256K)
;               /sel4 = 00000-1FFFF (128K)

; String Substitutions:
        string mem_cycle 'mem_io'
        string io_cycle  '/mem_io'

Equations

        sel1 = a19 * a18 * mem_cycle

        sel2 = a19 * /a18 * a17 * a16 * /a15 * /a14 * mem_cycle

        sel3 =   (/a19 * a18 * /a17 * mem_cycle)
               + (a19 * /a18 * /a17 * mem_cycle)

        sel4 = /a19 * /a18 * /a17 * mem_cycle

        mrd = mem_cycle * rd

        mwr = mem_cycle * wr

        iord = io_cycle * rd

        iowr = io_cycle * wr

Simulation

        trace_on   /sel1 /sel2 /sel3 /sel4 /mrd /mwr /iord /iowr

        setf    mem_io ; specify memory access
```

```
; check output '/sel1':
    setf    a19 a18 a17 a16 a15 a14
    check   sel1 /sel2 /sel3 /sel4
    setf    a19 a18 a17 /a16 a15 /a14
    check   sel1 /sel2 /sel3 /sel4
    setf    a19 a18 /a17 /a16 /a15 /a14
    check   sel1 /sel2 /sel3 /sel4

; check output '/sel2':
    setf    a19 /a18 a17 a16 /a15 /a14
    check   /sel1 sel2 /sel3 /sel4
    setf    a19 /a18 a17 a16 /a15 a14
    check   /sel1 /sel2 /sel3 /sel4

; check output '/sel3':
    setf    /a19 a18 /a17 a16 a15 a14
    check   /sel1 /sel2 sel3 /sel4
    setf    /a19 a18 /a17 /a16 /a15 /a14
    check   /sel1 /sel2 sel3 /sel4
    setf    /a19 a18 /a17 a16 /a15 a14
    check   /sel1 /sel2 sel3 /sel4
    setf    a19 /a18 /a17 a16 a15 a14
    check   /sel1 /sel2 sel3 /sel4
    setf    a19 /a18 /a17 /a16 /a15 /a14
    check   /sel1 /sel2 sel3 /sel4
    setf    a19 /a18 /a17 a16 /a15 a14
    check   /sel1 /sel2 sel3 /sel4

; check output '/sel4':
    setf    /a19 /a18 /a17 a16 a15 a14
    check   /sel1 /sel2 /sel3 sel4
    setf    /a19 /a18 /a17 /a16 /a15 /a14
    check   /sel1 /sel2 /sel3 sel4
    setf    /a19 /a18 /a17 a16 /a15 a14
    check   /sel1 /sel2 /sel3 sel4

    setf    /mem_io ; specify I/O access

; check output '/sel1':
    setf    a19 a18 a17 a16 a15 a14
    check   /sel1 /sel2 /sel3 /sel4

; check output '/sel2':
    setf    a19 /a18 a17 a16 /a15 /a14
    check   /sel1 /sel2 /sel3 /sel4

; check output '/sel3':
```

```
        setf    /a19 a18 /a17 a16 a15 a14
        check   /sel1 /sel2 /sel3 /sel4

;   check output '/sel4':
        setf    /a19 /a18 /a17 a16 a15 a14
        check   /sel1 /sel2 /sel3 /sel4

;   check strobes:
        setf    mem_io; memory access
        setf    /rd
        check   /mrd /iord
        setf    rd
        check   mrd /iord
        setf    /wr
        check   /mwr /iowr
        setf    wr
        check   mwr /iowr

        setf    /mem_io ; I/O access
        setf    /rd
        check   /mrd /iord
        setf    rd
        check   /mrd iord
        setf    /wr
        check   /mwr /iowr
        setf    wr
        check   /mwr iowr

        trace_off

; End of PDS File: PAL2BK.PDS
```

General information about the file is provided at the top of Listing 5-1; the PAL type (PAL16L8) is also specified. The pin list follows, specifying the signal names that are defined on the 20 pins of the PAL (some signals are inputs, while others are outputs). This is followed by a description section (comments) and a brief string substitution section. The 'Equations' section is next, and is the main section of the PDS file. It provides the Boolean equations for all of the PAL outputs. Finally, an optional 'Simulation' section provides simulation information to test the functionality of the design. The resulting test vectors can also later be placed into the output (JEDEC) file for testing programmed parts.

The simulation capability of PALASM 2 is noteworthy. The compiler supports a flexible set of simulation commands (instructions) that can allow the logic of a PAL design to be tested with a high level of completeness. Indeed, the simulation capability is more impressive than that offered by some of the third-party PLD language vendors, which have generally superior products. Simulation features include:

- FOR loops to iterate a set of commands a fixed number of times.
- WHILE-DO loops to iterate a set of commands until a specified condition becomes false.
- IF-THEN-ELSE conditional branching.

Aside from its simulation capability, PALASM 2 is a simple-minded compiler that lacks important features helpful for most medium- and high-complexity PAL designs. Again, these are standard features on the more-advanced, third-party PLD languages. Let's look at three specific problem areas of PALASM 2.

The first problem area is the lack of logic minimization capability. Since PLDs have only a limited amount of internal logic, logic minimization is critical in many applications. PALs, for example, typically support only seven or eight product terms per output. While this is adequate for most requirements, it is not uncommon to specify an equation for an output that consists of more than eight product terms. Often, however, the number of product terms can be reduced by a minimization algorithm, allowing a function to fit into a device that originally seemed too small. Here is a simple example of an equation that is clearly reducible, but generates an error message with PALASM 2:

$$
\begin{aligned}
\text{output} = \; & \text{sig1} * \text{sig2} \\
+ \; & \text{sig2} * \text{sig3} \\
+ \; & \text{sig1} * \text{sig3} \\
+ \; & \text{sig3} * \text{sig1} \\
+ \; & \text{sig2} * \text{sig1} \\
+ \; & \text{sig3} * \text{sig2} \\
+ \; & \text{sig1} * \text{sig4} \\
+ \; & \text{sig4} * \text{sig1} \\
+ \; & \text{sig1} * \text{sig2}
\end{aligned}
$$

Logic minimization is a standard part of all third-party PLD compilers.

Another PALASM 2 problem area is its inability to adequately handle multiple levels of parentheses. For example, while the equation,

$$
\begin{aligned}
\text{sel3} = \; & (/a19 * a18 * /a17 * \text{mem+cycle}) \\
+ \; & (a19 * /a18 * /a17 * \text{mem+cycle})
\end{aligned}
$$

is acceptable to PALASM 2, the equivalent equation,

$$
\text{sel3} = ((/a19 * a18 * /a17) + (a19 * /a18 * /a17)) * \text{mem+cycle}
$$

causes PALASM 2 to generate an error message.

Finally, PALASM 2 uses a rudimentary rule to determine if an equation is acceptable for an active-low output pin. If the polarity of the output signal name specified in the pin list is opposite the polarity of the same signal name specified in the output equation, the compiler will accept the output equation. If the polarities are the same, an error message is generated. The compiler does not even perform a simple DeMorgan transformation to see if the equation could work with the output. For example, assuming the pinlist for a PAL16L8 PDS file has an output signal named '/output' (with active-low polarity), the following equation is acceptable to PALASM 2,

$$\text{output} = /\text{sig1}$$

but the equivalent equation,

$$/\text{output} = \text{sig1}$$

causes the compiler to generate an error message.

In addition to the basic PALASM 2 compiler, MMI's PAL development software package includes some other utilities to aid the designer. *PLEASM* is MMI's compiler for programmable logic elements (PLEs—MMI's term for PROMs). Whereas PALASM 2 outputs a JEDEC file which can be downloaded to a PLD programmer, PLEASM generates an Intel Hex/ASCII file which is more commonly used by PROM programmers. *TIMING* is a utility that allows the user to enter a timing diagram for a state machine or sequencer application. The program then translates the specified timing diagram into PALASM 2 source code (a PDS file).

ZHAL indicates whether or not a PAL design can be put into a mask-programmed ZHAL (CMOS, "zero-power" Hard Array Logic) device. *PINOUT* displays (or prints out) a graphic image of the specified PLD, along with the signal names assigned to each pin. Figure 5-1 shows the PINOUT output for the PALASM 2 file shown in Listing 5-1. *VTRACE* is a utility that converts the output of the PALASM 2 simulator into a timing diagram. Figure 5-2 shows the VTRACE output for the PALASM 2 file shown in Listing 5-1. Other utilities are also included with the PALASM 2 package.

```
                Monolithic Memories PAL16L8

             *********   *********
             *             ***        *
    A19  **   1                  20  **  Vcc
             *                          *
    A18  **   2                  19  **  IOWR
             *                          *
    A17  **   3                  18  **  IORD
             *                          *
    A16  **   4                  17  **  MWR
             *                          *
    A15  **   5                  16  **  MRD
             *                          *
    A14  **   6                  15  **  SEL4
             *                          *
 MEM_IO  **   7                  14  **  SEL3
             *                          *
     RD  **   8                  13  **  SEL2
             *                          *
     WR  **   9                  12  **  SEL1
             *                          *
    Gnd  **  10                  11  **  NC
             *                          *
             ***********************
```

Figure 5-1. The output of MMI's PINOUT utility for the PALASM 2 file shown in Listing 5-1.

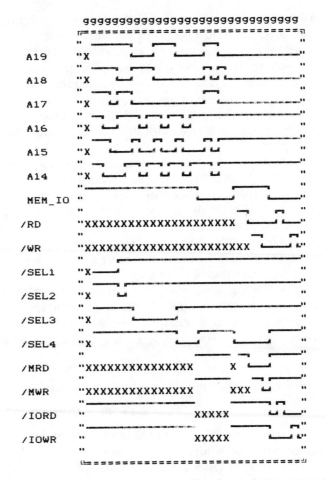

Figure 5-2. The output of MMI's VTRACE utility for the PALASM 2 file shown in Listing 5-1.

Despite its pitfalls, PALASM 2 is widely used in the PLD industry. This is largely due to the initial acceptance of "PALASM 1" as the first available PLD compiler, and AMD/MMI's continued dominance of the PLD marketplace. The price of the compiler is also a factor. It sells for approximately $200, and is often provided at no charge to volume PAL users. This is clearly less costly than the $2,000 or more typically needed to purchase a third-party PLD language.

The PALASM 2 compiler is available for the IBM PC and compatibles (including PS/2 models), as well as the Digital Equipment Corp. VAX/VMS. The PASCAL source code for PALASM 2 is also available from MMI, and can be easily ported to other systems. Most of the utilities included with the PALASM 2 package operate only on IBM PCs and compatibles.

AMAZE—Automatic Map And Zap Equations (Signetics)
To support its programmable logic devices, Signetics Corp. offers its *AMAZE* software package. It is often provided at no charge to corporate customers who use—or will potentially use—Signetics' PLDs. Like PALASM 2, AMAZE lacks

many of the more-advanced features of its third-party counterparts, but provides adequate functionality for most low- to medium-complexity PLD designs.

AMAZE uses essentially the same logic syntax as PALASM 2, although the ':=' assignment operator is not used. The main program module in the AMAZE software package is *BLAST* (Boolean Logic and State Transfer). BLAST translates the input information (found in several files) into a Signetics Standard Program Table file (having a '.STD' extension). Other programs can then use the information in the Standard Program Table file for various purposes, such as test vector simulation.

When a new PLD file is being defined, BLAST prompts for the PLD type to be used (e.g., PLS153), then displays a graphical image of the device on the terminal screen. The user must then assign signal names to each pin, as appropriate, and specify the input, output, or bidirectional operation of each pin (within the limits of the chosen device). This information is stored in the pin list file, having a '.PIN' extension. Once the pin list information has been entered, the logic for the design must be entered. BLAST accepts both Boolean equation input and State Transfer input.

The Boolean equation input format is straightforward. While AMAZE can adequately handle multiple levels of parentheses (unlike other, simpler PLD software packages), it requires its equations to conform to a fairly strict syntax. For example, if the output 'OUT1' is defined as active-low, the equation,

$$OUT1 = /(/INP1)$$

is acceptable, while the simpler, logically equivalent equation,

$$OUT1 = INP1$$

is not acceptable. This syntax limitation, however, is common to many of the manufacturer-dependent PLD compilers

The State Transfer input capability provides a good means to implement state machines. AMAZE allows several inputs, outputs, or state registers to be grouped together as *sets*, where a set is treated as a unit. For example, the three registers of a 3-bit (eight-state) state machine might be grouped together as,

$$[reg3 , reg2, reg1]$$

to form the state machine set. Set capability can be a powerful feature, and is highly supported in the third-party PLD languages.

While the basic logic entry capability is present in AMAZE, the compiler still lacks minimization capability—an essential feature for intermediate and complex combinatorial and state machine designs. Although AMAZE does eliminate redundant product terms (which is more than some simple PLD compilers do), that is the extent of its minimization capability.

AMAZE supports test vector simulation, and is even capable of automatically generating test vectors for a specified design. It also comes with a copy of the "shareware" PC Write word processing program for use as a text editor.

An example AMAZE design document is shown in Listing 5-2. The design uses a Signetics PLS153 to generate four memory chip selects and four system read/write strobes. The functionality of the design is identical to the PALASM 2 design presented in Listing 5-1. This example shows how a part with one architecture (PAL16L8, with a PAL architecture) can have a functional, pin-for-pin replacement part with a different architecture (PLS153, with an FPLA architecture).

Listing 5-2. Example AMAZE Design

```
@DEVICE TYPE
PLS153
@REVISION: A
@DATE: 01/16/88
@SYMBOL: AMZBK
@COMPANY: none
@NAME: Roger C. Alford


@DESCRIPTION

        This AMAZE file defines the memory select outputs
        generated by a PLD153 device. Memory and I/O read and
        write strobes are also generated.

        Input Signals:
            a14-a19 are address lines
            mem_io is active low for I/O accesses
            /wr and /rd are the write and read strobes, respectively

        Output Signals:
            /mrd is the memory read strobe
            /mwr is the memory write strobe
            /iord is the I/O read strobe
            /iowr is the I/O write strobe
            The following memory select ranges are defined:
                    /sel1 = C0000-FFFFF (256K)
                    /sel2 = B0000-B3FFF (16K)
                    /sel3 = 40000-5FFFF or 80000-9FFFF (256K)
                    /sel4 = 00000-1FFFF (128K)

@COMMON PRODUCT TERM
        mem_cycle = mem_io;
        io_cycle = /mem_io;


@I/O DIRECTION
        D0 = 0;          " /wr signal is always an input "
        D2 = 1;          " /sel1 output always enabled "
        D3 = 1;          " /sel2 output always enabled "
        D4 = 1;          " /sel3 output always enabled "
        D5 = 1;          " /sel4 output always enabled "
        D6 = 1;          " /mrd output always enabled "
        D7 = 1;          " /mwr output always enabled "
```

```
        D8 = 1;              " /iord output always enabled "
        D9 = 1;              " /iowr output always enabled "

@LOGIC EQUATION

      sel1 = /(a19 * a18 * mem_cycle);

      sel2 = /(a19 * /a18 * a17 * a16 * /a15 * /a14 * mem_cycle);

      sel3 = /((((/a19 * a18 * /a17) + (a19 * /a18 * /a17)) *
                 mem_cycle);

      sel4 = /((/a19 * /a18 * /a17 * mem_cycle);

      mrd = /(mem_cycle * rd);

      mwr = /(mem_cycle * wr);

      iord = /(io_cycle * rd);

      iowr = /(io_cycle * wr);

" End of AMAZE file: AMZBK "
```

Other AMAZE utility programs include *TOJED* to create a JEDEC output file from the '.STD' file, *DPI* (Device Programmer Interface) to communicate with the PLD programmer, and *PTP* to convert a PAL JEDEC file (uploaded from a PLD programmer) to a functionally equivalent Signetics PLD Standard file.

AMAZE also includes a utility that permits an entry format that is becoming increasingly popular with more-advanced PLD development packages: schematic entry. On a limited basis, AMAZE can translate schematic designs from FutureNet Corp.'s DASH schematic entry system or OrCAD Systems Corp.'s OrCAD:SDT schematic entry system into logic source files that can be read by the AMAZE compiler.

AMAZE operates on IBM PCs and compatibles.

PLAN—Programmable Logic Analysis (National)

To support its PLDs, National Semiconductor Corp. offers its IBM PC-based *PLAN* software. Like the PALASM 2 and AMAZE languages, PLAN is a simple language, acceptable only for low- to medium-complexity applications. Of the three compilers PLAN is perhaps the simplest, offering no logic minimization, no parentheses support (with limited exception), and a restrictive input file syntax. It is even particular about where comments are placed in the source file. Only Boolean equation input is supported, making state machine designs particularly difficult to develop. Nevertheless, PLAN offers some features that are not available on the other languages.

PLAN offers an interactive mode of operation, where the pin list (input and output signal names) and logic equations can be entered. PLAN uses the same assignment and logic operators as PALASM 2. Instead of using PLAN's interactive input mode, the user can optionally enter the information into a source file (with a '.BEQ' extension) using any ASCII text editor. After the pin list information has been entered, including the active state of each output (high or low), PLAN selects the PLD from its library that best fits the design, and automatically assigns the input and output signals to the appropriate pins on the selected PLD. The selected device is intended to be the least costly (i.e., least complex) PLD that will accommodate the specified pin list configuration. The user has the option to manually change the pin assignments or PLD selection (using an editor), if desired.

Once a complete source file has been developed, it can be compiled into a JEDEC file and downloaded to a PLD programmer. PLAN also supports device functional simulation using test vectors, so designs can be simulated and debugged before programming real parts.

An example PLAN design document is shown in Listing 5-3. The design is functionally identical to those presented earlier in Listing 5-1 (PALASM 2) and 5-2 (AMAZE), and uses a PAL16L8 to generate four memory chip selects and four system read/write strobes.

Listing 5-3. Example PLAN Design

```
PAL16L8
A19 A18 A17 A16 A15 A14 MEM_IO /RD /WR GND
NC /SEL1 /SEL2 /SEL3 /SEL4 /MRD /MWR /IORD /IOWR VCC
MEM_CYCLE.TERM = MEM_IO
IO_CYCLE.TERM = /MEM_IO
/SEL1 = A19 * A18 * MEM_CYCLE
/SEL2 = A19 * /A18 * A17 * A16 * /A15 * /A14 * MEM_CYCLE
/SEL3 =   /A19 * A18 * /A17 * MEM_CYCLE
        + A19 * /A18 * /A17 * MEM_CYCLE
/SEL4 = /A19 * /A18 * /A17 * MEM_CYCLE
/MRD = MEM_CYCLE * RD
/MWR = MEM_CYCLE * WR
/IORD = IO_CYCLE * RD
/IOWR = IO_CYCLE * WR
;
; Description:
;
;       This PLAN file defines the memory select outputs
;       generated by a PAL16L8 device. Memory and I/O read and
;       write strobes are also generated.
;
; End of PLAN File: PLANBK.BEQ
```

In addition to its basic operation, PLAN offers other helpful features, including the ability to print a graphic image of the PLD used in the design (similar to that shown in Fig. 5-1 from PALASM 2), and the ability to communicate with a PLD programmer.

HELP—Harris Enhanced Language for Programmable Logic (Harris)

Harris Corp. has developed *HELP* for its programmable logic customers. The HELP user interface is similar to that of National's PLAN software, although there are several differences. Both software packages feature an interactive approach to information entry. HELP does not automatically select the PLD to be used, and PLAN does not offer the extensive error checking (at data entry time) implemented in the HELP software. Both software packages are logically simple, disallowing parenthetical expressions, and requiring equations to be input in sum-of-products form.

HELP incorporates an interactive design entry system which Harris calls the Silicon Breadboard. It is designed to be a goof-proof method for design entry. The user is prompted at each step of the design entry process—starting with device selection—and error checking is performed as information is entered. After the HELP design has been entered, the Silicon Breadboard is exited causing the design to automatically compile. HELP includes a simple built-in full-screen editor to permit design changes. After a design change, the Silicon Breadboard is re-entered. To compile the new design, the software puts on a little show by prompting for all of the design information, and automatically answering its own prompts with the information from the HPL (Harris Programmable Logic) design specification file.

HELP is particular about the format of its design specification file, and it is unsafe for the designer to modify the file with a standard text editor. It is, therefore, difficult to add documentation to the file.

Listing 5-4 shows an example HELP design specification document, functionally identical to those presented earlier for the other PLD languages. The HELP design uses a PAL16LC8 (a CMOS version of the PAL16L8), and generates four memory chip selects and four system read/write strobes.

Listing 5-4. Example HELP Design

```
HPL16LC8                          HPL DESIGN SPECIFICATION
                                         01-22-1988

HELP TEST DESIGN

A19 A18 A17 A16 A15 A14 MEMIO /RD /WR GND
NC /SEL1 /SEL2 /SEL3 /SEL4 /MRD /MWR /IORD /IOWR VCC

IF (VCC)
/SEL1       = A19*A18*MEMCYCL

IF (VCC)
/SEL2       = A19*/A18*A17*A16*/A15*/A14*MEMCYCL

IF (VCC)
/SEL3       = /A19*A18*/A17*MEMCYCL
            + A19*/A18*/A17*MEMCYCL

IF (VCC)
/SEL4       = /A19*/A18*/A17*MEMCYCL
```

```
IF (VCC)
/MRD       = MEMCYCL*RD

IF (VCC)
/MWR       = MEMCYCL*WR

IF (VCC)
/IORD      = IOCYCLE*RD

IF (VCC)
/IOWR      = IOCYCLE*WR


MACRO FUNCTIONS:

MEMCYCL    = MEMIO

IOCYCLE    = /MEMIO

COMMENTS:

END
```

While the standard HELP software package does not perform any logic minimization, Harris offers an optional Advanced Utilities Module for HELP which includes a logic minimizer, and other functions. The Advanced Utilities Module also includes an automatic test vector generator.

HELP runs on the IBM PC and compatibles.

PLPL—Programmable Logic Programming Language (AMD)

Advanced Micro Devices' entry into the PLD language arena came in 1984 with the introduction of its IBM PC-based *PLPL* language. It is the most advanced of the "basic" manufacturer-dependent programmable logic languages (the languages described above), and offers features commonly found in the more-advanced packages available from third-party vendors. Supporting only its own devices, AMD generally offers the software package at no charge to volume users of its PLDs.

The features of PLPL are many. The language supports set capability—to a much greater extent than AMAZE—and allows groups of signals to be defined and used in pin definitions and Boolean equations. For example, the pin definition for the four lines of a data bus can be specified as,

$$D[0:3] = 6,7,8,9$$

instead of,

$$D0 = 6$$
$$D1 = 7$$
$$D2 = 8$$
$$D3 = 9$$

PLPL also supports complex equations with multiple levels of parentheses. Since the compiler knows how to apply DeMorgan's theorem, the Boolean equations do *not* have to be entered in sum-of-products form, allowing a reasonably flexible syntax.

Like AMAZE, PLPL supports a structured state machine description format, allowing complex state machines to be entered. Unlike any of the other languages described above, however, PLPL also includes an "optimize" option to minimize the compiled logic equations using the Quine-McCluskey reduction algorithm (see Chapter 2). The PLPL software also includes device simulation capability. It is relatively simple and similar to that offered by nearly all other languages mentioned. PALASM 2 is the notable exception, supporting a structured simulation input format for more-advanced simulation descriptions.

The Boolean operators and assignment operators used by PLPL are the same as those used by PALASM 2 and the other PLD languages.

Listing 5-5 shows an example PLPL design document, functionally identical to those given before for the other manufacturer-dependent languages. A PAL16L8 is used to generate memory chip selects and read/write strobes. Notice how the equation for 'sel3' is defined as a two-level parenthetical expression.

Listing 5-5. Example PLPL Design

```
DEVICE          Memory_Selects_Strobes (PAL16L8);

"

FILE            PLPLBK
REVISION        A
AUTHOR          Roger C. Alford
COMPANY   none
DATE            1/21/88


; Description:
;
;       This PLPL file defines the memory select outputs
;       generated by a PAL16L8 device. Memory and I/O read and
;       write strobes are also generated.
;
;       Input Signals:
;           a14-a19 are address lines
;           mem_io is active low for I/O accesses
;           /wr and /rd are the write and read strobes, respectively
;
;       Output Signals:
;           /mrd is the memory read strobe
;           /mwr is the memory write strobe
;           /iord is the I/O read strobe
;           /iowr is the I/O write strobe
;           The following memory select ranges are defined:
;               /sel1 = C0000-FFFFF (256K)
```

```
;                  /sel2 = B0000-B3FFF (16K)
;                  /sel3 = 40000-5FFFF or 80000-9FFFF (256K)
;                  /sel4 = 00000-1FFFF (128K)
"


PIN
        a19     = 1                      " IN - address line 19 "
        a18     = 2                      " IN - address line 18 "
        a17     = 3                      " IN - address line 17 "
        a16     = 4                      " IN - address line 16 "
        a15     = 5                      " IN - address line 15 "
        a14     = 6                      " IN - address line 14 "
        mem_io  = 7                      " IN - memory/I/O select signal
"

        /rd     = 8                      " IN - read strobe "
        /wr     = 9                      " IN - write strobe "
        /sel1   = 12                     " OUT - memory select 1 "
        /sel2   = 13                     " OUT - memory select 1 "
        /sel3   = 14                     " OUT - memory select 1 "
        /sel4   = 15                     " OUT - memory select 1 "
        /mrd    = 16                     " OUT - memory read strobe "
        /mwr    = 17                     " OUT - memory write strobe "
        /iord   = 18                     " OUT - I/O read strobe "
        /iowr   = 19;                    " OUT - I/O write strobe "

" Internal Equations: "
DEFINE
        mem_cycle = mem_io;
        io_cycle  = /mem_io;

" Logic Equations: "
BEGIN
        sel1 = a19 * a18 * mem_cycle;

        sel2 = a19 * /a18 * a17 * a16 * /a15 * /a14 * mem_cycle;

        sel3 =((/a19 * a18 * /a17) + (a19 * /a18 * /a17)) * mem_cycle;

        sel4 = /a19 * /a18 * /a17 * mem_cycle;

        mrd = mem_cycle * rd;

        mwr = mem_cycle * wr;

        iord = io_cycle * rd;

        iowr = io_cycle * wr;
```

```
END.

" End of PLPL File: PLPLBK "
```

Since PLPL supports DeMorgan equation transformations, the designer has the freedom to specify active high output signals (even with a PAL16L8, which has inverted outputs); the compiler takes care of the translation. For example, if the I/O-write signal were active high (iowr) instead of active low (/iowr), the iowr logic equation could be changed to,

$$iowr = /(io\_cycle * wr)$$

which will be translated by PLPL into,

$$iowr = /io\_cycle + /wr$$

PLPL does not, however, give complete freedom to the designer. Merely removing the slash (/) in front of 'iowr' in the pin list to indicate an active high output causes PLPL to generate an error message.

In late-1987 AMD also came out with an alternative PLD language for its customers. Through an arrangement with Personal CAD Systems, Inc.—then owner of the CUPL compiler—AMD introduced *AmCUPL*, a special version of CUPL that supports only AMD's devices. Aside from the limited device library, AmCUPL is a full-featured version of CUPL, supporting all of the compiler's powerful features. CUPL is a third-party (manufacturer-independent) language that is described in more detail later in this chapter.

APEEL—Assembler for Programmable Electrically-Erasable Logic (ICT)

In 1987 International CMOS Technology (ICT) introduced its *APEEL* compiler to supports its PEEL EEPLD devices. Like the other PLD compilers described above, APEEL is a relatively simple compiler, adequate for low- to medium-complexity design tasks. It offers a nice user interface, and supports simulation and test vector fault grading (see Chapter 7). It also includes a built-in full-screen editor, and outputs a standard JEDEC output file. Logic minimization is not supported.

In addition to supporting the conventional logical and assignment operators used by the other PLD languages described above, APEEL also supports the logical operators used by the third-party CUPL and ABEL software packages (described later). CUPL and ABEL use the pound sign (#) for the OR operator, the ampersand (&) for the AND operator, and the exclamation point (!) for the NOT operator. Thus, APEEL defines the following logical operators:

    * & = AND operators
    + # = OR operators
    / ! = NOT operators

Listing 5-6 shows an example APEEL design document, functionally identical to those given above for the other manufacturer-dependent languages. In this case, a PEEL18CV8 EEPLD is used to generate the memory select signals and memory and I/O read/write strobes. As with the PLS153 used in the AMAZE design, the PEEL18CV8 design is a pin-for-pin functional replacement (alternate source) for the PAL16L8-based design shown with the other languages.

Listing 5-6. Example APEEL Design

```
TITLE 'APEEL FILE: PEELBK.APL
DESIGNER: Roger C. Alford
DATE: 01/25/88'


PEEL18CV8


" Description:
"
"       This APEEL file defines the memory select outputs
"       generated by a PEEL16CV8 device. Memory and I/O read and
"       write strobes are also generated.
"
"       Input Signals:
"           a14-a19 are address lines
"           mem_io is active low for I/O accesses
"           /wr and /rd are the write and read strobes, respectively
"
"       Output Signals:
"           /mrd is the memory read strobe
"           /mwr is the memory write strobe
"           /iord is the I/O read strobe
"           /iowr is the I/O write strobe
"           The following memory select ranges are defined:
"               /sel1 = C0000-FFFFF (256K)
"               /sel2 = B0000-B3FFF (16K)
"               /sel3 = 40000-5FFFF or 80000-9FFFF (256K)
"               /sel4 = 00000-1FFFF (128K)
"
"
"                     ____  ____
"                    |    \/    |
"            a19  { 1      20 }  Vcc
"            a18  { 2      19 }  /iowr
"            a17  { 3      18 }  /iord
"            a16  { 4      17 }  /mwr
"            a15  { 5      16 }  /mrd
"            a14  { 6      15 }  /sel4
"          mem_io { 7      14 }  /sel3
"            /rd  { 8      13 }  /sel2
"            /wr  { 9      12 }  /sel1
"            Gnd  {10      11 }  I
"                    |_____|
"
```

```
"

" Pin Assignments:

  " Inputs:

        a19      pin 1                         " address line 19
        a18      pin 2                         " address line 18
        a17      pin 3                         " address line 17
        a16      pin 4                         " address line 16
        a15      pin 5                         " address line 15
        a14      pin 6                         " address line 14
        mem_io   pin 7                         " memory/I/O select
        !rd      pin 8                         " read strobe, active low
        !wr      pin 9                         " write strobe, active low
        nc       pin 11

   " Outputs:

        sel1     pin 12 = neg com feed_or      " memory select 1, active
low
        sel2     pin 13 = neg com feed_or      " memory select 2, active
low
        sel3     pin 14 = neg com feed_or      " memory select 3, active
low
        sel4     pin 15 = neg com feed_or      " memory select 4, active
low
        mrd      pin 16 = neg com feed_or      " memory read strobe,
active low
        mwr      pin 17 = neg com feed_or      " memory write strobe,
active low
        iord     pin 18 = neg com feed_or      " I/O read strobe, active
low
        iowr     pin 19 = neg com feed_or      " I/O write strobe,
active low


EQUATIONS

    sel1 = !(a19 & /a18 & mem_io)

    sel2 = !(a19 & !a18 & a17 & a16 & !a15 & !a14 * mem_io)

    sel3 = !((!a19 & a18 & !a17 & mem_io) #
            (a19 & !a18 & !a17 & mem_io))

    sel4 = !(!a19 & !a18 & !a17 & mem_io)
```

```
mrd = !(mem_io & rd)

mwr = !(mem_io & wr)

iord = !(!mem_io & rd)

iowr = !(!mem_io & wr)
```

" End of PEEL File: PEELBK.APL

The APEEL software runs on IBM PCs and compatibles, and is available from ICT as part of their no-charge PEEL Evaluation Kit, or as part of their PEEL Development System (PDS-1). The PEEL Development System (under $800) includes the APEEL software as well as a device programming unit for programming ICT's EEPLDs. The programmer includes a half-slot board that plugs into an IBM PC backplane slot. The APEEL software included with PDS-1 performs extra functions related to accessing the programming unit.

A+PLUS—Altera Programmable Logic User System (Altera)

To support its CMOS EPLDs, Altera has developed its *A+PLUS* software package. Unlike the other manufacturer-dependent languages described above, A+PLUS is in the same class as the third-party PLD languages (such as CUPL and ABEL) in terms of capability. Most PLD manufacturers tend to put their greatest effort into the development of new devices, with support software handled by a relatively small group of people that cannot practically develop an advanced PLD support package. Altera, on the other hand, sees the importance of PLD software support from a different perspective. Since many of its devices achieve a higher level of complexity than most other PLD manufacturers, Altera does not feel its devices can be adequately supported by existing third-party PLD languages.

Because Altera also realizes the importance of good software support for effective utilization of available logic resources within its devices, the company staffs nearly as many software designers as hardware designers. The result is advanced development software that keeps pace with new PLD architectures as they are introduced. A+PLUS supports design entry in several formats, including Boolean equation entry, state machine entry (optional), netlist entry, and schematic entry (optional). It accepts schematics generated by FutureNet's DASH, P-CAD's PC-CAPS, and Altera's own LogiCaps. Of course it works best with LogiCaps, since LogiCaps is optimized for use with A+PLUS.

Like APEEL, A+PLUS permits flexibility in the operators used in Boolean equations. It supports the conventional operators used by all of the languages described above, and also supports the operators popularized by CUPL and ABEL. A+PLUS also permits a "postfix" apostrophe (') to be used as a NOT operator. Thus, A+PLUS defines the following logical operators:

  * & = AND operators

  + # = OR operators

  / ! ' = NOT operators

And the following equations are equivalent:

$$out1 = /in1 * /in2 + in3$$
$$out1 = !in1 \& !in2 \# in3$$
$$out1 = in1' * in2' + in3$$

To minimize the EPLD logic requirements of compiled designs, A + PLUS includes a logic minimizer which incorporates a modified Quine-McCluskey logic reduction algorithm. The software can also intelligently apply DeMorgan's theorem, giving generous freedom in the format of Boolean equations. For example, A + PLUS will accept an active-low output equation in the format,

$$out = /(in1 * /in2 + in3)$$

as well as in the format,

$$/out = in1 * /in2 + in3$$

treating the two equations identically.

The A + PLUS software package includes several features to simplify the design effort for the designer. The software can automatically select the best (smallest) Altera EPLD for a specified design, and can also automatically assign the pin numbers to all input and output signals. Of course these automatic features can be overridden if desired.

For its LogiCaps schematic entry system, Altera also offers an optional MacroFunctions library. This library contains numerous 7400-series and 4000-series TTL and CMOS devices familiar to most logic designers. The PLD designer can then use these standard parts—MacroFunctions—to create designs. LogicCaps translates the resulting schematic designs into acceptable Altera Design Files (ADFs) which can then be processed by A + PLUS. LogiCaps uses an intelligent MacroFunction translation algorithm, and unused gates or functions are automatically eliminated. For example, if a 7474 dual D-type flip-flop MacroFunction is specified in a design but only one of the two flip-flops is used, the unused flip-flop is automatically eliminated from the design, and does not appear in the generated ADF.

Once a design has been entered, it can be compiled and minimized by the A + PLUS compiler. The final output is a standard JEDEC output file. Altera's optional Functional Simulator can then be used to test the functionality of the design before programming real parts. A + PLUS also generates a Utilization Report to indicate which of a part's resources have been utilized by the design, and how they have been used. For sequential (state machine) designs using Altera's SAM (Stand-Alone Microsequencer) devices, Altera offers a separate *SAM + PLUS* software package, which is used in conjunction with A + PLUS.

An example A + PLUS design (.ADF) file is shown in Listing 5-7. The design is functionally identical to those given for other manufacturer-dependent languages. In this case, an Altera EP310 EPLD is used to generate the memory select signals and memory and I/O read/write strobes. As with the PLS153 and PEEL18CV8 devices used in other designs, the EP310 design is a pin-for-pin functional replacement for the PAL16L8-based design. Notice in Listing 5-7 how the A + PLUS software accepts the multiple levels of parentheses used in the 'sel3' equation.

Listing 5-7. Example A + PLUS Design

```
Roger C. Alford
none
January 24, 1988
1.00
A
EP310
Memory Selector


%
Description:
      This A+PLUS file defines the memory select outputs
      generated by an EP310 EPLD device. Memory and I/O read
      and write strobes are also generated.

      Input Signals:
         a14-a19 are address lines
         mem_io is active low for I/O accesses
         /wr and /rd are the write and read strobes, respectively

      Output Signals:
         /mrd is the memory read strobe
         /mwr is the memory write strobe
         /iord is the I/O read strobe
         /iowr is the I/O write strobe
         The following memory select ranges are defined:
               /sel1 = C0000-FFFFF (256K)
               /sel2 = B0000-B3FFF (16K)
               /sel3 = 40000-5FFFF or 80000-9FFFF (256K)
               /sel4 = 00000-1FFFF (128K)
%

OPTIONS: TURBO=OFF
PART: EP310

INPUTS:
      a19@1,a18@2,a17@3,a16@4,a15@5,a14@6,
      mem_io@7,rd@8,wr@9

OUTPUTS:
      sel1@12,sel2@13,sel3@14,sel4@15,
      mrd@16,mwr@17,iord@18,iowr@19


NETWORK:

   % Inputs: %
```

```
        a19 = inp(a19)              % address line 19 %
        a18 = inp(a18)              % address line 18 %
        a17 = inp(a17)              % address line 17 %
        a16 = inp(a16)              % address line 16 %
        a15 = inp(a15)              % address line 15 %
        a14 = inp(a14)              % address line 14 %

    % Outputs: %
        sel1 = conf(sel1c,)         % memory select 1, active low %
        sel2 = conf(sel2c,)         % memory select 2, active low %
        sel3 = conf(sel3c,)         % memory select 3, active low %
        sel4 = conf(sel4c,)         % memory select 4, active low %
        mrd  = conf(mrdc,)          % memory read strobe, active low %
        mwr  = conf(mwrc,)          % memory write strobe, active low %
        iord = conf(iordc,)         % I/O read strobe, active low %
        iowr = conf(iowrc,)         % I/O write strobe, active low %


EQUATIONS:

    % Intermediate Equations %

        mem_cycle = mem_io;
        io_cycle  = /mem_io;

    % Output Equations %

        sel1c = /(a19 * a18 * mem_cycle);

        sel2c = /(a19 * /a18 * a17 * a16 * /a15 * /a14 * mem_cycle);

        sel3c = /(((/a19 * a18 * /a17) + (a19 * /a18 * /a17)) *
                    mem_cycle);

        sel4c = /(/a19 * a18 * /a17 * mem_cycle);
        mrdc  = /(mem_cycle * rd);

        mwrc  = /(mem_cycle * wr);

        iordc = /(io_cycle * rd);

        iowrc = /(io_cycle * wr);

END$
```

Altera's development software operates on IBM PCs and compatibles.
Altera's basic PLD development system—PLCAD4—includes the A + PLUS compiler and an EPLD device programmer. The programmer consists of a box with

ZIF (zero insertion force) sockets, and a full-size IBM PC plug-in controller board. PLCAD4 sells for approximately $3,000 without options.

iPLDS II—Intel Programmable Logic Development System II (Intel)

Intel Corp. offers its *iPLDS II* software to support its family of EPLDs. Like Altera's A + PLUS software, iPLDS II offers a complete, high-level programmable logic development environment competitive with the third-party languages. Intel's initial iPLDS software was merely a repackaged version of Altera's software, since Intel was the foundry and an alternate-source for Altera's EPLDs. Since then, however, Intel has begun developing new EPLDs independent of Altera, and has, therefore, developed its own software support—iPLDS II.

The basic iPLDS II software permits design entry either in Boolean equations or netlist. Optional packages permit state machine and schematic entry as well. In addition to supporting FutureNet's DASH and P-CAD's PC-CAPS schematic entry software, Intel has made special arrangements with Ovation to offer a special version of the company's popular Schema II schematic entry software. It is called Schema II-PLD. Like Altera's LogiCaps software, Schema II-PLD includes a library of the most common SSI/MSI TTL devices and other EPLD primitives, and directly outputs Advanced Design Files (ADFs), compatible with the iPLDS II compiler.

For logic minimization, iPLDS II uses the ESPRESSO II-MV logic reduction algorithm, developed and copyrighted by the University of California at Berkeley. ESPRESSO II-MV reduces the equations to the least possible number of product terms to allow as much logic as possible into Intel's EPLDs. After a compilation, the iPLDS II compiler outputs a Resource Utilization Report, describing the device resources that were utilized by the design.

Like Altera's PLCAD4 development system, the iPLDS II package runs on IBM PCs and compatibles, and includes a device programmer with an IBM PC plug-in board, and software for controlling the programmer.

ERASIC Development System (Exel)

To support its family of ERASIC EEPLDs, Exel Microelectronics introduced its *ERASIC Development System*. Like the Altera and Intel packages, Exel's package is designed to operate on IBM PCs and compatibles, and includes a PC-based device programmer. Unlike the other languages, however, Exel does not offer complete software support. Instead, the company merely offers special software supplements that work in conjunction with the established, industry-standard ABEL software from Data I/O Corp.

While most conventional PLD architectures consist of AND-arrays followed by OR-arrays (two-level logic)—lending themselves nicely to standard sum-of-products Boolean equations—Exel's ERASIC devices incorporate a NOR-foldback array architecture (see Chapter 3), which supports the implementation of multiple-leveled logic. Since the advanced features of this architecture are not normally supported by the existing third-party PLD languages—particularly CUPL and ABEL—Exel saw the need to develop its own support software. Instead of developing an entire new language, however, Exel chose to develop a software enhancement for the ABEL language.

ABEL has several functional modules that perform different operations in the PLD compilation process. One module is called *FUSEMAP*, and is responsible for generating a JEDEC output file for the PLD specified in the design. Another module, called *SIMULATE*, is responsible for simulating the operation of the design, based on designer-generated test vectors. Working with Data I/O, Exel programmers developed MultiMap and MultiSim, which replace ABEL's FUSEMAP and SIMULATE modules for ERASIC designs.

With MultiMap, ERASIC designs can include multiple-level logic and buried logic functions (such as S-R latches), not normally supported with conventional PLDs and the standard ABEL software. MultiSim, of course, allows the compiled design to be simulated. Although ABEL itself is available for other systems as well, Exel's MultiMap and MultiSim operate only on IBM PCs and compatibles.

XACT—Xilinx Advanced CAD Technology (Xilinx)

Like Exel's ERASIC devices, Xilinx' Logic Cell Array (LCA) devices do not conform to conventional PLD architectures, and existing third-party languages proved to be inadequate to support these "programmable gate arrays" (see Chapter 3). To support its devices, Xilinx therefore introduced its IBM PC-based *XACT* software. XACT is clearly different from any other PLD development language, being graphic oriented to permit line routing between various on-chip Configurable Logic Blocks (CLBs) and I/O Blocks (IOBs).

When using the XACT design editor for design entry, each CLB must be separately defined in terms of Boolean equations or Karnaugh maps. Xilinx does, however, offer software that allows schematics to be generated using FutureNet's DASH schematic entry system and other schematic entry software packages, using a special Xilinx device library. The schematic is then automatically partitioned into CLBs.

Once the design has been entered and routed, it is compiled by the XACT software. XACT is also capable of determining signal propagation delays based on the signal routing and the speed of the part selected. This is helpful in analyzing a design.

Xilinx also offers a development support feature not offered by any other PLD manufacturer—an in-circuit emulator: *XACTOR*. The XACTOR emulator connects to the target system in place of the actual LCA, and is completely controlled by an IBM PC or compatible by means of an RS-232 port. The designer can then download a compiled LCA design to the emulator and verify its operation. XACTOR makes it easy to check quick design changes, and can speed the LCA development cycle considerably. Of course, as larger devices are used (such as Xilinx' 9,000-gate XC3090 device), the value of the XACTOR emulator becomes even more pronounced.

XACT also supports an optional simulation packages: *P-SILOS*. This is a version of the Silos logic and timing simulator from SimuCad Corp. that supports the Xilinx LCAs. After a design has been entered and compiled, P-SILOS can be used to simulate critical paths and ensure proper operation under varying process, voltage, and temperature conditions.

While Xilinx' advanced software and hardware design support give the designer a great deal of aid in developing LCA-based designs, the software does not support a state machine entry format, and is therefore weak in this area. This is unfortunate considering that LCA devices contain many more registers than any other PLD architecture, making them particularly suitable for supporting state machine designs. State machine entry is an area that is likely to be addressed by Xilinx in the future. In the meantime there are other alternatives for state machine support. They are described later. Nonetheless, Xilinx supports its PLDs with enough power and capability for most design requirements. The XACT software, without options, costs around $3,000.

Since MMI is an alternate-source for Xilinx' LCAs, MMI also offers the XACT software for its LCA devices.

Action Logic System (Actel)

To develop designs for its desktop-configurable channeled gate arrays, Actel Corp. offers its *Action Logic System*. This development package includes the Viewdraw schematic entry software and Viewsim simulation software from Viewlogic Systems, as well as Actel's own Activator device programmer and other support software. The Action Logic System purports to offer the designer the same capability as when designing with standard mask-programmed gate arrays.

Other Manufacturer-Dependent PLD Languages

Although we have covered the primary manufacturer-dependent PLD languages, there are other PLD software packages available that were developed by PLD manufacturers. These additional software packages generally support devices with unique architectures that cannot be easily supported on the primary languages. The devices, in fact, are generally application-specific PLDs (ASPLDs). AMD, for example, has software development packages for its Am2971 Programmable Event Generator (PEG) and its Am29PL141 Fuse Programmable Controller (FPC), two state-machine/sequencer devices. For maximum efficiency, the trend will probably be toward integrating support for all devices into the primary software packages, and eliminating the special, device-specific software packages.

Another example of a manufacturer-dependent software package (with a twist) is the LC-9000 language from Programmable Logic Technologies—but the company is not a PLD manufacturer. Nonetheless, their software only supports GAL devices (developed by Lattice and alternated-sourced by other manufacturers), and in that respect it is a PLD-manufacturer-dependent language. Programmable Logic Technologies additionally sells a GAL device programmer called the Logic Lab.

PLD-Manufacturer-Independent Languages

While there are numerous manufacturer-dependent languages from which to choose, using such a PLD language generally restricts the designer to the devices produced by the PLD manufacturer. For the greatest design flexibility, however, it is desirable to have access to the devices offered by all, or at least several, PLD manufacturers. This is the primary intent of the third-party, manufacturer-independent languages. This goal is achieved to varying degrees by the different third-party languages, but with so many new and complex device architectures available and being regularly introduced, no language currently supports *all* existing PLDs. Nonetheless, the statistics verify the obvious; designers lean heavily on the third-party languages for a majority of PLD design support, and the percentage of designers using third-party languages is likely to continue increasing.

In this section we will look at the PLD support software available from third-party vendors.

CUPL—Universal Compiler for Programmable Logic (Logical Devices)

In 1981 a company called Assisted Technology was formed to develop programmable logic design tools. The company was later purchased by Personal CAD Systems, Inc. (P-CAD), a manufacturer of personal computer-based schematic CAD software. In 1988 the programmable logic compiler that P-CAD had acquired changed hands again. It was sold to Logical Devices, a manufacturer of device programmers. Seeing the need for a universal PLD language offering support for the devices from all PLD manufacturers, Assisted Technology founder Bob Osann set out to pioneer such a language. In September, 1983, Assisted Technology released version 1.01a of its *CUPL (Universal Compiler for Programmable Logic* compiler, supporting 29 devices. CUPL has matured over the years, and now supports many devices from nearly all PLD manufacturers. CUPL's PLD support includes PROMs.

CUPL is a powerful language and supports Boolean equation, truth table, and state diagram design entry. The language also optionally supports schematic entry using P-CAD's PC-CAPS schematic capture software package and others. The compiler supports four levels of logic reduction, selectable by the designer. This flexibility can be very important since it is sometimes desirable to maintain redundant logic terms in a design.

As described earlier, CUPL uses the pound sign (#) for its OR operator, the ampersand (&) for its AND operator, and the exclamation point (!) for its NOT operator. The language also uses the dollar sign for its XOR operator, and the conventional '=' and ':=' assignment operators for combinatorial and registered equations, respectively.

With the exception of Altera's A+PLUS software, CUPL is considerably more advanced than virtually every manufacturer-dependent language described earlier (not counting XACT, since it cannot be easily compared). CUPL supports set operations, string substitution, file inclusion (i.e., multiple files can make up a design), and conditional compilation. It also supports simulation of user-specified test vectors.

Listing 5-8 shows an example CUPL design specification. The design is functionally the same as those given earlier for the manufacturer-dependent languages. A PAL16L8 is used to generate memory select signals and memory and I/O read/write strobes.

Listing 5-8. Example CUPL Design

```
Name          CUPLBK;
Partno        1234;
Date          1/16/88
Revision      A
```

```
Designer        Roger C. Alford;
Company ;
Assembly        A1234;
Location        U92;
Device          P16L8;

/* Description:

        This CUPL file defines the memory select outputs
        generated by a PAL16L8 device. Memory and I/O read and
        write strobes are also generated.

Input Signals:
        a14-a19 are address lines
        mem_io is active low for I/O accesses
        /wr and /rd are the write and read strobes, respectively

Output Signals:
        /mrd is the memory read strobe
        /mwr is the memory write strobe
        /iord is the I/O read strobe
        /iowr is the I/O write strobe
        The following memory select ranges are defined:
                /sel1 = C0000-FFFFF (256K)
                /sel2 = B0000-B3FFF (16K)
                /sel3 = 40000-5FFFF or 80000-9FFFF (256K)
                /sel4 = 00000-1FFFF (128K)
*/

/** Input Pin Definitions **/
Pin 1   = a19;                  /* address line 19 */
Pin 2   = a18;                  /* address line 18 */
Pin 3   = a17;                  /* address line 17 */
Pin 4   = a16;                  /* address line 16 */
Pin 5   = a15;                  /* address line 15 */
Pin 6   = a14;                  /* address line 14 */
Pin 7   = mem_io;              /* memory/I/O select */
Pin 8   = rd_n;            /* read strobe, active low */
Pin 9   = wr_n;           /* write strobe, active low */

/** Output Pin Definitions **/
Pin 12  = sel1_n;              /* memory select 1, active low */
Pin 13  = sel2_n;              /* memory select 2, active low */
Pin 14  = sel3_n;              /* memory select 3, active low */
Pin 15  = sel4_n;              /* memory select 4, active low */
Pin 16  = mrd_n;              /* memory read strobe, active low */
Pin 17  = mwr_n;              /* memory write strobe, active low */
Pin 18  = iord_n;             /* I/O read strobe, active low */
```

```
Pin 19  = iowr_n;                    /* I/O write strobe, active low */

/** Internal Logic Equations **/
        mem_cycle       = mem_io;
        io_cycle        = !mem_io;
        rd              = !rd_n;
        wr              = !wr_n;

/** Equations **/
        sel1_n = !(a19 & a18 & mem_cycle);

        sel2_n = !(a19 & !a18 & a17 & a16 & !a15 & !a14 & mem_cycle);

        sel3_n = !((((!a19 & a18 & !a17) # (a19 & !a18 & !a17)) &
                        mem_cycle);

        sel4_n = !(!a19 & !a18 & !a17 & mem_cycle);

        mrd_n = !(mem_cycle & rd);

        mwr_n = !(mem_cycle & wr);

        iord_n = !(io_cycle & rd);

        iowr_n = !(io_cycle & wr);

/** End of CUPL File: CUPLBK.PLD **/
```

Because the number of PLD types is constantly increasing, Logical Devices is committed to updating CUPL periodically to support new devices as they are developed. Ideally, of course, the availability of design support for new devices will be coincident with the introduction of the devices.

CUPL is available for IBM PCs and compatibles, as well as CP/M, VAX/Unix, and VAX/VMS machines. The IBM PC version sells for approximately $1,000.

ABEL—Advanced Boolean Expression Language (Data I/O)

Following in the footsteps of its Assisted Technology competitor, Data I/O Corp.—the leading manufacturer of EPROM and PLD device programmers—introduced the *ABEL* language. A functionally good compiler combined with the backing of a large corporation quickly put ABEL in the lead as the number-one-selling PLD development language.

ABEL is similar to CUPL in capability and syntax, offering Boolean equation, truth table, and state diagram design entry. ABEL also supports schematic entry using the FutureNet (a Data I/O company) DASH schematic entry system, in conjunction with the optional DASH-ABEL translator package. For logic minimization ABEL uses the PRESTO algorithm and, like CUPL, supports four levels of logic reduction.

For communicating with its PLD programmers from a personal computer, Data I/O offers its *PROMlink* program. Data I/O also offers another support package,

PLDtest, which can help generate test vectors for device test. PLDtest is primarily useful for production test of PLDs, and is described in Chapter 7.

An example ABEL design specification is shown in Listing 5-9. Again, the design is functionally the same as those given earlier. A PAL16L8 is used to generate memory select signals and memory and I/O read/write strobes. Notice the similarity between the ABEL and CUPL design specifications.

Listing 5-9. Example ABEL Design

```
module  ABELBK

title   'Memory Selector'

" Author: Roger C. Alford
" Date: 1/16/88
" File: ABELBK.ABL

ABELBKdv          device'P16L8';

" Description:
"
"       This ABEL file defines the memory select outputs
"       generated by a PAL16L8 device. Memory and I/O read and
"       write strobes are also generated.
"
"       Input Signals:
"         a14-a19 are address lines
"         mem_io is active low for I/O accesses
"         /wr and /rd are the write and read strobes, respectively
"
"       Output Signals:
"         /mrd is the memory read strobe
"         /mwr is the memory write strobe
"         /iord is the I/O read strobe
"         /iowr is the I/O write strobe
"         The following memory select ranges are defined:
"             /sel1 = C0000-FFFFF (256K)
"             /sel2 = B0000-B3FFF (16K)
"             /sel3 = 40000-5FFFF or 80000-9FFFF (256K)
"             /sel4 = 00000-1FFFF (128K)


' Input Pin Definitions:
a19     Pin     1;                  " address line 19
a18     Pin     2;                  " address line 18
a17     Pin     3;                  " address line 17
a16     Pin     4;                  " address line 16
a15     Pin     5;                  " address line 15
```

```
a14     Pin     6;                      " address line 14
mem_io  Pin     7;                      " memory/I/O select
rd_n    Pin     8;                      " read strobe, active low
wr_n    Pin     9;                      " write strobe, active low

' Output Pin Definitions:
sel1_n  Pin     12;                     " memory select 1, active low
sel2_n  Pin     13;                     " memory select 2, active low
sel3_n  Pin     14;                     " memory select 3, active low
sel4_n  Pin     15;                     " memory select 4, active low
mrd_n   Pin     16;                     " memory read strobe, active low
mwr_n   Pin     17;                     " memory write strobe, active low
iord_n  Pin     18;                     " I/O read strobe, active low
iowr_n  Pin     19;                     " I/O write strobe, active low

' Internal Logic Equations:
        mem_cycle = mem_io;
        io_cycle  = !mem_io;
        rd        = !rd_n;
        wr        = !wr_n;

Equations
        sel1_n = !(a19 & a18 & mem_cycle);

        sel2_n = !(a19 & !a18 & a17 & a16 & !a15 & !a14 & mem_cycle);

        sel3_n = !((((!a19 & a18 & !a17) # (a19 & !a18 & !a17))
                    & mem_cycle);

        sel4_n = !(!a19 & !a18 & !a17 & mem_cycle);

        mrd_n = !(mem_cycle & rd);

        mwr_n = !(mem_cycle & wr);

        iord_n = !(io_cycle & rd);

        iowr_n = !(io_cycle & wr);

end     ABELBK
```

Like its P-CAD counterpart, ABEL is regularly updated to include support for new devices as they are introduced. There are also unique situations, as with Exel Microelectronics (described earlier), where a company may develop software for its devices that merely supplements ABEL. Exel's software will not work with CUPL (or any other language), and ABEL was clearly chosen because of its volume lead in the PLD industry.

ABEL is available for a variety of different systems, including IBM PCs and compatibles, VAX/VMS, VAX/Unix, Sun, Valid, and Apollo/Mentor. The IBM PC version of ABEL sells for approximately $1,500.

PLDesigner—Programmable Logic Device Designer (Minc)

Feeling that existing third-party PLD languages were inefficient to design with, and inadequate for complex designs, a group of four Hewlett-Packard Co. employees left their secure environment to develop a new, more-advanced PLD language. The HP spinoff, Minc, Inc., began shipping its *PLDesigner* in February, 1988.

PLDesigner implements several new and unique features for advanced operation. In addition to Boolean equation, truth table, state machine, and schematic design entry methods, PLDesigner also supports *waveform* entry. Waveform entry allows the designer to graphically enter the input signals and desired output waveforms of a sequential device, and the compiler automatically generates the appropriate equations.

PLDesigner does not require the PLD to be specified at design time. A complete design can be entered and compiled without a device being selected. After a design has been compiled, PLDesigner will list all of the devices in its library that will accept the specified design, and allow the designer to select the desired device. For complex designs multiple devices can be specified, and PLDesigner can automatically partition the logic among the different devices.

Unlike other third-party PLD languages, PLDesigner supports complex devices and architectures, including advanced Altera/Intel devices, and foldback logic devices (such as those from Exel and Signetics). PLDesigner uses a structured Pascal-like language, and supports nested function macros. It also includes advanced simulation capability—again with Pascal-like commands (similar to PALASM 2), allowing loops and conditional branches.

In addition to the standard JEDEC output format, PLDesigner also supports the increasingly popular EDIF format (described later in this chapter), used for CAE (computer-aided engineering) system design transfer.

PLDesigner operates on IBM PCs and compatibles, and costs approximately $4,500.

PLD Design System (Hewlett-Packard)

Interestingly, at about the same time Minc introduced its PLDesigner software (early 1988), Hewlett-Packard Co. released its *PLD Design System* software package, touting many of the same features. Unlike most other PLD software packages, HP's PLD Design System does not run on IBM PCs and compatibles; instead, it operates on the company's own HP 9000 Series 300 workstations.

Like Minc's PLDesigner, the PLD Design System allows the PLD logic specification to be entered without regard to specific devices. After the logic design has been entered, the software can optionally select a device or devices that will support the defined logic (from the list of allowable devices specified by the designer), or it can provide a list of acceptable devices from which the designer can choose. The PLD Design System software is also capable of automatically partitioning a design into multiple PLDs. In addition, the software allows the designer to identify speed-critical signals. The software will then partition the design in such a way that the high-speed signals remain on a single chip for best performance.

HP's PLD Design System supports the same logic entry alternatives as Minc's PLDesigner, including waveform entry. It also can work in conjunction with HP's Electronic Design System, using the same schematic entry system. Unlike most third-party software packages, the PLD Design System even supports complex devices, like Altera's EP1800. An optional feature with the PLD Design System is automatic test vector generation, which creates test vectors that will detect all stuck-at-0 and stuck-at-1 faults in the devices, as well as fuses that are faulted in the opposite state.

Although the PLD Design System is certainly an advanced software package, its capability is unfortunately reflected in its price. The package costs between $8,000 and $14,500 depending on options.

FutureDesigner (FutureNet)

FutureNet Corp. has its FutureDesigner software package to assist in the development of complex PLD designs. FutureDesigner also bridges the gap to gate arrays and allows entered designs to be compiled for PLD or gate array implementation. This feature lets designs be implemented using PLDs for prototyping and/or initial production, then later changed to gate-array implementation for volume production. FutureDesigner supports semiautomatic design partitioning for multiple-PLD designs, and optionally supports advanced logic simulation.

The cost of FutureDesigner, which runs on IBM PCs and compatibles, is approximately $8,000 for the base package, $4,000 for the schematic entry software, and $6,000 for the CADAT simulator and translation software.

LOG/IC (Elan, Kontron, Isdata)

Elan Digital Systems, Kontron Electronics, and Isdata (in Europe) sell the *LOG/IC* (or *LOG/iC*) software package. LOG/IC is a screen-oriented PLD development tool that allows designs to be entered independent of the device(s) to be used. It also supports automatic design partitioning, as with Minc's PLDesigner and HP's PLD Design System. The software accepts design input in the form of logic equations, truth tables, state diagrams, and, optionally, schematic entry.

LOG/IC includes a test vector simulator, and is also capable of generating test vectors for full-fault coverage of programmed devices. As with Future-Designer, LOG/IC can also support gate array designs. An optional advanced simulator is also available.

The software is partitioned into modules, with each module sold separately. The software is available for IBM PCs and compatibles, as well as Apollo workstations, DEC VAX/VMS and VAX/UNIX computers, and Prime minicomputers. The base PC software costs approximately $2,000 (including PAL, FPLA, and PROM support). Additional modules for gate array or microprogramming support are sold at additional cost. The advanced simulator (available only for IBM PCs and compatibles and the DEC VAX) costs approximately $900.

PLDE—Programmed Logic Design Environment (ALDEC)

The *Programmed Logic Design Environment (PLDE)* is another PLD development tool that runs on IBM PCs and compatibles. It is available from Automated

Logic Design Co. (ALDEC). PLDE allows the designer to enter multiple-PLD designs with additional "glue" (support) logic, and is capable of simulating the entire design. The base price is approximately $3,000, with the optional compiler costing around $2,000.

Erasable Logic Development System (Pistohl)

Another PLD software package appeared on the market in early 1988 from Pistohl Electronic Tool Co., the *PET100-Series Erasable Logic Development System*. The basic unit includes an IBM PC-based device programmer, and Pistohl's Erasable Logic Assembler. The company also offers a Professional Erasable Logic Development System, which includes four personality modules for the device programmer, and telephone support. The assembler accepts only Boolean equations for input, and supports only CMOS programmable logic devices. The basic package sells for approximately $800, with the Professional package costing somewhere in the area of $1,000.

PLD Master (Daisy)

In 1986, Daisy Systems released a PLD design software package that runs on its workstations: *PLD Master*. PLD Master works in conjunction with other, standard PLD compilers, including ABEL, PALASM, and AMAZE, to create a highly integrated design environment for the system designer. It takes advantage of the system's multiwindow environment, and allows the designer to view several portions of the design simultaneously. For example, an output waveform, an ABEL source file, a system block diagram, and a JEDEC output file may all appear on the screen simultaneously.

PLD Master supports a hierarchical system design approach, allowing sections of a system design to be specified as blocks. Each block can be broken down into more, lower-level blocks having more-specific functionality. This hierarchy continues to the circuit level. The logic requirements for a circuit block—including inputs, outputs, and transfer functions—can be defined and simulated on the system, with the output presented as waveforms. The transfer functions can be defined in terms of schematic entry, Boolean equations, or state machine entry. Once a logic block has been defined, it can also be simulated within the context of the entire system, to see if the defined timing and logic functions work properly with other logic blocks. The iterative design/ simulation procedure can take place without ever prototyping any circuits or programming any PLDs.

Once the design definition is complete and ready for implementation, specific programmable logic devices can be specified to implement the logic requirements of the system. PLD Master outputs a standard JEDEC PLD file for compatibility with virtually all PLD programmers.

PLD Master sells for about $6,500, and is available for all of Daisy's systems. One of Daisy's systems—the Personal LOGICIAN—is IBM PC-based, but runs a propriety operating system.

Other Design Support Software

A number of other software packages are available that support various aspects of programmable logic design. Instead of being designed strictly for programmable logic design support, these software packages generally include program-mable logic as part of a larger design support objective. Some are oriented toward gate-array support, but include PLD support for prototyping or initial system production. Others are advanced, general-purpose CAE packages that include programmable logic support.

The *gate-level* simulation support offered by most of these advanced pack-ages is a much higher level of simulation than that offered by the PLD languages described above. Gate-level simulation can identify propagation delay problems in the PLD's interaction with other system components, and can also identify potential glitches and race conditions. Other conditions, such as register set-up and hold time violations, can also be detected.

Mentor Graphics is a manufacturer of workstations used for electronic system modeling and gate-level logic simulation. Logic Automation offers SmartModel simulation models for many PLDs; these models are designed to work with Mentor Graphics' systems.

Case Technology sells its Vanguard CAE Design System software for IBM PCs and DEC VAXes. Vanguard optionally incorporates CUPL for PLD develop-ment, and supports gate-level simulation of several PLDs.

Cadnetix offers gate-level simulation on the company's workstations for many PLDs. The Cadnetix simulator is based on the industry-standard CADAT logic simulator. In addition to PLDs (and standard logic devices), modeling is also available for memory devices, including RAM and ROM, which can also be used as programmable logic devices.

Matra Design Semiconductor offers a Gate-Array CAD software package for IBM PC compatibles, designed to allow gate-array development. The software features the ability to accept several PLD designs and integrate them into a single gate array.

Other advanced software packages support digital logic design in general, without supporting programmable logic devices specifically. Some of these packages can be valuable in the development of complex PLD designs, by aiding in logic minimization, simulation, or state-machine design. These software packages often take advantage of artificial-intelligence technology to find a more efficient means of expressing a given design. Packages include Socrates (Synthesis and Optimization of Combinational circuits using a Rule-based And Technology-independent Expert System) from Calma Co., Logic Consultant from Trimeter, and Design Advisor from NCR Microelectronics.

Table 5-1 provides a summary of the features and cost for most of the PLD design languages described here.

PLD Language Considerations

With so many PLD support languages available, the decision of which one(s) to use may not be obvious. As part of its *1987 Programmable Logic Devices Users Study*, the Research Department of *Electronic Engineering Times* magazine

Table 5-1. Summary of Most PLD Design Languages

Software Pkg.	Mfr. Dep./ Indep.	Devices Supported	Entry-Methods						Logic Reduction ?	Approx. Cost ($)
			Boolean Equ.	Truth Table	Schematic	Netlist	State Mach.	Waveform		
PALASM 2 MMI (AMD)	D	Company's Own	X				X			0
AMAZE Signetics	D	Company's Own	X	X			X			0
PLAN National	D	Company's Own	X							200
HELP Harris	D	Company's Own	X						Optional	0
PLPL AMD	D	Company's Own	X				X		X	0
APEEL ICT	D	Company's Own (PEEL)	X							0
A + PLUS Altera	D	Company's Own	X	X	X	X	X		X	3000
iPLDS II Intel	D	Company's Own	X	X	X	X	X		X	3500
ERASIC Dev. Exel	D	Company's Own	X	X	X	X	X		X	—
XACT Xilinx	D	Company's Own (LCA)	X	X	X				X	3000
Action Logic Actel	D	Company's Own	X	?	X	?			X	—
CUPL Logical Dev.	I	Many (Universal)	X	X	X	X	X		X	1000
ABEL Data I/O	I	Many (Universal)	X	X	X	X	X		X	1500
PLDesigner Minc	I	Many (Universal)	X	X	X	X	X	X	X	4500
PLD Design Sys HP	I	Many (Universal)	X	X	X	X	X	X	X	8000 +
LOG/IC Elan, others	I	Many (Universal)	X	X	X		X		X	2000
ELDS Pistohl	I	Several (CMOS PLDs)	X						?	800

NOTE: Software features and cost are subject to change. Check with vendors for current information.

asked PLD users to specify which PLD development software packages they use. While the two primary third-party languages—CUPL and ABEL—combined to support a majority of PLD users, at 22.0% and 44.6%, respectively, MMI's PALASM language was clearly dominant, at 52.4% (obviously a number of users used multiple languages). Altera's A + PLUS software followed CUPL at 16.1%.

The PLD marketplace has continued to change, however, and there is clearly an increasing trend toward the third-party languages, particularly in light of the more-complex PLDs that are becoming available. Similarly, the PLD software packages themselves are improving, and new, more-advanced packages, like PLDesigner, are becoming available. Let's take a look at the considerations involved in selecting a PLD development language.

Manufacturer-Dependent vs. Independent

Device support is an important consideration in selecting a PLD language. If, for example, a design intends to use one or more Xilinx LCAs, the language selection is limited to a single choice: XACT. If only PALs will be used, then one of the manufacturer-dependent languages may suffice, although the lack of logic minimization is a definite drawback. One of the third-party languages (e.g., CUPL, ABEL, or PLDesigner) may be the best choice. Similarly, if a designer wants to use a variety of PLDs, one of the third-party languages is quite likely to be the best choice (the only potential obstacle being cost).

Of course a designer could get a copy of AMAZE from Signetics, PLPL from AMD, and PALASM 2 from MMI. While this alternative may cost less money, there are several drawbacks. First, the design entry is inconsistent among the three languages. Instead of learning a single (third-party) language, the designer must learn three different languages. Second, logic reduction will be minimal at best with the manufacturer-dependent languages, and state machine and schematic entry are generally not supported as well as on the third-party languages. Third, the task of keeping all of the software packages updated quickly becomes arduous. Finally, the varying syntax of the different languages makes understanding and maintenance of the PLD design specifications—especially by other parties, such as technicians—extremely difficult, inefficient, and error-prone.

In general, a manufacturer-dependent language should only be used when only devices from the manufacturer (or an alternate-source) are being used, or when one or more devices being used in a design are not supported by a third-party language (such as a newly introduced part or a special ASPLD). Of course, there are exceptions to the general rule. If a design will only use MMI PALs, except for a single LCA, then XACT must be used in addition to the PAL compiler, which may be National's PLAN, AMD's PLPL, or MMI's PALASM 2 software.

From the standpoint of the designer, the primary advantage of using manufacturer-dependent languages (in addition to cost) is simply to support newly introduced devices not otherwise supported by the third-party languages. PLD manufacturers have ulterior motives. From the standpoint of the PLD manufacturers, the primary benefit of designers using their software is that the designers are more likely to buy their devices. As a general rule, it is best to rely primarily on a manufacturer-independent, third-party PLD language.

Logic Design Entry Methods

Another consideration in the selection of a PLD language is the design entry methods supported by the language. All languages support Boolean equation entry, although the languages vary in terms of parentheses support, and equation format flexibility. Some languages require sum-of-products form, others are less restrictive. Several of the languages support schematic entry, although to varying degrees and with different schematic entry packages. If a designer already uses a particular schematic entry package and wants to use schematic entry for his or her PLD designs, then a language that works with that schematic entry package should be considered.

If state machines are to be used, a language that supports state diagram entry is highly recommended. Truth table, netlist, and waveform entry are other design entry methods to consider. In some cases there are other alternatives for missing design entry methods. For example, if XACT is to be used for an LCA design and state machine input is required (though not normally supported by the software), the state machine entry of another software package, such as ABEL, could be used. By creating an ABEL design using a "dummy" PLD, the desired state machine design could be entered and compiled. The reduced Boolean output equations from ABEL could then be manually entered into the XACT design specification and integrated into the LCA.

User Interface

The PLD language user interface is very important, and has a large influence on how easy and efficient the language is to operate. Menu-oriented languages are often desirable—especially for designers new to programmable logic—but may become inefficient and troublesome for experienced designers. The software should at least provide the option to bypass the menu system and compile by command.

Similarly, beginners may find it helpful to use software that walks the designer through the entire design process, such as Harris' HELP. However, beware of languages that do not permit this feature to be bypassed. Once the design methodology is familiar, it is generally more efficient to enter designs and make modifications using a standard, familiar text editor, and to compile by command.

Logic Reduction

Except for most low- to medium-complexity designs, PLD logic minimization is *very* important, and is often lacking in manufacturer-dependent languages. Logic minimization is especially important for designs incorporating schematic or state machine design input, since these input methods frequently result in equations with numerous terms. Since PLDs are logic-limited, and the designer generally desires to include as much logic as possible in every device, logic minimization can become a costly option to be without.

Test Vector Generation and Simulation

Test vectors are important for verifying the operation of a design, and for testing programmed devices (see Chapter 7). Most PLD languages support test vectors, at least minimally. But test vector support varies greatly. Languages that support test vectors also support the simulation of the test vectors. Some languages require the test vectors to be manually generated using 0s and 1s for all of the input and output signals. This can be tedious and error-prone. Other languages (such as PALASM 2) support structured commands that are defined in a simulation description, allowing loops and conditional branches. Test vectors are generated as specified in the simulation description.

Still, other languages can automatically generate test vectors, which is no help for design verification, but is helpful for testing programmed parts in production.

Advanced Features

There are other, advanced features offered by some languages that may make the design task easier for the designer. These include automatic device selection, automatic design partitioning, device-independent compilation, waveform design input, and EDIF file output. Most are offered by newer languages, such as Minc's PLDesigner and HP's PLD Design System.

System Support

System support is another area that may be a consideration for some designers. If an IBM PC or compatible computer is used as the host system for PLD development, almost all languages described in this chapter can be used. If the PLD design software is to be placed on a VAX or other system, only languages supporting the target system can be considered.

Cost

Last, but not least, cost is always a consideration. Clearly, the manufacturer-dependent languages feature the lowest cost, but they also offer the least amount of capability, flexibility, and device selection. As mentioned earlier, the more-powerful third-party languages should be used whenever possible.

PLD Development Services

There may be times when designers would prefer to specify the logic requirements (including speed) of a PLD, and have another source create the PLD design specification and select an appropriate device. Because of the increasing popularity of PLDs, services have become available to fill this niche.

In order to encourage sales of their own PLDs, many manufacturers are offering design support through local representatives or through distributors. While choosing to use a manufacturer representative for a PLD design may accomplish the task, the obvious limitation is the PLD device selection from which the final device will be chosen. Also, such sources often do not provide test vectors—or "complete" test vectors—useful for production testing of programmed parts.

The best approach is to use a company that is not associated with a specific PLD manufacturer. A much wider variety of devices is then available, and the finished design is likely to be more complete. One company that performs PLD designs is Programmable Devices. Programmable Devices provides the system designer with complete PLD designs, including documentation, simulation results, and test vectors for full production fault coverage. Devices are chosen for minimal cost, at the same time meeting the speed and power consumption requirements specified by the system designer. The PLD design support is an addition to Programmable Devices' other operations, which includes volume programming of PLDs. (See Appendix B for the address of Programmable Devices.)

JEDEC PLD File Format Standard

Virtually all standard PLD languages generate an output file that conforms to *JEDEC (Joint Electron Device Engineering Council) Standard No. 3-A*, released May, 1986, entitled "Standard Data Transfer Format Between Data Preparation System and Programmable Logic Device Programmer." The Standard No. 3-A is an enhancement over the original Standard No. 3, released October, 1983. As its name implies, the standard was developed to allow necessary information to be transferred from the PLD compiler to the PLD programmer. Let's take a brief look at the JEDEC PLD standard file format.

Listing 5-10 shows an example JEDEC PLD file. Since the file is in ASCII format, it can be easily edited, viewed, or printed. The JEDEC file must start with an STX (start-of-text) character (02 hex), and end with an ETX (end-of-text) character (03 hex). The file is broken down into fields. Except for the first field—the Design Specification field—each field begins with a field identifier and ends with an asterisk (*). Each identifier is a single character (letter), although additional characters may be used to identify subfields. Fields have different priorities. Some fields are required to be supplied by the development language. Others are required to be recognized by the programmer, or by a tester, and some fields are simply optional. The fields and subfields defined by the JEDEC standard are listed in Table 5-2.

Listing 5-10. Example JEDEC PLD File

```
ABEL(tm)  Version 2.02a  JEDEC file for: P16R4
Created on: 17-Sep-88 09:51 AM
Example PLD file
     Roger C. Alford*
QP20* QF2048*
L0000
111111111111111111111111111111111111
111111111101101111101110111111111
11111111110111101111101101111111111
0000000000000000000000000000000000
```

```
0000000000000000000000000000000000
0000000000000000000000000000000000
0000000000000000000000000000000000
0000000000000000000000000000000000
1111111111111111111111111111111111
1111111111011110110111011111111111
0000000000000000000000000000000000
0000000000000000000000000000000000
0000000000000000000000000000000000
0000000000000000000000000000000000
0000000000000000000000000000000000
0000000000000000000000000000000000
0000000000000000000000000000000000
0000000000000000000000000000000000
0000000000000000000000000000000000
0000000000000000000000000000000000
0000000000000000000000000000000000
0000000000000000000000000000000000
0000000000000000000000000000000000
0000000000000000000000000000000000
1111101110111011111110111111111
1111101101011111110110111111111
1111101111011011110110111111111
0000000000000000000000000000000000
0000000000000000000000000000000000
0000000000000000000000000000000000
0000000000000000000000000000000000
0000000000000000000000000000000000
1111101101011011111110111111111
1111101111011001111111011111111
1111101111011110110110111111111
1111101111011101110111111111111
0000000000000000000000000000000000
0000000000000000000000000000000000
0000000000000000000000000000000000
0000000000000000000000000000000000
0111111111011101110110111111111
1111101101011011111110111111111
1111101111011001111111011111111
1111101111011101110111011111111
0000000000000000000000000000000000
0000000000000000000000000000000000
0000000000000000000000000000000000
0000000000000000000000000000000000
1111111111111111111111111111111111
1111111111011111101101101111111111
1111111111011101111111111111111
0000000000000000000000000000000000
```

```
OOOOOOOOOOOOOOOOOOOOOOOOOOOOOOOOOOO
OOOOOOOOOOOOOOOOOOOOOOOOOOOOOOOOOOO
OOOOOOOOOOOOOOOOOOOOOOOOOOOOOOOOOOO
OOOOOOOOOOOOOOOOOOOOOOOOOOOOOOOOOOO
OOOOOOOOOOOOOOOOOOOOOOOOOOOOOOOOOOO
OOOOOOOOOOOOOOOOOOOOOOOOOOOOOOOOOOO
OOOOOOOOOOOOOOOOOOOOOOOOOOOOOOOOOOO
OOOOOOOOOOOOOOOOOOOOOOOOOOOOOOOOOOO
OOOOOOOOOOOOOOOOOOOOOOOOOOOOOOOOOOO
OOOOOOOOOOOOOOOOOOOOOOOOOOOOOOOOOOO
OOOOOOOOOOOOOOOOOOOOOOOOOOOOOOOOOOO
OOOOOOOOOOOOOOOOOOOOOOOOOOOOOOOOOOO*
VOOO1 CX1XXXXXXNXXLHHHHHN*
VOOO2 C10XXXXXXNXXLLHHHHN*
VOOO3 CXO11XXXXNXXLLLHHHLN*
VOOO4 CX1XXXXXXNXXLHHHHHN*
VOOO5 C10XXXXXXNXXLLHHHHHN*
VOOO6 CXOOOXXXXNXXLLLHHHLN*
VOOO7 CXOOOXXXXNXXLLLHHHLN*
VOOO8 CXOO1XXXXNXXLHLHHHHN*
VOOO9 CXO11XXXXNXXHHLLHHLN*
VOO10 CX1XXXXXXNXXLHHHHHHN*
VOO11 C10XXXXXXNXXLLHHHHHN*
VOO12 CXOOOXXXXNXXLLLHHHLN*
VOO13 CXOO1XXXXNXXLHLHHHHN*
VOO14 CXOO1XXXXNXXLHLHHHHN*
VOO15 CXOOOXXXXNXXHHLLHHLN*
VOO16 CXOXX1XXXNXXHHLLHHLN*
VOO17 CXOXXOXXXNXXLHHLHLHN*
VOO18 CXOXXXXXXNXXLHHLHLHN*
VOO19 CX1XXXXXXNXXLHHHHHHN*
C40CF*
3C4B
```

The Design Specification field begins immediately after the initiating STX character. While the contents of this mandatory field are not explicitly specified, the JEDEC standard recommends that the field consist of:

1. User's name and company

2. Date, part number, and revision

3. Manufacturer's device number

4. Other information

The Design Specification field must end with an asterisk.

The Note (N) field is simply used to place notes into the file, and is generally ignored by the device programmer or tester.

The Quantity (Q) or Value field specifies numeric values or limits that must be supplied to the programmer. Three Q subfields are defined, QF, QP, and QV.

Table 5-2. JEDEC Std. No. 3-A Field Identifiers

Identifier	Description
(none)	Design Specification
N	Note
QF	Number of Fuses in Device
QP	Number of Pins in Test Vectors
QV	Maximum Number of Test Vectors
F	Default Fuse State
L	Fuse List
C	Fuse Checksum
X	Default Test Condition
V	Test Vectors
P	Pin Sequence
D	Device (obsolete identifier)
G	Security Fuse
R	Signature Analysis, Resulting Vector
S	Signature Analysis, Starting Vector
T	Signature Analysis, Test Cycles
A	Access Time

The QF subfield specifies the number of fuses in the device, the QP subfield specifies the number of pins the device has, and the QV subfield specifies the maximum number of test vectors in the file (to help the programmer with allocating memory to hold the test vectors).

The three fields F, L, and C are used for device programming information. Since each fuse in a PLD can be assigned one of two states—zero (connection made, or fuse intact) or one (connection broken, or fuse blown)—binary digits are used to specify the fuse patterns. Within the PLDs, fuses are numbered sequentially, beginning with fuse 0. A device with 1,024 fuses, for example, would have fuses numbered from 0 to 1,023. The F field specifies the default fuse state (for fuse values not explicitly specified in the file), which is always either 0 or 1. The L field specifies the fuse list. The field begins with a (decimal) starting fuse number, which is followed by a space or a carriage return and a list of the fuse values (0s and 1s). The C field specifies a fuse checksum value, to help detect communication errors.

A number of fields are used for device testing, i.e., test vectors. The X field specifies the default test condition for test vectors that are not explicitly defined, or for the "don't-care" test conditions. The V field specifies a test vector. There are generally many test vectors in a JEDEC PLD file, and they are executed in *numeric* order, regardless of the order they are specified in the JEDEC file. The V field begins with a (decimal) test vector number, followed by a space, then followed by the test conditions for the various device pins (one test condition is specified for each device pin). Valid test condition specifiers include:

0	Apply logic 0 to pin (input)
1	Apply logic 1 to pin (input)
X	Apply default logic value to device
C	Clock (0-1-0) pin (input)
K	Clock (1-0-1) pin (input)
2–9	Apply super voltage
N	Do not test pin (power pin, etc.)
L	Test pin for logic 0 level (output)
H	Test pin for logic 1 level (output)
Z	Test pin for high-impedance state
P	Preload registers
B	Preload buried registers

Super voltages (test condition specifiers 2-9) are used to place some PLDs into a special test mode. Register preload (test condition specifiers P and B) can only be performed on certain PLDs. This is not universally supported, and generally requires a super voltage to be applied to the device.

The test vector test conditions are normally applied to the device pins in numerical order, left to right. The Pin (P) field can, however, be used to specify a different pin number ordering, if desired.

The A field defines the propagation delay for the test vectors, in one nanosecond increments. This may be useful for some advanced testers, but is generally unused.

Some PLD testers support signature analysis. The R, S, and T fields are used for such applications.

The G field specifies whether or not the device's security fuse is to be programmed. Of course, this field is optional and applies only to devices that have a security fuse.

EDIF File Format Standard

In 1983, realizing the need for data-exchange standards in CAE, six manufacturers of CAE tools—Daisy Systems, Motorola, National Semiconductor, Mentor Graphics, Tektronix, and Texas Instruments—began an effort to establish a standard CAE design exchange format. Out of this effort was born the *Electronic Design Interchange Format (EDIF)*. Version 2.0.0 of the standard was released in 1987, and has already been adopted for implementation by a number of companies. EDIF is expected to achieve standardization by the Electronic Industries Association (EIA), further promoting its use among CAE vendors and users.

Although Minc is the only PLD software supplier that has announced EDIF support for its PLD designs, it seems likely that others will also adopt this standard as its popularity increases. If properly implemented, PLD designs would become portable between the different PLD languages that support EDIF, despite the differences in language syntax. EDIF standardization may also allow PLDs to be more-easily integrated into system designs that exist on CAE systems that support the standard. While the future of the EDIF standard as it applies to PLD designs is still uncertain, it looks very promising.

Chapter Summary

In this chapter we looked at the wide variety of PLD languages available for supporting PLD designs, including those developed by PLD manufacturers—the manufacturer-dependent languages. Also covered were those developed by third-party vendors—the manufacturer-independent languages. We then looked at some of the tradeoffs and considerations involved with selecting PLD languages. Finally, we took a look at the JEDEC and EDIF file format standards.

Chapter 6

Designing with PLDs

The essence of this book is distilled in this chapter. While the other chapters provide necessary support material for the information presented here, the main goal is to teach the designer how to design with programmable logic devices. The design task involves much more than simply choosing one or more devices, developing equations, and plopping the resulting parts into a system. Indeed, there are numerous considerations that must be pondered, and only after careful analysis can a programmable logic design be realized—if PLDs are even appropriate.

Chapter Overview

In this chapter we will look at the considerations involved with programmable logic design. We will see how to determine when PLDs should and should not be used, how to choose the right devices for the design task, how to select the appropriate design tools, and how to generate the logic definitions. We will also look at design simulation, debugging, and verification. Finally, we will conclude with a brief look at available "starter" kits and booklets for new PLD designers and examine a PLD design example.

Defining Design Goals

The first step in any system or subsystem design should be the establishment of design goals. The designer should consider the following; functions and features to be implemented, speed requirements, durability requirements, power consumption limitations, and space constraints. The designer must also establish acceptable limits for product cost, development cost, and development duration, i.e., time-to-market. Of course, each of these design considerations must be viewed in the context of available technology and resources. To attempt the development of a $100 supercomputer in six months is unrealistic in terms of both cost and development duration. It is not uncommon for the designer—often in conjunction with marketing and product planning personnel—to repeat the design goal definition process several times before settling on a design specification that is both adequate and realistic.

PLDs vs. Other Logic Alternatives

As discussed in Chapter 1, the designer has several logic alternatives available from which to choose for a digital design. These include standard SSI and MSI logic devices (represented by the ubiquitous 74xx00-series logic devices), standard LSI and VLSI devices (such as microprocessors and associated peripheral devices), programmable logic devices, gate arrays, standard-cell devices, and full-custom devices. Each logic alternative offers its own advantages and disadvantages, and most digital designs use a mixture of devices from two or more of these categories. Microprocessor-based systems, for example, commonly use standard LSI devices (the microprocessor and its peripheral devices), standard SSI and MSI parts (gates and bus buffers), and programmable logic devices (for address decoding, bus arbitration, etc.).

In determining which logic alternatives are best to use, the designer must consider the related issues of device architectures, circuit board space, development time, expected production volume, and cost. Other considerations may also apply, such as special speed or power consumption requirements. When considering the effective cost of the various logic alternatives, the designer must take into account absolute part costs, and also amortize nonrecurring engineering (NRE) costs over the expected number of parts to be purchased during the life of the product.

Full-custom devices offer the least space and cost for devices to be manufactured in very high volume, since silicon space is used very efficiently. Unfortunately, full-custom devices also require the greatest amount of development time, and the highest NRE costs of any of the available alternatives.

Like full-custom devices, standard-cell devices are also space- and cost-efficient, but are restricted to combinations of standard circuits (cells). The development time and NRE costs of standard-cell devices are substantially less than those of full-custom parts, but more than those of gate arrays and PLDs. Standard-cell devices are generally restricted to high-volume applications.

Gate arrays require less development time and involve lower NRE costs than full-custom and standard-cell devices, but use silicon space less efficiently and thus cost more to manufacture. For sufficiently high volumes, however, gate arrays are generally more cost-effective than PLDs. Gate arrays are generally used in medium-high- to high-volume applications.

Programmable logic devices are the least demanding of the custom/semi-custom alternatives in terms of NRE costs, and also require the least amount of development time. For many applications, such as address decoders and state machines, PLDs require even less development time than standard SSI/MSI logic—an important feature! Nonrecurring engineering charges for PLDs are generally *zero*, once the one-time costs for development software and hardware have been spent. And, unlike the other custom/semicustom alternatives, PLDs allow multiple design iterations without repeating NRE charges and development time delays.

While PLDs are most beneficial for low- to medium-volume applications, they are not infrequently incorporated into high-volume systems. This is sometimes done to permit address decoding or other logic changes. There is a wide range of PLDs available, some of which extend into gate array densities. Thus, PLDs not only offer short development cycles, but can save a substantial amount of circuit board space in most applications, compared to equivalent SSI/MSI devices.

Circuit debugging is also generally faster and less tedious when using programmable logic. This is because devices can be quickly modified, reprogrammed, and retried, often without adding any "cuts and jumpers."

Standard SSI/MSI parts have the advantage of offering "zero development time" and no NRE costs. Because so few gates are used in a single IC package, however, circuit board usage is very inefficient and relative cost (cost per gate) is high. Other "invisible" costs are also higher with SSI/MSI devices, compared to PLDs. Since a single PLD will generally replace many SSI/MSI devices, procurement, inventory, testing, and other costs are multiplied when using SSI/MSI devices, costing more than the programmable logic alternative. Like PLDs, SSI/MSI parts are most beneficial for low- to medium-volume applications, although they are also commonly found in high-volume applications. Standard MSI devices, such as bus buffers and latches, appear in many high-volume applications.

Standard LSI/VLSI devices are virtually perfect. They require no development time or NRE cost, and use silicon space to its maximum efficiency. They are also low in cost and are useful for any volume, from low to very high. As a general rule, standard LSI/VLSI devices should be used in designs whenever possible.

Table 6-1 summarizes the various logic alternatives, and their merits. With these considerations in mind, and any others that may be appropriate, the designer must determine which types of devices should be used. The design will most likely consist of parts from several of the logic device categories. The remainder of this chapter describes the procedures for selecting and designing with PLDs. The designer must, of course, determine whether or not programmable logic is appropriate for a particular design.

Table 6-1. Comparison of Logic Alternatives

Logic Alternative	NRE Costs (typical)	Development Time	Design Iteration Penalty	Relative Device Cost/Gate	Prod. Volume (typical)
full-custom	very high	> 1 year	NRE + months	very low	> 100K
standard-cell	> $50K	months	NRE + Dev. Time	low	> 20K
gate array	$10K–50K	weeks-months	NRE + Dev. Time	med.-low	> 5K
PLD	$0	hours-week	hours	medium	< 10K
Std LSI/VLSI	$0	none	–	very low	any
Std SSI/MSI	$0	none	–	high	any

Choosing the Right PLDs

Once it has been determined that the use of PLDs is appropriate, the designer must select the best devices for the task. The design will most likely require a variety of different PLDs, although it is common for some PLDs to appear multiple times in a design. Design considerations can be broken down into three primary categories: functionality; design and development support; and manufacturing concerns. While each of these areas is important when considering which devices to use, the relative "weight" assigned to each category must be determined by the designer, based on the specific requirements of the design. Above all, however, the desired functionality must be met in order to take advantage of the programmable logic alternative.

Functionality Considerations

The PLD functionality issues involve device specifications. These include architecture, speed, power consumption, output types, output current drive, logical capability, input/output pin count, and operating temperature range. Other specifications or features may also be important in specific instances, such as erasability or in-circuit programmability.

Some of the functionality issues will be apparent from the design specification. For example, if a battery-operated portable system is being developed, the designer will certainly want to use low-power CMOS PLDs. Other PLD requirements become more obvious as the design progresses.

If a complex circuit with many inputs and outputs is to be implemented with programmable logic, the designer must often choose between using a single (or few) complex part with many pins, or several less-dense parts that may have other advantages (such as higher speeds). If multiple PLDs are to be used for the circuit, how the logic is to be *partitioned* and the requirements for each device must be determined. If a simple circuit is to be implemented in programmable logic, the input/output requirements may be straightforward, and may easily fit within the package constraints of a typical 20-, 24-, or 28-pin device. In this case, there are no partitioning concerns, so the designer can more easily select the PLD that meets the logical requirements of the circuit.

Some designs may require logic that can be reprogrammed in-circuit. This allows diagnostic logic to be loaded into the PLDs, and permits software-based in-circuit logic upgrades for design fixes or system address map changes. There are currently only two types of PLDs that easily permit this: RAM-based devices such as the LCAs from Xilinx and MMI, and +5V-only EEPROM-based PLDs available from Lattice and its alternate sources.

The designer should choose an efficient architecture appropriate for the application. Although devices with generic architectures are valuable and acceptable for many applications, including simple address decoders, low-complexity state machines, and "glue" logic, specialized or *application-specific* PLDs (ASPLDs) are more efficient when used in the applications for which they were designed. For example, an advanced state machine design would likely benefit from using one of the special state-machine-oriented devices that are available. Even among the nonapplication-specific PLDs, the designer will find many devices optimized for certain applications. Some devices, for example, include XOR gates to gear themselves toward counter applications, such as the PAL20X10. Similarly, some devices support multiple clocks for special synchronization requirements, like the PAL20RA10 which supports *asynchronous clocking*, where each output can be clocked individually. Still other devices, such as the PAL16A4, are oriented toward arithmetic operations.

Functionality is clearly the most important of the PLD-selection considerations, since the other considerations are without value if the required circuit functionality is not attained. Chapters 3 and 4 discuss the available PLD families and architectures in detail.

Design and Development Support Considerations

Once the PLDs have been selected, the designer must make sure design support tools are available to support the development effort. In general, the designer should have access to one or more logic compilers and a device programmer. The designer may also want to have access to other development aids such as a logic simulation program and/or a logic minimizer.

Depending on the programmable logic being used, other hardware support may also be available. For example, Xilinx offers a hardware emulator for use with its Logic Cell Array (LCA) devices.

The quality and cost of the development tools should also be considered. Of course, development software is essentially a one-time expense (not counting updates), so if a company already owns acceptable PLD compilers, the cost can be considered zero. The quality of development software is difficult to define, and will be discussed in more detail. As a rule, the software should support the designer's desired logic entry methods, and should offer some form of logic minimization and test vector simulation capability.

Another form of development support comes in the form of erasable PLDs. Depending on the IC technology used in the production parts, PLD erasability may not be practical or cost-effective during production. It is desirable, however, to have access to erasable parts during the debugging stage of a design, since parts can be quickly and easily erased and reprogrammed, without having to throw away many devices.

If production parts will use EEPROM technology, electrical (window-less) erasability is inherent, and the same parts used for production may be used during debugging. If EPROM-based parts are to be used, erasability is only possible if expensive windowed-ceramic packaging is used. The parts in economical plastic packaging are one-time programmable (OTP). Nonetheless, all OTP EPROM-based parts have windowed, erasable counterparts that can be used during the development cycle. If nonerasable bipolar or CMOS devices are to be used in production, erasable counterparts may also be available for development. For example, the ubiquitous bipolar PAL16L8 cannot be erased, but a logically equivalent, erasable, EPROM-based PALC16L8-35 is available from Cypress Semiconductor, and can generally be substituted during the development cycle. While EEPROM-based parts are the most ideal because of their quick erase cycle, EPROM-based parts also work well.

Development support should not be taken lightly, since it can substantially impact both the ease of development and the development time. If the designer has the option of choosing from among multiple different PLDs, the availability of development software and hardware tools for the different devices should be strongly considered when determining which devices to use. (See Chapter 5 for a look at PLD development aids.)

Production Considerations

With the possible exception of manufacturing only a very few systems, production considerations of PLDs cannot be left out of the PLD-choosing process. There are many interrelated considerations to be taken into account. The importance of each consideration must be determined jointly by manufacturing personnel and the system designer. Production factors that affect the decision include volume, time schedule, quality (testability) requirements, security requirements, and other factors.

Perhaps the most obvious production consideration is device cost, although cost factors are also an inherent part of every other production consideration, at least indirectly. Unit price alone cannot be used to determine the effective cost of using a particular device. The cost must be viewed in perspective with other production considerations.

Programming requirements make up another important consideration. Is programming equipment readily available? Is the necessary programming equipment in-house, or does it need to be purchased? Can parts be programmed in high quantity quickly? Can the PLD distributor program the parts to save cost? Can the parts be reused if the logic needs to be changed? These are some of the questions pertaining to programming requirements that should be answered when considering specific PLDs.

Testability and reliability are two more related production considerations. Erasable devices are generally fully tested at the factory, since they can be programmed with special logic patterns, verified, and erased. Devices that are EEPROM-based are especially testable, since they are capable of more iterations of testing within a reasonable period of time. EPROM-based parts, in contrast, must experience a 20-minute (typical) erase cycle between programmings. Bipolar PLDs see only limited testing at the factory, since device fuses can only be "blown" (programmed) once, and cannot be erased. PLDs are also typically tested after programming in the system-production environment. The designer must consider the ease and completeness of this testing.

Availability is also important when selecting parts for production use. Delays can be very costly. To improve both availability and unit cost, alternate sourcing of devices (or "functionally equivalent" devices) is desirable.

Finally, inventory considerations must be taken into account. If a device having a more-generic architecture can be used in place of multiple other devices, inventory (and purchasing) costs would be lower. For example, if a design might use a PAL16L8 and a PAL16R4, it may be preferable to use a

GAL16V8, since this part can "emulate" both of these PALs. If there are a large number of devices already in inventory, it may be desirable to incorporate some of those devices in the new design.

Chapter 7 discusses production considerations of PLDs in detail.

Choosing the Right Development Tools

One of the primary advantages of using programmable logic is the fast development time. Circuits can be transformed from concept to silicon in a matter of hours. Circuits that once required many error-prone hours of logic simplification can now be minimized in minutes. Instead of pages of state tables and corresponding Karnaugh maps, state machine design becomes a simple state diagram or if-then-else definition. Similarly, circuit changes are no longer arduous, but often simply a matter of altering the logic definition in a file and recompiling.

To take full advantage of these benefits, the designer must choose the right development tools. Depending on the PLDs used, the designer may have many or few design tools available from which to choose.

The designer must weigh the tradeoffs of the various development tools to determine which are best for the design. Some of the considerations are obvious, while others are not. When evaluating PLD compilers, the designer should consider adequate device support, logic reduction capability, test vector generation, and simulation capability. Also, the ability to support complex Boolean equations (multiple parenthetical levels with "free" format—i.e., not requiring a specific format such as Sum-of-Products format). Design input flexibility is also important, and should include more than one of: Boolean equations, truth tables, state machine, waveform, net list, and schematic. In general, the more the better.

It is also advantageous for the designer to "standardize" on one or two PLD compilers for virtually all of his or her PLD design work. Popular *universal* compilers, such as ABEL, CUPL, and PLDesigner allow the designer to become familiar with only a single PLD development package, while being able to support a large majority of existing PLDs. Standardizing on a single package allows the designer to become very efficient with the package, which permits the greatest degree of productivity and minimizes the PLD design and development cycle. These universal compilers also tend to offer greater functionality than other, manufacturer-specific compilers.

Cost, of course, must also be considered. For a small organization with extremely limited funds, the inexpensive or free PLD compilers offered by many of the programmable logic manufacturers may be the only acceptable alternatives. For other organizations planning on using PLDs in production systems or ongoing development work—even moderately small organizations—it is probably best to spend the $2,000 or more required to get a flexible, capable universal PLD compiler. Cost, of course, can be deceiving, and the flexibility and time savings offered by a universal compiler will generally pay for itself, when compared to the functionality of a typical inexpensive manufacturer-dependent compiler.

There are times when the PLD compiler choice is limited. This typically happens for particularly complex parts, such as the Logic-Cell Arrays (LCAs) available from Xilinx and MMI; for recently introduced parts—which may not yet be supported on a universal compiler—and for special-architecture devices, which are not easily supported by universal compilers. In these cases, manufacturer-provided compilers are often the only alternative for development tools.

For most designers, the only programmable logic development aid used is a PLD compiler. For complex designs, however, it is often helpful to use a logic simulator program that goes beyond the simple test vector simulation capability of most PLD compilers. Logic simulators allow complex logic circuits—with multiple PLDs—to be simulated, generating an output that reveals potential race conditions, glitches, and hang-up states, and calculates circuit propagation delays.

Many designers will want to use schematic entry to enter portions of their PLD designs. As this option becomes increasingly popular, more PLD compilers will support most or all of the popular schematic entry software packages. Some PLD vendors prefer to offer their own schematic entry software, such as Altera with its LogiCaps package. Most others, however, prefer to support other, third-party schematic entry packages, such as FutureNet's DASH, Personal CAD System's PC-CAPS, Omation's Schema, and Oregon Software's OrCAD.

For a few devices, most notably LCAs, hardware development tools are also available. Xilinx offers an in-circuit emulator for its LCAs which allows the logic definition to be downloaded into the LCA, and also allows monitoring of certain device operation characteristics. Other PLD hardware support may become available as devices continue to increase in complexity.

PLD development tools are discussed in detail in Chapter 5.

Determining the Best Logic Definition Form(s)

Having chosen the PLDs and development software, the designer must determine the best method or methods for entering the logic definition. This is often simply a matter of preference, but there are general guidelines that can be used in selecting the best logic definition forms. Of course, the logic definition alternatives supported by the development software will determine the options. On the other hand, it is not unreasonable to select the development software based partly on its support for desired logic definition input formats.

While many designs may simply use a single design definition entry format—typically Boolean equations—it is common for designs to incorporate two or more different input alternatives, since different formats are better for different logic functions.

Boolean Equations

Boolean equation entry is the most basic and universal form of logic definition entry for PLD compilers, being supported by every compiler. Although Boolean entry is universally supported and a good choice for a wide variety of design situations, the designer must use caution when choosing this approach. The flexibility and syntax of Boolean equation entry vary considerably from one compiler to another—another good reason to standardize on a particular PLD compiler. For example, one compiler may define an output pin as "active low," causing the equation "true" condition to generate a low output. Another compiler may require the equation to explicitly state the output polarity. Thus one compiler would generate an active low output for IN1 and IN2 high with the equation,

$$OUT = IN1 * IN2$$

while another compiler would require the equation,

$$OUT = /(IN1 * IN2)$$

for an active-low output. This often causes confusion for new PLD designers, and can be a source of frustration and apprehension. Perhaps the best approach is to study the compiler's documentation and examples carefully, then experiment until the compiler's syntax is clear.

Truth Tables

Truth table entry is convenient for some applications, most notably decoders (e.g., a BCD to 7-segment decoder) and address decoders with unusual requirements (particularly when using PROMs).

State Diagram

State machine or state diagram entry is valuable, of course, for state machine and sequencer designs. Even simple, four- to eight-state designs can greatly benefit from this entry format. The compiler is responsible for converting the state definitions into the proper equations for the PLD, and minimizing the equations—a time-consuming and error-prone task when done manually. Additionally, changes are very simple to make, streamlining the development process. In general, state diagram entry can save the designer more time and effort over manual or Boolean equation entry than any other design entry method. Thus, state diagram entry capability should be considered a mandatory PLD compiler feature when medium- to high-complexity state machines are being designed, and should be seriously considered for even simple state machines.

Waveform Entry

Some PLD compilers support waveform entry. This is especially valuable in the creation of sequencers, but can also be used in other registered designs. Waveform entry offers the designer *WYSIWYG* (what you see is what you get) entry of sequential designs, without the use of any Boolean equations. The compiler converts the waveforms into the appropriate logic equations. This can be a valuable, time-saving approach to sequencer designs.

Schematic Entry

Schematic entry has been growing steadily as a desirable entry alternative for PLD designers. Most digital logic designers are already comfortable with schematics—generally more so than with Boolean equations—and so schematic entry provides a simple, low-resistance path into programmable logic design. Schematic entry bypasses many of the fears and much of the learning curve typical of first-time PLD design, and alleviates the apprehension often experienced when first attempting Boolean equation-based designs.

Schematic entry is, and can be, valuable for many circuits, but the designer should be careful not to use it simply as a crutch. Proficiency at Boolean equation entry should be attained by *all* programmable logic designers, although its usage may be limited if desired. In addition to its convenience in many situations, schematic entry offers good documentation to PLD designs, generally allowing other designers to easily follow or modify the designs.

Net List

The net list entry option offered by some compilers allows nonsupported schematic entry packages to be supported by creating a net list conversion utility. The net list generated by the schematic entry software can then be converted into the format acceptable to the PLD compiler. This entry alternative also allows the designer to create a logic preprocessor—such as a special minimization program—which can then output its information in the compiler's net list format. Net list format, itself, is not generally used as a direct entry format by the designer.

Developing the Logic Definitions

Once the PLDs and development software have been selected for a project, the designer must develop the logic definitions for the devices. This involves creating *source files* using the chosen logic definition formats, then compiling the source files to create output files that can be used to configure (program) the PLDs. When creating the logic definitions for the PLDs in a system, the designer must consider logic partitioning for complex circuits, and be aware of device and compiler limitations that can lead to elusive circuit problems. Equally important is good documentation. The designer should consider good source file documentation a critical part of the logic definition process.

Design Partitioning

Depending on complexity, the designer may need to determine how some circuits should be partitioned among two or more devices. The designer must also keep in mind the propagation delays in multiple-PLD designs. Of course, circuits that fit into a single PLD are preferred, since they are easier to work with and implement, but single-device solutions may be impossible or impractical in many situations.

Figure 6-1 shows an example circuit that must be partitioned into two devices. A brief study of the circuit shows a clear partition, as shown by the dashed line. The circuit on the left will easily fit into a 24-pin PLD, while the one on the right will fit comfortably into a 20-pin part. The resulting "black box" PLD circuit is shown in Fig. 6-2.

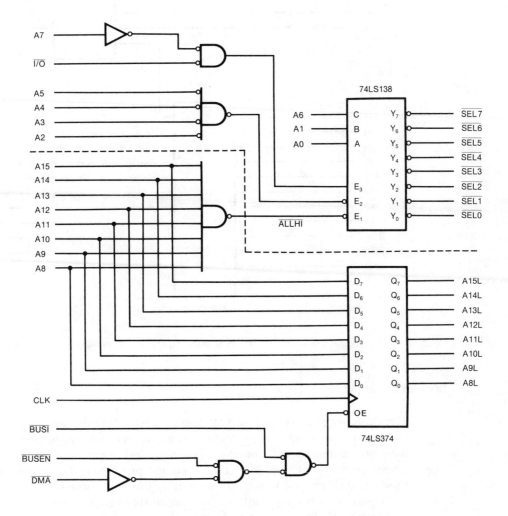

Figure 6-1. Example circuit that must be partitioned into two PLDs.

In many situations, the partitioning of a circuit will not be so obvious, and several iterations may be required before determining the optimum partition. Indeed, each iteration may find different PLDs being considered for implementing different portions of the circuit. For particularly large circuits, it may be beneficial to break the circuit down into smaller sections, then further partition these sections into manageable pieces for individual PLDs.

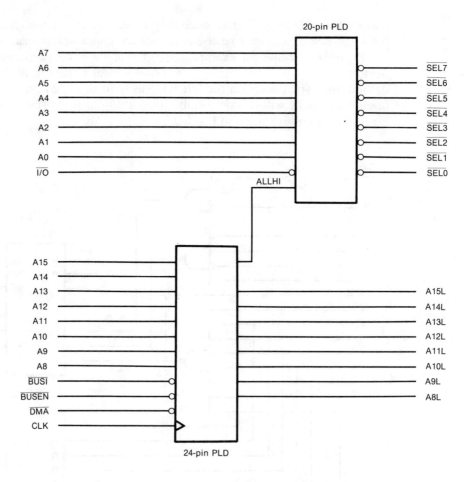

Figure 6-2. "Black box" PLD circuit equivalent of circuit shown in Fig. 6-1.

Boolean Equation Cautions

The designer should take several precautions when designing with Boolean equations. It is good design practice to avoid race conditions (see Chapter 2), have an awareness of how the PLD compiler operates, and how to avoid unexpected logic design changes. A common problem is the loss of *intentional* logic redundancy due to logic reduction by the PLD compiler.

Figure 6-3 shows a combinatorial circuit that suffers from a race condition, along with a timing diagram and the Boolean equation for the circuit. Figure 6-4 shows a similar, logically equivalent circuit having a redundant gate to eliminate the race condition. Notice the additional term in the Boolean equation. When the equation is minimized by the PLD compiler, the equation and circuit shown in Fig. 6-5 results. Note how the compiler "lost" the redundant gate.

Although it is generally desirable to minimize the Boolean equations in PLD designs, there are situations where the designer should not allow the PLD compiler to minimize the logic, in order to retain intentional redundancy. For

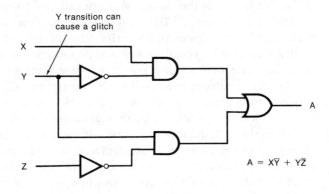

Figure 6-3. Combinatorial circuit with a race condition.

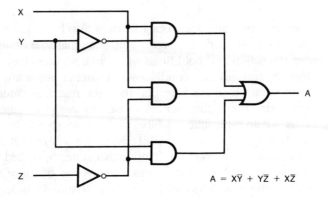

Figure 6-4. Improved combinatorial circuit with a redundant gate to eliminate the race condition.

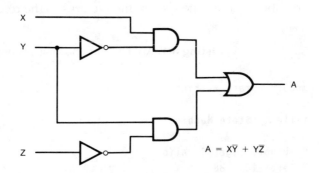

Figure 6-5. Improved combinatorial circuit after logic minimization; the redundant gate has been lost.

this reason, most PLD compilers that incorporate logic minimization either support different levels of logic reduction or permit the reduction to be turned off altogether. It is the designer's responsibility to make sure the compiler is operating as expected. This may involve looking at the reduced equations generated by the compiler to verify that the intended logic redundancy has been retained. Race conditions caused by lost redundant terms can be elusive to find, since the logic will still pass test vector simulation.

Another problem to be avoided is improper clocking when using PLDs that support asynchronous clocking. The clock signals to the output registers of these devices are generated by product term outputs. The timing of the input signals to the product terms must be regulated to avoid race conditions or other timing anomalies that may cause inadvertent clock signal generation. As with all registered devices, register set-up and hold times relative to the register clocks must be met—a design concern not infrequently overlooked in designs based on asynchronous clocking.

State Machine Cautions

The programmable logic designer must also be cautious when implementing state machine or sequencer designs. With state machine designs, he or she must ensure that the set-up and hold times of internal registers (registers internal to the PLDs) are met, and that race conditions and hang-up states are avoided (see Chapter 2). It is important to make sure that the state machine enters the appropriate state at power-up or reset time, and also that no states—even illegal ones—are inescapable. Thus, for an n-bit state machine, all 2^n states should be defined.

Listing 6-1 shows an ABEL listing for a three-bit state machine having five states (states 0 through 4). Notice that states 5, 6, and 7 have not been defined, and are treated as "don't cares." If any one of these states is entered inadvertently, the operation of the state machine is indeterminate—it may cause strange, erratic operation, or simply "lock up" by entering an infinite loop. A modified version of the state machine definition file is shown in Listing 6-2. Notice how states 5, 6, and 7 have been defined, and merely return the state machine to the reset state. Another possible approach to unused states is shown in Listing 6-3. In this case, if an invalid state is entered, the state machine sets an error bit to notify the system, then returns to the reset state.

Listing 6-1. ABEL Listing Showing a Simple Three-Bit,
Five-State State Machine

```
module   State_Machine_1

title    'State Machine 1'

" Author: Roger C. Alford
" Date: 10/4/88

STATEM1 device  'P16V8R';
```

```
            " Input Pin Definitions:
                    CLK     pin     1;      " SYNCH/STATE MACHINE CLOCK
                    AENn    pin     2;      " ADDRESS ENABLE
                    BUSEL1n pin     3;      " BUS 1 SEL
                    BUSEL2n pin     4;      " BUS 2 SEL
                    RESETn  pin     5;      " SYSTEM RESET
                    STARTCY pin     6;      " START CYCLE SIGNAL

            " Output Pin Definitions:
                    STATE2  pin     19;     " STATE MACHINE BIT 2
                    STATE1  pin     18;     " STATE MACHINE BIT 1
                    STATE0  pin     17;     " STATE MACHINE BIT 0
                    EN1n    pin     16;     " ENABLE 1
                    EN2n    pin     15;     " ENABLE 2
                    NOCYCn  pin     14;     " NO CYCLE IN PROGRESS IND.

            " Internal Logic Equations:
                    STATEM  = [STATE2,STATE1,STATE0];    " STATE MACHINE SET
                    AEN     = !AENn;
                    BUSEL1  = !BUSEL1n;
                    BUSEL2  = !BUSEL2n;
                    RESET   = !RESETn;

            " Logic Equations:
                equations

        EN1n    := !(!RESET & !(STATEM==0) & ((STATEM==1) # !EN1n));
        EN2n    := !(!RESET & !(STATEM==0) & ((STATEM==2) # !EN2n));
        NOCYCn  := !(RESET # (STATEM==0));

" State Machine Definition:
    state_diagram [STATE2,STATE1,STATE0]
        state 0: IF RESET THEN 0
                ELSE IF BUSEL1 & AEN THEN 1
                    ELSE IF BUSEL2 & AEN THEN 2
                        ELSE 0;

        state 1: GOTO 3;

        state 2: GOTO 3;

        state 3: IF RESET THEN 0
                ELSE IF STARTCY THEN 4
                    ELSE 3;

        state 4: IF RESET # (!BUSEL1 & !BUSEL2) THEN 0 ELSE 4;
end     State_Machine_1
```

Listing 6-2. ABEL Listing Showing the Three-Bit State Machine with the Unused States Defined

```
module  State_Machine_2

title'  State Machine 2'

" Author: Roger C. Alford
" Date: 10/4/88

STATEM2 device  'P16V8R';

" Input Pin Definitions:
        CLK      pin     1;      " SYNCH/STATE MACHINE CLOCK
        AENn     pin     2;      " ADDRESS ENABLE
        BUSEL1n  pin     3;      " BUS 1 SEL
        BUSEL2n  pin     4;      " BUS 2 SEL
        RESETn   pin     5;      " SYSTEM RESET
        STARTCY  pin     6;      " START CYCLE SIGNAL

" Output Pin Definitions:
        STATE2   pin     19;     " STATE MACHINE BIT 2
        STATE1   pin     18;     " STATE MACHINE BIT 1
        STATE0   pin     17;     " STATE MACHINE BIT 0
        EN1n     pin     16;     " ENABLE 1
        EN2n     pin     15;     " ENABLE 2
        NOCYCn   pin     14;     " NO CYCLE IN PROGRESS IND.

" Internal Logic Equations:
        STATEM  = [STATE2,STATE1,STATE0];  " STATE MACHINE SET
        AEN     = !AENn;
        BUSEL1  = !BUSEL1n;
        BUSEL2  = !BUSEL2n;
        RESET   = !RESETn;

" Logic  Equations:
   equations
            EN1n:= !(!RESET & !(STATEM==0) & ((STATEM==1) # !EN1n));
        EN2n:= !(!RESET & !(STATEM==0) & ((STATEM==2) # !EN2n));
        NOCYCn:= !(RESET # (STATEM==0));

" State Machine Definition:
    state_diagram [STATE2,STATE1,STATE0]
        state 0: IF RESET THEN 0
                ELSE IF BUSEL1 & AEN THEN 1
                    ELSE IF BUSEL2 & AEN THEN 2
                        ELSE 0;

        state 1: GOTO 3;
```

```
                state 2: GOTO 3;

                state 3: IF RESET THEN 0
                            ELSE IF STARTCY THEN 4
                                ELSE 3;

                state 4: IF RESET # (!BUSEL1 & !BUSEL2) THEN 0 ELSE 4;

                state 5: GOTO 0;
                state 6: GOTO 0;
                state 7: GOTO 0;

end         State_Machine_2
```

Listing 6-3. ABEL Listing Showing the Three-Bit State Machine with the Unused States Defined, Which Set an Error Flag Then Return the State Machine to the Reset State

```
module    State_Machine_3

title 'State Machine 3'

" Author: Roger C. Alford
" Date: 10/4/88

STATEM3  device 'P16V8R';

" Input Pin Definitions:
        CLK      pin     1;      " SYNCH/STATE MACHINE CLOCK
        AENn     pin     2;      " ADDRESS ENABLE
        BUSEL1n  pin     3;      " BUS 1 SEL
        BUSEL2n  pin     4;      " BUS 2 SEL
        RESETn   pin     5;      " SYSTEM RESET
        STARTCY  pin     6;      " START CYCLE SIGNAL

" Output Pin Definitions:
        STATE2   pin     19;     " STATE MACHINE BIT 2
        STATE1   pin     18;     " STATE MACHINE BIT 1
        STATE0   pin     17;     " STATE MACHINE BIT 0
        EN1n     pin     16;     " ENABLE 1
        EN2n     pin     15;     " ENABLE 2
        NOCYCn   pin     14;     " NO CYCLE IN PROGRESS IND.
        ERRORn   pin     13;     " STATE MACHINE ERROR SIGNAL

" Internal Logic Equations:
        STATEM = [STATE2,STATE1,STATE0];  " STATE MACHINE SET
        AEN    = !AENn;
```

```
              BUSEL1   =  !BUSEL1n;
              BUSEL2   =  !BUSEL2n;
              RESET    =  !RESETn;

" Logic  Equations:
   equations
        EN1n    := !(!RESET & !(STATEM==0) & ((STATEM==1) # !EN1n));
        EN2n    :=!(!RESET & !(STATEM==0) & ((STATEM==2) # !EN2n));
        NOCYCn  := !(RESET # (STATEM==0));
        ERRORn  := !(!RESET & ((STATEM==7) # !ERRORn));

" State Machine Definition:
   state_diagram [STATE2,STATE1,STATE0]
        state 0: IF RESET THEN 0
                   ELSE IF BUSEL1 & AEN THEN 1
                      ELSE IF BUSEL2 & AEN THEN 2
                         ELSE 0;

        state 1: GOTO 3;

        state 2: GOTO 3;

        state 3: IF RESET THEN 0
                   ELSE IF STARTCY THEN 4
                      ELSE 3;

        state 4: IF RESET # (!BUSEL1 & !BUSEL2) THEN 0 ELSE 4;

        state 5: GOTO 7;
        state 6: GOTO 7;
        state 7: GOTO 0;

end      State_Machine_3
```

A common oversight in the design of state machines is meeting the set-up times for the PLD registers. This is particularly true in circuits with asynchronous signals being used to determine the next state. Failure to adhere to set-up requirements can result in improper state sequencing or metastability problems. Refer to Chapter 2 for a discussion of the problems associated with state machines and metastability.

Design Documentation

In some ways the advent of programmable logic can be viewed as having reduced circuit design to a software task, since a good portion of the design effort involves entering and compiling the logic description on a computer. As with good software design, quality documentation is an essential part of good

programmable logic design. The designer should comment source files liber-
ally, summarizing the operation of each device, identifying all input and output
signals, and describing logic equations, truth tables, and state machines wherever ambiguity may exist. Even graphic entry forms, such as waveform and
schematic entry, should be supplemented with a written description of the logic
being implemented.

A properly documented source file is easier to debug and modify than one
that is undocumented or poorly documented. A designer should be able to
return to a PLD design after an extended absence—even years—and be able to
quickly determine the logic and operation of the design. Similarly, a well-
documented PLD source file allows other engineers to quickly "come up to
speed" with the circuit if ever necessary.

Another valuable documentation feature is the *modification history*. This is
a summary of the logic changes that have taken place for a PLD during its life.
Listing 6-4 shows an ABEL PLD source file with a modification history. The
modification history table summarizes the changes that have taken place, and is
usually found near the beginning of the source file. The table indicates the date
and reason for each change, and includes a special "search" code to help
identify the places in the file that each change affected. The table may also
include other information, as desired. If a person wishes to find all of the places
affected by a particular change, he or she needs merely to search for every
occurrence of the search code in the file. Note that in order to retain a complete
history, logic equations must not be deleted. They should, instead, be "commented out" (so that they are not compiled) and tagged with the appropriate
search code. A replacement equation can then be entered in place of the
equation that was commented out.

Listing 6-4. ABEL PLD Source File Showing a Modification History

```
module    SELECT

title     'Memory Selector'

" Author: Roger C. Alford

SEL              device    'P16L8';

" Modification History:
"
"   Date        Ini    Code              Reason for Change
"  --------     ---    ----    -------------------------------------

"  10/03/88     rca            Initial creation
"  10/18/88     rca    ++A1    Add redundant term to eliminate glitch
"                               (AF)
"  10/20/88     rca    ++A2    Change 'Sel' outputs to active high
"  10/26/88     rca    ++A3    Add STB output signal and equation
```

```
" Input Pin Definitions:
a19    Pin    1;                 " address line 19
a18    Pin    2;                 " address line 18
a17    Pin    3;                 " address line 17
a16    Pin    4;                 " address line 16
a15    Pin    5;                 " address line 15
a14    Pin    6;                 " address line 14
mem_io Pin    7;                 " memory/I/O select
rd_n   Pin    8;                 " read strobe, active low
wr_n   Pin    9;                 " write strobe, active low


" Output Pin Definitions:
sel1   Pin    12;                " memory select 1, active low
                                 " ++A2  CHANGED TO ACTIVE HIGH
sel2   Pin    13;                " memory select 2, active low
                                 " ++A2  CHANGED TO ACTIVE HIGH
AF     Pin    14;                " memory select 3, active low
STB    Pin    15;                " ++A3   memory strobe signal
mrd_n  Pin    16;                " memory read strobe, active low
mwr_n  Pin    17;                " memory write strobe, active low
iord_n Pin    18;                " I/O read strobe, active low
iowr_n Pin    19;                " I/O write strobe, active low


" Internal Logic Equations:
       mem_cycle      = mem_io;
       io_cycle       = !mem_io;
       rd             = !rd_n;
       wr             = !wr_n;


Equations
       mrd_n = !(mem_cycle & rd);
       mwr_n = !(mem_cycle & wr);
       iord_n = !(io_cycle & rd);
       iowr_n = !(io_cycle & wr);
       AF = (a19 & !a18)#(a18 & !a17) # (a19 & !a17);   " ++A1
       sel1 = a19 & a18 & mem_cycle;  " ++A2
       sel2 = a19 & !a18 & a17 & a16 & !a15 & !a14 & mem_cycle;   " ++A2
       STB = mem_cycle & (rd # wr);   " ++A3


" Deleted Equations:
"* ++A1 AF = (a19 & !a18)#(a18 & !a17);
"* ++A2 sel1_n = !(a19 & a18 & mem_cycle);
"* ++A2 sel2_n = !(a19 & !a18 & a17 & a16 & !a15 & !a14 & mem_cycle);

end    SELECT
```

In situations where several PLDs represent partitions of a larger circuit, it is also valuable to describe how the PLDs interact. This may be accomplished either by appropriate comments in each PLD source file, or by a master document file that encompasses the entire circuit. If a master document file is used, it should be referenced in the source file of each PLD in the circuit.

Developing and Using Test Vectors

Test vectors are signal patterns used to verify the logic of PLDs. Test vectors are simulated by software for design verification, and can also be physically applied to programmed devices to ensure proper operation of programmed parts. In this section we will take a look at how test vectors are used in design verification. In Chapter 7 we see how test vectors are used for testing programmed parts in a production environment.

Most popular PLD compilers support test vector simulation to varying degrees. Some compilers simply interpret individual test vectors sequentially, while others include a complete test vector "language." Test vector languages generally support structured Pascal-like statements for implementing multiple iterations and "what if" decisions. This capability provides the designer with a greater level of help in design verification.

Appropriately developed test vectors have the potential to save the designer a lot of time and cost in the development and debugging stages of a design. Test vectors for a PLD should be able to simulate most of the logic operation of the device, providing the designer with at least a minimal verification of the logic definition. Test vector device simulation will often show up logic definition problems before the time-consuming task of programming parts, placing them into a prototype system, and debugging the system—only to find PLD logic design errors. The use of test vectors for PLD design verification is particularly important because internal device nodes are not available outside the parts, in many instances making in-circuit debugging very difficult.

In addition to saving debugging time by using PLD test vector simulation, the designer can also save the cost of parts that might otherwise be lost to multiple design iterations. Although the designer should use erasable PLDs during the debugging stage of a design, this is not always possible. If a designer is forced to use one-time programmable parts during debugging, the cost savings from using test vector simulation can be sizeable, because of the reduction in the number of device logic changes.

For combinatorial circuits, it may not be possible to generate test vectors for every possible combination of inputs. However, a "representative" group of test vectors should be developed. The test vectors should also verify output-enable and feedback circuits, where appropriate. If a device is used for address-range decoding, the test vectors should check the address range boundaries for each select output. For example, if a device output goes active (low) for addresses in the range 04H–07H, test vectors with address inputs 03H, 04H, 07H, and 08H should be generated, verifying the appropriate output response for each address input. For latched circuits, the test vectors should verify that the latching operations work properly, and that registers are reset or preset, where appropriate. Note that the designer is still responsible for making sure that register set-up and hold times are met—this cannot be determined by test vector simulation.

State machines are generally more complex to test than combinatorial or simple latched circuits. The test vectors should test access to every defined state, and verify error traps for at least some unexpected conditions and illegal states. The test vectors should also verify proper reset operation.

Complex circuits often involve multiple PLDs. In these cases, the designer often has to write the test vectors for each PLD individually, and is therefore forced to simulate the operation of the other PLDs in the circuit when generating the test vectors. Some of the more-advanced PLD compilers, however, take more of a system-level approach to PLD design, and allow test vectors to be written for interconnected groups of PLDs. This can greatly reduce the debugging effort for multiple-PLD circuit designs.

The effort to develop test vectors strictly for design verification is clearly warranted. Fortunately, the same test vectors, or a subset of them, can (and should) also be used in the production environment to verify operation of programmed devices. As discussed in Chapter 7, the test vectors are often augmented with other vectors generated by a special program with the specific intent of being able to catch stuck bits in programmed parts. Caution must be used when applying design verification test vectors to programmed parts. Because of the way the test vectors are applied to programmed parts, some test vectors may fail when testing good programmed parts, even though the same vectors pass during test vector simulation. This is mostly true when implementing combinatorial latches. Figure 6-6 shows a combinatorial latch circuit and its corresponding timing diagram, with a PLD implementation of the circuit described by the ABEL listing in Listing 6-5. The test vectors in the ABEL listing pass test vector simulation (design verification), but fail programmed device testing on a Data I/O Model 29B PLD programmer.

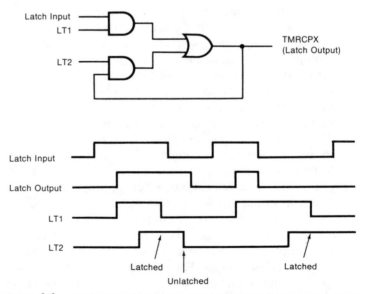

Figure 6-6. A combinatorial latch circuit and corresponding timing diagram.

Listing 6-5. ABEL PLD Source File with Test Vectors for the
Combinatorial Latch Circuit

```
module  WAITstates

title   'Combinatorial Latch Circuit'

" author: Roger C. Alford

WAITS            device'F82S153';

" Input Pin Definitions:
        MEMS      pin    1;        " MEMORY SELECT
        IOS       pin    2;        " I/O SELECT
        TIMER0    pin    3;        " TIMER COMPARE BIT 0
        TIMER1    pin    4;        " TIMER COMPARE BIT 1
        TIMER2    pin    5;        " TIMER COMPARE BIT 2
        TIMER3    pin    11;       " TIMER COMPARE BIT 3
        CLK       pin    13;       " SYSTEM CLOCK
        LT2       pin    14;       " LOAD TIMER 2 SIGNAL
        LT1       pin    15;       " LOAD TIMER 1 SIGNAL

" Output Pin Definitions:
        TMRACT   pin    12;        " TIMER ACTIVE SIGNAL
        TMRCP3   pin    16;        " TIMER BIT 3
        TMRCP2   pin    17;        " TIMER BIT 2
        TMRCP1   pin    18;        " TIMER BIT 1
        TMRCP0   pin    19;        " TIMER BIT 0
" Internal Logic Equations:
        H,L,X,Z = 1,0,.X.,.Z.;     " COMMONLY USED EQUATES
        TIMER   = [TIMER3,TIMER2,TIMER1,TIMER0];
        TMRCP   = [TMRCP3,TMRCP2,TMRCP1,TMRCP0];
        MEMTIME = [0,0,1,0];       " WAIT COUNT FOR MEMORY ACC. (2)
        IOTIME  = [0,1,1,1];       " WAIT COUNT FOR I/O ACC. (7)

" Output Equations:
    equations
        TMRCP    = (((MEMTIME & MEMS)#(IOTIME & IOS)) & LT1)
                    # (TMRCP & LT2);

        TMRACT  = !(((TMRCP==TIMER) & !CLK)
                    # (!TMRACT & LT2)
                    # (!LT1 & !LT2));

" Test Vectors:
    test_vectors
        ([TIMER,CLK,LT1,LT2,MEMS,IOS] -> [TMRCP,TMRACT])
                                      " TEST MEMORY CYCLE:
```

```
[  0, L,  H,  L,  H,   L ] -> [  2,   H  ];
[  2, L,  H,  L,  H,   L ] -> [  2,   L  ];
[  2, H,  H,  L,  H,   L ] -> [  2,   H  ];
[  5, L,  H,  L,  H,   L ] -> [  2,   H  ];
[ 10, L,  H,  L,  H,   L ] -> [  2,   H  ];
[ 15, L,  H,  L,  H,   L ] -> [  2,   H  ];
                                    " TEST I/O CYCLE:
[  0, L,  H,  L,  L,   H ] -> [  7,   H  ];
[  2, L,  H,  H,  L,   H ] -> [  7,   H  ];
[  5, L,  L,  H,  L,   H ] -> [  7,   H  ];
[  7, L,  L,  H,  L,   H ] -> [  7,   L  ];
[ 10, H,  L,  H,  L,   H ] -> [  7,   L  ];
[ 15, L,  L,  H,  L,   H ] -> [  7,   L  ];

end     WAITstates
```

Design Simulation

When designing complex circuits, it is often desirable to take a step beyond mere test vector simulation. Advanced logic simulators are available which will verify the interaction of multiple programmable and other logic devices, including the verification of gate delays and register set-up and hold times. As PLD-based designs become increasingly more complex, gate-level simulation will become more important, and will probably see a consistent increase in usage. Such advanced simulation capability is not, however, a standard part of existing PLD compilers, but must either be included with the engineering workstation or purchased separately.

Programming PLDs

In order to complete the development cycle, real PLDs must be programmed and tested in their target system. PLD programming is generally accomplished by downloading the JEDEC output file from the PLD compiler (via a computer's RS-232 serial port) to a PLD programmer, then using the programmer to program (or "burn") the part. This procedure may vary slightly from system to system and programmer to programmer. In some environments, the same device programmer used for production programming of PLDs will be used for programming the initial prototype devices. In other environments, different equipment may be used in engineering than in production. The designer must make sure that the production programmer can also program the parts.

Some small organizations may feel that they cannot justify the purchase of a PLD programmer, even though they wish to use PLDs in a system design. In this case, the organization can often work out an arrangement with a device representative or distributor, or other programmable logic consulting organization, to program the prototype and production devices. Chapter 7 discusses PLD programming in greater detail.

Final PLD Debugging and Verification

While the designer should take as much advantage of test vector-based design verification and gate-level design simulation as possible, in-circuit system-level debugging is the inevitable final stage in the design verification and check-out process. As mentioned earlier, erasable PLDs should be used for this stage of debugging if possible. Not only does the use of erasable devices save cost by allowing parts to be reused, but the added testability, and thus reliability, of erasable parts virtually eliminates one unknown in the debugging process. If bipolar OTP parts are used during the debugging stage, it is difficult to be sure whether a circuit problem is the result of an incorrect logic definition or a defective device, since these parts cannot be completely tested at the factory. Erasable parts, including CMOS UV-erasable devices and (especially) CMOS electrically erasable devices, can be 100% tested at the factory, virtually eliminating the possibility of a device being defective.

Depending on the complexity of the design, it is not unusual for PLDs to experience multiple logic definition iterations before settling on a final design. Since the designer cannot probe inside the system's PLDs, there must be a certain amount of reliance on information from the PLD compiler—especially from the test vector simulation. As the designer generates theories for operational problems, they should, if possible, be verified using test vector simulation prior to programming new devices with modified logic definitions.

Debugging PLD-based prototype systems is typically much easier than debugging traditional SSI/MSI logic boards. This is because the PLD design changes often require only device programming alterations, instead of the time-consuming and marginally reliable "cuts and jumpers" changes that typify the traditional systems. Combined with the help of computer-based logic design aids, PLD design and debugging is vastly more efficient than traditional SSI/MSI design.

PLD "Starter" Kits and Booklets

There are several PLD "starter" kits and primer booklets designed to help the first-time PLD designer make a smooth transition into the realm of programmable logic design. Virtually all of these resources are made available by companies which have a vested interest in teaching engineers to use *their* products—i.e., PLD manufacturers, PLD programmer manufacturers, and PLD compiler manufacturers. Following are some resources that may be helpful for new PLD designers.

Data I/O Corporation, a manufacturer of PLD programmers and producer of the ABEL compiler, offers a free booklet called, *Programmable Logic: A*

Basic Guide for the Designer. This booklet takes the reader through programmable logic basics (what is a PLD?, advantages of programmable logic, etc.) and briefly discusses PLD design, programming, and testing, and includes two design examples. Contact, Data I/O Corp., 10525 Willows Road N.E., C-46, Redmond, WA 98052 (206) 881-6444.

National Semiconductor Corporation, a manufacturer of PLDs, has a free booklet entitled, *Programmable Logic Primer*. This booklet is a basic introduction to National's PALs, including a basic architectural description and information on testing, reliability, and handling. It does not, however, provide much information relating to actual PLD design. Contact National Semiconductor Corp., P.O. Box 58090, Santa Clara, CA 95052-8090 (408) 721-5000.

Logical Devices, the manufacturer of the CUPL PLD compiler, offers its free *Programmable Logic User's Guide* on a disk, designed to be run on an IBM PC compatible system. This informative guide compares programmable logic architectures, describes advantages of PLDs, and provides useful PLD design information. Contact Logical Devices, 1321 N.W. 65th Place, Ft. Lauderdale, FL 33309 (305) 974-0967.

In a joint effort to promote programmable logic design and their own wares, Logical Devices and PAL-manufacturer Texas Instruments combined efforts to create the "PAL Starter Kit." As its name implies, the kit's goal is to initiate designers into the world of *PAL* design. This well-designed $49.95 kit offers a copy of Logical Devices' PC-disk-based *Programmable Logic User's Guide* and a copy of a booklet entitled, *My First PAL Design*. The booklet steps the reader through some PAL design basics, along with design examples. To put this new-found education into practice, the kit also includes four popular Texas Instruments PAL devices and a full-featured version of the CUPL compiler that supports only the four PAL devices included in the kit, along with a copy of CUPL's user's manual. Contact either Logical Devices at the address above or contact Texas Instruments, P.O. Box 225012, Dallas, TX 75265 (800) 232-3200.

In a similar agreement between Logical Devices and Samsung Semiconductor, Samsung is offering the "CPL Starter Kit," configured similar to the PAL Starter Kit described above. Contact Samsung Semiconductor, 5150 Great America Parkway, Santa Clara, CA 95054 (408) 980-1630.

A PLD Design Example

Perhaps the best way to understand how all the decisions come together in a PLD design is by example. Let's look at an example design that requires a variety of decisions that will lead us from conception to design completion. Some of the production economic decisions are touched on only lightly here, but are covered in detail in Chapter 7.

The scenario: We must design an arbitration circuit that allows two asynchronous processors to access a single, dual-ported RAM memory area—having already determined that it is best implemented using programmable logic. If a processor wait is required, the circuit must activate a wait signal to the processor within 250 ns of receiving the select signal from the processor. The circuit must also control all address and data bus buffers between the processors and the dual-ported RAM. Processor 1 is given priority when requests are made simultaneously. For write cycles, the address lines to the dual-ported memory must be set up at least 50 ns before the leading edge of the write strobe. Both read and write strobes have minimum widths of 50 ns *at the memory*. A 16 MHz clock signal is available in the system for timing. We will also assume that an ABEL compiler is accessible.

Inputs to the arbitration circuit include the select signals from the two processors (DPRCS1* and DPRCS2*), and the read and write strobes from the two processors (RD1*, WR1*, RD2* and WR2*), in addition to the system clock and RESET signals. Outputs include two address buffer enables (ADDEN1* and ADDEN2*), two data bus buffer enables (DATEN1* and DATEN2*), and two processor wait signals (WAIT1* and WAIT2*). Figure 6-7 shows a partial system block diagram, with the arbitration circuit shown as a "black box." (Note: Because this circuit involves asynchronous signals, metastability is a concern; while appropriate synchronizers will be incorporated, for simplicity the metastability MTBF calculations will not be shown.)

This circuit clearly lends itself to state machine implementation. A state machine must therefore be defined to perform the functions needed by the circuit. We will use the 16 MHz system clock for state machine synchronization. Figure 6-8 shows a state diagram for the arbitration circuit. The state machine has nine states, so it requires four bits to implement. The resulting 16-state state machine has seven unused states. In addition to the four state bits, the state machine also requires two (internal) flag bits. The final input/output pin/signal count for the arbitration circuit is:

- 8 inputs (2 latched)
- 8 outputs (6 latched)
- 4 state machine bits (4 latched)
- 2 state machine flag bits (2 latched)

Now that the circuit signal and operation requirements have been defined, the next step is to find acceptable PLDs to implement the circuit. In searching for one, or perhaps two, PLDs to implement the circuit, it should be realized that only 16 of the signals need to be accessible outside the arbitration circuit. The six state machine-related bits and the two input latch bits can all be "buried" (kept entirely inside the PLDs). A search reveals several single-chip and dual-chip solutions. Single-chip solutions include the Altera EP900 and the Lattice GAL6001. Dual-chip solutions include an AMD PAL23S8 sequencer in conjunction with a 74LS74 dual D-type flip-flop (to handle input latching); a PAL16P8 and a PAL16R6; two GAL16V8's; two PEEL18CV8's; and two PLS159's. The choice from among these is first narrowed based on which devices are supported by the available production programming equipment and development software tools (note, however, that these reasons can be "overruled" if other criteria prove more important). Realizing that EEPROM-based parts are the most desirable for production (why?—see Chapter 7), and that a number of GAL16V8 parts are currently available in stock and are acceptably cost-effective, we choose to use two GAL16V8's to implement the arbitration circuit. (Note:

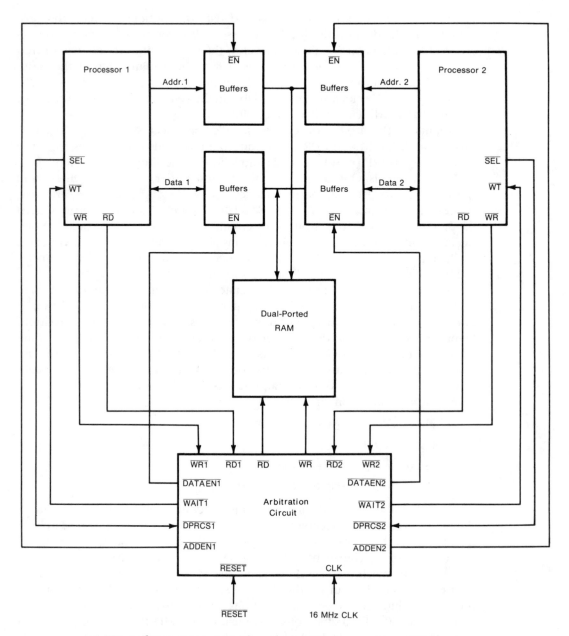

Figure 6-7. Partial block diagram of example system requiring a PLD-based synchronizer circuit.

This choice was made strictly for this example, and other alternatives might have been chosen under other circumstances.)

Now that the devices have been chosen and we already have acceptable software and programming tools, we must determine how the design is to be partitioned. This step, of course, is only necessary if multiple PLDs are involved in the circuit design. A logical partitioning for the arbitration circuit is shown in

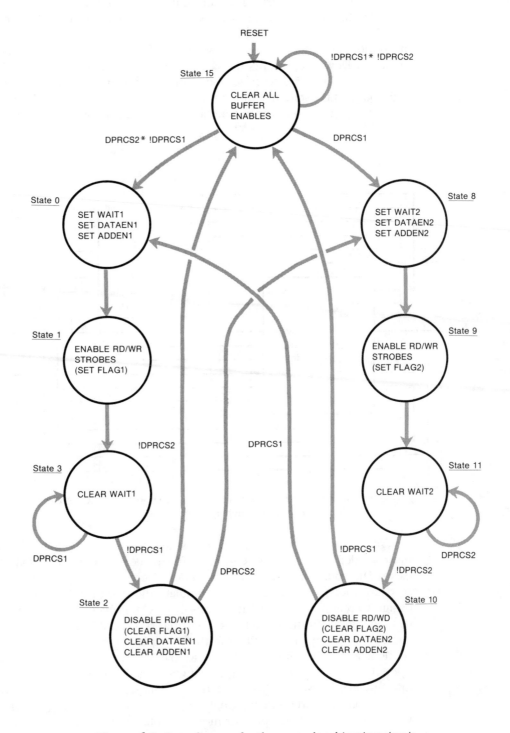

Figure 6-8. State diagram for the example arbitration circuit.

Fig. 6-9. Both of the GAL16V8 devices use the 16 MHz clock signal for timing, and accept the RESET signal as an input. Device 1 accepts the DPRCS1∗ and DPRCS2∗ input signals from the system, in addition to the four state machine bits from device 2. Device 1 also generates the six latched outputs of the arbitration circuit, and passes two latched (synchronized) select signals to device 2. Device 2 accepts the latched select signals from device 1, and also accepts the four read/write strobes from the system. Device 2 uses six of its eight outputs for state machine functions (including the two flag bits), and uses the remaining two outputs to generate output read and write signals to the dual-ported RAM.

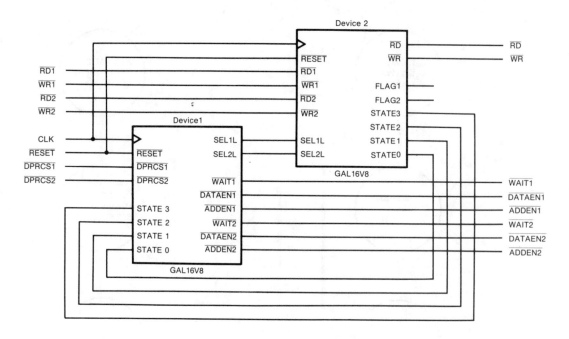

Figure 6-9. Partitioning of the example arbitration circuit using two GAL16V8 devices (device pin numbers are not shown).

The next step in the design cycle is straightforward—the logic for the circuit must be defined using the chosen software development tool (ABEL in this case). The source file should be well-documented, and test vectors (or other software tools) should be used to simulate the design before committing the design to real parts. Several iterations of this step may be required before the desired logic definition is achieved. Listings 6-6 and 6-7 show acceptable ABEL source listings for the two PLDs in the example circuit.

Finally, the circuit should be breadboarded or prototyped to verify proper operation in a real circuit. If logic changes are still required, they will generally only involve software, alleviating the circuit board wiring changes that were once required in circuit debugging! For production, additional (or different) test vectors should be developed for more-complete device testing, as described in Chapter 7.

Listing 6-6. ABEL Source Listing for GAL1 in the Example Arbitration Circuit

```
module  Arbitration_State_1flag'-r2'

title   'Abitration Circuit State Machine Device 1'

" Author: Roger C. Alford
" Date: 10/5/88

ARBSTAT1         device 'P16V8R';

" Input Pin Definitions:
        CLK      pin    1;       " SYNCH/STATE MACHINE CLOCK
        DPRCS1n  pin    2;       " CPU 1 SHARED RAM SELECT SIGNAL
        DPRCS2n  pin    3;       " CPU 2 SHARED RAM SELECT SIGNAL
        STATE3   pin    4;       " STATE MACHINE BIT 3
        STATE2   pin    5;       " STATE MACHINE BIT 2
        STATE1   pin    6;       " STATE MACHINE BIT 1
        STATE0   pin    7;       " STATE MACHINE BIT 0
        RESETn   pin    8;       " SYSTEM RESET

" Output Pin Definitions:
        WAIT1n   pin    19;      " CPU 1 WAIT SIGNAL
        DATAEN1n pin    18;      " CPU 1 DATA BUFFER ENABLE
        ADDEN1n  pin    17;      " CPU 1 ADDRESS BUFFER ENABLE
        WAIT2n   pin    16;      " CPU 2 WAIT SIGNAL
        DATAEN2n pin    15;      " CPU 2 DATA BUFFER ENABLE
        ADDEN2n  pin    14;      " CPU 2 ADDRESS BUFFER ENABLE
        SEL1L    pin    13;      " LATCHED CPU 1 SELECT SIGNAL
        SEL2L    pin    12;      " LATCHED CPU 2 SELECT SIGNAL

" Internal Logic Equations:
        STATEM  = [STATE3,STATE2,STATE1,STATE0];  " STATE MACHINE
SET
        DPRCS1  = !DPRCS1n;
        DPRCS2  = !DPRCS2n;
        RESET   = !RESETn;

" Logic  Equations:
   equations
        SEL1L     := DPRCS1;

        SEL2L     := DPRCS2;

        WAIT1n    := !((SEL1L & !(STATEM==3) & !(STATEM==2)) &
                      !RESET);

        WAIT2n    := !((SEL2L & !(STATEM==11) & !(STATEM==10)) &
                      !RESET);
```

```
        DATAEN1n  := !(((STATEM==0) # !DATAEN1n) & !(STATEM==2) &
                        !RESET);

        DATAEN2n  := !(((STATEM==8) # !DATAEN2n) & !(STATEM==10) &
                        !RESET);

        ADDEN1n   := !(((STATEM==0) # !DATAEN1n) & !(STATEM==2) &
                        !RESET);

        ADDEN2n   := !(((STATEM==8) # !DATAEN2n) & !(STATEM==10) &
                        !RESET);

end     Arbitration_State_1
```

Listing 6-7. ABEL Source Listing for GAL2 in the
Example Arbitration Circuit

```
module  Arbitration_State_2     flag'-r2'

title   'Abitration Circuit State Machine Device 2'

" Author: Roger C. Alford
" Date: 10/5/88

ARBSTAT2        device   'P16V8R';

" Input Pin Definitions:
        CLK     pin     1;          " SYNCH/STATE MACHINE CLOCK
        SEL1L   pin     2;          " LATCHED CPU 1 SELECT (DPRCS1)
        SEL2L   pin     3;          " LATCHED CPU 2 SELECT (DPRCS2)
        WR1n    pin     4;          " CPU 1 WRITE STROBE
        RD1n    pin     5;          " CPU 1 READ STROBE
        WR2n    pin     6;          " CPU 2 WRITE STROBE
        RD2n    pin     7;          " CPU 2 READ STROBE
        RESETn  pin     8;          " SYSTEM RESET

" Output Pin Definitions:
        STATE3  pin     19;         " STATE MACHINE BIT 3
        STATE2  pin     18;         " STATE MACHINE BIT 2
        STATE1  pin     17;         " STATE MACHINE BIT 1
        STATE0  pin     16;         " STATE MACHINE BIT 0
        WRn     pin     15;         " SHARED MEMORY WRITE STROBE
        RDn     pin     14;         " SHARED MEMORY READ STROBE
        FLAG1   pin     13;         " STATE MACHINE FLAG 1
        FLAG2   pin     12;         " STATE MACHINE FLAG 2
```

```
" Internal Logic Equations:
        STATEM  = [STATE3,STATE2,STATE1,STATE0];  " STATE M. SET
        RD1     = !RD1n;
        RD2     = !RD2n;
        WR1     = !WR1n;
        WR2     = !WR2n;
        RESET   = !RESETn;

" Logic  Equations:
   equations
        FLAG1   := ((STATEM==1) # FLAG1) & !(STATEM==2) & !RESET;

        FLAG2   := ((STATEM==9) # FLAG2) & !(STATEM==10) & !RESET;

        WRn     = !((FLAG1 & WR1)#(FLAG2 & WR2));

        RDn     = !((FLAG1 & RD1)#(FLAG2 & RD2));

' State Machine Definition:
   state_diagram [STATE3,STATE2,STATE1,STATE0]

   " State numbers chosen to facilitate reduction to minimum #
    of product terms, to allow fit into the selected device.

        state 15: IF RESET THEN 15
                     ELSE IF SEL1L THEN 0
                         ELSE IF SEL2L THEN 8
                             ELSE 15;

" CPU 1:
        state 0: GOTO 1;

        state 1: GOTO 3;

        state 3: IF RESET THEN 15
                    ELSE IF !SEL1L THEN 2
                        ELSE 3;

        state 2: IF SEL2L THEN 8 ELSE 15;

" CPU 2:
        state 8: GOTO 9;

        state 9: GOTO 11;

        state 11: IF RESET THEN 15
                     ELSE IF !SEL2L THEN 10
                         ELSE 11;
```

```
          state 10: IF SEL1L THEN 0 ELSE 15;

" Invalid States:
          state 4:  GOTO 15;
          state 5:  GOTO 15;
          state 6:  GOTO 15;
          state 7:  GOTO 15;
          state 12: GOTO 15;
          state 13: GOTO 15;
          state 14: GOTO 15;

end       Arbitration_State_2
```

Chapter Summary

In this chapter we discussed the considerations involved in designing with programmable logic. We covered other logic alternatives, device selection, design support tools, production considerations, design entry formats, and the process of developing the logic definitions. Also, the use of test vectors for design verification, design simulation alternatives, device programming, and the debugging of PLD-based systems. We then concluded with a look at available PLD starter kits and booklets, and a PLD design example.

Production with PLDs

The ultimate goal of most designs incorporating PLDs is to achieve production of a product. Depending on the product and the application, this may involve only a few systems or as many as tens of thousands. Although the designer is required to consider certain manufacturing concerns during the design phase of PLD-based systems (as discussed in the previous chapter) there are many considerations that must be dealt with by the production department. Too often, PLD production concerns are not adequately considered or dealt with, frequently resulting in frustration, higher production costs, and even manufacturing delays.

Chapter Overview

In this chapter we will consider the product manufacturing aspects of PLD usage. Manufacturing considerations include device selection, acquisition, alternate-sourcing, programming, security, and testing. Cost considerations are encompassed in all of the above, and manufacturers invariably desire and attempt to keep *real* costs to a minimum. This involves more than simply purchasing the least expensive PLDs. Since many production costs are "hidden," they are sometimes difficult to identify and are often overlooked. Because of the important, though elusive, nature of production costs, a discussion on PLD production cost analysis will also be presented.

PLD Packaging and Power Consumption Considerations

PLDs come in a wide variety of packages and IC technologies and are available in bipolar and CMOS technologies, with varying power consumption, speed, and current drive specifications. Packaging options also tend to vary widely among different devices, depending on the number of pins, power consumption, reprogrammability, and space-saving features. Since by their nature PLDs tend to save board space—minimizing or eliminating SSI and MSI devices in a design—they tend to be available in some of the newer, more space-efficient packages. Space-efficient packages include 300 mil-wide (0.3 inch-wide) 24- and 28-pin Dual In-line Packages (DIPs), Surface Mountable Small Outline Packages (SOs), Pin Grid Arrays (PGAs), Flat Packs, J-Leaded Chip Carriers (JLCCs), Plastic Leaded Chip Carriers (PLCCs), and Leadless Chip Carriers (LCCs). Figure 7-1 shows a number of PLDs in varying packages.

Figure 7-1. Photo showing a variety of different PLD packages.

Reasons exist for the wide variety of package options, and no single choice is best for all applications. It is, therefore, worthwhile to look at the tradeoffs offered by the different package choices.

Ceramic packages offer better cooling properties than plastic packages, but are more expensive than their molded plastic counterparts. Ceramic's higher thermal conductivity allows heat generated by the die to be more readily dissipated into the surrounding air. Ceramic can also withstand higher temperatures than molded plastic. Thus, ceramic packages are generally chosen for ICs that dissipate much heat or that will be operated in high-temperature environments (such as industrial and military environments).

Ceramic and quartz have similar thermal expansion characteristics, allowing them to be combined in a single IC package without separating during changing temperature. The thermal expansion characteristics of plastic, on the other hand, differ considerably from those of quartz, disallowing plastic and quartz to be combined in an IC package. Since ultraviolet (UV) light-erasable EPLDs use transparent quartz windows to provide light access to the die, these devices are always manufactured using ceramic packaging.

Since all existing EPLDs are made using CMOS technology, the heat generated by these devices does not typically justify a ceramic package. When conditions permit, molded plastic seems to be the preferred packaging choice for CMOS devices. Since device erasability may no longer be required after the design phase of a project, most EPLDs are also available in lower-cost, one-time programmable (OTP) molded plastic packages. Since these parts lack the transparent window found on their erasable counterparts, they cannot be erased after programming, and are thus not reusable (reprogrammable). The plastic packaging, however, can reduce device costs considerably.

This is one area where the beauty of EEPROM technology shines. Unlike the EPROM technology-based EPLDs, EEPLDs—based on electrically erasable EEPROM technology—can be erased and reprogrammed in windowless plastic packages. Since EEPLDs are erased using electric current instead of light, windows are not needed. And since all existing EEPLDs are made using CMOS technology, their low power consumption makes them compatible with economical molded plastic packaging. They are, however, also available in ceramic packages for industrial and military applications. EEPLDs provide other benefits in the area of testability, as described later.

The need for PLD reprogrammability must be ascertained before beginning production. As discussed in Chapter 5, it is generally wise—whenever possible—to use reprogrammable PLDs during the development stage of a product. It is important, however, to minimize device costs during manufacturing, and selecting OTP parts is often the most effective way to reduce PLD costs. For example, a designer may use EPLD PALs during product development, but choose standard OTP bipolar parts for production to reduce parts costs. A designer may also use certain EPLDs during the design stage, then choose to use OTP EPLDs (in windowless plastic packages) for production. EEPLDs are the only devices that allow erasability to be retained when using economical plastic packaging. Even when designing with EEPLDs, however, it is sometimes more cost-effective to use a functionally similar part in a different technology for production.

If the circuitry of a product is expected to be upgraded sometime after being shipped, it may be beneficial to use reprogrammable PLDs in production systems. Systems that may not be fully debugged or that are produced in low volume may also benefit from using reprogrammable PLDs.

Reprogrammable devices are forgiving. If a programming error is made during manufacturing, affected parts can be simply erased and reused, whereas OTP parts must be discarded. Similarly, if a design change is made after starting production, reprogrammable parts can simply be erased and reprogrammed, while OTP parts must be discarded—wasting money and valuable time. Nonetheless, reprogrammability generally comes at a price, so the tradeoffs should be carefully considered prior to device purchases.

Saving printed circuit (P.C.) board space is a common objective for using PLDs. Even in designs primarily using PLDs for other reasons, space savings is a natural byproduct. The amount of P.C. board space available for a design is application-dependent, varying from one design to the next. The value of board real-estate also varies, and depends on the size of the P.C. board and the amount of circuitry that needs to be placed on the board. In some applications, board size is fixed, such as designs for standard bus systems like VMEbus, Multibus, and PC bus. In other applications, the board size can vary to meet circuitry requirements.

Determining printed circuit board development and production costs is sometimes difficult. For higher production volumes, design costs become less significant, so production costs should be minimized. For smaller production volumes, the development cost becomes more significant. The higher the chip density on a P.C. board, the more time, effort, and cost is involved with the layout. As chip density increases, additional layers can be added to allow easier line routing, but extra layers also increase board manufacturing costs.

Such manufacturing dilemmas are common. The designer and production manager must determine the best combination of tradeoffs to minimize production costs. If reducing component size is desired to minimize the required number of P.C. board layers, it may be beneficial to choose SO, PGA, PLCC, or LCC device packages to save board space. Although these packaging options are typically more costly than their DIP counterparts, the additional cost may be justified by lower P.C. board cost. Similarly, it may be worthwhile to alter the circuit design to incorporate higher-density PLDs, saving additional board real estate. If board size is flexible, on the other hand, it may be more economical to increase the size of the board to reduce component density, while maintaining use of economical DIP packages.

Another consideration that affects larger systems is the number of P.C. boards in the system. In some cases, the use of higher-density PLDs and/or higher-density IC packages can permit a design to fit onto fewer boards than might otherwise be possible. Under these circumstances, it is generally more economical (and electrically more beneficial—i.e., less noisy) to incur the higher PLD costs associated with the use of advanced PLDs and dense IC packages.

Power consumption is another area to consider before beginning production, though it should be considered during the design stage. The use of CMOS parts in place of power-hungry bipolar parts, though typically more expensive, can substantially reduce system power consumption, thereby reducing power supply and cooling requirements, and allowing components and boards to be placed in closer proximity to each other.

Whenever PLD substitutions are considered—for power consumption, reprogrammability, cost, or other reasons—the design engineer should be consulted, and should ultimately decide whether such substitutions are acceptable. Since timing, output current drive, and other factors must be considered when substituting devices, it is important to ensure that the devices included in the final product meet the design requirements determined by the board or system designer.

Availability and Alternate-Sourcing

Few things are more frustrating in a manufacturing environment than holding up production because one or more components have not yet arrived. Such delays are also costly. It is even more frustrating when the missing parts are sole-sourced, and manufacturers are quoting availability in months instead of days or weeks. While the designer should be careful to choose PLDs—and other components—that will not lead to such a predicament, situations like this are sometimes unpredictable and unavoidable.

Sole-sourced PLDs should be used cautiously. When possible, devices with multiple manufacturers should be used. Most manufacturers realize the importance of alternate-sourcing, and attempt to arrange alternate sources for new products as they are developed. When new devices are first introduced, however, it generally takes months—and sometimes even years—before an alternate-source is established and producing parts. It is wise to be wary of manufacturers indicating "impending" alternate-sources.

Alternate-sourcing of PLDs can come in several forms. The most obvious is an identical device from a different manufacturer, produced using identical IC masks. A similar alternate-source is a functionally identical device offered by a different manufacturer in an enhanced or different IC technology (such as a more-advanced bipolar process, or CMOS instead of bipolar).

Another form of alternate-sourcing involves the use of a device that is similar architecturally. For example, if a PAL22V10 could not be obtained when desired, a V750 could substitute, since it is a functional superset of the PAL22V10. Similarly, if an EP320 is unavailable, a GAL16V8 or PEEL18CV8 may be able to fill the need.

A final alternate-sourcing approach involves the use of devices with dissimilar architectures. This was not uncommon in the early days of PLDs, when multiple PAL or FPLA suppliers were not available. A P.C. board could be laid out so that either a PAL (PAL16L8, for example) or an FPLA (such as a PLS153) could be placed in the board's 20-pin PLD socket. Similarly, the new foldback architecture of the ERASIC family from Exel Microelectronics allows functional emulation of most PAL, FPLA and FPLS devices.

Whenever a device substitution is being considered, the design engineer should be consulted, and should verify that such a substitution would not cause timing or other problems with the product. The designer must also make sure that software and programming support is on-site or readily available for substitute devices.

Design Security

When a company spends tens of thousands—perhaps even millions—of dollars developing a product that may include several man-years of development and testing, there is a justifiable reluctance to allow competitors to have free access to the design specifics. This is clearly IBM's position with its PS/2 family of computers, which incorporates many semicustom devices, as well as numerous patents. For this reason, most PLDs include a security provision which can be enabled during production, if desired.

Physical—Security Fuses

A security fuse, while varying slightly in operation for different devices, essentially prevents the internal fuse pattern of a PLD from being read. Of course, this also prevents the internal pattern from being verified after programming, so verification must take place before blowing the security fuse.

Some manufacturers get a little more elaborate with their security fuse operation. Exel Microelectronics, for example, has a special SecurityPlus security mechanism in its ERASIC devices. When the security fuse of an ERASIC device is blown, the device's entire fuse pattern—including the security fuse— can be read and verified. The security function does not go into effect until after the chip has been powered down then powered up again.

Even with blown security fuses, it is not difficult to determine the internal logic pattern of simple PLDs if someone is serious about finding out what is inside. Most bipolar PALs can simply be opened-up and looked at under a microscope—blown fuses are clearly visible (see Fig. 7-2). Some manufacturers of bipolar PALs, such as Fairchild Semiconductor Corp.—use vertical fuse technology, preventing blown fuses from being viewed under a microscope. Since CMOS devices employing EPROM and EEPROM technology do not incorporate fuses in the same sense as bipolar devices, the logic configuration of these devices cannot be determined by viewing under a microscope. Newer PLDs with more-complex, higher-density architectures cannot be deciphered as readily as simpler PLDs, making their security fuses much more effective at securing internal logic secrets.

While most PLDs incorporate a security fuse feature, there are many that do not. Logic Cell Arrays and most FPLAs, for example, do not have security features. If design security is an important consideration for a product, PLDs should be chosen that support such a feature.

Legal—Copyrights and Patents

Design security can also be implemented through copyrights and patents, although most manufacturers feel less comfortable with these alternatives. The copyright laws in the United States and many other countries now protect software and binary patterns. Although legal precedents have yet to be set in this area for the PLD industry specifically, the trend seems to indicate likely coverage of PLD designs. Of course, once a competitor becomes familiar with the logic inside a device, the logic functions can be rewritten—perhaps using a different PLD—making copyright infringement difficult to prove.

Certain PLD designs may also be patentable, but the same basic drawbacks of copyrights apply. A patent attorney should be consulted to determine the patentability of a PLD design.

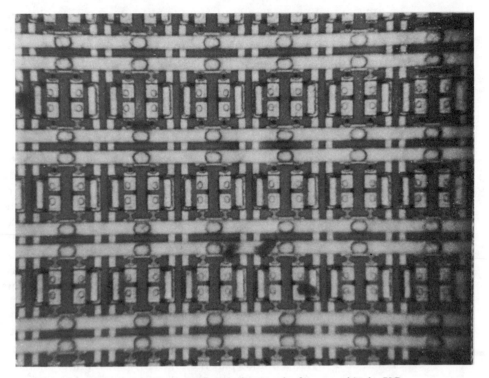

Figure 7-2. Photomicrograph showing the fuses on a bipolar PLD.
Courtesy Advanced Micro Devices.

PLD Inventorying and Numbering

As described in Chapter 1, one of the hidden costs that is part of producing boards with integrated circuits is inventorying. If parts remain in inventory for an extended period of time they become more costly, since the money invested in the parts is sitting idle, not producing income, or even drawing interest. Indeed, the trend for most ICs, and for PLDs in particular, is for prices to drop as products and manufacturing techniques mature. Thus, the value of inventoried devices often becomes less over a period of time, making extended inventorying less palatable.

Since the use of PLDs can substantially reduce the number of components on a P.C. board, inventory cost savings are realized because fewer parts need to be supported. Some PLDs are more effective at reducing inventory costs than others. For example, if a design includes a number of standard PAL devices—say a PAL16R8, a PAL16R4, a PAL16L8, a PAL14L4, and a PAL14H4—a device having a more-generic architecture (such as an EP320, a GAL16V8, or a PEEL18CV8) can often emulate all such devices. The use of generic devices, therefore, could reduce the number of different devices to be inventoried from several to one or two. Generic devices have the added advantage of being more likely to be usable in other designs, reducing the likelihood of becoming stagnant inventory parts. Although generic parts are typically more expensive than the fixed-architecture devices, the cost difference may be offset by inventory and other savings.

PLD testability—described later in this chapter—also has an effect on inventory costs. Since fuse-based PLDs (i.e., bipolar PLDs and fused-CMOS PLDs) are OTP devices, the fuses cannot be blown during chip manufacturing to verify operation. This would make the devices unusable. While most such devices include special on-chip circuitry to test at least portions of the chips' operation, the customer can expect a certain number of devices to fail programming or operation. Generally, a 95%–98% success rate can be expected with bipolar PLDs, with 97% being about average. With IC and testing technologies improving, however, these numbers are getting higher.

Unlike fuse-based PLDs, devices based on EPROM or EEPROM technologies can be fully tested and erased at the factory (and in-house, if desired), providing a nearly 100% functional yield. Even OTP EPROM-based devices can be fully tested before being packaged (though they cannot be tested at the customer site). Thus, reprogrammable PLDs can minimize the number of "extra" parts that must be ordered and inventoried for a product, saving inventory costs. Since failed OTP devices must be returned to the manufacturer for refund or credit—another procedure involving time and money, and one that is generally neglected—reprogrammable devices minimize or eliminate this expense, as well.

Different manufacturers have different approaches for keeping track of blank and programmed PLDs. Regardless of the part numbers used to store blank PLDs in inventory, when approaching production each PLD in a system should be assigned a unique part number. The part number should be included in a company document, indicating the P.C. board the device goes on, its position on the P.C. board (unit number, or U#), PLD type (including the blank part number used by the company's inventory system) and logic source file for the device. It may also list acceptable alternate devices. The part number should also have an extension indicating the revision level of the logic inside the device.

For example, a device may have number P1123.A indicating programmable device #1123, revision A. If the logic or device type is modified, the device number changes to P1123.B, and so on. A company document then references device number P1123, providing the following information:

Device: P1123
P.C. board: D6170.E
Position: U34
Device type: PAL16R4A-2 (internal #A48C043)
Manufacturer: MMI, National, AMD
Acceptable Alternates: GAL16V8, EP320
Source Description Language: ABEL
Source Description Filename: INTCTL.ABL
JEDEC Filename: P1123x.JED   (x = revision)
Notes: New file compilation required if a substitute device is chosen.

Notice how the PLD part numbering approach is essentially the same as that used for other programmable devices, such as EPROMs that contain system software. By assigning a unique part number to each programmed PLD on a board, the devices can be labelled with their assigned numbers and easily referenced on other company documents, including assembly drawings and parts lists (bills of materials).

When storing PLDs in inventory, devices should be in their blank state. This permits last-minute logic changes to be made without rejecting (or reprogramming) a lot of programmed parts. This also allows leftover devices to be used for other applications.

In some instances, devices that have already been programmed will need to be returned to stock. This may be due to reduced production, excessive device programming, or other reasons. If the programmed parts are OTP devices, or are expected to be needed—as programmed—in the foreseeable future, it is best to return the parts to inventory under the assigned *programmed* part numbers (e.g., P1123.A). Do not return programmed parts to stock under their blank part numbers! If the programmed parts are erasable, and will not be needed as programmed in the foreseeable future, it may be most beneficial to erase the parts and return them to inventory under their assigned blank part numbers. Note that EEPROM-based EEPLDs do not need to be erased before being placed back into inventory, since these devices can be electrically erased later, as part of the reprogramming process.

PLD Programming and Testing

Like EPROMs containing system software in microprocessor-based systems, PLDs must be programmed, or "burned," before they can be used in a system. There are a number of PLD programming options available to the product manufacturer. Manufacturers of PLD-based systems should be aware of some of the intricacies of preparing PLDs for use in manufactured products. In this section, we will look at how PLDs are programmed, and the programming-related concerns of the product manufacturer.

People familiar with programming EPROMs will not feel uncomfortable programming PLDs; the process is very similar. In fact, it is not uncommon to find device programmers that are capable of programming both EPROMs and PLDs, though often an adapter change is required. Programming PLDs is less tedious than programming EPROMs, since typical PLDs are programmed in only a few seconds, compared to several minutes for most EPROMs.

A means must exist to transfer the compiled program (for EPROMs) or logic (for PLDs) information from a computer to the device programmer. There are several standard file formats in existence to support the transfer of compiled program code; the most common are Intel's Hex/ASCII format and Motorola's similar S-record format. Some PLD compilers support the Intel Hex/ASCII format for PROMs (PLEs), but a different format, developed by the Joint Electron Device Engineering Council (JEDEC), is the standard for PLDs.

In October 1983, the JEDEC Solid State Products Engineering Council released the first version of JEDEC Standard No. 3, "Standard Data Transfer Format Between Data Preparation System and Programmable Logic Device Programmer." The standard was later revised and released as Standard No. 3-A, in May 1986. Fortunately for the PLD industry, the need for such a format was recognized relatively early on, before the explosive growth that has since become the industry's trademark. The JEDEC standard has become universally accepted and adopted by the PLD industry, the only exceptions coming from companies because of their special needs. In the case of Xilinx' XACT system, the output file can be generated in any of three standard formats: Intel Hex/ ASCII, Motorola S-record, or Tektronix Hex. This is because the information is generally placed into an EPROM or PROM.

PLD programmers are capable of accepting JEDEC file information downloaded from a host computer via a serial RS-232 port, and are also capable of duplicating existing PLDs—provided that device security fuses, if present, are still intact. For production, it is *very poor practice* to duplicate PLDs from a master device. The risk is too high that the master has become defective (by static electricity or otherwise), resulting in the repeated duplication of a bad part. The result is unpleasant, and is particularly devastating if OTP devices are used.

Device testing should be considered an integral and important part of PLD programming. Most PLD programmers accept PLD *test vectors* for testing devices after they have been programmed. Any number of test vectors may be developed and applied to a device, although the practical limitation is usually the amount of memory available—either in the computer used for development, or in the programmer itself. The lack of test vectors is another reason not to duplicate PLDs from a master device.

When using OTP parts—particularly bipolar parts—a certain number of device failures can be expected, since complete factory testing is impossible. The number (percentage) of devices that pass the basic PLD programming operation—blowing fuses, then verifying that the correct fuses are, indeed, blown—is known as the programming yield. The number (percentage) of devices that pass the programming operation *and* operate properly—being ready for use in a product—is known as the post-programming functional yield (PPFY). The object is to keep this number as high as possible. Note that a PLD can pass the basic PLD programming operation, and yet not function properly—this is why post-programming device testing is important.

Devices made using reprogrammable technologies, such as LCAs (SRAM cell), EPLDs (EPROM cell), and EEPLDs (EEPROM cell), can be tested to a much higher degree at the factory than can bipolar or other devices that are not reprogrammable. The SRAM- and EEPROM-based devices lend themselves particularly well to complete testing, since they can be erased, reprogrammed, and tested many times in only a few seconds. EPROM-based devices, on the other hand, must go through a 20-minute (nominal) erase cycle between reprogramming, making numerous test patterns impractical during the manufacturing process. While EPLDs are tested to a much greater extent than fuse-based devices, and offer an almost perfect PPFY, they cannot be tested to the same degree as SRAM- and EEPROM-based devices.

Some manufacturers of reprogrammable PLDs suggest that post-programming functional testing is unnecessary with their devices, because of the completeness of factory testing. Even though the degree to which post-programming testing is needed is clearly not as high as with nonreprogrammable devices, reprogrammable PLDs, are subject to damage from such things as improper programming and electrostatic discharge (ESD). Indeed, being CMOS, reprogrammable devices are generally more susceptible to ESD damage than bipolar devices. For this reason, post-programming functional testing should be performed on *all* PLDs; especially when using fuse-based PLDs, such testing should not even be considered optional.

Because of their sensitivity to ESD, production operations with CMOS devices, including programming, testing, and insertion, should be performed at anti-static workstations. This precaution will minimize the number of devices damaged or destroyed by ESD.

There are a variety of testing alternatives available to the product manufacturing community. Let's take a look at some of the alternatives, and discuss their relative merits.

Test Vectors with a PLD Programmer

The use of test vectors with a PLD programmer is the most common—and most convenient—method of testing programmed PLDs. Test vectors are typically generated by the PLD designer or test engineer as part of the device definition source file. All popular PLD programming languages support test vector generation. The test vectors should be defined so that as much logic as possible on the PLD can be tested. Although such tests are limited in their capability—disallowing open-collector outputs to be verified, for example—they generally provide an adequate test for programmed PLDs.

As described in Chapters 5 and 6, test vectors are designed for two different purposes: for design verification, and for programming verification. Design verification test vectors are often used with device simulation software (as well as with the PLD programmer), and are intended to ensure that the operation of the PLD is what the designer expects. The intention of programming verification test vectors is to make sure that the PLD actually performs the logic functions specified by the device's logic definition, and to test as much of the device circuitry as possible. The production department is only concerned with programming verification testing, since the PLD designs are expected to be complete and verified.

It is difficult to know how much of the circuitry within a PLD is actually being tested by test vectors. To provide assistance in this area, a number of PLD languages are capable of generating test vectors that provide complete fault coverage. The most common form of fault coverage is *stuck-at-0* and *stuck-at-1* coverage, where the test vectors will catch any (or almost any) logic signals stuck in one state or the other.

Several companies also provide separate software packages to assist in generating production test vectors. Data I/O Corp., for example, has developed its *PLDtest* program. PLDtest can perform fault grading; i.e., it can analyze the test vectors written for a specific device and provide a report indicating how complete the vectors are at testing the whole device. PLDtest can also generate supplementary test vectors to the designer's "seed" vectors to provide additional fault coverage, or it can generate a complete set of test vectors if seed vectors do not exist.

The "Operation" section of the PLDtest manual describes the theory of operation of the program, as well as some of its limitations. It also provides tips on designing for testability. This section should be reviewed thoroughly before using the program for large production volumes. By understanding the concepts presented, the test engineer can assure the fullest possible device testing.

As described in the PLDtest manual, certain designs are beyond its capability, and test vectors are best written by the designer or test engineer. Registered devices, in particular, can pose problems. PLDtest makes extensive use of *register preloading* for registered devices. Devices lacking this capability can be severely restricted in testability, and with their support under PLDtest.

State machine and sequencer applications are popular uses of PLDs. Since certain states may be reachable only after executing many test vectors, it can be difficult to test certain portions of the operation of state machine devices. To circumvent this problem, most newer registered PLDs support *register preloading*. This allows device registers to be preloaded to an initial state to test hard-to-reach states and conditions. In order to take advantage of register preloading, the programmer must also support this feature. The most popular programmers include register preloading support.

One final note regarding PLD test. It may not support newer devices, or devices with special architectures (foldback architecture, for example). When considering PLDtest or any similar PLD test program for test vector generation, the program's device repertoire should be consulted to make sure that pertinent PLDs are supported.

Another program that generates production test vectors is *Anvil ATG* from Anvil Software. Anvil ATG, which runs on IBM PC compatibles, provides 90%–100% fault coverage for sequential designs, and includes a time-based simulator, a fault simulator, and an automatic test vector generator.

Structured Design also offers its PC-based *TestPLA* software for generating test vectors.

The capability of programs like PLDtest, ATG, and TestPLA is limited, but they can assure good fault coverage for most PLD designs.

When test vectors are generated, either by the test engineer using development software, or by a program such as PLDtest (or both), the test vectors become part of the PLD's JEDEC output file, and are downloaded to the PLD programmer as part of the JEDEC file. Most programmers automatically apply the downloaded test vectors to the PLD after programming, and generate an error code or message if a failure occurs.

When developing test vectors, there are a number of situations that must be approached cautiously. Some test vector problems will be revealed during software simulation, if this is done before device programming. Others are more elusive, and will pass software simulation, but cause programmed devices to fail. The circuits that cause most of the problems are those involving feedback paths.

Figure 7-3 shows a circuit that will oscillate under certain logic conditions. If test vectors are not carefully written for such a circuit, the output oscillation will cause unpredictable and inaccurate test results.

Figure 7-4 shows a circuit that is partial to race conditions. When the B and C inputs in Fig. 7-4 change simultaneously, for example, a glitch can occur at the

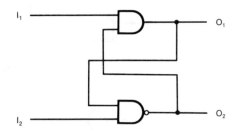

Figure 7-3. Circuit that will oscillate under certain conditions.

S input to the S-R latch because of propagation time differences, resulting in an undesirable latch output change. Such a problem may not show up during software simulation (because of the static-value approach used by most software simulators), but will appear when applying the test vectors to a programmed device.

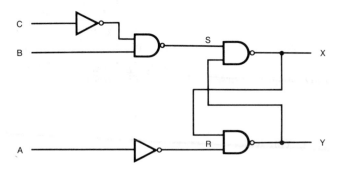

Figure 7-4. Circuit with race conditions.

Figure 7-5 illustrates yet another potential problem circuit. This circuit uses two control signals, CTRL1 and CTRL2, in conjunction with a feedback circuit to latch signal IN. When CTRL1 is high and CTRL2 is low, signal IN appears at the output of the circuit, OUT. When CTRL2 goes high, the circuit output remains unchanged. CTRL1 can then go low, with CTRL2 and the OUT feedback retaining the value of IN. If, when writing test vectors to test this circuit, CTRL2 is brought high and CTRL1 is brought low at the same time, a software simulator may very well pass the test vectors. The same test vectors applied to a programmed device by a PLD programmer may fail, however, since the programmer may clear CTRL1 before setting CTRL2 when setting-up the test vectors. Beware when testing combinatorial latches.

Signature Analysis

Signature analysis is another feature that can be used to test PLDs. This approach involves the use of a circuit to generate a sequence of nearly random logic patterns, which are applied to the inputs of a known-good PLD. As each pattern is applied to the device inputs, the outputs of the device are recorded as

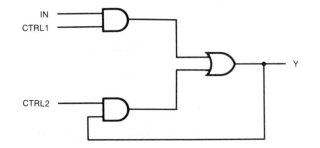

Figure 7-5. Circuit that may cause test vector problems.

a binary number and added to a running test-sum. At the completion of the process, the final test-sum is the device's *signature*. This signature value can then be compared to that of other programmed devices to determine if they are functioning properly. Of course, such an approach lends itself more easily to some device architectures than others, but can be an effective testing method.

Some companies offer special machines purely for signature analysis applications. These machines also tend to carry relatively high price tags. Others do, however, offer programmers with signature analysis capability. Data I/O, for example, includes its Logic Fingerprint signature analysis feature in some of its PLD programmers. Each Logic Fingerprint test cycle generates 128,000 test patterns.

Integrated Circuit Testers

Some integrated circuit testers can also be used for PLD testing. While many IC testers can only test devices that are already supported in their resident device libraries, others allow the end user to develop test vectors to support new or custom devices. The testing concept is similar to the test vector approach used with PLD programmers, although IC testers usually have more capability. They can test outputs under load conditions, and can also vary open-collector and high-impedance outputs. Some of the more-expensive units can also perform certain parametric tests, such as logic thresholds.

An economical IC tester that supports custom vector generation is the Circuit Cellar IC Tester, sold for $349 in kit form from Circuit Cellar, Inc., P.O. Box 428, Tolland, CT 06084; phone: (203) 875-2751. The tester, shown in Fig. 7-6, was also presented in the November and December, 1987 issues of *BYTE* magazine. It comes complete with IBM PC-compatible software for supporting custom devices, and a standard library of supported devices. The Circuit Cellar IC Tester tests devices under load conditions, and can verify high-impedance and open-collector outputs. It can also detect shorted inputs. The tester is capable of testing 14-, 16-, 20-, and 24-pin devices.

Listing 7-1 shows an example Circuit Cellar IC Tester device definition file for a PAL device. The logic equations for the PAL are also provided in the device definition file. The vector compiler reads the information from the vector definition file, and compacts the information into a module usable by the

Figure 7-6. Photo of the circuit cellar IC tester.

execution program. If numerous custom device definitions are combined together into a single vector compaction file, the IC tester is capable of identifying the device installed in its test socket. It must, however, be in its library. This can be helpful, for example, if a PLD is programmed but is inadvertently not labelled or mislabelled. The tester can determine which device it is. For complete flexibility, don't-care (X) conditions are supported by the tester.

Listing 7-1. Sample Device Definition File, with Test Vectors

```
* CIRCUIT CELLAR IC TESTER_VECTOR DEFINITION FILE
*
* Roger C. Alford
* 10/5/88
*
* This file contains the definition for PAL #1234 (a PAL16L8),
* having the output equations:
*
*      MRD\  = !(MEMIO & !RD\)
*      MWR\  = !(MEMIO & !WR\)
*      IORD\ = !(!MEMIO & !RD\)
*      IOWR\ = !(!MEMIO & !WR\)
*
* The device has the following pinout:
*
*   Inputs:
*        Pin 7   = MEMIO
*        Pin 8   = RD\
*        Pin 9   = WR\
*   Outputs:
*        Pin 16  = MRD\
*        Pin 17  = MWR\
*        Pin 18  = IORD\
*        Pin 19  = IOWR\
*   Power:
```

```
*          Pin 10  = GND
*          Pin 20  = +5V
*
*
# 1234                                              * PAL device #1234
S 20 10 20                                          * Define power, GND, # of pins
* MEMIO RD\ WR\    MRD\ MWR\ IORD\ IOWR\            * Specify signals
F   I   I   I       0    0    0    0                * Define signals as In/Out
P   7   8   9      16   17   18   19                * Specify signal pin numbers
* TEST INACTIVE STATES:
I   1   1   1       0    0    0    0                * Generate "output" vector
R                   1    1    1    1                * Specify "readback" vector
I   0   1   1       0    0    0    0
R                   1    1    1    1
* TEST MEMORY STROBES:
I   1   0   1       1    0    0    0                * Memory Read
R                   0    1    1    1
I   1   1   0       0    1    0    0                * Memory Write
R                   1    0    1    1
* TEST I/O STROBES:
I   0   0   1       0    0    1    0                * I/O Read
R                   1    1    0    1
I   0   1   0       0    0    0    1                * I/O Write
R                   1    1    1    0
*
E                                                   * End of definition
```

VLSI Testers

On the high end of the PLD testing alternatives are VLSI (Very Large Scale Integration) device testers. These testers are expensive. They are primarily used for PLDs when already owned by a company and are being used for other purposes. The cost of these testers is often too high to justify solely for PLD testing. VLSI testers are capable of test vector support, as well as device parametric testing—including logic thresholds, input and output currents, and propagation delays. Since these testers have become popular in many applications for gate array and standard cell device testing, they also work well at testing PLDs.

One company that produces VLSI device testers is Teradyne, Inc., 321 Harrison Ave., Boston, MA 02118; phone: (617) 482-2700. In 1986 Teradyne released a new software product called Circuit Breaker, intended specifically to support programmable logic. Designed to run on a VAX/VMS computer system in conjunction with the company's logic and fault simulator software, Circuit Breaker generates tests for a variety of PLD fault types, even for PLDs that are highly sequential. Teradyne claims that Circuit Breaker is the first PLD test program to generate tests for dynamic (time-related) faults as well as static faults.

At a price of $50,000, plus $2,000 for each PLD model generator (specific to each PLD type to be tested), the software is clearly aimed at high-volume manufacturers. Nonetheless, when used in conjunction with a capable VLSI device tester, unmatched testing completeness is the clear result.

PLD Programming Options

As described in the cost analysis section in this chapter, programming involves cost. Therefore, the different programming alternatives should be carefully considered before making a final decision. The decision must be determined based on production volume, time frame, money available for initial equipment investment, and manpower availability.

On-Site PLD Programmer

The most common approach to PLD programming is for a company to have its own PLD programming equipment. Depending on production volume and PLD device support needs, the cost of this equipment ranges from several hundred to tens of thousands of dollars. While few manufacturers currently produce "gang" PLD programmers—allowing multiple devices to be programmed simultaneously—PLDs are typically programmed in only a few seconds. This is in contrast to the several minutes generally needed to program standard EPROMs. Individual device programming is, therefore, generally adequate for most levels of production. Automatic device handlers that work in conjunction with device programmers are also available for high-volume production.

On-site programming does, of course, require the use of company personnel. They must be able to download compiled logic information from a computer into the PLD programmer. This is generally in the form of a JEDEC PLD output file. They must also direct the programmer to program the parts. Labels must be printed for all PLDs, and must be placed on the devices as they are programmed. Many companies prefer to coat the labels to prevent smearing. The labels are best printed by a computer using special software and an acceptable printer.

PLD Programming Services

For system manufacturers that do not want to purchase their own equipment, or do not have the personnel to spare, there are companies that provide PLD programming services. These companies will program and test the PLDs in accordance with prearranged test procedures and delivery schedules. Three primary categories of programming services exist: PLD manufacturers, PLD distributors, and third-party services. Of course, when considering any PLD programming service, the delivery schedule must be considered in conjunction with cost.

PLD Manufacturers

The most obvious source of programming support is probably the PLD manufacturer. While not all PLD manufacturers provide programming and testing services for their devices, a number of them do. Notice that testing is always associated with programming. The importance of this was described earlier. Since device testing is an integral part of PLD programming, PLD manufacturers should have the best insight into how to test their devices.

If the manufacturer programs and tests parts before shipping, there is little concern for failures and factory returns. The PPFY should always be virtually 100%. One level of shipping is also eliminated when the manufacturer programs the parts. In comparison, if a distributor is used to program the PLDs, the parts must be shipped to the distributor, programmed, then shipped to the customer. If a third-party service is used to program the parts, the parts are generally first shipped by the manufacturer to the customer (sometimes by way of a distributor), then they are shipped to the programming company, programmed, then shipped back to the customer for production use.

On the down side, PLD manufacturers generally charge a set-up fee for each different PLD (or PLD logic pattern) to be programmed. For example, if a design consists of eight PLDs to be programmed by the manufacturer, the purchasing company would have to pay eight set-up fees, the cost of the PLDs, and an additional programming fee for each device programmed. Another drawback is that only parts from that manufacturer can be programmed. This is limiting when PLDs from multiple manufacturers are used in a design, and also limits alternate-sourcing flexibility.

PLD Distributors

The United States, like many other countries, is inundated with electronic parts distributors. Distributors are the primary sources of parts for companies involved with small- and medium-scale production, and are thus likely sources for PLD programming. While not all distributors of PLDs provide programming services, the major ones do—and the idea is becoming increasingly popular.

Since many product manufacturers purchase their PLDs from a distributor anyway, the distributor tends to be a convenient place to have the devices programmed. They can be programmed before being shipped. Traditionally, distributors do not charge a set-up fee, although this is subject to change. They usually require their customers to supply the PLD JEDEC files on an IBM-compatible diskette, so the files can be downloaded from an IBM PC compatible to the device programmer. The distributor generally adds a fee-per-device programming charge to the cost of the PLDs, although some do not.

One drawback in using distributors for device programming is that, similar to manufacturers, they will only program PLDs that they sell. While this may be less limiting than a single PLD manufacturer, it may not encompass all of the PLDs within a particular design.

Third-Party Services

Some "third-party" vendors have begun offering programming services. A set-up fee is usually charged in addition to a fee per PLD. The third-party service also works with its customers to establish acceptable device testing procedures and delivery schedules.

The primary advantage of using third-party services is that the widest variety of PLDs has manufacturer support. These services can generally handle large volumes, and keep their programming equipment updated to support new devices as they become available.

Mask-Programmed PLDs

Another manufacturing option not to be overlooked is mask-programmed devices. Unlike standard PLDs, mask-programmed devices are not programmed by blowing fuses (or configuring EPROM or EEPROM cells). They are pre-programmed by changing the IC masks used to manufacture the parts. The parts are manufactured as function-specific, and cannot be programmed to function differently. These devices are essentially like gate arrays (and, in fact, *are* gate arrays in some cases), and require only one or two mask layer changes to be configured to customer requirements.

A set-up fee (higher than that for programming set-up) is charged for setting-up the PLD masks—usually several thousand dollars. As with other gate arrays, this process requires time, so lead times are longer for mask-programmed PLDs than for blank or manufacturer-programmed devices. There are two primary advantages of mask-programmed devices. First, no device programming or test-ing is required by the customer, since this is done during the manufacturing process. This, of course, saves money. Second, the cost of the manufactured PLDs is lower than that of standard, blank PLDs. Since the mask-programmed devices do not have fuses, and because fuses consume a large amount of silicon area, the amount of silicon required to produce mask-programmed parts from some suppliers is much less than that required to produce fused parts. As a result, manufacturing yields are higher. In some cases, the fuse layers of standard PLDs are replaced with metallized interconnect layers, so the die size remains the same, but manufacturing yields are still higher.

Several PLD manufacturers offer their devices in mask-programmed form, such as MMI with its Hard Array Logic (HAL and ZHAL) devices, and National Semiconductor with its National Masked Logic (NML) parts. There are also third-party suppliers who offer gate arrays specifically designed to replace many standard PLDs. A few third-party suppliers are listed in Appendix A.

Because of the substantial set-up charge, it is best to consider mask-pro-grammed devices only when preparing for high-volume production. The prod-uct manufacturer should consider programming, testing, and parts cost savings when considering the mask-programming approach, to determine if the savings could be adequately amortized over the expected production volume.

Although the mask-programming approach makes the associated PLDs sole-sourced, standard, programmable parts can be substituted if there is a schedule delay or an increase in production volume.

Keep in mind that PLD design changes are more costly. Mask programming should only be considered after a design has been completely verified, and has achieved a high confidence level. Also, inventorying of mask-programmed parts is more expensive than that of blank parts. This is because different logic configurations must be separately inventoried, even if multiple devices are masked from the same basic PLD type.

Some companies, like Compaq Computer Corp., look to standard, off-the-shelf PLDs for initial systems production, but later resort to mask-programmed PLDs or gate arrays for final production. This gives them the opportunity to resolve all design bugs and to make sure that the logic is firm before committing to "hard" silicon.

Production Cost Analysis

How much does it cost to include PLDs in products? Most cost-related information has been presented in other forms in this chapter, but it is worthwhile to analyze the PLD-related production costs in an attempt to make production decisions clearer.

Some cost areas are optional, while others are not. Note that this discussion disregards one-time expenses, such as programming and test equipment purchases, which can be substantial. Areas that involve cost in PLD use include:

- Device purchase
- Extra devices to compensate for bad devices
- Device unavailability/shipping delays
- Incoming inspection/testing
- Inventory
- Programming
- Post-programming testing
- Bad device returns
- Last-minute design changes
- Post-programming design changes
- Post-shipment design changes
- In-system PLD failures (at production site)
- Post-shipment (field) PLD failures

Device purchase is clearly an expense that cannot be avoided. It is up to the design engineer to determine what PLD types are acceptable, including alternates. The buyer then is responsible for finding the parts that have the lowest prices with acceptable availability. Beware! Device prices can be deceiving. PLD costs must be viewed in perspective with the other production costs listed above. The production manager should work together with the buyer to determine the best PLD alternatives.

It is difficult to assign specific costs to such things as inventory, device programming, and device testing. These costs can vary considerably not only from one company to another, but from one product to another within the same company. For discussion purposes we will present a look at a hypothetical situation, pulling some arbitrary numbers out of a hat. These numbers are for example purposes only, and *should not* be used as accurate values for decision-making in real applications. To minimize costs in an actual production environment, the production manager should attempt to estimate real costs as accurately as possible. Once all of the costs have been estimated and viewed in terms of production volume and the other considerations presented here, it becomes reasonably straightforward to make the best possible decisions.

For our example, let's assume we have just developed a new widget that is ready for production. The widget design includes five PLDs, listed here with their acceptable alternates. For the purposes of this example, we will not concern ourselves with part speeds or packages—plastic packaging is acceptable for all devices.

Device Name: PLD1
Device Type: PAL16L8
Alternates: PAL16P8, GAL16V8, EP320, PLS153

Device Name: PLD2
Device Type: PAL22V10
Alternates: PAL32VX10, XL78C800

Device Name: PLD3
Device Type: X2064 (LCA)
Alternates: none

Device Name: PLD4
Device Type: PAL16R6
Alternates: PAL16RP6, GAL16V8, EP320

Device Name: PLD5
Device Type: PLS153
Alternates: none

Widget production is expected to be about 1,000 units per year, with the initial production run being 500 units, beginning in three weeks.

Upon contacting various distributors, we acquire the delivery schedules and prices for the PLDs, as presented in Table 7-1 (*Note: these are not real prices!*).

Since bipolar PLDs tend to experience a 95%–98% PPFY—with 97% being typical—orders for bipolar PLDs are always increased by 4% at the Widget company. Thus bipolar PLD prices are internally considered to be 4% higher than actual prices. Since additional cost would also be involved with returning bad bipolar PLDs for replacement (estimated at $2.00 per returned device) such devices are discarded. Because bipolar devices ultimately also result in a 4% inventory increase, higher inventory costs also result. Bipolar PLD testing is mandatory, and estimated at $0.15 per device. No incoming inspection is performed.

EPLDs and EEPLDs (including OTP EPLDs) are considered 100% factory-tested. To compensate for production damage or post-production failure, the quantity of parts ordered is 0.5% higher than needed for production. Thus, the prices for these devices are considered to be 0.5% higher. Post-programming testing requirements are also less than those for bipolar PLDs. EPLD and EEPLD testing cost is estimated at $0.07 per device.

Table 7-1. Hypothetical Widget PLD Prices

Device	Price*	Delivery Schedule
PAL16L8	2.00	STOCK
PAL16P8	2.50	2 WEEKS
PAL16R6	2.00	STOCK
PAL16RP6	2.50	2 WEEKS
GAL16V8	2.40	3 WEEKS
EP320	7.00	3 WEEKS
EP320 otp	2.50	3 WEEKS
PLS153	2.30	1 WEEK
PAL22V10	6.00	2 WEEKS
PAL32VX10	9.00	4 WEEKS
XL78C800	12.00	3 WEEKS
X2064	18.00	2 WEEKS

*Note: prices are reduced 10% if quantity is doubled.

Each PLD must be programmed, and therefore has an associated programming cost. The logic programming information for the SRAM-based X2064 LCA will be combined with system software and stored in the system's EPROMs, so the programming cost for this device is considered zero. The remaining devices have variable programming times, ranging from about 5–15 seconds. However, we will consider the programming cost to be constant for all of the devices. Device programming includes producing labels, downloading JEDEC files from a PC to the PLD programmer, programming, and labelling the devices. Let's assume from experience we know that device programming costs us about $0.12 per device (keep in mind, this is strictly hypothetical).

Inventory costs are a little more difficult to estimate. They are based on three primary factors: (1) the (small) inventory usage rate for repairs and replacements; (2) the estimated revenue lost due to idle money in inventoried parts; and (3) the cost of inventory maintenance. Based on these factors, the cost of part inventory is estimated at 2% of the part cost, plus $0.04 per device for maintenance. It should be noted that if multiple device types are merged into a single type—eliminating an inventoried device—an estimated $0.05 per device is saved in inventory costs.

Finally, there's the "risk factor." We need to determine how solid the design is, and if there's any likelihood of the design changing after PLD programming. If PLD logic changes may be required in the foreseeable future, it may be best to consider reprogrammable parts instead of OTP parts. Although the Widget design looks fairly solid, it is the first of its kind, so a certain modification risk is involved. Based on a risk factor determined by engineering and marketing, the cost of OTP parts is considered to be 15% higher than actual cost to compensate for the possibility of having to scrap them due to a reprogramming change.

With all of these cost factors in mind, we can now create a new device cost table for all of the parts, and determine the best PLD choices. Table 7-2 shows the new cost table.

Table 7-2. Effective Cost Table for Widget PLDs

PLD#	PART	BASE-$	EXTRA-$	PROG-$	TEST-$	INV-$	RISK-$	TOTAL-$
1	PAL16L8	2.00	0.08	0.12	0.15	0.08	0.30	2.73
1	PAL16P8	2.50	0.10	0.12	0.15	0.09	0.38	3.34
1/4	GAL16V8	2.40	0.02	0.12	0.07	0.09	0.00	2.70
1,4	GAL16V8	2.16	0.01	0.12	0.07	0.03	0.00	2.39
1/4	EP320	7.00	0.04	0.12	0.07	0.18	0.00	7.41
1,4	EP320	6.30	0.03	0.12	0.07	0.12	0.00	6.64
1/4	EP320 otp	2.50	0.02	0.12	0.07	0.09	0.38	3.18
1,4	EP320 otp	2.25	0.01	0.12	0.07	0.04	0.34	2.83
1/5	PLS153	2.30	0.10	0.12	0.15	0.09	0.35	3.11
1,5	PLS153	2.07	0.08	0.12	0.15	0.03	0.31	2.76
2	PAL22V10	6.00	0.24	0.12	0.15	0.16	0.90	7.57
2	PAL32VX10	9.00	0.36	0.12	0.15	0.22	1.35	11.20
2	XL78C800	12.00	0.06	0.12	0.07	0.28	0.00	12.53
3	X2064	18.00	0.09	0.00	0.07	0.40	0.00	18.56
4	PAL16R6	2.00	0.08	0.12	0.15	0.08	0.30	2.73
4	PAL16RP6	2.50	0.10	0.12	0.15	0.09	0.38	3.34

Notes:

BASE	=	PLD base price
EXTRA	=	Add'l cost for extra devices
PROG	=	Programming cost
TEST	=	Testing cost
INV	=	Inventory cost
RISK	=	Risk factor cost
TOTAL	=	Effective total device cost
x/y	=	x *or* y
x,y	=	x *and* y

With all items now identified, we can determine which devices would minimize production costs. The decision for PLD3 and PLD5 is simple, since these devices do not have listed alternates. For PLD1, the GAL16V8 is the most cost-effective choice. Similarly, PLD4 is best served by the GAL16V8. Finally, the PAL22V10 is the most economical choice for PLD2. Notice how the GAL16V8 proved to be the most economical choice for PLD1 and PLD4 even though it does not have the lowest base price.

Confidence factor also plays a part in the decision-making process. It is often easier to feel a higher level of confidence with EPLD and EEPLD devices than for bipolar devices. Unlike fuse-based technologies, the erasable technologies permit complete testing at the factory. In some cases, then, the higher confidence level offered by devices using reprogrammable technologies should be included in the risk factor estimate. This depends primarily on how complete the post-programming testing is for fuse-based devices.

Research has shown that the later a device fails in a product, the more costly it becomes, increasing by a factor of 10 each time a device gets to a new stage. For example, if it costs $3.00 to replace a failed PLD at the programming stage, it may cost $30 to replace the part after it has been installed in a board, and $300 after it has been shipped to a customer. Thus, testing is important at both the post-programming IC level and the post-insertion board level to minimize the effective economic loss from bad devices. If post-programming testing of fuse-based devices is complete, there should be an associated high level of confidence that nearly all bad parts will be found during post-programming IC testing. If the testing is incomplete, the risk is higher that a device failure will be found at a later stage, resulting in a higher effective cost.

Chapter Summary

In this chapter we considered the factors involved with selecting, programming, and testing PLDs for the production environment. We considered the various approaches to PLD testing and their tradeoffs, and discussed device technology-related issues. We concluded with a brief study of production economics, as it applies to manufacturing with programmable logic devices.

Chapter 8

PLD Application Examples

As we have seen, there are many programmable logic devices from which to choose, and many potential applications for which they are suitable. Since PLDs are being used in an increasingly wider variety of applications, it is impossible to look at all applications. However, to help better understand how PLDs are selected and used, it is often useful to look at real applications. This information can then be used "as is" in other designs, or can be extrapolated to meet the needs of similar designs. Guiding designers to implement real PLD-based designs is the ultimate goal of this book. Hopefully, the example applications presented here will help new designers become familiar with how PLD designs are commonly implemented.

Chapter Overview

In this chapter we will cover five diverse example PLD applications that were selected from electronic industry trade journals and PLD-manufacturer data books. The examples are presented in the order of their complexity, and each is preceded by a brief summary of the application and a credit to its source.

Basic Gates

The *Basic Gates* reprint (Fig. 8-1) is an application note from a National Semiconductor data book. It uses a simple PAL (PAL12H6) and the PALASM I compiler to show how basic logic gates can be implemented in PLDs. The note includes the AND, OR, NAND, NOR, XOR, and INVERT logic functions.

8.1 BASIC GATES

This example demonstrates how fusable logic can implement the basic inverter, AND OR, NAND, NOR and exclusive -OR functions. The PAL 12H6 is selected because it has 12 inputs and 6 outputs.

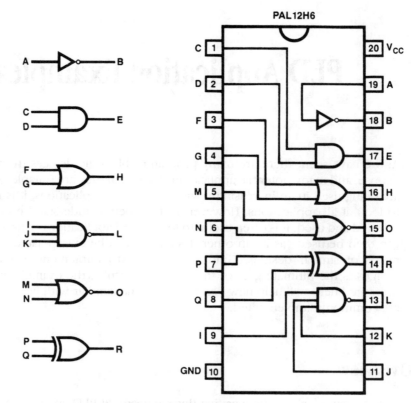

Figure 8.1.1 Basic Gates

* **Applications contained in this chapter are for illustration purposes only and National makes no representation or warranty that such applications will be suitable for the use specified without further testing or modification.**

Figure 8-1. *cont.* Basic Gates. *Reprinted from* Programmable Logic Design Guide,

```
PALASM VERSION 1.5

PAL12H6
TOM WANG
BASIC GATE
NSC SANTA CLARA
C D F G M N P Q I GND J K L R O H E B A VCC
B = /A
E = C*D
H = F + G
L = /I + /J + /K
O = /M*/N
R = P*/Q + /P*Q
FUNCTION TABLE
A B C D E F G H I J K L M N O P Q R
-------------------------------------------
L H  X X X  X X X  X X X X  X X X  X X X ;TEST INVERTER
H L  X X X  X X X  X X X X  X X X  X X X ;TEST INVERTER
X X  L L L  X X X  X X X X  X X X  X X X ;TEST AND GATE
X X  L H L  X X X  X X X X  X X X  X X X ;TEST AND GATE
X X  H L L  X X X  X X X X  X X X  X X X ;TEST AND GATE
X X  H H H  X X X  X X X X  X X X  X X X ;TEST AND GATE
X X  X X X  L L L  X X X X  X X X  X X X ;TEST OR GATE
X X  X X X  L H H  X X X X  X X X  X X X ;TEST OR GATE
X X  X X X  H L H  X X X X  X X X  X X X ;TEST OR GATE
X X  X X X  H H H  X X X X  X X X  X X X ;TEST OR GATE
X X  X X X  X X X  L L L H  X X X  X X X ;TEST NAND GATE
X X  X X X  X X X  L L H H  X X X  X X X ;TEST NAND GATE
X X  X X X  X X X  L H L H  X X X  X X X ;TEST NAND GATE
X X  X X X  X X X  H L L H  X X X  X X X ;TEST NAND GATE
X X  X X X  X X X  H H H L  X X X  X X X ;TEST NAND GATE
X X  X X X  X X X  X X X X  L L H  X X X ;TEST NOR GATE
X X  X X X  X X X  X X X X  L H L  X X X ;TEST NOR GATE
X X  X X X  X X X  X X X X  H L L  X X X ;TEST NOR GATE
X X  X X X  X X X  X X X X  H H L  X X X ;TEST NOR GATE
X X  X X X  X X X  X X X X  X X X  L L L ;TEST EXCLUSIVE OR GATE
X X  X X X  X X X  X X X X  X X X  L H H ;TEST EXCLUSIVE OR GATE
X X  X X X  X X X  X X X X  X X X  H L H ;TEST EXCLUSIVE OR GATE
X X  X X X  X X X  X X X X  X X X  H H L ;TEST EXCLUSIVE OR GATE
-------------------------------------------
DESCRIPTION

BASIC GATE


           *************** ***************
           *             *  *   *        *
           ****             ****
     C     * 1*    P A L    *20*    VCC
           ****             ****
           *      1 2 H 6   *
           ****             ****
     D     * 2*             *19*    A
           ****             ****
           *                *
           ****             ****
     F     * 3*             *18*    B
           ****             ****
           *                *
           ****             ****
     G     * 4*             *17*    E
           ****             ****
```

National Semiconductor Corp., May 1986, pp. 157–161, with permission.

```
                    *                              *
                   ****                           ****
          M       * 5*                           *16*    H
                   ****                           ****
                    *                              *
                   ****                           ****
          N       * 6*                           *15*    O
                   ****                           ****
                    *                              *
                   ****                           ****
          P       * 7*                           *14*    R
                   ****                           ****
                    *                              *
                   ****                           ****
          Q       * 8*                           *13*    L
                   ****                           ****
                    *                              *
                   ****                           ****
          I       * 9*                           *12*    K
                   ****                           ****
                    *                              *
                   ****                           ****
          GND     *10*                           *11*    J
                   ****                           ****
                    *                              *
                   *********************************
```

BASIC GATE

```
                    11 1111 1111 2222 2222 2233
              0123 4567 8901 2345 6789 0123 4567 8901

BEG*FPLT PAL12H6    8

    8 ---- ---X --00 --00 --00 --00 ---- ---- /A
    9 XXXX XXXX XX00 XX00 XX00 XX00 XXXX XXXX
   10 XXXX XXXX XX00 XX00 XX00 XX00 XXXX XXXX
   11 XXXX XXXX XX00 XX00 XX00 XX00 XXXX XXXX

   16 X-X- ---- --00 --00 --00 --00 ---- ---- C*D
   17 XXXX XXXX XX00 XX00 XX00 XX00 XXXX XXXX

   24 ---- X--- --00 --00 --00 --00 ---- ---- F
   25 ---- ---- X-00 --00 --00 --00 ---- ---- G

   32 ---- ---- --00 -X00 -X00 --00 ---- ---- /M*/N
   33 XXXX XXXX XX00 XX00 XX00 XX00 XXXX XXXX

   40 ---- ---- --00 --00 --00 X-00 -X-- ---- P*/Q
   41 ---- ---- --00 --00 --00 -X00 X--- ---- /P*Q

   48 ---- ---- --00 --00 --00 --00 ---- -X-- /I
   49 ---- ---- --00 --00 --00 --00 ---- ---X /J
   50 ---- ---- --00 --00 --00 --00 ---X ---- /K
   51 XXXX XXXX XX00 XX00 XX00 XX00 XXXX XXXX

END*FPLT

LEGEND:  X : FUSE NOT BLOWN (L,N,0)   - : FUSE BLOWN    (H,P,1)
         0 : PHANTOM FUSE   (L,N,0)   0 : PHANTOM FUSE (H,P,1)

NUMBER OF FUSES BLOWN =  306
```

Figure 8-1. *cont*. Basic Gates. *Reprinted from* Programmable Logic Design Guide,

```
BASIC GATE                                    BASIC GATE

 1 XXXXXXXXXXXXXXXXXHO1                        1 XXXXXXXXXXXXXXXXXHO1
 2 XXXXXXXXXXXXXXXXXL11                        2 XXXXXXXXXXXXXXXXXL11
 3 OOXXXXXXXXXXXXXXXLXX1                        3 OOXXXXXXXXXXXXXXXLXX1
 4 O1XXXXXXXXXXXXXXXLXX1                        4 O1XXXXXXXXXXXXXXXLXX1
 5 1OXXXXXXXXXXXXXXXLXX1                        5 1OXXXXXXXXXXXXXXXLXX1
 6 11XXXXXXXXXXXXXXXHXX1                        6 11XXXXXXXXXXXXXXXHXX1
 7 XXOOXXXXXXXXXXXLXXX1                         7 XXOOXXXXXXXXXXXLXXX1
 8 XXO1XXXXXXXXXXXHXXX1                         8 XXO1XXXXXXXXXXXHXXX1
 9 XX1OXXXXXXXXXXXHXXX1                         9 XX1OXXXXXXXXXXXHXXX1
10 XX11XXXXXXXXXXXHXXX1                        10 XX11XXXXXXXXXXXHXXX1
11 XXXXXXXOXOOHXXXXX1                          11 XXXXXXXOXOOHXXXXX1
12 XXXXXXXOXO1HXXXXX1                          12 XXXXXXXOXO1HXXXXX1
13 XXXXXXXOX1OHXXXXX1                          13 XXXXXXXOX1OHXXXXX1
14 XXXXXXX1XOOHXXXXX1                          14 XXXXXXX1XOOHXXXXX1
15 XXXXXXX1X11LXXXXX1                          15 XXXXXXX1X11LXXXXX1
16 XXXXOOXXXXXXXHXXX1                          16 XXXXOOXXXXXXXHXXX1
17 XXXXO1XXXXXXXLXXX1                          17 XXXXO1XXXXXXXLXXX1
18 XXXX1OXXXXXXXLXXX1                          18 XXXX1OXXXXXXXLXXX1
19 XXXX11XXXXXXXLXXX1                          19 XXXX11XXXXXXXLXXX1
20 XXXXXOOXXXXLXXXX1                           20 XXXXXOOXXXXLXXXX1
21 XXXXXO1XXXXHXXXX1                           21 XXXXXO1XXXXHXXXX1
22 XXXXX1OXXXXHXXXX1                           22 XXXXX1OXXXXHXXXX1
23 XXXXX11XXXXLXXXX1                           23 XXXXX11XXXXLXXXX1

PASS SIMULATION        230         24


PASS SIMULATION        230         24
  PRODUCT:   1 OF EQUATION.   4      UNTESTED(SAO)FAULT
  PRODUCT:   2 OF EQUATION.   4      UNTESTED(SAO)FAULT
  PRODUCT:   3 OF EQUATION.   4      UNTESTED(SAO)FAULT

NUMBER OF STUCK AT ONE (SA1)  FAULTS ARE = 10

NUMBER OF STUCK AT ZERO (SAO) FAULTS ARE =  7

PRODUCT   TERM   COVERAGE         = 85%
```

National Semiconductor Corp., May 1986, pp. 157–161, with permission.

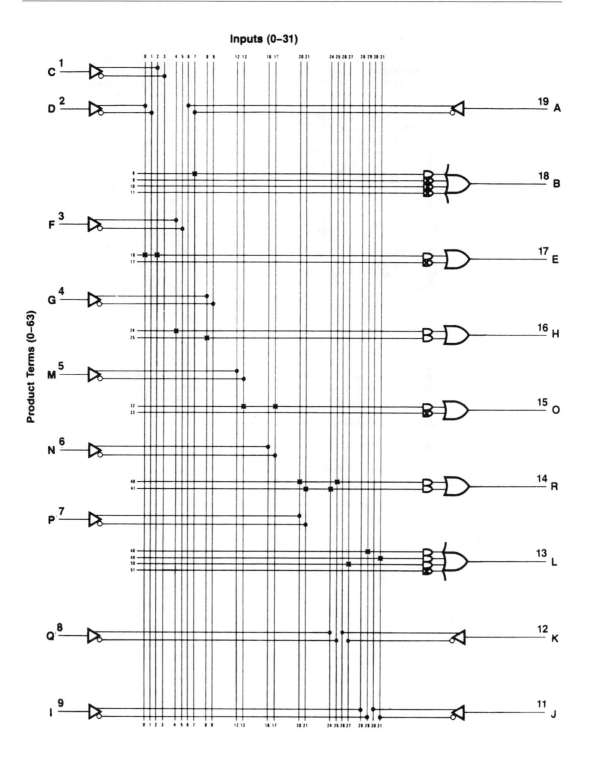

Figure 8-1. *cont.* Basic Gates. *Reprinted from* Programmable Logic Design Guide,

8.2 BASIC CLOCKED FLIP FLOPS

This example demonstrates how fusable logic, PAL16R8, can implement the basic flip-flops; J-K flip-flop; T flip-flop, D flip-flop, and S-R flip-flop. A PAL16L8 can be substituted for this application. Then, the clock input (CLK) would be gated with the data inputs to implement the basic flip-flop.

```
PALASM VERSION 1.5

PAL16R8
BFLIP
BASIC
NSC
CLK J K T PR CLR D S R GND
/OC /SRC /SRT /DC /DT /TC /TT /JKC /JKT VCC
JKT:=J*/JKT*/CLR
    +/K*JKT*/CLR
    +PR
JKC:=/J*K*/PR
    +/J*/JKT*/PR
    +K*JKT*/PR
    +CLR
TT:=T*/TT*/CLR
    +/T*TT*/CLR
    +PR
TC:=/T*/TT*/PR
    +T*TT*/PR
    +CLR
DT:=D*/CLR
    +PR
DC:=/D*/PR
    +CLR
SRT:=S*/CLR
    +/R*SRT*/CLR
    +PR
SRC:=/S*R*/PR
    +/S*/SRT*/PR
    +CLR
FUNCTION TABLE
CLK /OC PR CLR J K JKT JKC T TT TC D DT DC S R SRT SRC
-----------------------------------------------------
X H X X   X X Z   Z   X Z Z   X Z Z   X X Z   Z;HI-Z

C L L H   X X L   H   X X X   X X X   X X X   X;CLEAR
C L L L   L L L   H   X X X   X X X   X X X   X;
C L L L   L H L   H   X X X   X X X   X X X   X;
C L L L   H H H   L   X X X   X X X   X X X   X;TOGGLE
C L L L   H L H   L   X X X   X X X   X X X   X;
C L L L   L L H   L   X X X   X X X   X X X   X;
C L L L   L H L   H   X X X   X X X   X X X   X;
C L H L   X X H   L   X X X   X X X   X X X   X;PRESET
C L L L   H H L   H   X X X   X X X   X X X   X;TOGGLE
C L L L   H L H   L   X X X   X X X   X X X   X;

C L L H   X X X   X   X L H   X X X   X X X   X;CLEAR
C L L L   X X X   X   L L H   X X X   X X X   X;
C L L L   X X X   X   H H L   X X X   X X X   X;TOGGLE
C L L L   X X X   X   H L H   X X X   X X X   X;TOGGLE
C L H L   X X X   X   X H L   X X X   X X X   X;PRESET
```

National Semiconductor Corp., May 1986, pp. 157–161, with permission.

9-Bit Parity Generator/Checker

This reprint (Fig. 8-2) is an application note from a Signetics data book. It describes the design of a 9-bit parity generator/checker circuit using a PLS153 FPLA device (the article uses the part's older "82S153" number) and the company's AMAZE compiler. The first part of the note describes the operation of the parity generator/checker circuit and how it is to be implemented. It then shows a block diagram of the circuit along with truth tables for the various sub-circuits. Finally, an AMAZE source file and related AMAZE output files are provided to show the implementation of the circuit.

PLD Provides Chip Select and Wait States

This reprint (Fig. 8-3) is an article that appeared in the industry journal, *EDN*, and describes the use of a PAL22V10 device to generate chip selects and wait states in a Z80-based system. The article shows a block diagram of the circuit being implemented, and a PLD source listing showing the PAL22V10 logic definition. The listing appears to be for AMD's PLPL compiler.

High Speed Asynchronous SCSI Controller

This reprint (Fig. 8-4) comes from a Cypress Semiconductor data book, and describes the use of the company's CY7C330 Synchronous State Machine PLD to implement a basic, asynchronous SCSI (Small Computer System Interface) controller. The SCSI is an ANSI standard, and is popular for interfacing to disk drives, tape drives, and optical storage drives. The application note provides a reasonably detailed discussion of the SCSI timing to be implemented, and discusses several design considerations. It concludes with a circuit diagram showing the CY7C330 as the coordinator for the SCSI controller, which includes a few support circuits. The note falls short of providing a source listing for the CY7C330 logic.

Use Logic Cell Array to Control a Large FIFO Buffer

This final reprint (Fig. 8-5) is an article from *Electronic Design* magazine. It describes the use of a logic-cell array (LCA) in conjunction with some dynamic RAM to implement a FIFO (first in, first out) buffer. The article describes why FIFO buffers are useful in certain applications and the limitations of small FIFOs. It then proceeds into a discussion of the design of the FIFO buffer, and how it can be implemented using an LCA. Circuit diagrams are used to illustrate the logic functions being placed into the LCA. An M2018 LCA is used in the article, having approximately 1,800 equivalent gates.

Signetics

Application Specific Products

AN21
9-Bit Parity Generator/Checker With 82S153/153A

Application Note

INTRODUCTION

This application note presents the design of a parity generator using Signetics PLD, 82S153 or 82S153A, which enables the designers to customize their circuits in the form of "sum-of-products". The PLA architecture and the 10 bi-directional I/O's make it possible to implement the 9-bit parity generator/checker in one chip without any external wiring between pins. A logic diagram of the device is shown in Appendix A.

The parity of an 8-bit word is generated by counting the number of "1's" in the word. If the number is odd, the word has odd parity. If the number is even, the word has even parity. Thus, a parity generator designed for even parity, for example, will generate a "0" if the parity is even, or a "1" if parity is odd. Conversely, an odd parity generator will generate a "0" if the parity of the word is odd, or a "1" if the parity is even. This bit is then concatinated to the word making it 9-bits

long. When the word is used elsewhere, its parity may be checked for correctness.

FEATURES

* **Generates even and odd parities (SUM$_E$ and SUM$_O$)**
* **SUM$_E$ = "1" for even parity, "0" for odd parity**
* **SUM$_O$ = "1" for odd parity, "0" for even parity**
* **Generate parity or check for parity errors**
* **Cascaded to expand word length**

DESCRIPTION

The most straight forward way of implementing the parity generator/checker is to take the 9-input truth table (8 inputs for the 8-bit word, and 1 input for cascading the previous stage) and put it in a 256 × 4 PROM. Since there are 2^9 combinations and half of them is odd,

the other half is even, the circuit will take 256 terms. An alternative is to divide the 9-bits into 3 groups of 3-bits as shown in Figure 1. If the sum of the 3-bits is odd, then the intermediate output SU1, or SU2, or SU3 equals 1. Otherwise it equals 0. The intermediate results are grouped together and SUM$_O$ becomes "1" if the sum is odd, otherwise SUM$_O$ equals "0". The circuit is implemented using AMAZE as shown in Figure 3. SU1 is an intermediate output for inputs I_0, I_1 and I_2. In the same manner, SU2 and SU3 are intermediate outputs for I_3, I_4, I_5 and I_6, I_7, I_8. The design uses up 16 product terms and 5 control terms leaving 16 product terms and 4 bi-directional I/O's to implement other logic designs.

The design is tested by using the logic simulator provided by AMAZE. The input test vector is chosen to exhaustively test for all 8 input combinations at all 4 sections of the circuit.

Figure 8-2. 9-Bit Parity Generator/Checker with 82S153/153A.

Reprinted from Programmable Logic Data Manual, *Signetics Corp., November 1986, pp. 9–125 through 9–130, with permission.*

9-Bit Parity Generator/Checker With 82S153/153A   AN21

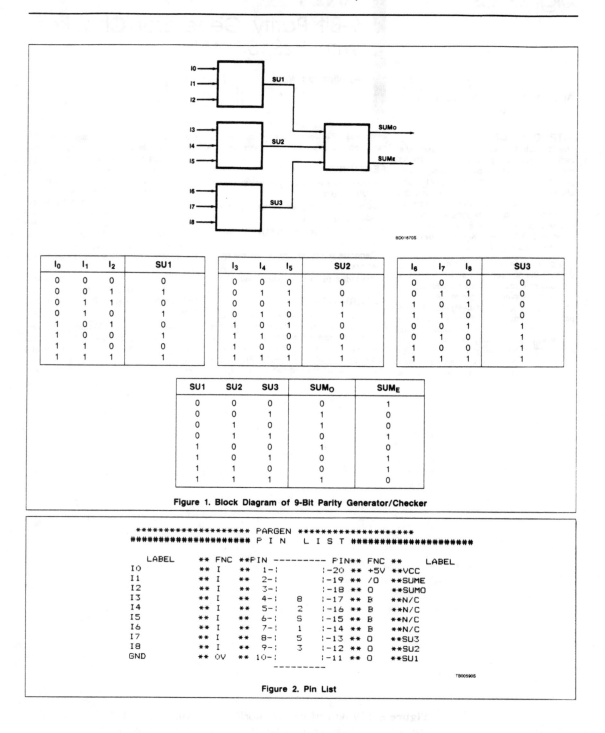

Figure 1. Block Diagram of 9-Bit Parity Generator/Checker

I_0	I_1	I_2	SU1
0	0	0	0
0	0	1	1
0	1	1	0
0	1	0	1
1	0	1	0
1	0	0	1
1	1	0	0
1	1	1	1

I_3	I_4	I_5	SU2
0	0	0	0
0	1	1	0
0	0	1	1
0	1	0	1
1	0	1	0
1	1	0	0
1	0	0	1
1	1	1	1

I_6	I_7	I_8	SU3
0	0	0	0
0	1	1	0
1	0	1	0
1	1	0	0
0	0	1	1
0	1	0	1
1	0	0	1
1	1	1	1

SU1	SU2	SU3	SUM_O	SUM_E
0	0	0	0	1
0	0	1	1	0
0	1	0	1	0
0	1	1	0	1
1	0	0	1	0
1	0	1	0	1
1	1	0	0	1
1	1	1	1	0

```
****************** PARGEN ******************
###################### P I N   L I S T ######################

        LABEL    ** FNC **PIN --------- PIN** FNC **    LABEL
    IO           ** I  **  1-|       |-20 ** +5V **VCC
    I1           ** I  **  2-|       |-19 ** /O  **SUME
    I2           ** I  **  3-|       |-18 ** O   **SUMO
    I3           ** I  **  4-|   8   |-17 ** B   **N/C
    I4           ** I  **  5-|   2   |-16 ** B   **N/C
    I5           ** I  **  6-|   S   |-15 ** B   **N/C
    I6           ** I  **  7-|   1   |-14 ** B   **N/C
    I7           ** I  **  8-|   5   |-13 ** O   **SU3
    I8           ** I  **  9-|   3   |-12 ** O   **SU2
    GND          ** OV **  10-|      |-11 ** O   **SU1
                           ---------
                                                    TB00590S
```

Figure 2. Pin List

Figure 8-2. *cont.* 9-Bit Parity Generator/Checker with 82S153/153A. *Reprinted from*

9-Bit Parity Generator/Checker With 82S153/153A AN21

```
******************** PARGEN ********************
@DEVICE TYPE
82S153
@DRAWING
******************************* PARITY GENERATOR/CHECKER
@REVISION
****************************** REV. -
@DATE
****************************** xx/xx/xxxx
@SYMBOL
****************************** FILE ID: PARGEN
@COMPANY
****************************** SIGNETICS
@NAME
@DESCRIPTION
*******************************************************************
*    This circuit is a 9-bit parity generator/checker commonly used  *
*    for error detection in high speed data transmission/retrieval.  *
*    The odd parity output (SUMO) is high when the sum of the data    *
*    bits is odd. Otherwise it is low.                                *
*    The even parity output (SUME) is high when the sum of the data   *
*    bits is even. It is low otherwise.                               *
*******************************************************************
@COMMON PRODUCT TERM
@I/O DIRECTION
"
*******************************************************************
*    SU1, SU2 and SU3 are outputs which are defined in the PIN LIST   *
*    and therefore they don't need to be defined here again.          *
*******************************************************************
"
@OUTPUT POLARITY
"
*******************************************************************
*    The output polarities of different outputs are defined in the   *
*    PIN LIST. They don't have to be defined again here.              *
*******************************************************************
"
@LOGIC EQUATION
"
*******************************************************************
*    SU1, SU2, and SU3 are intermediate terms                        *
*******************************************************************
                        TRUTH TABLE
        INPUTS                    OUTPUTS
   ------------------        ---------------------
   SU3    SU2    SU1         SUMO      SUME = /SUMO
   I8     I7     I6          SU3
   I5     I4     I3          SU2
   I2     I1     I0          SU1

    0      0      0           0          1
    0      0      1           1          0
    0      1      0           1          0
    0      1      1           0          1
    1      0      0           1          0
    1      0      1           0          1
    1      1      0           0          1
    1      1      1           1          0
"

SU1 = /I2 * /I1 *  I0 + /I2 *  I1 * /I0 +
       I2 * /I1 * /I0 +  I2 *  I1 *  I0 ;
SU2 = /I5 * /I4 *  I3 + /I5 *  I4 * /I3 +
       I5 * /I4 * /I3 +  I5 *  I4 *  I3 ;

SU3 = /I8 * /I7 *  I6 + /I8 *  I7 * /I6 +
       I8 * /I7 * /I6 +  I8 *  I7 *  I6 ;

SUMO = /SU1 * /SU2 *  SU3 + /SU1 *  SU2 * /SU3 +
        SU1 * /SU2 * /SU3 +  SU1 *  SU2 *  SU3 ;

SUME = /(/SU1 * /SU2 *  SU3 + /SU1 *  SU2 * /SU3 +
         SU1 * /SU2 * /SU3 +  SU1 *  SU2 *  SU3) ;
```

TB005800

Figure 3. AMAZE Implementation of the Parity Generator/Checker Circuit

Programmable Logic Data Manual, *Signetics Corp., November 1986, pp. 9–125 through 9–130, with permission.*

9-Bit Parity Generator/Checker With 82S153/153A   AN21

Table 1. Programming Table

```
         ******************** PARGEN ********************
         Cust/Project -
         Date        - ****************************** xx/xx/xxxx
         Rev/I. D.   - ****************************** REV. -

         82S153                                  !      POLARITY      !
    ---                                          --------------------------
    T  !                                         !L:H:H:H:H:H:H:H:H:H:H!
    E  !---------------------------------------  --------------------------
    R  !       I          !       B(i)        !       B(o)           !
    M  !---------------------------------------  --------------------------
    ---!7_6_5_4_3_2_1_0!9_8_7_6_5_4_3_2_1_0!9_8_7_6_5_4_3_2_1_0!
     0!- - - -,- L L H!- -,- - - -,- - - -!. .,A A A A,. . A A!
     1!- - - -,- L H L!- -,- - - -,- - - -!. .,A A A A,. . A A!
     2!- - - -,- H L L!- -,- - - -,- - - -!. .,A A A A,. . A A!
     3!- - - -,- H H H!- -,- - - -,- - - -!. .,A A A A,. . A A!
     4!- - L L,H - - -!- -,- - - -,- - - -!. .,A A A A,. A . A!
     5!- - L H,L - - -!- -,- - - -,- - - -!. .,A A A A,. A . A!
     6!- - H L,L - - -!- -,- - - -,- - - -!. .,A A A A,. A . A!
     7!- - H H,H - - -!- -,- - - -,- - - -!. .,A A A A,. A . A!
     8!L H - -,- - - -!- -,- - - -,- - L L!. .,A A A A,A . . A!
     9!H L - -,- - - -!- -,- - - -,- - L L!. .,A A A A,A . . A!
    10!L L - -,- - - -!- -,- - - -,- - H L!. .,A A A A,A . . A!
    11!H H - -,- - - -!- -,- - - -,- - H L!. .,A A A A,A . . A!
    12!- - - -,- - - -!- -,- - - -,H L L -!A A,A A A A,. . . A!
    13!- - - -,- - - -!- -,- - - -,L H L -!A A,A A A A,. . . A!
    14!- - - -,- - - -!- -,- - - -,L L H -!A A,A A A A,. . . A!
    15!- - - -,- - - -!- -,- - - -,H H H -!A A,A A A A,. . . A!
    16!0 0 0 0,0 0 0 0!0 0,0 0 0 0,0 0 0 0!A A,A A A A,A A A A!
    17!0 0 0 0,0 0 0 0!0 0,0 0 0 0,0 0 0 0!A A,A A A A,A A A A!
    18!0 0 0 0,0 0 0 0!0 0,0 0 0 0,0 0 0 0!A A,A A A A,A A A A!
    19!0 0 0 0,0 0 0 0!0 0,0 0 0 0,0 0 0 0!A A,A A A A,A A A A!
    20!0 0 0 0,0 0 0 0!0 0,0 0 0 0,0 0 0 0!A A,A A A A,A A A A!
    21!0 0 0 0,0 0 0 0!0 0,0 0 0 0,0 0 0 0!A A,A A A A,A A A A!
    22!0 0 0 0,0 0 0 0!0 0,0 0 0 0,0 0 0 0!A A,A A A A,A A A A!
    23!0 0 0 0,0 0 0 0!0 0,0 0 0 0,0 0 0 0!A A,A A A A,A A A A!
    24!0 0 0 0,0 0 0 0!0 0,0 0 0 0,0 0 0 0!A A,A A A A,A A A A!
    25!0 0 0 0,0 0 0 0!0 0,0 0 0 0,0 0 0 0!A A,A A A A,A A A A!
    26!0 0 0 0,0 0 0 0!0 0,0 0 0 0,0 0 0 0!A A,A A A A,A A A A!
    27!0 0 0 0,0 0 0 0!0 0,0 0 0 0,0 0 0 0!A A,A A A A,A A A A!
    28!0 0 0 0,0 0 0 0!0 0,0 0 0 0,0 0 0 0!A A,A A A A,A A A A!
    29!0 0 0 0,0 0 0 0!0 0,0 0 0 0,0 0 0 0!A A,A A A A,A A A A!
    30!0 0 0 0,0 0 0 0!0 0,0 0 0 0,0 0 0 0!A A,A A A A,A A A A!
    31!0 0 0 0,0 0 0 0!0 0,0 0 0 0,0 0 0 0!A A,A A A A,A A A A!
    D9!- - - -,- - - -!- -,- - - -,- - - -!
    D8!- - - -,- - - -!- -,- - - -,- - - -!
    D7!0 0 0 0,0 0 0 0!0 0,0 0 0 0,0 0 0 0!
    D6!0 0 0 0,0 0 0 0!0 0,0 0 0 0,0 0 0 0!
    D5!0 0 0 0,0 0 0 0!0 0,0 0 0 0,0 0 0 0!
    D4!0 0 0 0,0 0 0 0!0 0,0 0 0 0,0 0 0 0!
    D3!- - - -,- - - -!- -,- - - -,- - - -!
    D2!- - - -,- - - -!- -,- - - -,- - - -!
    D1!- - - -,- - - -!- -,- - - -,- - - -!
    D0!0 0 0 0,0 0 0 0!0 0,0 0 0 0,0 0 0 0!

         I I I I I I I I S S N N N N S S S I S S N N N N S S S I
         7 6 5 4 3 2 1 0 U U / / / / U U U 8 U U / / / / U U U 8
                         M M C C C C 3 2 1   M M C C C C 3 2 1
                         E 0                 E 0
```

Figure 8-2. *cont.* 9-Bit Parity Generator/Checker with 82S153/153A. *Reprinted from*

9-Bit Parity Generator/Checker With 82S153/153A   AN21

```
"
*****/*************************************************************
*    This is a test pattern for the 9-bit parity generator/checker  *
*    circuit. The simulator will use this file as an input to        *
*    simulate the logical function.                                  *
*****************************************************************
"         SS              EXPECTED
"         UU     SSS      OUTPUTS
"IIIIIIII MMBBBBBUUUI      BBBBB
"76543210 E076543218       98321
 LLLLLLLL ////////////L    "HLLLL
 HLHHLHLL ////////////H    "LHLLH
 LHHLLHHL ////////////H    "LHLHL
 HHLHLLHL ////////////L    "HLLHH
 LLHLHHLH ////////////H    "LHHLL
 HLLHHLLH ////////////L    "HLHLH
 LHLLHLHH ////////////L    "HLHHL
 HHHHHHHH ////////////H    "LHHHH
QUIT
```

TB00600S

a. Input Pattern PARGEN.TST

```
82S153   A:pargen.STD
" This file is the result of logic simulation of the parity generator/checker
" circuit. The inputs are read from input file PARGEN.TST
"
"   INPUTS  <=B(I/O)=>   TRACE TERMS
"   76543210 9876543210
"
   00000000 HL....LLLO ;
   10110100 LH....LLH1 ;
   01100110 LH....LHL1 ;
   11010010 HL....LHHO ;
   00101101 LH....HLL1 ;
   10011001 HL....HLHO ;
   01001011 HL....HHLO ;
   11111111 LH....HHH1 ;
"
" -------- ----------   I/O CONTROL LINES
"         OOIIIIOOOI   DESIGNATED I/O USAGE
"         OOIIIIOOOI   ACTUAL I/O USAGE
"
" PIN LIST...
" 08 07 06 05 04 03 02 01 19 18 17 16 15 14 13 12 11 09 ;
```

TB00601S

b. Output File From SIMULATOR

Figure 4. Test Vectors

Programmable Logic Data Manual, *Signetics Corp., November 1986, pp. 9–125 through 9–130, with permission.*

9-Bit Parity Generator/Checker With 82S153/153A

APPENDIX A

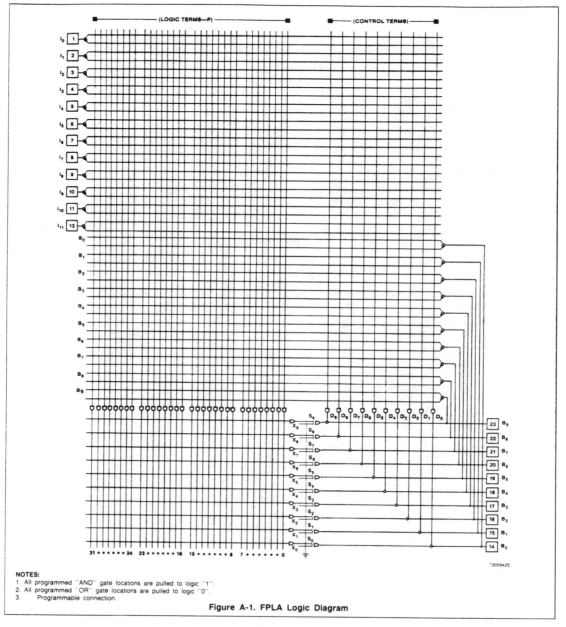

NOTES:
1. All programmed "AND" gate locations are pulled to logic "1".
2. All programmed "OR" gate locations are pulled to logic "0".
3. Programmable connection.

Figure A-1. FPLA Logic Diagram

Figure 8-2. *cont.* 9-Bit Parity Generator/Checker with 82S153/153A.
Reprinted from Programmable Logic Data Manual, *Signetics Corp., November 1986,*
pp. 9–125 through 9–130, with permission.

PLD provides chip select and wait states

Vineet Dujari
Advanced Micro Devices, Sunnyvale, CA

You can combine a memory-address decoder and wait-state generator in one 24-pin DIP by programming an AmPAL22V10 or equivalent device according to **Listing 1**. With this device, your microprocessor clock can accommodate the fastest memory chip in your system instead of the slowest.

The example in **Fig 1** is based on a Z80 CPU and assumes a memory system that includes two blocks of 16k-byte addresses (enabled by CS01 and CS23) and four blocks of 8k-byte addresses (enabled by CS4, CS5, CS6, and CS7). You can support other memory configurations by changing the outputs specified in the chip-select-decoder specification in **Listing 1**.

The AmPAL22V10 generates chip-select signals for the memory when the MREQ signal is active; in addition, it loads an appropriate count value in the wait-state counter at that time. This counter's high-level bit connects to the CPU's WAIT signal, so the CPU waits until the high-level bit is set before terminating that memory cycle. The internal CTSTATE

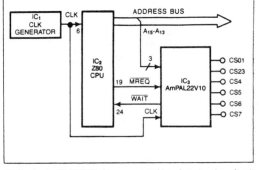

Fig 1—An AmPAL22V10 chip generates chip-select signals and wait states for the memory of a Z80-based system.

signal determines if the counter is in the load or the count mode. This example inserts from zero to three wait states in every memory cycle. **EDN**

To Vote For This Design, Circle No 749

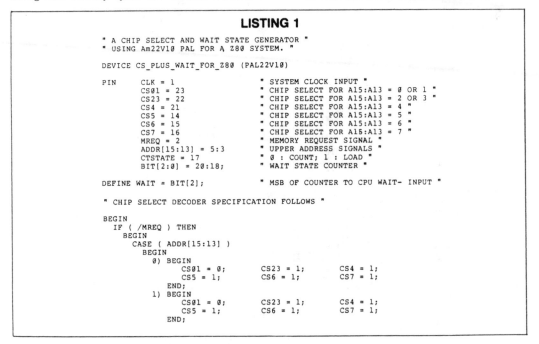

```
                            LISTING 1

        " A CHIP SELECT AND WAIT STATE GENERATOR "
        " USING Am22V10 PAL FOR A Z80 SYSTEM. "

        DEVICE CS_PLUS_WAIT_FOR_Z80 (PAL22V10)

        PIN     CLK = 1             " SYSTEM CLOCK INPUT "
                CS01 = 23           " CHIP SELECT FOR A15:A13 = 0 OR 1 "
                CS23 = 22           " CHIP SELECT FOR A15:A13 = 2 OR 3 "
                CS4 = 21            " CHIP SELECT FOR A15:A13 = 4 "
                CS5 = 14            " CHIP SELECT FOR A15:A13 = 5 "
                CS6 = 15            " CHIP SELECT FOR A15:A13 = 6 "
                CS7 = 16            " CHIP SELECT FOR A15:A13 = 7 "
                MREQ = 2            " MEMORY REQUEST SIGNAL "
                ADDR[15:13] = 5:3   " UPPER ADDRESS SIGNALS "
                CTSTATE = 17        " 0 : COUNT; 1 : LOAD "
                BIT[2:0] = 20:18;   " WAIT STATE COUNTER "

        DEFINE WAIT = BIT[2];       " MSB OF COUNTER TO CPU WAIT- INPUT "

        " CHIP SELECT DECODER SPECIFICATION FOLLOWS "

        BEGIN
          IF ( /MREQ ) THEN
            BEGIN
              CASE ( ADDR[15:13] )
                BEGIN
                  0) BEGIN
                        CS01 = 0;      CS23 = 1;      CS4 = 1;
                        CS5 = 1;       CS6 = 1;       CS7 = 1;
                     END;
                  1) BEGIN
                        CS01 = 0;      CS23 = 1;      CS4 = 1;
                        CS5 = 1;       CS6 = 1;       CS7 = 1;
                     END;
```

Figure 8-3. PLD Provides Chip Select and Wait States, by Vineet Dujari.

Reprinted from EDN, August 21, 1986 (pp 184–185), with permission
© *1988 Cahners Publishing Company, a Division of Reed Publishing USA*

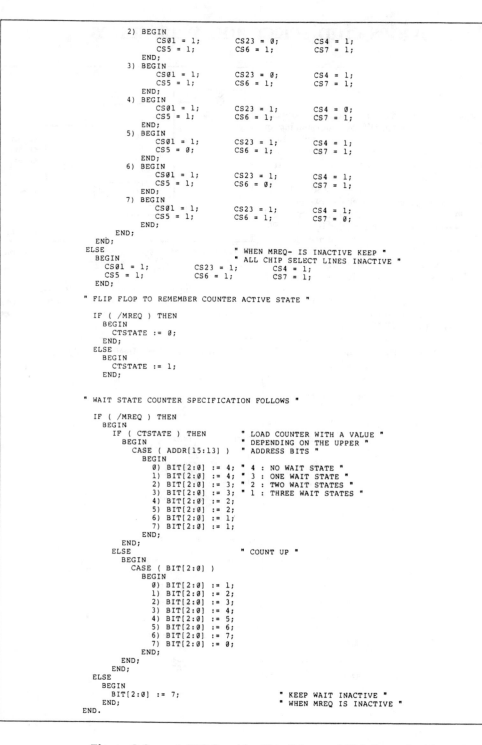

```
            2) BEGIN
                 CS01 = 1;        CS23 = 0;        CS4 = 1;
                 CS5 = 1;         CS6 = 1;         CS7 = 1;
               END;
            3) BEGIN
                 CS01 = 1;        CS23 = 0;        CS4 = 1;
                 CS5 = 1;         CS6 = 1;         CS7 = 1;
               END;
            4) BEGIN
                 CS01 = 1;        CS23 = 1;        CS4 = 0;
                 CS5 = 1;         CS6 = 1;         CS7 = 1;
               END;
            5) BEGIN
                 CS01 = 1;        CS23 = 1;        CS4 = 1;
                 CS5 = 0;         CS6 = 1;         CS7 = 1;
               END;
            6) BEGIN
                 CS01 = 1;        CS23 = 1;        CS4 = 1;
                 CS5 = 1;         CS6 = 0;         CS7 = 1;
               END;
            7) BEGIN
                 CS01 = 1;        CS23 = 1;        CS4 = 1;
                 CS5 = 1;         CS6 = 1;         CS7 = 0;
               END;
          END;
      END;
  ELSE                              " WHEN MREQ- IS INACTIVE KEEP "
    BEGIN                           " ALL CHIP SELECT LINES INACTIVE "
      CS01 = 1;           CS23 = 1;        CS4 = 1;
      CS5 = 1;           CS6 = 1;        CS7 = 1;
    END;

" FLIP FLOP TO REMEMBER COUNTER ACTIVE STATE "

  IF ( /MREQ ) THEN
    BEGIN
      CTSTATE := 0;
    END;
  ELSE
    BEGIN
      CTSTATE := 1;
    END;


" WAIT STATE COUNTER SPECIFICATION FOLLOWS "

  IF ( /MREQ ) THEN
    BEGIN
      IF ( CTSTATE ) THEN        " LOAD COUNTER WITH A VALUE "
        BEGIN                    " DEPENDING ON THE UPPER "
          CASE ( ADDR[15:13] )   " ADDRESS BITS "
            BEGIN
              0) BIT[2:0] := 4;  " 4 : NO WAIT STATE "
              1) BIT[2:0] := 4;  " 3 : ONE WAIT STATE "
              2) BIT[2:0] := 3;  " 2 : TWO WAIT STATES "
              3) BIT[2:0] := 3;  " 1 : THREE WAIT STATES "
              4) BIT[2:0] := 2;
              5) BIT[2:0] := 2;
              6) BIT[2:0] := 1;
              7) BIT[2:0] := 1;
            END;
        END;
      ELSE                       " COUNT UP "
        BEGIN
          CASE ( BIT[2:0] )
            BEGIN
              0) BIT[2:0] := 1;
              1) BIT[2:0] := 2;
              2) BIT[2:0] := 3;
              3) BIT[2:0] := 4;
              4) BIT[2:0] := 5;
              5) BIT[2:0] := 6;
              6) BIT[2:0] := 7;
              7) BIT[2:0] := 0;
            END;
        END;
      END;
    ELSE
      BEGIN
        BIT[2:0] := 7;                  " KEEP WAIT INACTIVE "
      END;                              " WHEN MREQ IS INACTIVE "
  END.
```

Figure 8-3. *cont.* PLD Provides Chip Select and Wait States, by Vineet Dujari.

Reprinted from EDN, *August 21, 1986 (pp 184–185), with permission*

© *1988 Cabners Publishing Company, a Division of Reed Publishing USA*

CY7C330 Design Example: High Speed Asynchronous SCSI Controller

Introduction

This application note describes a minimal, though extremely fast SCSI (Small Computer Systems Interface) controller that is built up from a few parts surrounding a CY7C330 synchronous state machine PLD. The controller is compliant with the SCSI standard for a host-based minimally featured interface.

A speed of 12 Megacycles is achieved by efficiently using various features of the CY7C330. The 50 MHz speed, the input registers, and the device size including the array size are all features which help to achieve this level of performance.

At 50 MHz, the register to register transfers can occur at 20 ns intervals which is fast enough to keep datapath transfers out of the way of SCSI transfers. In order to achieve optimal throughput, the SCSI handshake transfer must be made the limiting factor, so this clock speed is necessary.

The input registers are used to synchronize external signals. Synchronization is necessary so that the state machine can respond to these signals, and the input section of the state machine is the correct place to perform the task. Since the signals are synchronized at the input to the array, adherence to grey code transitions can be ignored in the design and thus time critical transitions can be made in less cycles.

The device and array size of the CY7C330 are sufficient to accommodate the entire control section of the interface. In fact, because the device is large enough, several signals are shared and therefore more features can be accommodated in this design than would be the case if the interface was constructed from smaller PLDs.

The minimally featured SCSI Host implementation is a complete interface to one or more SCSI controllers from a single host.

Conventions

In this document, conventions are followed so that signal names in timing and state diagrams can be related to schematics unambiguously.

If a signal name appears suffixed by a minus sign ($-$) then that signal is active low. The minus sign is part of the signal name, and not an operator. As an example, the signal ACK$-$ appears on several timing diagrams and the minus is there to remind the reader that a low on the timing diagram is the asserted state.

In state diagrams the asserted states appear as 1's. This makes the diagram easier to read than one with T's and F's. In any case there is no ambiguity because the boolean variables which are used in state diagrams are not circuit level signals. For example, the variable CDIT is used in a state diagram with a 1 being true, while the corresponding signal name in the schematic and the timing diagram is CDIT$-$ with a low assertion level.

The slash '/' is the inversion operator. This is similar to the BAR operator in boolean algebra, so /A has the same

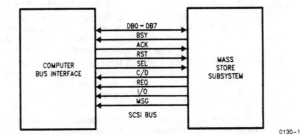

Figure 1. Mass Store Subsystem and Minimal SCSI Implementation

0130-1

Figure 8-4. CY7C330 Design Example: High Speed Asynchronous SCSI Controller. *Reprinted from* CMOS Data Book, *Cypress Semiconductor Corp., pp. 10–87 through 10–92 with permission.*

meaning as $\overline{A}$. An operator does not signify activity level, so the inclusion of a signal suffix ($-$ or blank) is additional information.

The PLD definitions and equations, the signal assertion level should only appear in the pin name declaration. PLD equations should then be written referring only to variable names as they appear in state diagrams and truth tables.

The design file for this CY7C330 application has not been included in this note, but is available from Cypress Semiconductor.

History

The SCSI standard evolved from the SASI controller specification by DTC and Shugart which was a widely adopted parallel interface for disk controllers. The current SCSI standard is upwards compatible from this original specification.

Apart from the more rigorous timing and electrical specifications, most SCSI additions (i.e. reselection, arbitration, and synchronous mode) apply when the interface is being used as a network. If the sole use of the interface is to access a mass storage subsystem, then these features may be omitted and the resultant SCSI implementation will be smaller and faster.

The current SCSI interface is 8 bits wide, and it is possible to operate in asynchronous mode for a minimally featured interface at a rate of up to 16 Megacycles. The interface may be widened to 16 bits at some time in the near future; if so, then the SCSI throughput rate will double to a theoretical maximum of about 32 Megabytes per second.

The SCSI standard is likely to prevail in storage system interfaces. The only competing standard is ESDI which, being a serial data interface, has a much lower data throughput.

System Considerations

A block diagram of a minimal SCSI implementation is shown in *Figure 1*. Normally the Mass Store Subsystem is inside the same enclosure as the computer; if it is not, then for emission considerations differential drivers and receivers should be used. In this application note, it is assumed that the flat cable SCSI bus is about a foot long so that transmission delays are minimal (5 ns).

The Mass Store Subsystem consists of one or more disk drives or other high density storage devices, and one or more controllers with SCSI ports. Unused lines in the SCSI bus are not shown in *Figure 1*.

The computer system itself will access the SCSI controller from its own bus. For this example, a simple asynchronous interface has been implemented. This interface has only one data strobe and there are two signals — RTS (Request to send) and CTS (Clear to send) to request or acknowledge data access cycles. These signals allow for the connection of a DMA device or another data interface.

The SCSI Transfer Protocol

A SCSI data access consists of a command transfer followed by a data transfer. The command transfer proceeds as follows:

1) The host waits for BSY to go inactive, then asserts SEL and one of the 8 data bits (to select one of 8 controllers).

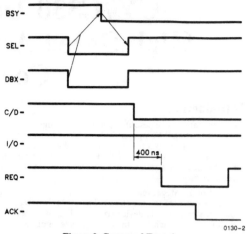

Figure 2. Command Transfer

2) The controller drives BSY active when this selection combination is detected.

3) The host releases SEL and the data bit used for selection.

4) The controller assets C/D and REQ to read a command byte from the host.

5) The host outputs the first byte of the command and asserts ACK.

6) The controller accepts the data and deasserts REQ.

7) The host then deasserts ACK.

8) Steps 4 through 7 are repeated for 6 bytes (more in special cases).

After the command has been read in by the controller, the operation is either performed or aborted. After executing a command, a status byte (C/D asserted) is sent to the host to indicate success or an error condition.

If the command is a write command, then data is first transferred from the host to a buffer on the controller. After the data is written to the disk, a command complete status message is sent to the host.

If the command is a read command, then data is read from the disk, checked for validity, and passed to the host. Some controllers offer a 'Fly-by' mode which means data is passed to the host as soon as it is read, and an error condition is signalled afterwards.

The normal data transfer protocol follows the above description (steps 4 to 7). At the end of the access, the status byte is transferred, then activity ceases. BSY goes inactive to signal the end of the access.

Interface Timing Considerations

There is one major delay and one minor delay to be observed during selection, and there is a data setup delay to be observed during data transfer.

For the host interface, under the single initiator option in the SCSI specification, there is a 400 ns 'bus settle delay' to

---

Figure 8-4. *cont.* CY7C330 Design Example: High Speed Asynchronous SCSI Controller.

be observed after BSY goes false, and before SEL is asserted. Additionally, SEL is to be deasserted at least two deskew delays after BSY is asserted. A deskew delay is 45 ns.

Data is to be setup for a minimum of one deskew delay
plus one cable skew delay (45 + 10 ns) before the ACK
signal is given.

Like the host interface, the controller interface has timing
constraints associated with selection and data access.

The controller implements the same data setup delay as the
host, but the strobe which is accommodated from the controller side is REQ.

The response to SEL must be shorter than 200 microsec-
onds.

The setup time allowed for I/O and C/D [control signals]
is specified as one 'bus settle delay' or 400 ns.

It is worth nothing here that the response to SEL, and the
various 'bus settle delay' constraints, are really system level
response times, and need not be of concern in the hardware
design at this level.

Performance Considerations

The 7C330 is a Moore machine; there are no combinatorial
paths from the inputs to the outputs. One problem that
arises in state machine design with Moore machines is that
the turnaround time or handshake delay to external signals
becomes the limiting factor in throughput. This problem is
most obvious in asynchronous interfaces.

Figure 3 shows a hypothetical synchronized transfer cycle.
This is the cycle as it could be implemented with a 7C330
synchronous state machine, if the ACK − signal was directly controlled by the 7C330.

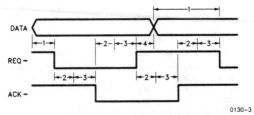

0130–3

Figure 3. Synchronized Transfer Cycle

Definitions for Figure 3:

1. T_{SU}: 55 ns setup time for data.

2. T_{LA}: Latency time delay; this consists of device propagation delays plus 0 or 1 clock cycles. For preliminary estimates, assume a 20 ns clock and 15 ns of delay.

3. T_C: Clock period.

4. T_D: Data delay (max) after REQ deasserted.

The time for one cycle using synchronized transfer cycles is
about 180 ns. This cycle time corresponds to a throughput
rate of just under 6 MHz, which is not as high a rate as the
7C330 is capable of supporting.

The problem is that for every edge there is a synchronization or latency delay plus a clock delay before the corre-

sponding handshake signal is given. These delays are undesirable and for the most part unnecessary, since the data
path is capable of accepting data at a higher rate.

This result underscores the need for supervisory control
over the handshake sequence. If the output data is ready
and waiting, there is no need to delay the handshake sequence until the state machine synchronizes to the event
and reacts. Likewise, if the input buffer is empty then it can
be asynchronously loaded.

In the schematic *(Figure 10)* a NOR buffer is used to drive
the output strobes, and to perform the asynchronous handshake, and to latch ACK − until the state machine has had
sufficient time to react. The signal CDIT − is used by the
7C330 to supervise the handshake sequence.

The SCSI Interface: Transfer to the Controller

For transfers to the controller, the asynchronous signal
that needs to be controlled is ACK − (active low acknowledge). This signal should go low soon after REQ − is asserted by the controller, but only after data has been setup
for a minimum of 55 ns. This signal should go high when
REQ − is deasserted.

To guarantee that the state machine sees the cycle take
place, ACK − is latched low until released by a controlling
signal (CDIT −) that comes from the state machine. The
same signal is used to hold off ACK − until the data setup
has been met (refer to Schematic for latch circuit details).

Another signal is required to clock data into the output
register (CAB). This signal has a duration of two clock
cycles for data setup timing. In *Figure 4* the signal CAB__D
is a delayed feedback version of CAB which is used to add
a delay cycle.

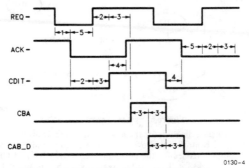

0130–4

Figure 4. Host to Controller Transfer Cycle

Definitions for Figure 4:

1. TAT: Asynchronous turnaround time (8 ns).

2. TLA: Latency time delay; this consists of device propagation delays plus 0 or 1 clock cycles. For preliminary estimates, assume a 20 ns clock and 15 ns of delay (25 ns
average).

3. TC: Clock period (20 ns).

4. TDO: Delay to output (15 ns).

5. Asynchronous turnaround time for controller end (8 ns).

Reprinted from CMOS Data Book, *Cypress Semiconductor Corp., pp. 10–87 through 10–92 with permission.*

Figure 4 shows the resultant transfer cycle to the controller from the host. The cycle time can be estimated from one REQ— rising edge to another. This time works out to an expected value of 108 ns.

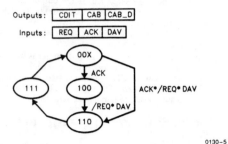

Figure 5. SCSI Transfer to Controller

The state diagram for the part of the controller that handles the interface timing is shown in *Figure 5*. At the start of the cycle, CDIT — is active because it is assumed that data has been at the interface for at least the setup requirement. CAB is the register clock for the output register, and it goes high after REQ— goes inactive (high), if there is data available (DAV, which is a logic function yet to be defined). The cycle then proceeds to completion and as CDIT — goes active another cycle can start.

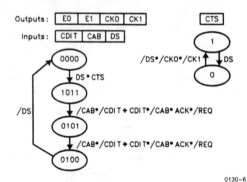

Figure 6. System Transfer to SCSI

The state diagram for the associated system transfer to the SCSI controller is shown in *Figure 6*. E0— and E1— are output enables for the two input registers; CK0 and CK1 are clocks for the same two registers; CTS — is a signal to the Host system that these registers are empty.

At the beginning [state 0000], E0— and E1 — are inactive, the clocks are low, and CTS— is active [0]. When DS — is asserted, the clocks go high to capture the data, E0— goes active and CTS— goes inactive to signal that the registers have been loaded [state 1011, CTS— = 1].

When either CK0 or CK1 are high, data is considered available by the state machine in *Figure 5* and consequently, DAV = CK0 + CK1. After CAB goes high, E1 — goes active, E0— inactive, and CK0 goes low [state 0101].

The next time CAB goes high, CK1 goes low to signify that the input registers are empty again [state 0100]. The state counter then automatically progresses [0000].

The machine waits for DS — to go inactive before allowing another cycle so that double clocking does not occur on one write cycle.

Transfer to the Host

When data is transferred to the Host from the controller, the handshake happens so quickly that there is a possibility that the interface will not see it and for this reason ACK — must be latched until the 7C330 signals [moves CDIT— high] to release it.

In this case, CDIT — is a signal that signifies that there is room in the receiving buffer for a data transfer. CBA is the clock for the input buffer and it goes high when CDIT — goes low or afterwards.

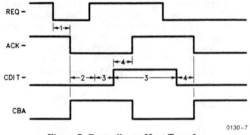

Figure 7. Controller to Host Transfer

Definitions for Figure 7:

1. TAT: Asynchronous turnaround time (8 ns).

2. TLA: Latency time delay; this consists of device propagation delays plus 0 or 1 clock cycles. For preliminary estimates, assume a 20 ns clock and 15 ns of delay. (25 ns average).

3. TC: Clock period. (20 ns).

4. TDO: Delay to output (15 ns).

Figure 7 shows the relevant timing for this transfer cycle. The cycle time can be estimated from the rising edge of CDIT — to the next similar edge. In this case, it is reasonable to expect a cycle time of about 80 ns.

Figure 8-4. *cont.* CY7C330 Design Example: High Speed Asynchronous SCSI Controller.

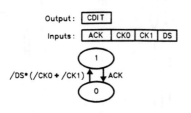

Figure 8. SCSI Tranfer to Host

Figure 8 shows the state diagram for this cycle.

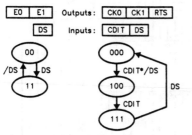

0130-9

Figure 9. Transfer to Host System

Figure 9 shows the data diagram for the system to interface transfer cycle.

Staging Considerations

Staging considerations include the initialization, startup, and change of direction of the interface. The signal 'I/O'

from the SCSI port mandates the direction of transfer, and this changes during the process of command completion, so there is a need to make sure that the relevant state machines are all qualified by 'IO'.

A readback path is provided for the CPU on the Host system to be able to read the SCSI signals directly. The signal DS− is reserved for normal data, but the signals CS0− thru CS1− allow D0 on the system data bus to be used to read SCSI signals.

The following addresses apply:

CS0 = 0: enable readback to D0

CS0 = 1: disable readback

CS2,CS1: 00 - BSY

CS2,CS1: 01 - C/D

CS2,CS1: 10 - I/O

CS2,CS1: 11 - REQ

The reset function for SCSI Controllers is independent of the Host interface controller. In the schematic of *Figure 10*, the signal RST is set by the Host system and this simply forces the RST− signal low on the interface.

The controller can be reset at any time by asserting INIT− from the Host system. If the code 001 is on CS2, CS1, CS0 then a select is performed: SEL− is pulled low until BSY− appears.

The transfer of data to the interface, in particular the device select code, should be done before the selection sequence is performed. After INIT− is released, data can be transferred normally and the REQ, ACK handshake will operate properly.

The transfer of diagnostic data (i.e. sense byte, errors) to the Host will be indicated by the DIAG− flag which is set until INIT− is asserted.

Reprinted from CMOS Data Book, *Cypress Semiconductor Corp., pp. 10–87 through 10–92 with permission.*

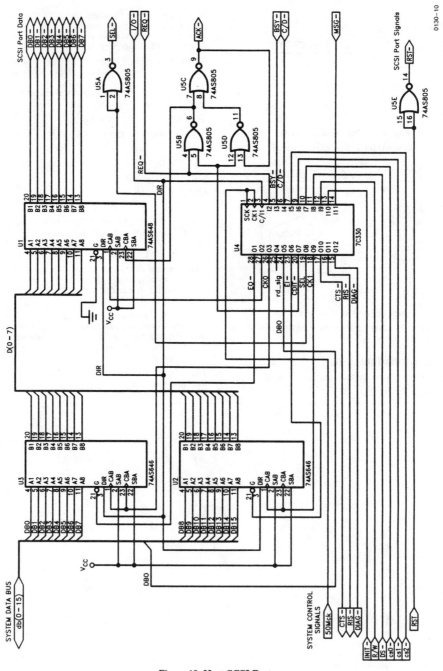

Figure 10. Host SCSI Port

Figure 8-4. *cont.* CY7C330 Design Example: High Speed Asynchronous SCSI Controller. *Reprinted from* CMOS Data Book, *Cypress Semiconductor Corp., pp. 10–87 through 10–92 with permission.*

Use logic cell array to control a large FIFO buffer

Chris Jay and Karen Spesard
Advanced Micro Devices Inc., 2175 Mission College Blvd., MS 10-02, Santa Clara, CA 95054; (408) 235-7081.

First-in-first-out (FIFO) buffers store data and offer a communications link for two devices that operate asynchronously. Typical applications for such a buffer are in a dot-matrix printers connected to PCs or in teleconferencing systems that store video images. With video, it might take 1 Mbyte of data (1000 by 1000 pixels) to generate an image, but the information can be crammed into 32 kbytes of memory space. The data would reside in a temporary FIFO storage buffer while waiting to be processed by the imaging device.

The amount of data to be stored determines the way a buffer is designed. If the data array is small, say 9 bits by 64 words, it can be implemented with a register-based FIFO architecture. But larger data arrays—128 words and up—require a RAM-based FIFO buffer that can pack more data in less pc-board area than registers. Not only that, RAM designs offer further advantages over the register approach. The readback process doesn't destroy the data contents and it's possible to implement a retransmit function. Because data doesn't "shuffle" through a stack of registers, a RAM buffer also lacks the so-called "fall-through time". Data is simply written to and read out from RAM locations until the buffer is empty, and then the process repeats.

Once a RAM-based FIFO buffer is indicated, the question boils down to which type of RAM to use—static or dynamic. Static RAMs require less control than dynamic RAMs, though they occupy more board space for a given memory size. Generally, static RAMs give a solution for medium sized FIFO buffers (between 128 bytes and 8 kbytes). When it comes to printer and imaging applications with large buffer sizes (64 kbytes and greater), a dynamic RAM solution can be built on a much small-

er circuit board than a static RAM can. The problem, however, is that a dynamic RAM FIFO buffer is tough to control logically, and a refresh function must be supplied.

A typical dynamic RAM-based FIFO buffer consists of a controller, dynamic RAM drivers, and the dynamic RAMs for data storage *(Fig. 1)*. All control lines ($\overline{\text{RAS}}$, $\overline{\text{CAS}}$, $\overline{\text{OE}}$, and $\overline{\text{WE}}$) and dynamic RAM address lines are buffered through Am2966 dynamic RAM driver chips. The handshake logic between the dynamic RAM controller and system CPU consists of the REQRD (Request to Read), REQWR (Request to Write), RDY Read (Read Ready), and RDY Write (Write Ready) signals. Other output lines from the controller indicate the amount of data in the buffer: full, half full, or empty. (Not shown in *Fig. 1* are two resistor-ca-

Simplify the design of a dynamic RAM-based FIFO buffer controller with a programmable logic array that regulates logic and refresh.

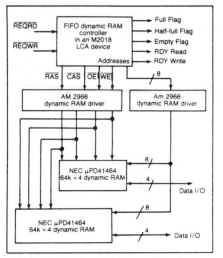

1. One PLD chip from Advanced Micro Devices generates all the logic control and refresh signals for a 64-kbyte dynamic RAM-based FIFO buffer. The only external devices required are dynamic RAM driver chips to buffer signals between the controller and memory.

Figure 8-5. Use Logic Cell Array To Control a Large FIFO Buffer, by Chris Jay and Karen Spesard. *Reprinted with permission from* Electronic Design, *(Vol. 36 No. 11), May 12, 1988.* © *1988 VNU Business Publications, Inc.*

pacitor networks used for oscillator circuits. The oscillators generate clock signals to control the timing of dynamic RAM refresh and read-write access.)

This dynamic RAM FIFO buffer circuit uses a high-density CMOS programmable logic device—the M2018 Logic Cell Array (LCA) from Advanced Micro Devices. User-programmable, it can perform a number of VLSI functions. In this application, it controls DRAM as a FIFO buffer.

The M2018 LCA itself is a static RAM array-based device consisting of a cluster of 100 configurable logic blocks (CLBs) arranged in a 10 by 10 matrix. Through programming, each block can be interconnected to other blocks. To handle I/O operations, the LCA also contains 74 I/O blocks (IOBs) for transferring signals to and from the bonding pads. Like CLBs, IOBs are configurable. The M2018 LCA is packaged in a 68-terminal, plastic leadless chip carrier.

For dynamic RAM control, five basic circuit functions must be programmed into the LCA *(Fig. 2)*. With its system- and refresh-clocks, the control circuitry is essentially a state machine that controls the $\overline{\text{RAS}}$ (the row address strobe), $\overline{\text{CAS}}$ (the column address strobe), $\overline{\text{OE}}$ (the Out-

put Enable or "Read" signal), and $\overline{\text{WR}}$ (the "Write" signal) sequence and address multiplexers. Output signals RDY READ and RDY WRITE tell other parts of the system that no read or write activity is currently occurring, and that a REQRD or REQWR command can be input to the controller. Two 16-bit binary counters—one for read, one for write—are selected by the read-write multiplexer. The dynamic RAM address is separated by a row-column select multiplexer to generate distinct row and column address cycles for the dynamic RAMs. From a design standpoint, the most logic-intensive circuit is the 16-bit up-down status counter that tracks the amount of data in the buffer. The counter increments for write operations and decrements for reads.

Three events—Request Refresh, REQRD, and REQWR— are prioritized by the dynamic RAM controller *(Fig. 3, top)*. The highest priority is accorded to Refreshing, followed by Read and Write (if a Read and Write request occur simultaneously, Read will be processed first). Refresh must be given the highest priority to maintain the dynamic RAM array's data integrity.

Three registers in the controller—$\overline{\text{RAS}}$, $\overline{\text{CAS}}$, and ROW/COL SEL—perform the $\overline{\text{RAS}}$, $\overline{\text{CAS}}$, and address multiplexing for read-write cycles. This brings active $\overline{\text{CAS}}$ before $\overline{\text{RAS}}$ refreshing during the active refresh period. The three registers are typically in the set condition; when a Request Refresh signal comes in, the "SET" register will be set on the following System Clock signal.

The ENAC (Enable Access) output of the controller is designed such that ENAC and Refresh are considered as mutually exclusive events. That is, if ENAC is true, Refresh is automatically false, and vice versa. This is because a dynamic RAM can't be refreshed and accessed simultaneously.

Logic equations for $\overline{\text{RAS}}$, $\overline{\text{CAS}}$, and ROW/COL SEL are derived with Karnaugh maps and truth tables and the resulting equations are implemented using a PC-based program called XACT. The design starts by defining the mutual exclusivity of ENAC and Refresh. One Karnaugh map defines a read or write cycle while the second defines the refresh cy-

2. The basic dynamic RAM, implemented on the M2018 LCA, performs handshaking to a system CPU, generates memory- and refresh-clocks, and controls write and read operations to and from the dynamic RAMs.

Figure 8-5. *cont.* Use Logic Cell Array To Control a Large FIFO Buffer, by Chris Jay and Karen Spesard.

cle. Using map minimization techniques, logic equations can be developed for the variables. For example, the logic equation for $\overline{RAS}$ turns out to be

$$RAS := \overline{RAS}*(ROW/COL\ SEL)*(\overline{CAS}) + RFSH*CAS$$

where * indicates the logical AND operation and + indi-

cates logical OR. Similar logic equations can be developed for $\overline{CAS}$ and ROW/COL SEL *(Fig. 3, bottom)*.

The RDY READ and RDY WRITE signals are generated by gating the output of the REQRD and REQWR registers with the output of the Request Refresh register. In the absence of read or write activity, the handshake signals indicate that the FIFO dynamic RAM is ready for an

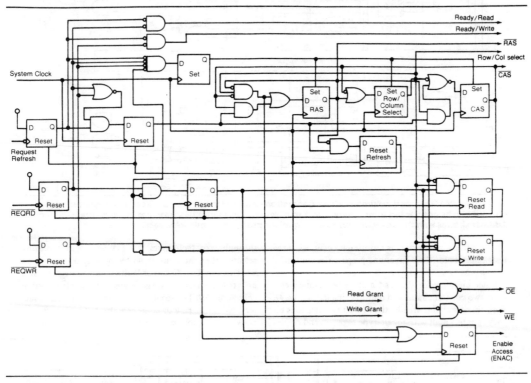

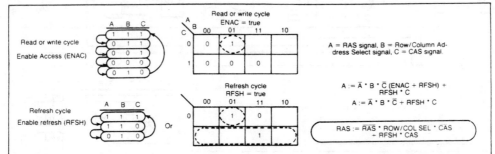

3. The control section of the M2018 PLD establishes the priority of operations occurring in the dynamic RAMs (refresh, read, write). D-type registers perform the set and reset functions of the control signals (top). The control logic is designed as a state machine, with ENAC (Enable Access) output configured so that ENAC and refresh are mutually exclusive events. If ENAC is true, Refresh is automatically false (bottom).

Reprinted with permission from Electronic Design, *(Vol. 36 No. 11), May 12, 1988. © 1988 VNU Business Publications, Inc.*

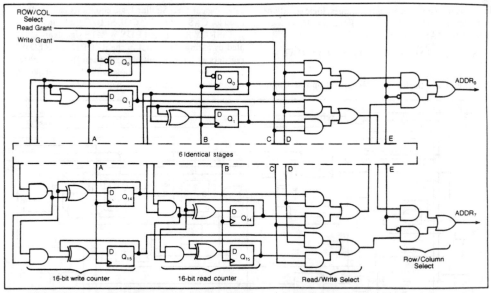

4. Dynamic RAM row- and column-address generation occurs through two identical 16-bit synchronous counter chains connected to an 8-way, 2-to-1 multiplexer. This circuit synchronizes the Row- and Column-Address strobes with the Row-Column Select signal for proper dynamic RAM sequencing.

access. After a read, write, or refresh has occurred, three reset registers for these functions prepare the controller for the next cycle.

Logic circuitry for the read and write channels employs two counter chains and multiplexing gates *(Fig. 4)*. Both counter chains are identical 16-bit synchronous binary counters built with toggle-type registers and ripple-

through-carry techniques. The first level of multiplexing selects either the read or write counter, depending on whether the Read Grant or Write Grant control signal is asserted. Both signals are generated in the control portion *(Fig. 3, again)*. The second layer of multiplexing gates selects either the row or column address. The sequence of active $\overline{RAS}$ followed by a ROW/COL SEL and an active

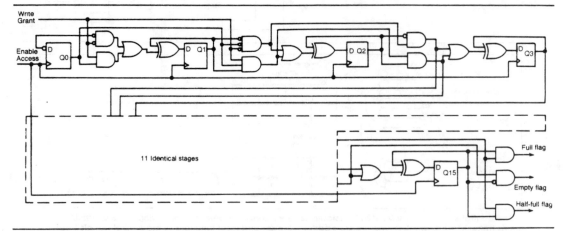

5. Status information on the amount of data in FIFO buffer memory is monitored by a 16-bit up-down counter. Three flags (full, half-full, empty) relay the buffer's current data load to other control elements.

Figure 8-5. *cont.* Use Logic Cell Array To Control a Large FIFO Buffer, by Chris Jay and Karen Spesard.

$\overline{CAS}$ synchronizes valid row and column addresses to the falling edges of $\overline{RAS}$ and $\overline{CAS}$, respectively. This occurs through the eight way, 2-to-1 multiplexer.

To supply buffer status information to external circuits that interface to the FIFO dynamic RAM controller, a status counter is included to convey the amount of data in storage (full, half full, or empty). Any external system sending data to the dynamic RAMs must cease transmission when the Full flag is asserted. The Half-Full flag can be monitored by external circuits to supply information on the timing of data flow through the buffer. Continual monitoring of the Half-Full flag, rather than the Full flag, is a better indicator of the buffer's status.

The status counter is a 16-bit up-down type *(Fig. 5)*. Each time a write operation is granted, the counter is incremented by the clock edge of the Enable Access output of the control circuitry. The Write Grant signal is in fact the up-down control because during a read cycle this signal is inactive and the counter will decrement. Combinational decoding from the status counter gives the necessary flag information at the output.

Two internal oscillators must be configured to supply the system clock and refresh timing. The general equation for oscillator timing to establish an even mark-space ratio clock is

$$T = N[(C1 \times R1) + (C2 \times R2)]$$

where N is a multiplying factor equal to 0.35 for TTL logic levels and 0.75 for CMOS levels.

The actual design of a 64-kbyte controller has been implemented and is available from Advanced Micro Devices in a PROM format (filename XDES10.PRM). □

References:

LCA Applications Handbook, Advanced Micro Devices, 1987.

uPD41464 65536 x 4 Dynamic NMOS RAM data sheet, NEC Electronics, 1987.

Karen Spesard, Senior Systems Applications Engineer at Samsung Semiconductor, previously worked for Advanced Micro Devices. She holds a BS in Chemical Engineering from the University of Illinois, and an MSEE degree from the University of Santa Clara.

Chris Jay is Applications Manager for the Logic Cell Array at AMD. He holds a BS from the University of Essex in England.

How Valuable?	Circle
Highly	544
Moderately	545
Slightly	546

Chapter Summary

In this chapter we looked at five example PLD applications to illustrate how PLDs are used in real applications. The applications range from simple gates to complex controllers, providing a broad look at how different PLD architectures fit into different applications.

Chapter 9

The Future of PLDs

The past decade or so has seen the birth and exponential growth of the programmable logic industry. An increasing number of semiconductor manufacturers are jumping onto the programmable logic bandwagon, and the number and variety of PLDs is growing at a phenomenal rate. While early devices were power hungry and had simple, general-purpose architectures, the onslaught of new PLD architectures and semiconductor technologies has resulted in a large selection of general- and special-purpose parts. The growth of this industry appears to be continuing unimpeded, and its future looks even brighter.

Chapter Overview

In this chapter we will summarize the current state of the PLD industry and take a look at its future. We will discuss current industry trends, device architectures, IC technologies, software support, manufacturing support, and other PLD support services.

What Is an "Ideal" PLD?—Industry Trends

The description of a perfect or "ideal" PLD—within the realm of current IC technology—is subjective and tends to change as technology and user-expectations change. The term "ideal" refers to more than architecture. It encompasses packaging, power consumption, cost, testability, reliability, ease of use, and other factors. It is clear that these factors involve tradeoffs. Compromises must be made in some areas to improve others.

It is because of these many tradeoffs that the PLD industry has become so diverse. Early PLDs were high-power devices with simple, general-purpose architectures and, at least by today's standards, moderately slow speeds. The demands for greater flexibility, higher-density, more outputs, faster speeds, lower power consumption, reprogrammability, lower cost, and better software support were not overlooked by PLD manufacturers. However, no manufacturer could combine all of these requests into a single new part. Instead, more and more PLD families were created to meet various subsets of these requests. AMD, for example, pioneered the flexible macrocell architecture with its PAL22V10, while Altera began producing high-density devices using erasable CMOS technology. Similarly, Lattice introduced its EEPROM-based GAL devices (also incorporating macrocell architecture); Xilinx introduced the CMOS RAM-based programmable gate array; and Signetics and Exel pioneered and introduced devices based on the foldback array architecture.

Initially, all of the new PLD families still included only general-purpose devices. Devices within a family would differ by some basic architectural factors—such as the number of product terms, number of inputs and outputs, and number of registers. All had architectural similarities that reflected their general-purpose design. While this proved adequate for most applications, it quickly became clear that an increasing number of potential applications could not be reached, and that general-purpose devices having sufficient functionality for these applications would be too complex or expensive to be practical. This realization spurred a whole new division of the PLD industry, and will affect its foreseeable future.

To meet the needs of special applications that couldn't be met with general-purpose devices, many PLD manufacturers introduced *application-specific PLDs (ASPLDs)*, sometimes called *function-specific PLDs*. By optimizing these devices for specific applications, PLD manufacturers were able to offer advanced functionality at reasonable cost. Address decoders, state machines, and microprocessor busses were the first applications targeted by ASPLDs. The trend in developing new ASPLDs is continuing, and will likely diversify into other application areas.

It seems reasonable to predict an extension of the ASPLD concept into more-conventional LSI devices. Microprocessors, video display controllers, communications controllers, and other popular LSI devices will eventually incorporate programmable logic to permit optimization and customization. Single-chip microcomputers, for example, may include on-chip programmable logic to incorporate peripheral address decoding and state-machine-control of I/O lines. Similarly, digital signal processors (DSPs) may include programmable logic to permit optimized interaction with other devices in a system. This outlook clearly indicates that programmable logic—and knowledge of its use and application—will play an increasingly important role in the design of digital systems.

High-end PLDs are already infringing on the territory previously held by the low-end gate-array market. More and more designers are choosing programmable logic over similar gate-array alternatives because of the short development cycle, low development cost, and other advantages. But as PLD technology continues to improve, gate-array technology is also improving. The complexities of both low-end and high-end gate arrays are increasing such that PLDs are unlikely to "take over" the gate-array marketplace any time soon.

They will, however, continue to help "push" gate arrays into higher densities, and dominate portions of the low-end gate-array market.

Architectural Trends

In the days when PALs were first available, early PLD users had only three architectural choices: PROM, FPLA, and PAL. Although each architecture category included a variety of devices having different configurations, the designer was, nonetheless, limited. The PLD industry seemed to lack desire for architectural innovation, so virtually all of the new devices that were developed fit into these three basic architectures.

In the early 1980s new PLD architectures began to appear. In particular, device manufacturers were beginning to realize that existing architectures were too inefficient. Only a small percentage of overall device logic was being utilized, and much was being wasted. Silicon area requirements increased dramatically whenever additional inputs or feedback terms were added to an AND-array. PROMs were the worst: for each additional input (address line), the number of fuses *doubled*. PALs and FPLAs shared a similar problem, since the number of fuses in the AND-array on these devices would increase geometrically with the addition of outputs and associated product terms.

Altera took some first steps at changing the architecture of its complex devices by breaking them down into independent regions. Each region was like its own PAL, and they could interact with each other using a small number of global lines. This approach kept the AND-arrays down to reasonable sizes, making the devices practical to manufacture. The first real architectural innovation came from Xilinx, with its *logic-cell array (LCA)* architecture. This gate-array-like architecture bypassed the conventional AND-OR approach to PLD design, and instead consisted of a matrix of configurable logic blocks (CLBs) surrounded by a perimeter of I/O blocks (IOBs). Programmable interconnects were then used to interconnect the various blocks. While the LCA architecture came with some associated penalties, it also offered many advantages, not the least of which was (generally) more efficient use of device logic resources.

Another PLD architecture breakthrough followed sometime later—in the mid-1980s—with Signetics and Exel introducing devices based on an innovative *foldback* architecture. Although the foldback architecture still suffered from the problem of having a logic array (NAND or NOR) that would increase substantially in size with additional array terms, its architecture allowed on-chip resources to be used very efficiently. Logic functions could be "buried" and interconnected inside these devices, and multiple-level logic could be easily implemented. Since it supports programmable output interconnects and buried logic functions, the foldback architecture, in many respects, offers gate-array-like functionality. However, this is not obvious from a first look at the architecture.

Application-specific device architectures have also become prevalent in the PLD industry, although these are not truly new PLD architectures in the same sense as the LCA or foldback array architectures. ASPLDs often combine a variety of different architectural features to form a device optimized for a specific application. For example, an ASPLD designed for state-machine applications may incorporate a PAL for logic functions combined with a registered PROM, and perhaps additional buried (internal) registers. While the PAL and PROM portions of the device are well-established conventional PLD architectures, the combination of these architectures in a specific way can be considered a new architecture.

The number and variety of ASPLDs is growing steadily, and will probably continue to do so for several years. It is difficult to speculate about the development of new, innovative architectures of the same magnitude as the LCA and foldback architectures, except perhaps to say that they are inevitable. But experience has shown that well-established architectures have a strong foothold, and manufacturers of PLDs with newer architectures have a lot of resistance to overcome in order to convince designers to choose their wares. Nonetheless, if a clearly superior architecture is introduced and an established manufacturer can provide a smooth, painless upgrade path from the older architectures, the PLD industry may change direction quickly.

PLD IC Technology Trends

As with all semiconductor devices, advances in integrated circuit (IC) technology are going to affect the PLD industry and its future devices. It is easy to predict the continuation of certain trends that have been taking place for several years. Current IC technologies will continue to show increased speed, lower power consumption, smaller die (chip) sizes, higher integration, smaller packages, packages with more pins, lower costs, and various combinations of these. CMOS technologies will soon achieve sub-12 ns propagation delays, standard biplor PLDs will achieve sub-7 ns propagation delays, and ECL (Emitter-Coupled Logic) will achieve sub-6 ns propagation delays. Also, Gallium-Arsenide (GaAs) technology will likely see increased use by the PLD industry to produce fast, moderate-power PLDs with improved *speed-power products* compared to other technologies.

As IC technologies improve, signal line geometries tend to decrease. Devices using sub-one-micron line geometries are becoming increasingly more commonplace. This reduction in line geometries allows existing PLD designs to be implemented using less silicon area, resulting in lower device costs and increased speed. Similarly, improved geometries permit more components to be placed on a die, allowing future PLDs to support more-complex circuits.

New ways to implement certain functions will also play a part in improving PLD functionality and cost. For example, while EEPROM technology is very desirable for PLDs—offering the best overall technology for programmable logic—EEPROM cells tend to consume more silicon real-estate than EPROM cells. At least two companies, Seeq and Intel, have developed new "Flash" EEPROMs that use smaller EEPROM cells. This type of advancement may be applicable to PLDs, and would be as beneficial as smaller line geometries, but would offer these advantages without the drawbacks of going to smaller lines.

Because of the benefits offered to PLDs, it seems likely that EEPROM and similar technologies, i.e., electrically erasable technologies, will become more prevalent in the PLD industry. EEPROM technology permits a high level of testability and permits reprogrammability in economical, plastic IC packages, albeit at lower component densities and higher cost than some other technologies. Nevertheless, the benefits of electrically erasable technology in the PLD industry—and other industries—are great enough that research will likely continue until breakthroughs are achieved that will improve component densities and reduce costs.

Along with the semiconductor industry in general, PLD manufacturers are increasingly supporting high-density, surface mount packaging. More and more devices will continue to appear in Plastic Leaded Chip Carrier (PLCC) and Small Outline (SO) surface mountable packages.

Development Support Trends

The availability of development software was a key element in initially making programmable logic viable for wide-scale use by logic designers. Since MMI's first PALASM compiler, many other PLD software development tools have appeared, as outlined in Chapter 5. While early PLD compilers—such as PALASM itself—were simple and had few features, modern third-party PLD compilers are comparatively much more advanced. They support a wide variety of devices and offer the designer several design entry formats. These compilers also offer advanced logic reduction and design simulation.

PLD manufacturers have been quick to realize the importance of development software support for their products. Newly introduced PLDs are considered virtually nonexistent by most designers if adequate development software is not available at the time of their introduction. Because of this, most PLD manufacturers work closely with third-party PLD-compiler producers during the development of new PLDs, helping to ensure the availability of development software when the new devices are introduced. Despite this, designers must often wait several months after the introduction of new devices before they can obtain a software update. Most of the major PLD manufacturers are aware of this and have developed their own PLD compilers to support their own devices. These compilers support new devices as they are introduced, and are generally available to designers at low or no cost. However, they also generally lack the advanced features of the third-party compilers.

The large size of the PLD industry and the ever-present need for more-advanced compilers—particularly as new devices and designs increase in complexity—will ensure that existing third-party compilers will continue to improve, and that other development aids will enter the scene.

As PLD development software improves, the features most likely to develop or improve include automatic complex-design partitioning; more-advanced logic- and gate-level design simulation capability; better logic reduction algorithms; and improved support for newer PLD architectures, such as the foldback array architecture. Other utility programs are also likely to appear, including ones that help designers select the best PLDs for their designs, and ones that help in creating and maintain "libraries" of logic functions.

Over the last decade it has become apparent that programmable logic development software has been unable to keep pace with PLD advancements. Although software support is certainly available for the new, complex PLDs at the time they are introduced to the market, the *level* of support is often insufficient to take full advantage of the architectural features of these devices. Thus, usage becomes restricted, and designers sometimes find themselves working with a device that is clearly capable of meeting their needs logically, but are unable to determine a method to implement the desired functionality.

The level of software support will probably continue to lag behind device complexity for some time, and increasing device complexities will make the support chasm more apparent. This will force the industry to apply more resources into improved development software. The gap will then narrow, but will still be hard-pressed to keep up with the advancing silicon.

It is also possible that other segments of the semiconductor industry will assist the PLD industry in the area of development software. For example, existing gate-array development software may be modified to support programmable logic, making some advanced design software available to programmable logic designers.

Manufacturing Support Trends

To make PLDs easier, more reliable—and ultimately less expensive—to use, PLD manufacturers must continue to improve their support of PLDs in the product-manufacturing environment. When PLDs are being used in a production environment, there are several costs incurred by the system manufacturer related to the use of PLDs. These include procurement, incoming test, programming and labelling, post-programming test, programming-failure returns, in-circuit test, in-circuit failure returns, post-shipment failure returns, inventory, and design-change-related part losses. While any particular product or company may only see a subset of these costs (many companies, for example, do not perform incoming tests on their semiconductors), most will see a majority of them, to varying degrees. The more costs can be reduced, the more cost-effective PLDs ultimately become in system manufacturing.

Costs can be reduced merely by the choice of IC technologies used in the PLDs. For example, EPROM- and EEPROM-based devices, being erasable, feature a much higher level of testability at the factory than do (nonerasable) bipolar parts. This can lower (or eliminate) incoming test costs, failure costs (such as programming-failure returns costs), and design-change-related costs. Similarly, the number of different PLD types used in a design can be minimized by using devices with "generic" (flexible) architectures, resulting in reduced procurement and inventory costs.

Other manufacturing-related costs can be reduced using improved test software. Most PLD programmers designed for the manufacturing environment support device simulation using test vectors, but the big question is, how much of the device do the test vectors test? The test vectors used in the development stage may not be the best to use in production. More programs are now becoming available to assist in producing manufacturing-level test vectors for PLDs. These programs generate test vectors that often test 90–100% of the potential "stuck-at-0" and "stuck-at-1" PLD failures, as well as other possible failures. These test vectors are generally much more effective at testing PLDs than design-level test vectors, and result in lower costs because device problems are caught earlier in the manufacturing process.

As PLDs become even more complex, and as new architectures become available, the need for improved manufacturing support software will become more dominant. A number of third-party vendors are already supporting the PLD industry with test software to support the use of PLDs in production, although only a relatively few parts are generally supported by these programs. The number of devices and types of architectures supported by these and other programs will, however, continue to increase.

PLD programmers are also important in the manufacturing environment. Ideally, production-worthy programmers should support a wide variety of devices, and should support test vector simulation. This includes the special "preload" modes now allowed by many PLDs—with the ability to handle a large number of test vectors. Likewise, programmers must be able to program parts quickly, and—at least for moderate- to large-volume production—should be able to support "gang" (multiple device) programming, or the automatic insertion, programming, testing, and removal of devices to/from the PLD programmer. Only a handful of PLD programmers currently meet all of these criteria. However, more programmers are destined to support these features because of increased demand from designers and production supervisors. Improving programmer testing capability and programming throughput results in lower production costs.

Finally, a number of PLD support services are popping up to ease the programming and testing burden involved with manufacturing PLD-based systems. These services may be the most cost-effective approach to PLD-based manufacturing for many small companies, or companies new to manufacturing with PLDs.

PLD Support Services

As with any industry that generates many sales, the booming PLD industry has contributed its share of secondary support industries. Among these, some PLD support services have become available to help companies use PLDs—from conception to production. These services generally have access to several different development tools and are able to support devices from a variety of PLD manufacturers. Working with a product designer, they develop the logic definition, design-level test vectors, and, often, production-level test vectors. These services then assist in getting the parts to production, or offer production services themselves.

A similar, though vastly more-limited, rendition of this is appearing from many of the major semiconductor distributors. For the PLDs they sell, these distributors will often program and test parts at no cost, or for a nominal charge. Parts are then shipped to the system manufacturer already programmed, tested, and labeled, eliminating these and related costs normally associated with in-house PLD programming.

Since manufacturers, through their Field Application Engineers (FAEs), and distributors are trying harder to support end-users, it is difficult to speculate about the future of these and other PLD support services. While a few well-established services may continue to flourish, the industry trend may be toward local consultants and consulting firms that are familiar with a wide variety of different PLDs.

Chapter Summary

In this chapter we looked at the PLD industry and where it is heading. We discussed the current industry trends in device architecture, IC technology, software support, manufacturing support, and the outlook for other PLD support services.

PLD Manufacturers Names and Addresses

This appendix includes a list of all current (March 1989) PLD manufacturers, including names, addresses, and telephone numbers, in alphabetical order. Only manufacturers of non-PROM PLDs are listed. All addresses given are in the USA unless otherwise specified.

Actel Corp.
320 Soquel Way
Soquel, CA 94086
(408) 732-2835

Advanced Micro Devices, Inc. (AMD)
901 Thompson Place
P.O. Box 453
Sunnyvale, CA 94086
(408) 732-2400

Note: AMD and MMI merged in 1987, and while separate names have so far been retained, MMI's name may later be dropped in favor of the AMD name.

Altera Corp.
3525 Monroe Street
Santa Clara, CA 95051
(408) 984-2800

Atmel Corp.
2095 Ringwood Avenue
San Jose, CA 95131
(408) 434-9201

Cypress Semiconductor Corp.
3901 North First Street
San Jose, CA 95134
(408) 943-2600

Exel Microelectronics, Inc.
2150 Commerce Drive
San Jose, CA 95131
(408) 432-0500

Note: Exel is a subsidiary of Exar Corp.

Fairchild Semiconductor Corp.
P.O. Box 5000, M/S 2C17
Puyallup, WA 98373-0900
(206) 841-6000

Note: Fairchild was acquired by National Semiconductor Corp. in 1987.

Gazelle Microcircuits, Inc.
2300 Owen Street
Santa Clara, CA 95054
(408) 982-0900

Gould, Inc.
3800 Homestead Road
Santa Clara, CA 95051
(408) 246-0330

Harris Semiconductor Corp.
P.O. Box 883
Melbourne, FL 32901
(305) 724-7000

Hyundai Semiconductor Corp.
Hyundai Electronics America
2191 Laurelwood Road
Santa Clara, CA 95054
(408) 986-9800

Intel Corp.
1900 Prairie City Road
Folsom, CA 95630
(916) 351-8080

**International CMOS Technology,
Inc. (ICT)**
2125 Lundy Avenue
San Jose, CA 95131-1849
(408) 434-0678

Lattice Semiconductor Corp.
P.O. Box 2500
Portland, OR 97208
(503) 629-2131

Monolithic Memories, Inc. (MMI)
2175 Mission College Boulevard
Santa Clara, CA 95050
(408) 970-9700

Note: MMI merged with AMD in 1987.
While separate names have so far been
retained, MMI's name may later be
dropped in favor of the AMD name.

**National Semiconductor Corp.
(NSC)**
P.O. Box 58090
2900 Semiconductor Drive
Santa Clara, CA 95052-8090
(408) 721-5000

Note: National Semiconductor
acquired Fairchild Semiconductor
Corp. in 1987.

Panatech Semiconductor Corp.
3375 Scott Boulevard, Suite 440
Santa Clara, CA 95054
(408) 727-8144

Note: Panatech is a division of Ricoh
Co., Ltd. of Japan.

PLX Technology Corp.
625 Clyde Avenue
Mountain View, CA 94043
(415) 960-0448

Samsung Semiconductor, Inc.
5150 Great America Parkway
Santa Clara, CA 95054
(408) 980-1630

Seeq Technology, Inc.
1849 Fortune Drive
San Jose, CA 95131
(408) 432-9550

Seiko Semiconductor Ltd.
281, Fujimi, Fujimi-machi
Suwa-gun, Nagano-ken,
399-02
JAPAN
(0266) 62-4112

SGS Semiconductor Corp.
1000 East Bell Road
Phoenix, AZ 85022
(602) 867-6100

Signetics Corp.
811 East Arques Avenue
P.O. Box 409
Sunnyvale, CA 94086
(408) 739-7700

Sprague Electric Co.
3900 Welsh Rd.
Willows Grove, PA 19090

(215) 657-8400

Note: Sprague has indicated that it is exiting the PLD market.

Texas Instruments, Inc.
P.O. Box 225012
Dallas, TX 75265
(214) 995-6611

VLSI Technology, Inc.
1109 McKay Drive
San Jose, CA 95131

(408) 434-3100

Note: VLSI Technology has indicated that it is exiting the PLD market.

WaferScale Integration, Inc.
47280 Kato Road
Fremont, CA 94538
(415) 656-5400

Xilinx, Inc.
2069 Hamilton Avenue
San Jose, CA 95125
(408) 559-7778

PLD Development Aid Manufacturers Names and Addresses

This appendix contains a list of manufacturers of PLD development aids (primarily software). The first section lists third-party development aid producers (i.e., non-PLD-manufacturers), and includes names, addresses, telephone numbers, and product(s) offered; note that other, nonlisted products may also be offered by these companies. The second section lists the PLD manufacturers that offer software support for their own products; Appendix A lists the names and addresses of these PLD manufacturers. All company names are listed in alphabetical order.

Third-Party Development Aid Manufacturers

American Computer Automated Systems, Inc.
P.O. Box 20127
San Jose, CA 95160
(408) 997-3333

Product: PLD simulator.

Anvil Software
369 Massachusetts Avenue, Suite 192
P.O. Box 901
Arlington, MA 02174
(617) 641-3861

Product: Automatic Test Generator (ATG) for generating PLD test vectors.

Automated Logic Design Co. (ALDEC)
3525 Old Conejo Road, #111
Newbury Park, CA 91320
(805) 499-6867

Products: SUSIE logic simulator, Programmed Logic Design Environment (PLDE), ALEC for using single-chip microcomputers as PLDs.

Bytek Corp.
1021 S. Rogers Circle
Boca Raton, FL 33431
(305) 994-3520

Product: Universal Logic Array Development System (LADS).

CAD Group
3911 Portola Drive
Santa Cruz, CA 95062
(408) 475-5800

Product: Salt logic simulator with PLD support.

Cadnetix Corp.
5757 Central Avenue
Boulder, CO 80301
(303) 444-8075

Product: Logic simulation systems with PLD models.

Case Technology, Inc.
633 Menlo Avenue
Menlo Park, CA 94025
(415) 322-4057

Product: Vanguard CAE Design System with PLD support.

Capilano Computing
P.O. Box 86971
North Vancouver, BC V7L 4P6
CANADA
(604) 669-6343

Product: LPLC compiler.

Daisy Systems Corp.
700 Middlefield Road
Mountain View, CA 94039
(415) 960-6593

Product: PLD Master, and VSS logic simulator with PLD support.

Data I/O Corp.
10525 Willows Road N.E.
P.O. Box 97046
Redmond, WA 98073-9746
(206) 881-6444

Products: ABEL compiler, PLDtest test software, DASH-ABEL schematic interface, FutureDesigner CAE software.

Douglas Electronics
718 Marina Boulevard
San Leandro, CA 94577
(415) 483-8770

Product: Logic simulator with PLD support.

Elan Digital Systems/USA
P.O. Box 1610

San Anselmo, CA 94960
(408) 734-2226

Product: LOG/IC compiler.

Epic
3080 Olcott Street, Suite 203-B
Santa Clara, CA 95051
(408) 988-2944

Genrad
510 Cottonwood Drive
Milpitas, CA 95035
(408) 432-1000

Product: System Hilo logic simulator with PLD support.

Harris Scientific Calculations
7796 Victor-Mendon Road
P.O. Box H
Fishers, NH 14453
(716) 924-9303

Product: Cadat logic simulator with PLD support.

Hewlett-Packard Co.
1820 Embarcadero Road
Palo Alto, CA 94303
(415) 857-1501

Product: PLD Design System (PLDDS), and Hilo-3 logic simulator with PLD support.

HHB Systems
1000 Wyckoff Avenue
Mahwah, NJ 07450
(201) 848-8000

Isdata GmbH
Haid-und-Neu-Strasse 7
D-7500 Karlsruhe 1
WEST GERMANY

Product: LOG/IC compiler.

Kontron Electronics
1230 Charleston Road
Mountain View, CA 94039-7230

(415) 965-7020

Product: LOG/IC compiler.

Logic Automation
19500 N.W. Gibbs Drive
P.O. Box 310
Beaverton, OR 97075
(503) 690-6900

Product: PLD "SmartModels" for logic simulation on Mentor Graphics engineering workstations.

Logical Devices
1321 N.W. 65th Place
Ft. Lauderdale, FL 33309
(305) 974-0967

Product: CUPL compiler

Matra Design Semiconductor
2840-100 San Thomas Expressway
Santa Clara, CA 95051
(408) 986-9000

Product: Gate array software that includes PLD conversion, and Gateaid Plus/PC logic simulator with PLD support.

Minc, Inc.
1575 York Road
Colorado Springs, CO 80918
(719) 590-1155

Product: PLDesigner compiler.

Personal CAD Systems, Inc. (P-CAD)
1290 Parkmoor Avenue
San Jose, CA 95126
(408) 971-1300

Product: PLD Schematic entry software.

Pistohl Electronic Tool Co.
22560 Alcalde Road
Cupertino, CA 95014
(408) 255-2422

Product: Compiler and utilities for CMOS PLDs.

Programmable Devices, Inc.
155-T New Boston Street
Woburn, MA 01801
(617) 935-9530

Product: PLD manufacturing services.

Programmable Logic Technologies, Inc.
P.O. Box 1567
Longmont, CO 80501
(303) 772-9059

Product: LC-9000 compiler.

Qwerty, Inc.
5346 Bragg Street
San Diego, CA 92122
(619) 455-0500

Product: PLAQ compiler.

Royal Electronics Ltd.
1314 Kilborn Avenue
Ottawa, Ontario CANADA
(613) 723-0725

Product: Logicsim simulator.

Silvar-Lisco
1080 Marsh Road
Menlo Park, CA 94025
(415) 324-0700

Product: Helix logic simulator with PLD support.

Teradyne
Design and Test Automation Group
321 Harrison Avenue
Boston, MA 02118
(617) 482-2700

Product: Lasar logic simulator with PLD support; Circuit Breaker logic and fault simulation software for PLDs, for use with the company's VLSI testers.

Valid Logic Systems
2820 Orchard Parkway
San Jose, CA 95134
(408) 432-9400

Product: Validsim logic simulator
with PLD support.

Viewlogic Systems
275 Boston Post Road W
Marlboro, MA 01752
(617) 480-0881

Product: Viewsim logic simulator
with PLD support.

PLD Manufacturers With Software Support

Actel Corp.
Advanced Micro Devices (AMD)
Altera Corp.
Exel Microelectronics, Inc.
Intel Corp.
International CMOS Technology, Inc. (ICT)
Lattice Semiconductor Corp.
Monolithic Memories, Inc. (MMI)
National Semiconductor Corp. (NSC)
Panatech Semiconductor Corp.
Signetics Corp.
Xilinx, Inc.

PLD Programmer Manufacturers Names and Addresses

This appendix includes an extensive list of manufacturers of (non-PROM) PLD programmers, including names, addresses, and telephone numbers. Manufacturers are listed in alphabetical order. Since the list of devices supported by the programmers from these manufacturers tends to change frequently, contact the manufacturers for current supported-device lists.

PLD manufacturers that offer programming equipment for their own devices are listed at the end of this appendix. See Appendix A for the addresses of these manufacturers.

Third-Party PLD-Programmer Manufacturers

**Advanced Microcomputer
Systems, Inc.**
2780 SW 14th Street
Pompano Beach, FL 33069
(305) 975-9515

Advin Systems, Inc.
1050-L East Duane Avenue
Sunnyvale, CA 94086
(408) 984-8600

American Reliance, Inc.
9241 E. Valley Boulevard
Rosemead, CA 91770
(818) 287-8400

BP Microsystems
10681 Haddington

Houston, TX 77043
(713) 667-1636

**Bytek Corp.
Instrument Systems Division**
1021 S. Rogers Circle
Boca Raton, FL 33437
(305) 994-3520

Click Instruments
P.O. Box 851013
Richardson, TX 75085-1013
(214) 783-9072

Curtis Electro Devices, Inc.
P.O. Box 4090
Mountain View, CA 94040
(415) 964-3846

Data I/O Corp.
10525 Willows Road NE
Redmond, WA 98073
(206) 881-6444

Destron Technologies, Inc.
385 Elliot Street
Newton, MA 02164
(617) 332-4621

Digilec, Inc.
1602 Lawrence Avenue
Ocean, NJ 07712
(201) 493-2420

Digital Media, Inc.
11770 Warner Avenue, Suite 225
Fountain Valley, CA 92708
(714) 751-1373

DLS Associates
1 Gale Road
Brick, NJ 08723
(201) 920-6807

Dynatec International
3594 West 1820 South
Salt Lake City, UT 84104
(801) 973-9500

Eden Engineering
P.O. Box 2200
Grass Valley, CA 95945
(916) 272-2770

Elan Digital Systems, Inc.
516 Marin Drive
Burlingame, CA 94010
(415) 964-5338

Electramotive Computers
142 Nevada Street
El Segundo, CA 90245
(213) 772-9208

GTEK, Inc.
399 Highway 90, Drawer 1346

Bay St. Louis, MS 39520
(601) 467-8048

Inlab, Inc.
2150-I W. 6th Avenue
Broomfield, CO 80020
(303) 460-0103

International Microsystems, Inc.
790 E. Arques Avenue
Sunnyvale, CA 94086
(916) 885-7262

JDR Microdevices, Inc.
110 Knowles Drive
Los Gatos, CA 95030
(408) 378-8927

Kontron Electronics
633 Clyde Street
Mountain View, CA 94039
(415) 965-7020

Link Computer Graphics, Inc.
4 Sparrow Drive
Livingston, NJ 07039
(201) 994-6669

Logical Devices, Inc.
1321 N.W. 65th Place
Ft. Lauderdale, FL 33309
(305) 974-0967

Microway
P.O. Box 79
Kingston, MA 02364
(617) 746-7341

Nicolet Instrument Corp.
Test Instruments Division
215 Fourier Avenue
Fremont, CA 94539
(415) 490-8870

Oliver Advanced Engineering, Inc.
320 Arden Street
Glendale, CA 91203
(818) 240-0080

One/D, Inc.
1050 East Duane Avenue
Sunnyvale, CA 94086
(415) 969-9900

Pistohl Electronic Tool Co.
22560 Alcalde Road
Cupertino, CA 95014
(408) 255-2422

**Programmable Logic
Technologies, Inc.**
P.O. Box 1567
Longmont, CO 80501
(303) 772-9059

**Promac Division
Adams-MacDonald Enterprises,
Inc.**
2999 Monterey Salinas Highway
Monterey, CA 93940
(408) 373-3607

Quantec Systems
500 Alden Road, Unit 11
Markham, Ontario L23 5H5
CANADA
(416) 479-0248

Qwerty, Inc.
5346 Bragg Street
San Diego, CA 92122
(619) 455-0500

Retnel Systems
P.O. Box 1348
Lawrence, MA 01842
(617) 683-4659

Royal Electronics
1314 Kilborn Avenue
Ottawa, Ontario K1H 6L3
CANADA
(613) 738-1202

Sherman Pirkle
782 Massachusetts Avenue

Lexington, MA 02173
(617) 861-6688

Southern Computer Corp.
141 W. Wieuca Road, Suite 300-B
Altanta, GA 30342
(404) 252-3340

Stag Microsystems, Inc.
1600 Wyatt Drive
Santa Clara, CA 95054
(408) 988-1118

Storage System Engineering
3105 El Camino, #201
Santa Clara, CA 95051
(408) 554-0841

Storey Systems
3201 N. Highway 67, Suite E
Mesquite, TX 75150
(800) 852-2022

Structured Design
333 Cobalt Way, Unit 107
Sunnyvale, CA 94086
(408) 988-0725

Sunrise Electronics, Inc.
524 S. Vermont Avenue
Glendora, CA 91740
(818) 914-1926

Swisscomp, Inc.
5312 56th Commerce Park
Tampa, FL 33610
(813) 628-0906

System General Co.
3rd Floor, #6, Lane 4
Tun Hwa N Road
Taipei, Box 53-591
TAIWAN, R.O.C.
(02) 721-2613

Varix
P.O. Box 850605
Richardson, TX 75085-0605
(214) 437-0777

Xeltek
473 Sapena Court, Unit 24
Santa Clara, CA 95054
(408) 727-6995

PLD Manufacturers that Offer Programming Equipment

Actel Corp.
Altera Corp.
Cypress Semiconductor Corp.
Exel Microelectronics, Inc.
Gazelle Microcircuits, Inc. (Internal)
Intel Corp.
Lattice Semiconductor Corp.
Xilinx, Inc.

Bibliography

Chapter 2

Blakeslee, Thomas R. *Digital Design with Standard MSI & LSI*. 2d ed. New York: John Wiley & Sons, 1979.

Brown, Douglas W. "A State-Machine Synthesizer—SMS." *The Proceedings of the 18th Design Automation Conference*. New York: IEEE Press, 1981, pp. 301–5.

Comer, David J. *Digital Logic and State Machine Design*. New York: CBS College Publishing, 1984.

Kopec, Stan. "State Machines Solve Control-Sequence Problems." *EDN* (May 26, 1988): 177–88.

Kopec, Stan. "Asynchronous State Machines Challenge Digital Designers." *EDN* (June 9, 1988): 179–86.

Mano, M. Morris. *Digital Logic and Computer Design*. Englewood Cliffs, NJ: Prentice-Hall, 1979.

Nagle, H. Troy Jr., B. D. Carroll, and J. David Irwin. *An Introduction to Computer Logic*. Edited by Franklin F. Kuo. Englewood Cliffs, NJ: Prentice-Hall, 1975.

Roth, Charles H. Jr. *Fundamentals of Logic Design*. 3d ed. St. Paul: West Publishing, 1985.

Svoboda, Antonin. "The Concept of Term Exclusiveness and Its Effect on the Theory of Boolean Functions." *Journal of the Association for Computing Machinery* (July 1975): 425–40.

Wakerly, John. "Designer's Guide to Synchronizers and Metastability, Part 1." *Microprocessor Report* (September 1987): 4–8.

Wakerly, John. "Designer's Guide to Synchronizers and Metastability, Part 2." *Microprocessor Report* (October 1987): 4–8.

Chapter 3

Andrews, Warren. "Architectural and Process Enhancements Deliver Faster, More Flexible PLDs." *Computer Design* (January 1, 1988): 31–42.

Bursky, Dave. "Faster, More Complex PLDs Arrive with Better Programming Tools." *Electronic Design* (April 1987): 13–25.

Bursky, Dave. "Dense Programmable Logic Chips Away at Gate Arrays." *Electronic Design* (August 11, 1988): 43–58.

Cole, Bernard C. "Programmable Logic Devices: Faster, Denser, and a Lot More of Them." *Electronics* (September 17, 1987): 61–72.

Collett, Ron. "A Glance at the PLD Industry." *ESD* (March 1987): 24.

El-Ayat, Khaled, Abbas El Gamal, Richard Guo, John Chang, Esmat Hamdy, John McCollum, and Amr Mohsen. "A CMOS Electrically Configurable Gate Array." *The Proceedings of the 1988 IEEE International Solid-State Circuits Conference*. New York: IEEE Press, 1981, pp. 76, 77, 309.

Goetting, Erich, and Mikael Hakansson. "Foldback Design Cuts Wasted Gates." *Electronic Engineering Times* (May 4, 1987): T8.

Lewis, Sasha. "Update: High-Density PLDs." *Electronic Products* (January 15, 1988): 14–16.

Marrin, Ken. "PLDs Slow Advance of Gate Arrays in Low-End Designs." *Computer Design* (February 1, 1986): 43–54.

Small, Charles H. "Programmable-Logic Devices." *EDN* (February 5, 1987): 112–33.

Smith, David. "Programmable Logic Devices." *EDN* (May 15, 1986): 94–109.

Wilson, Ron. "New PLD Architectures Deliver Needed Flexibility." *Computer Design* (June 1, 1988): 22–6.

Manufacturer Literature

Actel Corp. *An Architecture for Electrically Configurable Gate Arrays*. (1988).

Actel Corp. *Desktop Configurable Channeled Gate Arrays: The First No Compromise, No Wait ASIC Solution*. (1988).

Advanced Micro Devices, Inc. *Programmable Logic Handbook/Data Book*. (1987).

Advanced Micro Devices, Inc. *PAL Device Data Book*. (1988).

Advanced Micro Devices, Inc. *PGA 3000 Series Data Sheet*. (1988).

Altera Corp. *Data Book*. (1987).

Cypress Semiconductor Corp. *CMOS Data Book*. (January 1988).

Exel Microelectronics, Inc. *XL78C800 ERASIC Multi-Level E² PLDs Data Sheet*. (1987).

Intel Corp. *Programmable Logic Handbook*. (1988).

International CMOS Technology, Inc. *PEEL 18CV8 CMOS Programmable Electrically Erasable Logic Device Data Sheet*. (February 1988).

Lattice Semiconductor Corp. *GAL Data Book*. (Spring 1988).

Monolithic Memories, Inc. *PAL/PLE Device Programmable Logic Array Handbook*. 5th ed. (1986).

National Semiconductor Corp. *Programmable Logic Design Guide*. (May 1986).

Signetics Corp. *Programmable Logic Data Manual*. (1986).

Texas Instruments, Inc. *Programmable Logic Data Book*. (1988).

Xilinx, Inc. *The Programmable Gate Array Design Handbook*. 1st ed. (1986).

Chapter 4

Cole, Bernard C. "Programmable Logic Devices: Faster, Denser, and a Lot More of Them." *Electronics* (September 17, 1987): 61–72.

Collett, Ron. "Application-Specific PLDs Fill Big Niche." *ESD* (February 1987): 28–30.

Collett, Ron. "PLDs: On the Road to State-Machine Design." *ESD* (April 1988): 34–43.

Kopec, Stan, and David A. Laws. "Function-Specific Architectures Enhance Programmable State Machine Solutions." *Electronic Engineering Times* (May 4, 1987): T18, T24.

Martin, Steven L. "Programmable Devices Tailored to State Machine Needs." *Computer Design* (November 15, 1986): 37–41.

Small, Charles H. "Programmable-Logic Devices." *EDN* (February 5, 1987): 112–33.

Smith, David. "Programmable Logic Devices." *EDN* (May 15, 1986): 94–109.

Manufacturer Literature

Advanced Micro Devices, Inc. *Programmable Logic Handbook/Data Book*. (1987).

Advanced Micro Devices, Inc. *PAL Device Data Book*. (1988).

Altera Corp. *Data Book*. (1987).

Cypress Semiconductor Corp. *CMOS Data Book*. (January 1988).

Fairchild Semiconductor Corp. *Programmable Logic Array Data Sheet*. (1987).

Harris Corp. *CMOS Digital Data Book*. (1986).

Intel Corp. *Programmable Logic Handbook*. (1988).

Monolithic Memories, Inc. *PMS14R21/A PROSE Programmable Sequencer Data Sheet*. (1987).

Monolithic Memories, Inc. *Designing with the PROSE PMS14R21 Device technical note (TN-003)*. (1987).

Panatech Semiconductor, Inc. *CMOS EPL*. (1986).

PLX Technology, Inc. *PLX 448 High Drive Current, Programmable Logic Device for Bus Interface Applications Data Sheet*. (1988).

Samsung Semiconductor, Inc. *CMOS Programmable Logic (CPL) Data Book*. (1988).

Seeq Technology, Inc. *EEPAL 20RA10Z Data Sheet*. (1987).

Texas Instruments, Inc. *Programmable Logic Data Book*. (1988).

Texas Instruments, Inc. *A Designer's Guide to the PSG507*. (1987).

Chapter 5

Andrews, Warren. "What Do the Users Want from PLDs?" *Electronic Engineering Times* (May 4, 1987): T4, T20.

Angevine, Wayne. "An Introduction to EDIF." *Semicustom Design Guide* (1987): 26–35.

Bloom, Michael. "Smart Schematic Capture Systems Catch Mistakes Before Simulation." *Computer Design* (June 15, 1986): 44–6.

Clawson, Harvey. "Understand EDIF Conventions to Transfer Circuit Data." *Electronic Design* (October 1987): 49-56.

Electronic Engineering Times 1987 Programmable Logic Devices Users Study. New York: CMP Publications, December 1986.

Grant, John L. "State Machine Tools for ASIC Design." *Semicustom Design Guide* (1987): 92–6.

Gregory, David, Aart de Geus, and Tim Moore. "Automating Logic Design with Socrates." *Digital Design* (October 1986): 44–6.

Holley, Michael, and Dave Pellerin. "Choose Design Tools That Accommodate Many PLDs." *Electronic Engineering Times* (May 16, 1988): T6, T20.

JEDEC Standard No. 3-A: Standard Data Transfer Format Between Data Preparation System and Programmable Logic Device Programmer. Washington, D.C.: Electronic Industries Association, May 1986.

Marx, Esther. "EDIF: The Standard for Workstation Intercommunication." *IEEE Micro* (October 1985): 68–75.

Marx, Esther, Hart Switzer, and Mike Waters. "EDIF Format Brings Uniformity to CAE/CAD Data." *EDN* (January 22, 1987): 153–8.

Small, Charles H. "PLD-Design Software Meets the Challenge of Multiple-Device PLD Applications." *EDN* (February 18, 1988): 61–4.

Chapter 6

Andrews, Warren. "Options Grow as Programmable Devices Join Standard Parts and Semicustom Circuits." *Electronic Engineering Times* (September 29, 1986): T4, T42–3.

Andrews, Warren. "What Do the Users Want from PLDs?" *Electronic Engineering Times* (May 4, 1987): T4, T20.

Baker, Marc A. "Universal PALs Speed Time-to-Market." *Electronic Engineering Times* (May 16, 1988): T10.

Britt, Ronald. "Programmable-Logic Sequencers Solve Timing Problems." *EDN* (February 20, 1986): 209–20.

Caplow, Stephen. "Integrating PLD Design and Test." *Electronic Engineering Times* (May 16, 1988): T23.

Coli, Vincent J. "Introduction to Programmable Array Logic." *BYTE* (January 1987): 207–19.

Darbonne, Thomas. "Erasable PLDs and Software Help Forge State Machines." *Electronic Design* (August 21, 1986): 140–6.

de Bruyn Kops, Peter. "Testability Is Crucial in PLD-Circuit Design." *EDN* (August 18, 1988): 191–7.

Desai, Naushik, and Steven Grossman. "Tradeoffs Between CMOS and Bipolar PLDs." *Electronic Engineering Times* (May 4, 1987): T9, T30.

Durwood, Brian H. "PLD Testing: Why, When and How." *Computer Design* (April 1, 1988): 71–5.

Electronic Engineering Times 1987 Programmable Logic Devices Users Study. New York: CMP Publications, December 1986.

Faria, Don. "EPLD Macrocells and Feedback Signals Ease Circuit Design." *EDN* (April 17, 1986): 200–209.

Freedman, Robert A. "Getting Started with PALs." *BYTE* (January 1987): 223–30.

Goetting, Erich, and Mikael Hakansson. "Foldback Design Cuts Wasted Gates." *Electronic Engineering Times* (May 4, 1987): T8.

Grossman, Steven, and Alexandra Huff. "Implementing a State Machine." *Electronic Engineering Times* (September 29, 1986): T29, T50.

"Hidden Costs in PLD Usage." *GAL Data Book*. Lattice Semiconductor Corp. (Spring 1988): 47–51.

Jay, Chris. "XOR PLDs Simplify Design of Counters and Other Devices." *EDN* (May 28, 1987): 205–10.

Jigour, Robin J., and Greg Lara. "Benefits from EEPLDs Are Company-Wide." *Electronic Engineering Times* (May 16, 1988): T22.

Laws, David A. "High-Density EPLDs Make an Attractive Alternative to Gate Arrays for ASIC Designs." *Electronic Engineering Times* (September 29, 1986): T22.

Marshall, Trevor G. "PALs Simplify Complex Circuits." *BYTE* (January 1987): 247–59.

Mayer, John H., "Device Programmers Struggle to Catch Up with IC Developments." *Computer Design* (November 15, 1987): 107–14.

McClure, Mike. "PLDs Open the Way for Soft Prototyping." *Electronic Engineering Times* (May 4, 1987): T13, T24.

Milne, Bob. "Verify Your Circuit Designs with a Modular Simulator." *Electronic Design* (June 9, 1988): 57–8.

Osann, Bob. "Different PLDs Meet Different Design Needs." *Electronic Engineering Times* (September 29, 1986): T10.

Palley, Lawrence S. "EPLDs Provide for Fast Design Changes." *Electronic Engineering Times* (September 29, 1986): T8, T48.

Patterson, Wes. "Architectural Subtleties Make the Difference in the Selection of a Programmable Logic Device." *Electronic Engineering Times* (September 29, 1986): T5, T18.

"PLD Economics." *Programmable Logic Data Manual*. Signetics Corp. (1986): 2-6–2-7.

Programmable Logic: A Basic Guide for the Designer. Data I/O Corp. (1983).

Programmable Logic Primer. National Semiconductor Corp. (1986).

Small, Charles H. "Programmable-Logic Devices." *EDN* (February 5, 1987): 112–33.

Small, Charles H. "Automatic Test Generator for PLDs Clean Up Your Logic Designs." *EDN* (September 17, 1987): 59–64.

Swift, Art. "A Road Map for First-Time Users of Programmable Logic." *Electronic Engineering Times* (September 29, 1986): T6.

Vargas, Pedro. "EPLDs, PLAs, and TTL: Comparing the 'Hidden Costs' in Production." *Programmable Logic Handbook*. Intel Corp. (1988): 2-212–2-233.

Vithayathil, Joseph. "PLDs Are Now a Real Option for ASIC Users." *Electronic Engineering Times* (September 29, 1986): T14, T18.

Chapter 7

Baker, Marc A. "Universal PALs Speed Time-to-Market." *Electronic Engineering Times* (May 16, 1988): T10.

de Bruyn Kops, Peter. "Testability Is Crucial in PLD-Circuit Design." *EDN* (August 18, 1988): 191–7.

Denton, Donald L. "Quality and Reliability Screens Impact the Cost of Owning ICs." *Electronic Design* (November 20, 1986): 105–10.

Durwood, Brian H. "PLD Testing: Why, When and How." *Computer Design* (April 1, 1988): 71–5.

Durwood, Brian H., and Gary O'Donnell. "Mastering PLD Test Aspects Eases System Testing." *Electronic Design* (February 18, 1988): 103–8.

"PLD Economics." *Programmable Logic Data Manual*. Signetics Corp. (1986): 2-6–2-7.

"User-Benefits of Programmable Logic." *Programmable Logic Design Guide*. National Semiconductor Corp. (May 1986): 4–9.

Vargas, Pedro. "EPLDs, PLAs, and TTL: Comparing the 'Hidden Costs' in Production." *Programmable Logic Handbook*. Intel Corp. (1988): 2-212–2-233.

Hepner, Terry L. "PLDs: The Device Programmer's View." *Electronic Engineering Times* (September 29, 1986): T33, T40, T50.

"Hidden Costs in PLD Usage." *GAL Data Book*. Lattice Semiconductor Corp. (Spring 1988): 47–51.

Jigour, Robin J., and Greg Lara. "Benefits from EEPLDs Are Company-Wide." *Electronic Engineering Times* (May 16, 1988): T22.

Laengrich, Norbert. "Understanding Test Vectors in CAE." *Electronic Products* (March 15, 1987): 47–51.

Negrin, Alan E. "Complex Factors Underlie Universal-Programmer Selection." *EDN* (May 15, 1986): 167–72.

Small, Charles H. "PLD Programmers." *EDN* (March 31, 1987): 118–32.

Small, Charles H. "Automatic Test Generator for PLDs Clean Up Your Logic Designs." *EDN* (September 17, 1987): 59–64.

Stern, Richard H. "Field-Programmable Logic Devices—Are They Hardware or Software? Can Their Programmed Configurations Be Protected Against Copying?" *IEEE Micro* (October 1986): 61–62, 78.

Stern, Richard H. "Microcode Revisited: Further Implications of the NEC vs. Intel Case—Microcode, Instruction Sets, and Compatibility." *IEEE Micro* (April 1987): 81–3, 92.

"Testing Programmable Logic Devices Application Note." Supplement to Data I/O Corp. Update, vol. 2, no. 1 (1985).

Chapter 8

"Basic Gates." *Programmable Logic Design Guide*. National Semiconductor Corp. (May 1986): 157–161.

"CY7C330 Design Example: High Speed Asynchronous SCSI Controller." *CMOS Data Book*. Cypress Semiconductor Corp. (1988): 10-87–10-92.

Dujari, Vineet. "PLD Provides Chip Select and Wait States." *EDN* (August 21, 1986): 184–5.

Jay, Chris, and Karen Spesard. "Use Logic Cell Array to Control a Large FIFO Buffer." *Electronic Design* (May 12, 1988) 113–117.

"9-Bit Parity Generator/Checker with 82S153/153A." *Programmable Logic Data Manual*. Signetics Corp. (November 1986): 9-125–9-130.

Chapter 9

Andrews, Warren. "ASICs Outlook: Dust Off Predictions from 1986 and Use Them Again in 1987." *Electronic Engineering Times* (December 8, 1986): T40–T44.

Andrews, Warren. "What Do the Users Want from PLDs?" *Electronic Engineering Times* (May 4, 1987): T4, T20.

Baker, Stan. "The New PLD Era." *Electronic Engineering Times* (February 2, 1987): 17.

Bursky, Dave. "Programmable Logic Devices 1986 Technology Forecast." *Electronic Design* (January 9, 1986): 122–9.

Electronic Engineering Times 1987 Programmable Logic Devices Users Study. New York: CMP Publications, December 1986.

Rettig, Cynthia B. "Military-ASIC Market Grows at 18% Rate Through 1991." *EDN* (June 25, 1987): 350.

Index

Data Communications, Networks, and Systems

Thomas C. Bartee, Editor-in-Chief

Data Communications, Networks, and Systems is the most current publication in its field, written by 11 experts and edited by prominent Harvard University professor Thomas C. Bartee. It presents a comprehensive overview of state-of-the-art communications systems, how they operate, and what new options are open to system users.

Use this reference book to learn the advantages and disadvantages of local area networks; how modems, multiplexers and concentrators operate; the characteristics of fiber optics and coaxial cables; and the forces shaping the structure and regulation of common carrier operations. The book's ten chapters contain a wealth of information for all communications professionals.

Topics covered include:

■ Transmission Media
■ Carriers and Regulation
■ Modems, Multiplexers, and Concentrators
■ Protocols
■ PBX Local Area Networks
■ Baseband and Broadband Local Area Networks
■ Computer and Communications Security
■ Local Area Network Standards

368 Pages, 8 x 10-¼, Hardbound
ISBN: 0-672-22235-3
No. 22235, $39.95

Data Communications Testing and Troubleshooting

Gil Held

This book is a comprehensive guide to the operation and utilization of over 10 different test instruments in a data communications network. Written for technicians, network analysts, network engineers, and technical control center personnel, it provides a foundation for understanding, performing, testing, and troubleshooting for data communications equipment and transmission facilities.

Beginning with basic measurements and line parameters, the book serves as a tutorial to the basic uses and operation of the test instruments. It covers digital and analog testing and the digital interface in detail, and reviews the use of modem and multiplexer built-in test features. It also introduces the reader to traffic engineering and capacity planning.

Topics covered include:

■ Basic Measurements
■ Data Channel Parameters
■ Digital and Analog Testing
■ The Digital Interface
■ Diagnostic Hardware
■ Integral Diagnostic Testing
■ Capacity Planning
■ Appendices: Equipment Sizing Tables, Glossary, Abbreviations, Answers to Questions

192 Pages, 7-½ x 9-¾
ISBN: 0-672-22616-2
No. 22616, $29.95

Understanding Data Communications, Second Edition

Revised by Gilbert Held

One of our best-selling books in the Understanding Series, this revised edition is the ideal book for anyone wanting a broad, but not too technical introduction to data communications. Like the other titles in the series, this book combines a general overview of data communications with more detailed explanations of specific technologies within the field.

This new edition emphasizes asynchronous and synchronous modems, network design and management, and digital multiplexing as well as coverage of V.22bis and Packetized Ensemble Protocol modems.

Topics covered include:

■ Data Terminals
■ Messages and Transmission Channels
■ Asynchronous Modems and Interfaces
■ Synchronous Modems and Digital Transmission
■ Fiber Optic and Satellite Communications
■ Protocols and Error Control
■ Architectures and Packet Networks
■ Network Design and Management
■ ISDN (Integrated Services Digital Network)

300 Pages, 7 x 9, Softbound
ISBN: 0-672-27270-9
No. 27270, $17.95

Understanding Digital Electronics, Second Edition

Gene W. McWhorter

Learn why digital circuits are used. Discover how AND, OR, and NOT digital circuits make decisions, store information, and convert information into electronic language. Find out how digital integrated circuits are made and how they are used in microwave ovens, gasoline pumps, video games, cash registers, and other high-technology products.

Topics covered include:

■ Let's Look at a System
■ How Digital Circuits Make Decisions
■ Building Blocks that Make Decisions
■ Building Blocks with Memory
■ Why Digital?
■ Digital Integrated Circuits
■ Mass Storage and Digital Systems
■ How Digital Systems Function
■ Programmed Digital Systems
■ Digital Electronics Today and in the Future

264 Pages, 7 x 9, Softbound
ISBN: 0-672-27013-7
No. 27013, $17.95

**Visit your local book retailer or call
800-428-SAMS**

Understanding Digital Troubleshooting, Second Edition

Don L. Cannon

Digital electronic systems are more reliable than the systems they replace, yet, at some point, they will need repair and maintenance. This book provides an insight into this highly technical world in a language that both technicians and non-engineers understand. It presents the basic concepts and fundamental techniques needed to locate faults in digital systems and how to repair them.

■ Digital Systems Fundamentals
■ Digital Systems Functions
■ Troubleshooting Fundamentals
■ Combinational Logic Problems
■ Sequential Logic Problems
■ Memory Problems
■ Input/Output Problems
■ Basic Timing Problems
■ Advanced Techniques

272 Pages, 7 x 9, Softbound
ISBN: 0-672-27015-3
No. 27015, $17.95

Understanding Digital Computers

Forrest Mims, III

This book is for computer users and prospective computer users who want to understand the fascinating circuits and principles behind the digital computer. Learn what computers do, how they work, how it all began, and how to program a computer.

You will discover the basics of binary, sequential, and arithmetic logic and the power of computer meories and memory devices from magnetic tape and floppy disks to magnetic bubbles and laser disks.

Topics covered include:
■ What's A Computer?
■ Number Systems
■ Binary Logic
■ Combinational Logic
■ Sequential Logic
■ Arithmetic Logic
■ Memories
■ Computer Organization
■ Computer Programming

320 Pages, 7 x 9, Softbound
ISBN: 0-672-22597-2
No. 22597, $15.95

The 555 Timer Applications Sourcebook With Experiments

Howard M. Berlin

This book explains the 555 timer and shows how to use it, either alone or with other solid-state devices. Learn how to use the 555 timer and its counterpart, the 556 dual timer, in various specialized applications. Study the internal workings of the timer IC and how to connect it in monostable or astable multivibrator circuits. Experiments allow you to gain a basic practical knowledge.

Topics covered include:
■ Introduction to the 555 Timer
■ Monostable Operation
■ Astable Operation
■ Power Supply Circuits
■ Measurements and Control
■ Playing Games with the 555 Timer
■ Circuits for the Automobile and Home
■ The 555 and Ma Bell
■ Hobbies
■ Experimenting with the 555 Timer

160 Pages, 5-1/2 x 8-1/2, Softbound
ISBN: 0-672-21538-1
No. 21538, $9.95

Crash Course in Digital Technology

Louis E. Frenzel, Jr.

Back by popular demand, the "crash course" format is applied to digital technology. This concise volume provides a solid foundation in digital fundamentals, state-of-the-art components, circuits, and techniques in the shortest possible time.

Its objective is to give a solid foundation in digital fundamentals. It builds the specific knowledge and skills necessary to understand, build, test, and troubleshoot digital circuitry. No previous experience with digital technology is necessary.

Topics covered include:
■ Digital Data
■ Digital Logic Elements
■ Basic Digital Circuits
■ Digital Integrated Circuits
■ Using Logic Gates
■ Combinational Logic Circuits
■ Flip-Flops and Applications
■ Sequential Circuits: Counters, Shifts Registers, and One-Shots
■ Troubleshooting Digital Circuits
■ Appendices: Schmitt Trigger and Relocating Logic Diagrams to Physical Circuits

208 Pages, 8-1/2 x 11, Softbound
ISBN: 0-672-21845-3
No. 21845, $19.95

Understanding Digital Logic Circuits

Robert G. Middleton

Designed for the service technician engaged in radio, television, and audio troubleshooting and repair, this book painlessly expands the technician's expertise into digital electronics. Beginning with digital logic diagrams, the reader is introduced to basic adders and subtracters, flip-flops, registers, and encoders and decoders. Memory types are also discussed in detail.

Topics covered include:

■ The Anatomy of Digital Logic Diagrams
■ Additional Logic Gates and Cicuit Operation
■ Additional Gate Types and Logic Families
■ Flip-Flops and Clock Circuitry
■ Registers
■ Counters
■ Encoders and Decoders
■ Parity Generator/Checkers and Interfacing
■ Code Converters, Multiplexers, Demultiplexers, and Comparators
■ Addition, Multiplication, Division, and Video Games
■ Types of Memories
■ Miscellaneous Bipolar and MOS Memories
■ Digital Voltmeter Circuitry
■ Transmission Lines in Digital Systems

392 Pages, 5-1/2 x 8-1/2, Softbound
ISBN: 0-672-21867-4
No. 21867, $18.95

Advanced Digital Troubleshooting

Alvis J. Evans

Advanced Digital Troubleshooting provides comprehensive coverage of digital test equipment for intermediate-level electronics technicians, maintenance technicians, technical students, and hobbyists. The book emphasizes practical troubleshooting techniques, going into specifics at the board and component level where necessary.

Beginning with a brief review of digital circuits, it presents successful approaches to troubleshooting and includes digital test instruments such as digital logic probes, oscilloscopes, logic analyzers, and an in-circuit emulator.

Topics covered include:

■ Electrical Characteristics of Digital Systems
■ Digital Troubleshooting Methodology and Approaches
■ Microcomputer Fundamentals
■ Meet the Main Chips
■ Software and the Diagnostic Program
■ Using Basic Digital Troubleshooting Instruments
■ The Logic Analyzer
■ An In-Circuit Emulator
■ Signature Analysis
■ Repair Checkout and Preventive Maintenance

208 Pages, 8-1/2 x 11, Softbound
ISBN: 0-672-22571-9
No. 22571, $19.95

Computer-Aided Logic Design

Robert M. McDermott

This reference uses practical, everyday examples such as burglar alarms and traffic light controllers to explain both the theory and the technique of electronic design. CAD topics include common types of logic gates, logic minimization, sequential logic, counters, self-timed systems, and tri-state logic applications. Packed with practical information, this is a valuable source book for the growing CAD field.

Topics covered include:

■ Computer-Aided Design
■ Fundamentals of Boolean Logic
■ Logic Gates
■ Combinational Logic Design and Verification
■ Logic Minimization
■ Sequential Logic (Memory Elements)
■ Counters
■ Sequential Logic (Parallel/Serial Converters)
■ Finite State Machines
■ Self-Timed Systems
■ Tri-State Logic
■ Appendices: PROTOSIM Logic Simulation Program, MINLOG Logic Minimization Program, Common 7400-Series Logic Gates, Clock and Pulse Generator Circuits

448 Pages, 7-1/2 x 9-3/4, Softbound
ISBN: 0-672-22436-4
No. 22436, $25.95

IC Op-Amp Cookbook, Third Edition

Walter G. Jung

Earlier editions of *IC Op-Amp Cookbook* have been considered a "classic" in the industry.

The new edition has been greatly expanded in terms of device coverage in keeping with state-of-the-art advancements. Numerous charts make selecting data on a particular device much easier.

Topics covered include:

■ Op-Amp Basics
■ IC Op-Amps: The Evolution of General-Purpose and Specialized Types
■ General Operating Procedures and Precautions in Using Op-Amps
■ Voltage Regulators, References, and Power Supplies Using Op-Amps
■ Signal-Processing Circuits
■ Logarhythmic and Multiplier Circuit Techniques
■ Comparators
■ The Integrator and Differentiator
■ Signal-Generation Circuits

608 Pages, 5-1/2 x 8-1/2, Softbound
ISBN: 0-672-22453-4
No. 22453, $21.95

Visit your local book retailer or call
800-428-SAMS